THE BEST OF
ROYKO

THE BEST OF
ROYKO
THE TRIBUNE YEARS

MIKE ROYKO

Edited by David Royko

Chicago Tribune

MIDWAY

AN AGATE IMPRINT

CHICAGO

Chicago Tribune: R. Bruce Dold, Publisher & Editor-in-Chief; Peter Kendall, Managing Editor, Content; Christine W. Taylor, Managing Editor, Audience; Amy Carr, Director of Content.

Library of Congress Cataloging-in-Publication Data

Names: Royko, Mike, 1932-1997 author. | Royko, David, 1959- editor.
Title: The best of Royko : the Tribune years / Mike Royko ; edited by David Royko.
Description: Chicago : Midway, 2018.
Identifiers: LCCN 2018019299| ISBN 9781572842557 (hardcover) | ISBN 1572842555 (hardcover)
Classification: LCC PN4874.R744 A25 2018 | DDC 818/.5409--dc23
LC record available at https://lccn.loc.gov/2018019299

First printing: August 2018

10 9 8 7 6 5 4 3   19 20 21 22 23

Midway Books is an imprint of Agate Publishing. Agate books are available in bulk at discount prices. For more information, visit agatepublishing.com.

CONTENTS

CHAPTER 4: THE BELEAGUERED LITTLE GUY'S BEST FRIEND

CHAPTER 5: SPORTS AND THE CREATURES WHO DO IT

CHAPTER 8: COME ON IN, MEET THE FAMILY, HER FATHER PROBABLY WON'T BITE

CHAPTER 9: SONNY, BACK IN MY DAY . . .

CHAPTER 10: AIN'T TOO PROUD TO BEG

CHAPTER 11: WAR—BEEN THERE, DONE THAT, SEEN IT, HATE IT

CHAPTER 12: THE FUNNIEST GUY IN THE ROOM

CHAPTER 13: ME, MYSELF AND I

CHAPTER 14: POOPERY, ER, POTPOURRI

FOREWORD
by John Kass

W HEN I WAS A ROOKIE REPORTER and my newspaper hero, the legendary columnist Mike Royko, came over to the Tribune, I did a very stupid thing.

He asked me for the telephone number of a source. And I refused. That's right. I refused Mike Royko.

Mike wanted the number for Mayor Harold Washington's top aide, a former panderer and pimp with a ridiculous wig named Clarence McClain.

I was new, but not that new. Reporters live and die by their sources, and I wasn't going to give up Clarence's number for anyone. So I told Mike's legman that I didn't have it. The next day, passing in the lobby, Mike gave me a look, then a sneer, and I felt my world was coming to an end.

I mean, he was Mike Royko. What the hell did I think I was doing?

Later, I was asked into his office. It was about 3 o'clock, which, for columnists, is a time when the deadline drums begin pounding and the stomach acids growl. But he was gracious and asked me to sit down.

We sat and smoked and talked. I don't remember exactly what we talked about. For someone like me who grew up in Chicago wanting to be a reporter, the chance to sit around with Mike Royko was just too fantastic to comprehend. If you were a rookie basketball player and Michael Jordan wanted you to hang out with him, you probably couldn't deal with it either. But this wasn't a basketball player. This was Royko.

Finally, I realized that the room had been silent for some time. Then he growled something like: You didn't give me McClain's number.

And I replied in a tiny voice: Yes, that's right.

He didn't hold it against me. And periodically, he gave me good career advice on how to write and how to think about things and what to read. He was just so damn interesting, and he'd come out with things that you wouldn't associate with him.

For instance, he liked "And Quiet Flows the Don" by Mikhail Aleksandrovich Sholokhov, an epic tale of the Cossacks of the Don River Valley. I know why he liked it. Not for the politics as much as for the ways of the people in the villages, their petty jealousies, their rude ambition, their love of family and clan. It was very much like Chicago.

Mike could be gruff and even vicious in print. But in our occasional talks I saw a gentle kindness in the guy. I know that's not how people remember him, not if they met him late at night at some bar. But you can imagine what he had to endure, meeting guys in bars, strangers devoid of their inhibitions, competitive and intent on proving they were tougher, smarter, more knowledgeable than he. Who wouldn't have developed a sneer?

What I remember is that he was kind to me.

From time to time he'd call and I'd go over and we'd smoke and he'd tell stories. When he got stuck on jury duty while I was covering City Hall, we'd have lunch. And when he asked me for a phone number, I gave it to him.

Mike Royko was the greatest newspaperman of his generation, perhaps all generations, and he wrote his daily columns in the great days of newspapers.

He didn't tweet, and he didn't think about Internet clicks. He came to work and wrote his column every day whether he felt like it or not. And if you were lucky enough to have been born here in Chicago and you grew up reading Royko, you eventually got the sense that he was talking to all of us.

Why? Because he was one of us. He typed the truth out as he knew it, and we understood.

Of course Mike received all the awards, including the Pulitzer Prize, and he won praise from all the great and learned committees. But there is one award that newspaper people covet more than anything, perhaps even more so in this electronic age marking the slow demise of the printed paper. And he won it almost every day:

The Refrigerator Prize.

It is the one prize awarded without any intrigue or speeches. We'd read Mike's column, and either laugh or cry or become angry, and then we'd read it again. Finally, we'd cut it out of the paper and fix it to the front of the refrigerator for the entire family or workplace to see.

There have been several books written about Royko, including biographies, and I suppose a biography is a great way to learn about a complicated, sometimes troubled man. But perhaps it's not the best way. If you want to know about a teacher, you study the students. If you want to know about a farmer, look at the fields.

And if you want to learn about a columnist like Mike Royko, then the best way is to read his columns. And don't just read the great ones that people remember, but also the not-so-great columns that few remember. You'll see how he struggled, and how he came back the next day, and the next and the next. That is what's remarkable.

It's quite all right if you read these Royko columns merely for nostalgia about the old Chicago. But if you read just a bit more closely, you'll find more: his relentless professionalism, his attention to detail, his pacing and, of course, his humanity.

When he had it all working, it was just perfect.

He was the best at his trade. And he was all Chicago. ■

INTRODUCTION
by David Royko

"**H**OW I WISH your dad was around to write about this."
People often say this to me, and I always agree. "Oh boy, he would've had a field day."

Yep.

"I bet he would've said something like . . . ."

And that's where I can't disagree more, whatever that "something like" might be. Because that's one of the things that made Dad Mike Royko: Nobody ever knew what he'd say. He was not predictable, but even if you weren't expecting—or agreeing with—his take, it was worth thinking about and considering. If it didn't shift your own point of view, it probably made you defend it, if only in your mind, because his argument was always deeply considered and tightly constructed. It was never devised out of vain desire to be different or to attract attention. And the way he wove that argument through 900 words engrossed and entertained.

So I still wonder, "What would Dad have to say about this?"

The first big story his readers missed out on was Tiger Woods breaking into mainstream consciousness one April weekend at the 1997 Masters. Dad sure knew about it. Home from the hospital recovering from the aneurysm that would kill him later that month at 64, he was, as always, paying attention to the world.

1

He had to. For 33 years, he dragged himself out of bed knowing a blank page was waiting, daring him to fill it with words that would keep him at the top of the heap—and employed. Dad always considered himself a working man first, not above the other working stiffs who were taking the time to read him. Hard work was what won him a Pulitzer Prize in 1972.

Dad wrote five days a week since late 1963. It is a staggering record. Full-time columnists typically turn out two, maybe three columns a week—and his were the best. That's not a son bragging on his dad. Canvas the world of hypercompetitive columnists for confirmation. Or just read on. He performed this feat first for the Chicago Daily News, and after that paper folded in 1978, for the Chicago Sun-Times until Rupert Murdoch bought it. "No self-respecting fish would want to be wrapped in a Murdoch paper" is a quote of Dad's that still turns up regularly. The sale drove him across the street to the Chicago Tribune.

It took him a while to get used to that last post. When he came into the world, the Trib was the archconservative nemesis of the liberal, and, to the very end, Dad's late, lamented and beloved Daily News. By the time he joined the Trib, political dividing lines between the two remaining papers were blurring, and he was able to rationalize his defection. But it still bugged him.

It's the reason the chapter "Ain't Too Proud To Beg"—a chapter devoted to my dad's columns on the Tribune's annual charity fundraiser—doesn't have columns from 1984 or 1985. He was grumpy and resented the Trib for "asking" him, as they did all their columnists, to promote the year-end drive. But eventually Dad caved, telling me he'd realized it was a worthy cause and that he was being a jerk. A Trib exec later told me that the amount generated by his columns was always the biggest—and by a wide margin. It wasn't simply because his columns were the most widely read but because they are laugh-out-loud funny. He never did things halfway. Oh, and the one from 1991 about the drunken uncle? It's 100 percent true. It was my maternal granddad's twin, Uncle Frank.

When Dad died, he'd written nearly 8,000 columns, about half of them for the Trib. At 900 words per column, that's more than seven million words. (Those are the kinds of calculations Dad loved to do for columns, like figuring out how many days over his lifetime a friend stared at his bare feet every morning before getting out of bed.) His columns are about everything, because when you write that many, you have to become an "expert on lots of stuff," like his fictional consultant and one of his alter egos, Dr. I. M. Kookie.

Dad was certainly an expert on sports. When the book "The Best American Sports Writing of the Century" was published, it was no surprise to see Dad in there shoulder to shoulder with the specialists. And it's why I wanted to ask him about Tiger Woods. I knew he'd have opinions, because it was (a) about sports, (b) golf, in particular, and (c) race—all topics he knew well and wrote about many times.

I should have known he would be thinking along different lines. He thought the "experts" proclaiming that this would change golf and bring a flood of African-

Americans into the game were idiots. The demographics of golf were driven by socioeconomics, class and culture—not role models—and that was the column he was planning to write when he got a chance. He never did.

Years later, I read an "expert" explaining the lack of African-Americans in golf, even after Woods. He said the reasons reflected socioeconomics, class and culture.

Dad knew that, predicted it and would have beaten him to it by a decade.

Of course. ▪

CHAPTER 1
The Curmudgeon at Work and Play

Don't blow smoke—just get even

TUESDAY, APRIL 24, 1984

I rode a cab the other day that had a hand-drawn sign on the dashboard that said, "No Smoking."

Although I smoke, complying with the sign wasn't a problem. I'm not the kind of smoker who makes a fuss about being deprived. If somebody doesn't want me to smoke in his presence, I don't. As nonsmokers everywhere are angrily saying, why should they be subjected to somebody else's smoke?

After we had gone about a block, I said, "Will you please turn off the noise?"

The cabdriver, a shaggy-haired man in his 30s, looked in his mirror and said, "The what?"

"The noise."

"You mean my radio?"

"Yes, the radio."

"What's wrong with it?" he said.

"It's giving me a headache. The music is bad and there's static. You ever hear of the problem of noise pollution? That's noise pollution."

He shook his head and turned it down.

"I can still hear it," I said.

"You want a different station? Some other kind of music?"

"No. I hate music. I haven't liked any music since Spike Jones' band."

He shook his head again but snapped the radio off. We rode in silence for less than a minute, when he said:

"You know, it's a funny thing about music. Some people, they like. . . ."

I interrupted. "Say, no offense meant, but do you mind if we don't talk?"

"You don't want me to talk?" he said, sounding incredulous.

"Right."

"All right," he said, obviously offended. "Then I won't talk."

7

He probably thought I was rude or worse. Maybe you do, too. And maybe I sounded that way.

But just as he didn't want to be exposed to my smoke, why should I be exposed to his lousy taste in music, his radio's static and the sound of his voice?

Now, I have to admit that if the no-smoking sign hadn't been there, I might have felt differently. I would have opened the window a couple of inches so the smoke could escape, had a cigarette and listened to his music or his views on life.

But it's now my policy to meet intolerance with intolerance. I don't know if that's fair, but when it's over, I feel better.

It began a while ago with one of two women at the next table in a restaurant. She was my first exposure to the antismoking crusaders.

I was having dinner with a pal. We hadn't even ordered when she turned toward me and said very firmly, "I'd appreciate it if you didn't smoke."

Before I could do anything but look surprised, she launched a California-style lecture. "Respecting rights of others . . . menace to the environment . . . intruding on my space . . ."

Before she was finished, I had squashed my cigarette and said, "OK, OK."

Because I'm a fair person, I could see her point. A little of my smoke might have drifted in her direction, although the place seemed well ventilated.

About halfway through the meal, I turned toward her and said, "Excuse me, but could I tell you something?"

"Yes?" she said, glaring at me in anticipation of the request she *knew* would come: Could I have just one cigarette?

But I fooled her. I didn't mention smoking at all. I just said: "I really don't care about your neighbor's medical problems. Or your job. Or your vacation plans. Would you lower your voices so your conversation doesn't intrude on my space?"

She knew exactly what I was up to. She gave me a look of contempt and said: "Really. The tables here are so close that we'd have to whisper."

"Try," I said. "I'd appreciate it."

But they didn't. She said, loudly and clearly: "Oh, he just thinks he's being *clever*. Oh, he's so," and she dragged the word out, "so clevvvverrr." And they went on talking just as loudly.

That was it. War. I attacked on two fronts. First, I told my friend a dirty joke. No, it wasn't dirty, it was filthy. It had no swearing or gutter language. But a really good, filthy joke is even filthier if told in clinical terms.

Then I told another. And their nostrils quivered and they ate faster.

It seemed only fair. If I had to hear about their neighbor's intestinal malfunctions, why shouldn't they hear my filthy jokes?

While I told the jokes, I took out my cigarettes and lighter and put them on the edge of the table.

When my last bite was gone, and the coffee cups filled, I picked up the cigarette package and sort of fondled it. I could see them watching.

Then I slowly slid out a cigarette and tapped it on the table. And tapped and tapped it. Then I put it between my lips. She was not only watching, she was starting to look homicidal.

I just kept it there for a minute. I took it out while I said something. Then I tapped it some more.

I picked up the lighter. But I just held lighter and cigarette in my hands, as if distracted by conversation.

Finally, I snapped the lighter a couple of times. She cracked under the pressure. "Waiter," she said. "Check."

And they hadn't even had coffee or dessert.

As they rose, she glared at me and said, "Do you know what you are?"

I smiled, put down the unlit cigarette and said: "Thanks to you, much healthier."

So, you see, we can all coexist, if we just try. ∎

A smile a day . . . can be sickening

MONDAY, MAY 15, 1989

A clergyman has approached me with an idea he believes will make this a happier and more peaceful society. He wants all of us to make a habit of smiling at each other.

As Pastor T.L. Barrett Jr. put it, in his written proposal:

"The major objective of the 'Smile America' concept is to launch a nationwide campaign, which will inspire, enlighten and provide the incentive for the development of an inevitable consciousness of the acknowledgment of mankind, through a natural, genuine smile."

To remind people to smile, he wants to see the "Smile America" slogan plastered over T-shirts, headbands, bumper stickers, coffee mugs and dozens of other products.

And when the nation is thoroughly inundated in "Smile America" products, and we are all flashing our choppers at each other, he believes we will all be nicer and the crime rate will go down and we will feel relaxed and experience good vibrations.

In sending me his proposal, he said: "I would like you to review it. Your input would be helpful to me."

I'm afraid that Rev. Barrett has come to the wrong person for input on smiling.

As anyone who knows me is aware, I smile only when it is absolutely necessary and unavoidable, which isn't very often. I have friends of many years who can't say for certain that I have teeth.

There are many reasons I don't smile. For one thing, smiling is unnatural because it violates the laws of nature.

When you smile, your facial muscles resist gravity. It is far more natural for your face to let gravity do its thing and cause your face to droop. If nature intended us to be smiling all the time, we would have been made with our heads upside down.

So by defying gravity, smiling can be compared to bouncing up and down for no reason, or flapping your arms and trying to fly like a bird or bat. What kind of society would we be if everyone kept bouncing and flapping their arms? Pretty silly looking, I say.

Also, consider what other earthly creatures smile to show friendliness and happiness, sincere or otherwise.

The answer is none. When a dog or cat or any other beastie pulls back its lips and shows its teeth—an act we call a smile—it means that it is about to chomp on you and you'd better take off.

Only humans show their teeth as an act of friendliness. And even then, you can't be sure of the motive.

Think about it. Which humans smile the most? Politicians, used-car salesmen, quiz show hosts and drunken conventioneers, that's who.

Is that who this Rev. Barrett wants the whole country to emulate? Car salesmen, politicians, quiz show hosts and drunken conventioneers?

Look through history books and see if you can find one picture of Abe Lincoln smiling. Of course you can't. He knew what was going on, and if you know what's going on, you don't smile much.

On the other hand, turn on your TV and watch David Letterman. He never stops smiling, even when there isn't anything to smile about, which on his show is just about all the time. If you stuck your thumb in Letterman's eye, he'd smile.

So ask yourself: Would you prefer a nation of Abe Lincolns or David Lettermans? (Please don't send me your choice. I'm sure the results would be depressing.)

It might be unfair, but I don't trust people who smile all the time. As Slats Grobnik put it: "Anybody who smiles all the time is hiding something, even if it is only sore feet."

And many scientific surveys have shown that people who are habitual smilers are more inclined to say: "Have a nice day."

This dumb phrase is one of the nation's leading causes of mental stress and depression, because most people will not have a nice day. So after someone tells them to have a nice day, and they have a bad day, they wonder if there is something wrong with themselves for not having a nice day.

And, of course, they shouldn't blame themselves. Most people get up in the morning and go to work or to school. They buck traffic or wait for a dawdling bus. They confront a demanding boss, a nasty customer, a crabby teacher. They get traffic tickets. They have headaches. They fear getting bald, fat or wrinkled. They have debts. They see things in store windows that they can't afford. They lose a contact lens or suffer some other tragedy. They go home and find that the puppy has wet the rug.

With all this torment, how can they have a nice day? And why should they go around smiling or tolerating chronic smilers?

They shouldn't. They should do what comes naturally, which is to scowl. You can always trust a scowler. Have you ever walked into a car lot and been sold a lemon by a scowler?

Some sharp-eyed readers have probably noted that in my picture, I am smiling. It is a small smile, but a smile nonetheless.

So, you ask, if I am a scowler, why did I smile for the picture?

The photographer made me do it. He told me he had a terrible toothache. ■

Windshield-wiper lets in some light

FRIDAY, AUGUST 21, 1987

There are some mornings so lousy that you know the rest of the day is going to stink.

This one began with nature as the enemy in the form of a flooded basement. Nature is a frustrating enemy because no matter how much you rant and swear, it doesn't listen.

Then came the writing of a large check to the Internal Revenue Service. The IRS is a dangerous enemy because if you rant and swear you might be audited and have even more to rant and swear about.

And before the morning was half over, there was technology, an old and hated foe. It took the form of the Ohio Street bridge going up, then getting stuck and not coming down for 30 minutes, trapping thousands of us in our cars with nowhere to go.

There's not much point in cursing a Chicago bridgetender. If anything, we should have been grateful that he was sober enough not to raise the bridge while any of us were on it.

By the time the bridge lowered, and the traffic crept forward, I was hopelessly late for an interview with a source, my teeth were grinding and I was sure the entire world was plotting against me.

At Clark Street, I just caught the red light. That got me even angrier.

Suddenly, water was being sloshed across my windshield. At first, I didn't know where it was coming from.

Then I saw that a teenager had stepped from the curb with one of those gas-station tools, a combination sponge and squeegee, for cleaning windshields.

And he got me mad, too. My windshield was already spotless, so why was he cleaning it? Who asked him to? The light might change and I could lose a few more precious seconds.

Before he could use the squeegee, I gave him an angry glare, waved him off and turned on my wipers.

He stepped back on the sidewalk, shrugged, shook his head slightly and turned away.

About 16 and very skinny. His T-shirt was a grimy gray and his trousers looked like the kind that might have sold for $8 new a long time ago.

The light turned green, and I drove ahead. By the time I got to the next corner, I realized what I had just done.

That wasn't one of my sons on a corner, washing the windshields of strangers' cars, hoping some of them would be generous enough to hand him two bits. My sons never had to do anything that demeaning to put a few dollars in their pockets. They were fortunate enough to have been born Caucasian Americans, with an overpaid father.

And there I sat, in my big, black, fat-cat car, with air-conditioning blasting, stereo playing and enough electronic doodads to do everything but blow my nose.

I had enough money in my pocket to buy that skinny kid a suit, pay his family's rent for a month and maybe fill up their refrigerator and pantry.

But I hadn't had the decency to let him squeegee the windshield, then touch the button that lowers a window and give him a buck and a smile. I had given him a scowl and a wave-off, gestures that said he was a nothing.

And all the while, do you know what was playing on my stereo cassette? Peter, Paul and Mary singing that if they had a hammer, they'd hammer out love between their brothers and their sisters, all over the world—that's what was playing.

While I'm telling some ghetto kid to get lost.

Statistics ran through my mind. What's the teen-age black unemployment rate—40 or 50 percent? And we wonder why so many are into crime?

But there was a kid who wasn't grabbing my hubcaps, smashing and grabbing, mugging or heisting. All he was doing was cleaning windshields and hoping people like me might appreciate it.

Sure, it was a form of panhandling. But with that sponge and squeegee, he gave dignity to it. He was saying: "Look, I'm trying to work, I'm doing *something*."

And I tell him to bug off.

So I made a right turn at the next corner, then another one. I figured I'd double back and catch him a second time, and this time I'd give him a five-spot.

By the time I got back to the corner, he was gone. Maybe he moved to another corner. So I went around again, tried a couple more streets. But I couldn't find him.

So I drove to the office and parked. When I walked past my assistant, she said, "Good morning."

I told her it was a lousy, stinking morning.

Then I went in the men's room, looked in the mirror and saw the biggest reason for it being a lousy, stinking morning. ∎

Even darkest day has a bright side

TUESDAY, OCTOBER 20, 1987

As the Dow Jones plunged, I nervously pondered the possibility of another Great Depression and wondered what I should do to survive.

So I called my wife and said: "Buy coal."

"Why should I buy coal?"

"Because when I was a kid during the Depression, if you had coal in the basement for the furnace, you were all right."

"But we have a gas furnace."

"Buy some coal anyway in case they turn off the gas. The utilities are heartless. And buy potatoes."

"Why?"

"Because I remember that we ate a lot of potato pancakes. Cheap, and they stick to your ribs. And remember to switch off the lights."

But after we spoke, I turned on the TV and heard a financial expert say the stock plunge might merely be a long-overdue adjustment, and there is no reason to climb out on a window ledge.

Even more important, he said that this could be the time to take advantage of some shrewd buying opportunities.

Not wanting to miss any shrewd opportunities, I immediately headed for LaSalle Street, the heart of our city's financial district.

I saw a well-dressed young man stumbling along, holding his hands to his face and moaning.

"Excuse me," I said, "but can I ask you a personal question?"

"What is it?" he cried. "Make it quick, I'm heading for the nearest bridge."

"Are you a yuppie?"

"Yes, I am a devout yuppie."

"And you wouldn't happen to also be an MBA, would you?"

"To my lasting regret, yes."

"And are you a broker or a trader?"

"Yes, yes, but why are you asking me these questions."

"I just wondered what kind of watch you're wearing."

"A Rolex, of course. What kind of yuppie MBA broker-trader do you take me for?"

"Would you care to sell it?"

"Would I?" he cried, yanking it off and thrusting it at me.

I stuffed a few greenbacks in his hand and said: "Is that a Burberry trench coat you're wearing?"

"Yes, brand new," he said, tearing it off. "You want it?"

"Deal. And I can't help but notice a Mont Blanc pen in your pocket. Would you . . ."

"Name your price and you've got it. I've already used it to write a farewell note to my sweetheart, an assistant aerobics instructor."

"Thank you. And what about that Hermes scarf and the Porsche designer sunglasses, hmmmm?"

"As you can see, the scarf is newly tear-stained, so I'll knock off 10 percent."

"Make it 20. Now, let me ask what kind of wheels you have?"

He fell back against a wall as if stricken.

"You mean my . . ." And he began weeping.

"Is it a BMW?"

"Of course. Hand washed every second day since I've owned it. Oh, my Bavarian beauty."

"I know how you must feel. But at a time like this, you really should consider divesting yourself of this asset. It is a drain on your cash flow." He took the car keys from his pocket and said: "It has a list price of . . ."

I shook my head. "You don't understand. Now that the Dow has hit 1,700, the market is glutted with them."

I stuffed a few more bills into his hand and took the keys.

"Anything else?" I said.

"Well, there's my Olin skis, my Lotus Elan bike and my espresso machine."

"Where are they?"

"At my condo."

"Ah, you have a condo. Lakefront, I assume?"

"Are there condos elsewhere?"

"I'm sure we can agree on a reasonable price, including the furnishings. Deal?"

"I have little choice."

"Fine. Have we missed anything?"

"Well, yes, there is my . . . my . . . no, I can't bring myself to part with it."

"Be realistic. What is it?"

"No, I can't, it's more precious to me than anything else."

"What is it, your home multimedia center? Your Kangaroo golf bag and all-graphite clubs? Your Prince racket? You can't take them with you."

"No, it's my . . . membership in the East Bank Club. With my own locker."

"Ah, poor devil. But I'll take it. And to show you I'm not without heart, I'll bring you there one last time as my guest. Well, nice doing business with you. 'Bye.'"

"Wait," he said, as he searched through his pockets. Then he withdrew a small metal container.

"Here," he said. "You might as well have it all."

"What is it?"

"My coke," he said.

"No thanks. I prefer Pepsi." ▪

Quit smoking? That's nerve

TUESDAY, DECEMBER 3, 1985

Among the people I dislike most in the world are those who nod at the cigarette I'm smoking and say something they think is profound. Something like, "You know, those things are bad for you."

When they say that to me, I think, "Does this schnook think that I don't know the difference between a Pall Mall and a carrot stick?"

Of course I know smokes are bad for me. I've known that since I inhaled my first cigarette at age 16. I remember exactly where it was, what brand it was and why I did it.

It was at the Riverview Roller Rink, and my friend Slats suggested that if we were ever to fulfill our greatest hope in life—meeting a nice young lady and having a carnal experience—we should try to look older and more sophisticated.

Since the roller rink closed at 10 p.m., and we didn't have time to grow mustaches, we decided to smoke. And I immediately knew cigarettes weren't good for one's health. The first one made me dizzy. Then I got a splitting headache. And I went in the men's room and threw up.

The virtue of the young ladies at the roller rink was safe that day.

But we tried again. Listen, what's a little dizziness and a headache compared to the unfulfilled primal instincts of a 16-year-old? And what began as an attempt to look adult—or at least more adult than Andy Hardy—became a lifelong habit.

Which leads me to a second type of person I dislike as much as the one who tells me that cigarettes are bad for me.

He's the one who will casually say, "You know, you ought to quit smoking."

What a dummy. Does that kind of klutz think we smoke two packs a day because we're trying to get in shape to win the Olympic marathon?

If there's one thing that everybody who smokes cigarettes knows, it's that they ought to quit smoking cigarettes. They don't need the surgeon general to tell them. The morning coughing and wheezing, the panting when they pull on their socks, the shortness of breath when going uphill—even on an escalator—are broad enough hints.

If you stopped 1,000 smokers on the street and asked, "Should you stop smoking?" they'd all say yes. And if you asked all 1,000 why they were still smoking, most would say, "Because I can't stop."

Have you tried? "Sure." Then why have you failed? "Because I'm under personal pressure, job stress, it's a habit I just can't break. I am a weakling, sob, blubber, sniffle."

And they're truthful. It's a tough habit to break. And the longer you've been doing it, and the older you get, the harder it is to quit. (Oh, why can't sex be like smoking? Mother Nature must be an old prune.)

In my case, I've been smoking for 35 years. And the longest I ever went without a smoke was two and a half hours. It was a long movie.

In other words, I've never even tried because I knew I didn't have the will power.

If you've read this far, you're probably wondering why I'm going on this way and when I'm going to get to the point.

Right now.

First, I would like to admit to a lie. In Monday's paper, my column wasn't in its usual place. Instead, there was a tiny note at the bottom that said I was ill.

I wasn't ill. At least not in any conventional sense.

What happened was this: Last Friday, at 9:30 a.m., I went to a medical clinic that says it has an 85 percent success rate at breaking the smoking habit.

I didn't want to go, but my wife told me that if I smoked myself to death, she would punish me by going directly from the funeral to the Bahamas and spend all my money on skinny gigolos, rum drinks and wild living. Who wants to croak with that as a last thought?

So I went through the clinic's program, which lasts about three hours and includes being stuck with a few needles. When it was over I tossed my last pack of smokes out the car window.

Then I went home and spent the next 48 hours swallowing the pills they gave me, doing breathing exercises, chewing on carrot sticks and kicking the cats.

By Sunday afternoon, when it was time for me to go to the office and write my Monday column, my nerve endings were humming louder than the Mormon Tabernacle Choir. And I knew that if I left the house, I'd go straight to the gas station and buy a pack of smokes.

So I called in sick and spent the day swallowing the pills and chewing on more carrot sticks.

By Monday morning, I cranked up enough will power to come down here to do my job.

Which leads me to the last reason for writing on this subject.

Some of my friends are going to wonder why I have a cinnamon stick, which looks like a stubby cigar, jutting out of the corner of my mouth.

That's one of the things the doc suggested I chew on when I get the urge for a smoke. He agreed that I'd look silly walking around with a carrot sticking out of my mouth. And I'm too old to suck my thumb.

Now, if this program works and a month from now I'm still chomping cinnamon sticks instead of Pall Malls, I'm going to write about the program in detail. If as spineless a person as me can quit smoking, anybody can.

But if it fails, these will be the last words I'll write on the subject.

Except, of course, to change my will. ▪

It'll be no more Mr. Nice Guy

FRIDAY, JANUARY 2, 1987

Like most people, I make New Year's resolutions. And this year, I've resolved to be more open and honest with my friends.

That's always been a problem of mine—not saying what I really think for fear of hurting their feelings.

And in the long run, that's not good because they wind up kidding themselves about their own weaknesses and failings.

For example, when Sir Georg Solti calls me for a critique after a concert—as he usually does—I'm going to say: "Georgie, believe me, you're still the best. But that was a very sloppy adagio tonight. And, no, I will not sit in on rehearsals. There are only so many hours in the day, pal."

That goes for Mike Ditka, too. I'm going to tell him: "Don't ask me to draw up any more game plans. Why should I bother? You'll just lose your cool during the game and send in goofy plays anyway. But, okay, don't get upset, I'll sit up in the press box during the playoffs and phone down what I see. By the way, didn't I tell you in training camp to crack down on that fat kid's weight? When are you going to learn? You have to be tough."

It's not going to be easy. I'm dreading that next phone call from Meryl Streep. But I'm going to be blunt. "Meryl, you're married and I'm married. So forget me. As time goes by, your thoughts of us will fade. Almost. So goodbye. And here's looking at you, kid."

Some people are tougher than others, so I don't think Chuck Yeager will have trouble handling it when I tell him: "Sure it would be fun, but why don't we let the Voyager crew enjoy their glory. No, I won't design the plane, and I'm not going to fly it with you. Come on, do we need every record? Thanks, buddy, and you've got the right stuff, too."

A friend should try to lend a hand when it's needed. But there are limits. So I'm going to tell Dan Rather: "Of course, I've seen the slumping ratings, and I can feel for you. But my answer is the same—I'm not going to become your co-anchor. I'd have a schedule conflict because the show is on when I'm having a beer after work. No, it won't help if you ask Cronkite to call me."

Friends have to understand that they can't expect a person to spread himself too thin, to give up precious leisure time.

I hope Steve understands that. Martin, I mean. I'll give it to him straight: "Steve, I agree that it's a brilliant script. It could be the funniest thing you've ever done. But I just don't have the time to be your costar. And to ask me to also direct it? Hey, even for a friend, that's a bit much. Why don't you call Woody—he's dying for the part. Sure, it won't be great, but it'll be darned good. Chow, baby."

And a friend should understand how important privacy is. Not everybody loves the limelight.

That's hard for Robin Leach to accept, but for the 50th time I'm going to tell him: "Because we're friends, I know you're a good guy, and not the jerk you appear to be on 'Lifestyles of the Rich and Famous,' but I don't want your cameras coming into my home or tracking me on vacation. My hectic, jet-set life is something I prefer to keep to myself. I've told you before, Robin, that I'll do it when Bob De Niro does it. And I know that Bob told you that he'd do it only when I do. Catch-22, pal. Look, why don't you try one of the Saudi oil guys again. I'll give you his unlisted number."

And as much as I want to help any friend when he's down on his luck, sometimes you have to draw a line.

So when Ron calls, I'll have to say: "What have I been telling you for the last six years? Details, you have to pay attention to details. You can only delegate so much. Didn't I tell you to keep an eye on those guys in the basement? Didn't I warn you that there's more to the job than just getting on and off airplanes and waving at the cameras? I talk myself blue in the face and what do you do? You chop wood in California. So the answer is no, I'm not coming out there. I don't want Don's job. But I'll send you a white paper on how to handle this mess. Try to stay awake long enough to read it."

So that's my New Year's resolution, and I think I can do it. I'm confident because I made a resolution last year and I stuck with it.

I resolved to be more of a hard-eyed realist. ∎

Opportunity calls a wrong number

TUESDAY, JULY 12, 1988

In an aggressively cheerful voice, the caller said: "Mr. Royko? And how are you feeling this morning?"

I said: "Who are you and what do you want?"

That's the way I usually respond to bubbly people who phone and ask how I am feeling. How I'm feeling was none of his business, unless he was my physician, which he wasn't.

And I knew his question wasn't sincere. Strangers who call and ask how you are feeling really don't care. They almost always try to sell you something or put the arm on you for a favor.

So after I asked who he was and what he wanted, he said his name was David Roffman and he was a broker for a company called Blinder-Robinson.

Then he made his pitch. He said he would like to talk to me about some investment opportunities.

See? I told you he didn't really care how I was feeling.

But I was polite. Although he was interrupting me while I was trying to earn a living, I understood that he was just trying to earn a living.

So I thanked him for calling, but said that I was not interested in pursuing any investment opportunities.

That should have been the end of the conversation, but he pushed forward, asking if I bought stocks, if I made investments, and if so, what kind?

Again, I politely but firmly told him that I was working, I was busy and I was not interested in buying what he was selling. Then I said goodbye and hung up.

About three minutes later, my phone rang again. And once again it was David Roffman of Blinder-Robinson.

"We spoke earlier," he said.

Yes, we did. Three minutes ago. And three minutes ago I told you that I wasn't interested. Why are you calling me again?

"Well, I thought you might want to reconsider."

After three minutes?

"Yes, I thought you might have given it further thought and I'd . . . "

Ah, I understand. You thought that during the three minutes that elapsed, I sat back in my chair and thought: *I have blown an opportunity to become rich!* If only I had listened to that David Roffman, I might be well on my way to Easy Street by now. He could be making me rich. So, are you going to *make me rich*, Mr. Roffman?

He said: "Ha-ha, well, I don't know if I can make you rich."

You don't? Have you made anyone rich, Mr. Roffman? Can you give me the names of people who will swear under oath that your financial wisdom has built their vast fortunes?

He said: "Ha-ha, well, I can't say that, but some of them have done well."

Mr. Roffman, how old are you?

"I'm 24," he said.

You said 24?

"Yes, I'm 24."

Mr. Roffman, the day you were born, it's likely that I was doing what I'm doing today. Batting out a newspaper column and earning a decent living. My family had a sturdy roof over its head. We had food on our table. And our two dogs had food in their bowls. But do you know what has happened in those 24 years?

"What?"

I am still earning a decent living. My family still has a roof over its head. There is still food on the table and in the bowls, although the dogs have been replaced by cats. And do you know how I accomplished that?

"How?"

I did that by not being stupid enough to entrust my money to some 24-year-old guy who calls me on the telephone out of the blue and asks me to let him play games with my dough.

He was silent, so I went on. At that point I may have been ranting.

Mr. Roffman, I read the Wall Street Journal, which, with a straight face, calls itself the diary of the American dream. And all I read about are financial jackals tearing at each other's throats. I read about takeovers, insider deals, poison pills, Chapter 11s, indictments, investigations, betrayals, back-stabbings, swindles, cons and guys like Ivan Boesky going to a country club prison. I read about computers that bounce stock values like a yo-yo. And you expect me to throw my helpless, defenceless money into that den of thieves and vipers? I would be better off going to Vegas, sitting down at a blackjack table and taking hits all day on 15. Mr. Roffman, are you beginning to understand what my investment strategies are?

"Uh, you aren't interested."

Very good, Mr. Roffman. But don't feel bad. If you have a hot stock, you should call your ma, your pa, your sisters, brothers and friends and neighbors. Let them get rich. Share this golden opportunity with your loved ones. Why waste it on a stranger like me?

"I see," said Mr. Roffman. "Goodbye."

I waited three minutes. The phone didn't ring. Too bad. I never did get a chance to tell him how I was feeling that morning. ■

This hothead feels ugly, punk

WEDNESDAY, JULY 31, 1985

Maybe it's the muggy summer heat. Or it could be the position of the Moon. Or the slumping of the baseball teams. Whatever the causes, tempers seem to flare more easily at this time of the year, even among normally civil and restrained people.

An example of this could be seen a few days ago in a vignette that unfolded on a North Side street.

A man and his wife had gone out to a restaurant for dinner. They had driven separate cars because he had come from his job and she from a shopping trip.

After dinner, they left for home. He said he'd follow her—a small, protective gesture in the event of an accident, a flat tire or something of that kind.

On a main street, a few blocks from their home, they were in the right lane of traffic, waiting for the light to change so they could turn. Three or four cars were between them.

As they waited, a garishly painted clunker, with pretensions of being a hot rod, moved slowly in the other lane. Sticking out the windows were several goofily grinning young men.

They were shouting at people in the waiting lane of traffic. Things like: "Hey, baby, you turn me on. . . . Oh, doll, why don't we go out together and have a good time? . . . Hey, man, you got any grass you can spare?" As well as other youthful witticisms.

Before the light changed, their car stopped next to that of the man's wife, who happens to be an attractive blond.

The man couldn't hear what they were saying, but he saw them motion to his wife to roll down her window, which she did. And three of them were leaning out the window, pointing at her, waving their arms and laughing. And, it seemed to him, they appeared to be leering.

Anger welled up in the man. Right there on a city street, before his very eyes, his wife was being insulted, abused, molested, subjected to what were undoubtedly lewd and improper suggestions by a crew of punk barbarians. Why, it was right out of "A Clockwork Orange."

Then the light turned to green. Traffic began moving. His wife turned right.

But because a car had waited to make a left turn in the other lane, the car filled with the young men caught the next red light and stopped.

And the man found himself right next to them.

He pressed the electric button that lowered his window. Then he glared at them and snarled:

"You think you're funny, you [deleted] punk?"

One of the youths looked at him blankly and said, "Huh?"

"You're not funny," he said, his voice rising. "You're just a bunch of [deleted deleteds]."

"Hey, what's with you?"

"I'll tell you what's with me," the man shouted.

His right hand slid inside his suit jacket. At the same time, he opened his door slightly and put one foot on the pavement. And, as his face twisted into a look of magnificent menace, he bellowed:

"How would you like to have your [deleted] heads blown off, you rotten little [deleteds]."

They gaped, and one of them screamed, "Jeeeez, he's got a gun, he's got a gun!"

At that instant, the light changed. The driver, who had been looking bug-eyed, floored the gas pedal.

With a screech, the car roared into a left turn so sharp that one of the youths banged his head on the door frame. Tires squealing, it sped away.

The man clicked his door shut, turned right and pulled into the parking garage, where his wife was waiting.

"I really scared the hell out of those punks," he said, his face grim.

She looked at him in a puzzled way. "What punks?"

"Those punks in the car at the light who were molesting you."

She laughed. "They weren't molesting me. They were joking. They liked my car and asked me if I wanted to trade with them. They said they'd throw in a six-pack of beer. They were cute kids."

"Oh. I see."

"What did you say to them?"

"Uh, nothing much. I just said they shouldn't make so much noise, that's all."

"And that scared them?"

"Forget it."

And she did. But, boy, did I—uh, I mean, that guy—feel stupid. ∎

There goes another wasted 3 pounds

FRIDAY, FEBRUARY 16, 1990

The brain. What an amazing organ. Only 3 pounds or so in an adult, but containing millions of cells that create and transmit chemicals and electrical impulses controlling virtually everything we do. Every movement and thought. Every emotion. Our senses of hunger, thirst, smell, sight.

Think about that. It was that mere 3 pounds of gray and white matter in his skull that led Edison to create the phonograph, the light bulb and thousands of other devices we now take for granted.

From Einstein's 3 pounds of brain came thoughts that brought about the Atomic Age and opened new concepts of the universe.

The brains of Mozart and Beethoven brought forth sounds that today, centuries after they have died, still move audiences to joy and tears.

The brain of Shakespeare probed man's capacity for good and evil. The brain of Leonardo da Vinci conceiving of man flying four centuries before the brains of the Wright Brothers made it reality.

Remarkable machines took men to the moon and sustained their lives. But 3-pound brains created those machines. We have computers that, in a twinkling, solve mathematical problems that once took weeks, months or years. But the human brain created the computers.

All around us are soaring skyscrapers, incredible ground and air vehicles, shelf upon shelf of great literature, electronic impulses sending sights and sounds around the world in an instant. Everything from the superconducting supercollider to the humble yet gratifying McDonald's french fry—the products of that 3 pounds of gray matter in the skull of man.

But how often do most of us think about the brain, except when we have a headache. Many scientists study it, and they've solved many of its mysteries. But they still know less than they have learned.

The rest of us? Depending on our age and gender, we give far more thought to our biceps, breasts, buttocks, scalps, facial skin and reproductive organs. Ask yourself: When was the last time you thought about your brain? Or anyone else's brain, for that matter? Not lately, I'll wager.

And I'm as guilty as anyone. But just the other night I found myself pondering the amazing workings of this most incredible of organs.

It was during Wednesday's blizzard. I was behind the wheel of my car, waiting for the light to turn from red to green, so I could continue my homeward journey.

As I waited, I saw a car creep into the intersection, then stop directly in my path. The female person driving that car stopped because traffic ahead of her was jammed for blocks. She should have known that would happen. But she moved into the intersection anyway, then just sat there.

The light changed. Now it was my turn to go forward. But I couldn't. The man next to me couldn't. The dozens of people behind us couldn't. We just sat because the woman and her car barred our way.

That's when I began thinking about the incredible human brain. Einstein's equation: energy equals mass times the velocity of light squared. Edison searching the world for a filament that would light our homes and streets. Beethoven's Ninth Symphony. Popeil's Pocket Fisherman.

But there sat this creature, blessed with a 3-pound brain mass and those millions of cells. Yet she was incapable of a simple thought: "If I put my foot on the gas and creep a few more yards, I'll stop and when the light changes those people on my left won't get past me." Or a simple question:

"I'm not going anywhere anyway, so why should I block their way and make a bad situation even worse?"

The light changed again. And again. But she couldn't move. That was her bad luck, but why should she make her bad luck my bad luck? And the bad luck of dozens behind me.

Then she glanced to her left and saw me glaring at her. She quickly looked away. I guess the sight of a stranger's bared fangs was unpleasant.

It occurred to me that her brain's problem might be a lack of information. Input, as the computer people call it. I decided to give her some input.

I stepped out of my car and bellowed: "Lady, you know what you are? You are a [Editor's note: On rare occasions, Royko uses language that isn't appropriate for a family newspaper. In this case, it wouldn't be appropriate for an X-rated movie. So we have removed it. But you can use your imagination.]

"That's what you are, you stupid [Editor's note: Same disclaimer.]"

Because I have a loud voice, she heard every word. And her jaw dropped. A good sign. It meant the brain cells that receive and interpret crude, vile, obscene language were functioning. So were the brain cells that make jaws drop.

The driver on my right honked his horn. He waved and gave me a thumbs up gesture, an indication that his 3-pound cerebral mass was in good working order.

For a moment I thought about asking him if he would care to join me in getting out our tire irons and smashing her headlights and windows. But a portion of my brain told me that while it would be an act of true justice, it would accomplish nothing more than to make me feel good.

Eventually, she moved on. And as her wheels spun, she turned and stuck out her tongue. How disappointing. It meant that my input had been rejected and, when the opportunity arose, she'd block another intersection.

Nevertheless, I'm still amazed at the workings of the human brain. And someday science will figure out why brains are wasted on so many damn fools. ▪

Top grouch honors go to—yours truly

THURSDAY, AUGUST 24, 1989

Sometimes I am amazed by the incredible stupidity, insensitivity and poor judgment of Chicagoans. This is one of those times.

Recently I noted that a small town in Texas had held a contest to choose the town's biggest grouch.

So I thought it might be entertaining to invite my readers to send in their votes for the Top Well-Known Grouch in Chicago.

They did and the votes have been cast and tabulated. The results are in.

And in the view of those who voted, the Top Well-Known Grouch turns out to be me.

The contest wasn't even close. It was a stunning landslide.

I received 40 percent of the votes. Jesse Jackson was a distant second with 11 percent; Congressman Dan Rostenkowski and Bernie Lincicome tied with 8 percent; Jane Byrne and Ald. Dorothy Tillman had 6 percent; and the rest were scattered among Congressman Gus Savage, TV creatures Hugh Hill, Walter Jacobson and Bulldog Drummond, and Rev. Willie Barrow, George Dunne, Don Zimmer, Mike Ditka and a few others.

Forty percent consider me a grouch? The city's Grouchiest Grouch? I find that unbelievable.

It's true that like any normal human being I have an occasional day when I get up on the wrong side of the bed and am not in the best of spirits.

But the vast majority of the time, I am a good-natured, cheerful, optimistic, upbeat, fun guy. A joy to be around. When I sit down to do my job, my goal is to bring sunshine and joy to the readers, to leave them feeling happy and inspired, glad to be alive and whistling while they work or play.

And anyone who disputes that is a damn fool and ought to have his or her teeth bashed in.

When my assistant finished tabulating the vote, I expressed amazement that a chronic griper like Walter Jacobson would receive less than 2 percent.

"But Walter is kind of tiny and cute," she said.

"You think he is cute?" I asked.

"Sometimes," she said.

So I fired her. Let the ninny find a job with someone who is cute.

And when I told my wife about the results, she said, "I'm surprised."

"I thought you would be," I said, giving her a peck on the cheek.

"Yes, I would have expected you to get 90 percent."

"Shut up and make dinner," I said, giving her a cuff to the head.

Some of the voters, the few who were capable of constructing a simple sentence, added comments, such as that of J.M. Baggott, of Benton, Ill.

Mr. Baggott said: "You are so sour that if you looked at a cucumber, you would have an instant pickle."

Now, if I was a genuine grouch, Mr. Baggott's line might have offended me. But it didn't. In fact, it made me chuckle. However, I am surprised that a rube from a hick town like Benton would have even this tad of wit. My guess is that the yokel lifted it from a book of one-liners.

And someone named Maddie said: "Boy, I'd hate to have been one of your kids. They were probably too scared to color in their coloring books for fear they might go outside the lines."

I accept that comment with my usual good cheer. However, had you been one of my kids, you would not have been messing with coloring books. I would have told you to go outside and play in traffic.

My column photo seems to have swayed the thinking of some of the voters.

Leonard A. Stein, of Lincolnwood (as pretentious a community as I've ever seen), said: "No contest. Just look at the picture at the top of your column."

This sentiment was echoed by Mike Carter, of University Park, who said: "Everyone knows you are the grouchiest public figure in Chicago. And you're apparently getting grouchier if your new picture is any indication of your development."

That surprises me because I don't think my column photo conveys grouchiness. If anything, it reflects my kindly, gentle, caring, benign nature.

However, if it strikes anyone as looking grouchy, it's not my fault. The blame rests with the blatant, bumbling incompetence of the photographer who took the picture. And I'm going to demand that the editor fire him. If his wife and children end up hungry and homeless, that will serve as a good lesson to him to never again make a nice guy look grouchy.

As some of you may remember, the contest also included a category for the Top Unknown Grouch. I received a large stack of entries from those who claimed this title for their spouses, in-laws, siblings and co-workers. I'll share some of their cruel thoughts with you sometime next week.

Meanwhile, I want to thank everyone who took a few minutes out of their busy days to take part in this contest. I appreciate each and every comment, as dumb as they were. ∎

CHAPTER 2
For Better and For Worse, We All Gotta Eat

Hey, all you on the sauce . . .

TUESDAY, JUNE 5, 1984

S ome friends were going out for dinner and invited me along.

"We're going to get ribs," one of them said. "Do you know a good barbecue place?"

"Forget it," I said.

"Don't you like ribs?"

What a ridiculous question. Do I like ribs? That's like asking an alderman if he likes money. Considering that I am widely known as one of the great rib gourmets of the entire world, the question was almost an insult.

"Well then, let's go," they said.

"I'm sorry," I said. "But I no longer eat ribs in restaurants."

"But you said you love them."

"I do. And that is precisely why I don't ever eat them in restaurants."

"Why not? You can get good ribs in restaurants."

"Yes. Some are very good. But not good enough for me."

"Then where do you eat ribs?"

I explained that my standards for ribs are so high, my palate so demanding, my taste buds so sophisticated, that I could eat only the finest barbecued ribs known to civilized man. Ribs carefully selected from only the choicest piggies, then slowly smoked and cooked and finally covered with an incredible sauce containing 247 secret ingredients. Ribs so wonderful they defy description.

"My goodness," they said, "where do you get such ribs?"

There is only one source. I get them when this city's greatest rib cooker is in a mood to put them on the grill.

"And who is this person?" they demanded.

"You are looking at him," I said. "I hate false modesty."

29

"You?" they said, in disbelief.

"Yes, me. In some circles, I'm known as The Big Sauce. Or Super Bone. Or simply, Mr. Wonderful."

They scoffed. I'm used to that. It's human nature. To this day there are people who don't understand or appreciate Beethoven.

And one of them sneered: "But you're of the white persuasion. Everybody knows that the best rib cooks are of the black persuasion."

That's a common stereotype, and there might even be some truth in it. Yes, in general, blacks do cook ribs better than whites. That's because they don't go in for such terrible acts as preboiling or prebaking or any of the other sins against ribs. They cook the meat slowly over charcoal or wood chips.

But I know all the tricks. And I have the advantage of possessing a secret sauce recipe, created by my ancestor, Aunt Willie Mae Royko, who invented barbecuing 478 years ago in Warsaw, and handed down from generation to generation.

"If you are the best, prove it," they said.

I suppose I should. And there is only one way to do it.

So I am announcing the Second Annual Royko Ribfest, which will be held Sept. 16, a Sunday, in Grant Park.

As some of you will recall, the First Annual Royko Ribfest was held two years ago. I skipped a year because I don't like having annual events too often.

It was one of the biggest gatherings of amateur rib cooks in world history— with more than 400 of them gathered for a day of grilling, basting, nibbling, sipping, listening to a little blues music and thrilling to the drama of the judging and the awarding of the grand championship trophy.

Like the first one, this year's Ribfest will determine who the greatest of rib cooks really is. In other words, it will be me against the field.

Because of uncontrollable factors, I didn't win that first contest, making it only to the semifinals. I became preoccupied with the administrative duties of running so massive an event, and my cooking suffered. Also, the judges were stupid.

But this year, the outcome will be different, I'm sure. I'm ready for all challengers. And how can you become a challenger?

We will have space this time for 600 contestants, their grills, lawn chairs, tables, coolers, noisy brats, etc.

If you wish to enter, it's simple. All you have to do is send me a card or letter giving your name, address and phone number, and saying you want to compete in the Ribfest.

Address it to Royko Ribfest, Chicago Tribune, 435 N. Michigan Ave., Chicago 60611.

The first 600 entries will be accepted. So if you want to get in don't dawdle. Do it now.

When the first Ribfest ended, I promised the contestants that they would automatically get into the next one. You will. But you must also send a card or a letter.

Just mention in it that you are a past contestant. We'll check it against our old list to make sure you aren't fibbing.

Now, there are people who don't cook ribs, but fancy themselves to be rib experts and love to eat ribs that other people cook. In other words, you are moochers.

Well, there is a place for you in this contest. You could be selected as a judge. We will need more than 100 judges for the preliminaries.

To apply for this great honor—what a deal, all you do is eat—just send me a letter giving your qualifications. Brag all you wish. That's part of the rib culture. Send the letter to the same address. If you were a judge last time, mention that and you will have extra clout for being chosen again.

I'm sure there are many questions, and they'll all be answered in columns this week.

For now, mark your calendar, send in the card or letter and begin brewing your secret sauce.

The last time, we created a barbecue cloud that could be seen as far away as Indiana and Wisconsin. The simple folk thought we had been nuked.

This time, the cloud will be even bigger. And Chicago will never smell better. ∎

Men and washrooms: A commodious theory

FRIDAY, JANUARY 20, 1995

It's been a few days since the last terrifying food report. I believe a study showed that eating too much turkey can cause severe sneezing attacks if you fail to first remove the feathers.

So if you are looking for something to worry about, you might consider the concerns of Hank Blumenthal, of Highland Park.

The Blumenthals dine out a lot, and Blumenthal says he has noticed something that bothered him enough to bring it to my attention and suggest that the public be made aware of it.

"Have you ever gone to the men's room in a nice restaurant," he says, "and observed how few men wash their hands before leaving?"

I had to admit that I pay little attention to who does or doesn't wash their hands. It's always been a matter of indifference to me, since I seldom ask the waiter to bring me a plate of customer fingers.

Blumenthal agreed that the decision whether or not to wash one's hands is a private matter, unless a person is going to put his fingers in your food or mouth.

"In general, it is their own business," Blumenthal said. "However, I have a problem with those fellows who then stop by the reception counter and plunge their fingers into the mint candy dish and poke around until they find the flavor they want.

"I became aware of this situation recently when, after I washed my hands, another gentleman who had just zipped up exited the men's room at the same time as I, but stopped at the counter for a handful of candy before leaving.

"I have since become aware of this practice by some of my fellow diners. I have made a somewhat informal study of the men who come out of the washroom and let their fingers do the walking in the candy dish.

"A fair percentage of them wash their hands first, but others don't.

"As a result of my observations, I now skip the mints unless they are wrapped. I would just as soon stop somewhere else and buy myself a Snickers bar.

"But I thought you might be interested in following up my observations with an investigation.

"You might get a half-empty dish of candy from a few restaurants and have them examined by an independent laboratory and publish a urinalysis report on the findings."

Yes, I suppose an investigation of this sort could result in a potentially sensational headline: "Wee-Wee Germs Found On Bistro Mints! Dining Slobs Blamed!"

But there could be other headlines too. "Columnist Caught Lurking Near Restaurant Washrooms!" Or, "Columnist Seized Stealing Restaurant Mints!"

After I spoke to Blumenthal, I passed along his concerns to a restaurant operator, Sam Sianis, of the Billy Goat.

Sianis nodded and said: "I never eat mints in a restaurant."

Because you fear that they are contaminated by the fingers of those who don't wash their hands?

"No," he said, "because mints make me burp."

Giving it further thought, Sianis said: "Restaurants shouldn't put mint candy out like that."

Because of the threat of contamination?

"No," he said, "because if you give free candy some cheapskates won't order dessert."

Although he does not provide free mints, Sianis said he once had a problem with his mustard, which he puts out for hamburger eaters, along with onions and pickles.

"This woman is standing by the counter and she asks me if I have Grey Poupon. I told her I have American yellow, and it is better than Grey Poupon.

"So she puts her finger in the mustard pan. I ask her, 'Why you do that?' She says she wants to know how it tastes before she puts it on a hamburger. I told her that she shouldn't do that because I don't know where that finger has been.

"Her boyfriend says, 'Are you telling my girlfriend that there is something wrong with her finger?' I said, 'I don't know where her finger has been, and I don't know where your finger has been.' Nowadays, how do you know? So I have to put out a whole new pan of mustard.

"So the girlfriend said, 'I have never been talked to that way before.' And I told her, 'Well, you go around putting your finger in other people's mustard, and you'll get talked to that way a lot, and maybe you will also get a broken finger.'

"So the boyfriend says, 'Are you threatening my girlfriend?'"

"And I picked up my biggest knife and said: 'No, not your whole girlfriend; only her finger.'"

"After that, neither of them put their fingers in the mustard again. See, you explain things to people nice, they understand."

How true. In the meantime, though, we might be wise to skip the mints.

But Blumenthal, a man with sharp powers of observation, also said: "I sometimes wonder if the same threat exists with the bartender who tops off my vodka martini with a lemon twist.

"Of course, the alcohol would probably kill any germs. That's one of the benefits of a martini."

Advertising men can feel free to use that thought in a commercial. ∎

When 'prix fixe' is hard to swallow

MONDAY, JUNE 27, 1988

While browsing through a restaurant directory, I suggested to the blond that we might try a place that was newly listed.

She asked if it was expensive and I said that it had a "prix fixe" dinner.

"A *what*?" she said.

I repeated, "Prix fixe."

"How is it spelled?"

I spelled it aloud and again said: "Prix fixe."

"You're not pronouncing it correctly," she said.

Why not? I'm pronouncing it exactly the way it is spelled.

"No, no. If you say it that way, it sounds, well, it sounds obscene."

I said it again: "Prix fixe," the way it is spelled. And she may be right. It did sound like it might be a phrase describing some sort of male surgical procedure.

"The proper pronunciation," the blond said, flaunting her refined upbringing, "is pree feeks."

Then why isn't it spelled pree feeks?

"Because it is French. And in French, pree feeks is spelled prix fixe."

How stupid of me. I had forgotten that the first rule of the French language is that almost nothing is pronounced the way it's spelled. When the French invented their language, they rigged it that way just to make the rest of us feel inferior. They also thought that if they had a language that was almost impossible to learn, the Germans might not invade them.

"Pree feeks," the blond said. "It simply means fixed price."

I already knew that much. The question is, why do newspaper and magazine restaurant listings in the United States, where most of us speak one form of English or another, insist on using "prix fixe," which is pronounced "pree feeks" and means "fixed price," instead of "fixed price," which means fixed price and is pronounced "fixed price"?

My guess is that the vast majority of Americans do not know how to pronounce "prix fixe." And a great many don't even know what it means.

Why, if you went into some restaurants in Arkansas or Tennessee and asked if they had a "prix fixe" dinner—pronouncing it the way it is spelled—it's likely that the waiter would bellow, "Ya lowdown preevert," and hit you with a catfish.

This newspaper, I'm sorry to say, is no exception. We have "prix fixes" scattered all through our restaurant listings. I asked a few copy editors, who are experts in such matters, why we don't just say "fixed price." They weren't sure.

One of them said that he thought we did it when reviewing French restaurants.

If so, we're being inconsistent. We may even be discriminating.

For example, when we list a German restaurant, we don't say "fester preis," which is German for fixed price.

Fester preis. It has a pleasant, homey ring. It sounds like the name of somebody who lives deep in the Ozarks. "Howdy, I'm Fester Preis and this here is my brother Lester Preis and my uncle Chester Preis."

In our listings for Chinese restaurants, we don't write "Gu din jia ge," which I was told by a Chinese acquaintance means fixed price. Of course, he might have been pulling my leg. For all I know, it means: "The person who wrote this column is a geek." But I'll take his word for it.

I was going to include the Greek version of "fixed price," but Sam Sianis, who owns Billy Goat Tavern, said: "Feex price? You crazy? In Greek joints, we no got feex price. We charge what we can get."

Another copy editor told me that "prix fixe" is used so widely that it had become the accepted, common meaning for "fixed price."

That didn't make sense to me, either. I've never picked up the financial pages and read a story that said:

"Three steel companies have been accused by the antitrust division of the Justice Department of prix fixeing. The companies engaged in the fixe, sources say, to drive up the prix of steel."

Years ago, when Chicago was strictly a meat-and-potatoes town, we didn't have such linguistic problems.

I suppose that as we became more sophisticated, this was the prix we paid. ∎

Just think cheese, you have to laugh

WEDNESDAY, JANUARY 3, 1990

Several angry Chicagoans have sent me postcards, produced in Wisconsin, that they consider insulting to our city.

The postcard has a title that says "Street Art" and it shows two pictures.

One is a dingy alley. On the pavement is a chalk outline of a human figure. It's what the crime lab draws before it removes a murder victim. Under this picture is the word "Chicago."

The other picture shows a sidewalk with another chalk drawing. But this drawing shows the design of a hopscotch game, with a jump-rope lying across it. Under it are the words: "Fox River Valley, Wi."

Turning the card over, we read: "A graphic contrast: FBI statistics rate the Fox River Valley, Wisconsin, among the 10 safest areas in the nation. Here, children still play freely; women walk unescorted; and an unlocked car door does not necessarily mean an instant insurance claim. The Fox River Valley, Wisconsin, where the good life still exists!"

There are phone numbers on the card, so we phoned and discovered that it was produced by the Fox Cities Chamber of Commerce, which includes Fond du Lac, Appleton and Oshkosh.

The purpose of the cards is to lure Chicago industry to the safety and tranquility of their community.

"Basically, the postcard was designed somewhat tongue in cheek to compare the quality of life and the business climate in Chicago versus the Fox River Valley area in east-central Wisconsin," said Greg Hunt, vice president of economic development for the group. "I want to emphasize that it wasn't an effort to offend the Chicago area."

Of course not. Why should an attempt to steal industry and jobs by showing a homicide scene offend anyone?

Unfortunately, it did. As Tamara Delin, a North Sider who sent me her card, said: "I have never been so appalled. It is a disgraceful form of advertising, especially from a neighboring state. I have lived here all my life and for all good and bad, I still love this great city."

And as someone who signed his note only Fred said: "A guy at work showed me this card. Why don't you stick it to those hicks?"

I can't do that. The card might be offensive, but it's not sufficient provocation for a verbal feud.

Besides, there is some truth in the card's portrayal of Chicago. We do have more than our fair share of homicides, so why deny it?

And it is also true that cities like Fond du Lac are more tranquil. I've been to Fond du Lac, and most of the people appear so tranquil that their eyes are glazed, their jaws hang slackly and a few drooled.

No, I can't find it in my heart to lash out at those northern neighbors we josh as cheeseheads. I've traveled through much of Wisconsin, and I'm genuinely fond of it.

From its farms to its cities, you won't find kinder, simpler folk anywhere, except in custodial care.

Of course, a few of the farm folk are weird. Living out in the boonies can do that. There used to be a farmer named Ed, who was a loner and had a strange hobby. He turned the skin of some of his neighbors into lampshades. He pickled the rest.

Ed was an exception, of course, although it's still a good idea to lock your rustic cabin door. You never know what hobby might be going around.

Most of the cheeseheads are fine citizens, content to chomp on a bratwurst, burp, yank on the underside of a cow and wear long red underwear to formal social events. There's nothing wrong with long red underwear, but up there they wear it as an outer garment.

But there's more to Wisconsin than the farms and the fishing lodges, with the Japanese-made plastic muskies hanging behind the bars.

There's Milwaukee, a clean, well-run, orderly city. It was named after Chicago's Milwaukee Avenue because so many early Wisconsin travelers were impressed that the taverns on that street had separate washrooms. Or any washrooms.

Many sports fans have forgotten that Kareem Abdul-Jabbar played for the Milwaukee Bucks when he was still named Lew Alcindor. However, after every resident of Milwaukee asked him the same droll question, "How's the weather up there?" he demanded to be traded. When he left, a Wisconsin paper had an editorial that said: "And he never did tell us how the weather was up there, the ingrate."

There's also Madison, a progressive city with the campus of the renowned University of Wisconsin. Although some people still think of the university as a hotbed of radicals and leftists, I see nothing unusual about Midwestern students saying to their parents: "Mom, Dad, you are no-good, gringo imperialists."

Madison is also home to some of the most fervent feminists, who wear buttons that say: "Male is a four-letter word." I have to admire their spunk and unwillingness to conform. And I didn't think it was funny when a friend of mine returned from a visit to Madison and said:

"I saw this feminist woman near the campus and complimented her on her luxurious fur boots. She said: 'I'm not wearing boots.'"

So it is silly to get angry over a postcard. Like it or not, crime has a role in our history. Countless movies and TV dramas have been made about Chicago's gangsters. That's all part of our image. And while we might not be happy with it, when was the last time you saw a hit movie about a Wisconsin farmer kissing his cow? ■

Endorsements just a shell game

TUESDAY, JULY 16, 1985

The man from an advertising agency had an unusual proposition.

His agency does the TV commercials for a well-known chain of Mexican restaurants in Chicago.

"You may have seen our commercials," he said. "They include a cameo appearance by Lee Smith and Leon Durham of the Cubs. It shows them crunching into a tortilla."

No, I somehow missed seeing that.

"Well, anyway, we'd like to have you in a commercial."

Doing what?

"Crunching into a tortilla."

I thought tortillas were soft. I may be wrong, but I don't think you can crunch into a tortilla. Maybe you mean a taco.

"Well, you'd be biting into some kind of Mexican food."

What else would I have to do?

"That's it. It would be a cameo appearance. You'd be seen for about four seconds. You wouldn't have to say anything."

I'd just bite into a piece of Mexican food?

"Right. For a fee, of course."

How big a fee?

He named a figure. It was not a king's ransom, but it was more than walking-around money.

"It would take about 45 minutes to film," he said.

Amazing. In my first newspaper job almost 30 years ago, I had to work 12 weeks to earn the figure he had mentioned.

It was a small, twice-a-week paper, and I was the only police reporter, the only sports reporter, the only investigative reporter and the assistant political writer, and on Saturday I would edit the stories going into the entertainment page. The publisher believed in a day's work for an hour's pay.

Now I could make the same amount just for spending 45 minutes biting into a taco in front of a TV camera.

And when I was in the military, it would have taken eight monthly paychecks to equal this one taco-crunching fee. Of course, I also got a bunk and meals and could attend free VD lectures.

"Well, what do you think?" he asked.

I told him I would think about it and get back to him.

So I asked Slats Grobnik, who has sound judgment, what he thought of the deal.

"That's a lot of money just to bite a taco on TV. For that kind of scratch, I'd bite a dog. Grab the deal."

But there is a question of ethics.

"Ethics? What's the ethics in biting a taco? Millions of people bite tacos every day. Mexicans have been biting them for hundreds of years. Are you saying that Mexicans are unethical? Careful, some of my best friends are Mexicans."

No, I'm not saying that at all. I like Mexicans, though I'm opposed to bullfighting.

"Then what's unethical?"

The truth is, I can't stand tacos.

"What has that got to do with it? I can't stand work, but I do it for the money."

It has everything to do with it. If I go on TV and bite into a taco, won't I be endorsing that taco?

"So what? You've endorsed politicians and I've never met a politician that I liked better than a taco."

But endorsing a taco I didn't like would be dishonest.

"Hey, that's the American way. Turn on your TV and look at all the people who endorse junk. Do you think they really believe what they're saying?"

Then it's wrong. Nobody should endorse a taco if they don't like a taco.

"Then tell them you'll bite something else. A tortilla or an enchilada."

But I don't like them either. The truth is, I can't stand most Mexican food. The only thing I really like is the salt on the edge of a margarita glass. Oh, and I do like tamales.

"Good, then bite a tamale."

No, because the only tamales I like are the kind that used to be sold by the little Greeks who had hot dog pushcarts on the streets. They were factory-produced tamales about the size and weight of a lead pipe. But I don't think anybody would want me to do a TV commercial for hot dog stand tamales.

"Can't you just bite the taco and spit it out when the camera is turned off?"

That would be a sham. Besides, even if I liked tacos or tortillas, what does it matter? Why should somebody eat in a restaurant because they see me biting into that restaurant's taco? Am I a taco expert? What are my credentials to tell millions of people what taco they should eat? I'm not even a Mexican.

"You're as Mexican as Jane Byrne, and she's doing it."

To get the Hispanic vote, she would go on TV and eat a cactus.

"Well, you're a sucker to turn it down. Why, it's almost un-American. Do you think that in Russia any newsman would ever have an opportunity to make that much money by biting into a pirogi?"

That may be so. But maybe someday a food product will come along that I can lend my name to, something I can truly believe in.

"I doubt it. Not unless they start letting taverns advertise shots and beers on TV." ∎

Real Chicago pizza isn't 'Chicago pizza'

THURSDAY, MARCH 25, 1993

A publicity firm that represents a corporation has sent me a large package of information about pizza. More specifically, what has become widely known as "Chicago pizza."

It begins: "There are few legends in the culinary world. There are even fewer original ideas. But then again, Ike Sewell was one of a kind.

"Fifty years ago, Ike Sewell created the original deep-dish pizza and founded Pizzeria Uno, one of the most popular restaurants in Chicago and now across the country. The saga of Ike Sewell is a true American success story, which will be celebrated throughout this year.

"We think you will agree that America loves pizza. We believe that your readers will be surprised to learn that one of their favorite Italian dishes is American, created by an All-American football player who was raised on a Texas ranch."

The publicist goes on to describe the hoopla that will accompany the 50th anniversary of the late Ike Sewell's creation.

So what I have is information from a publicist for a corporation located near Boston that now owns the Chicago restaurant that was started by a Texan to sell an American version of an Italian dish.

Well, if I may be excused, I will skip the festivities. I really don't want to hurt the feelings of the corporation that now runs the chain of Pizzeria Uno clones around the country, but I can't stand deep-dish pizza.

And for years I have been fighting a lonely battle against calling this particular food "Chicago pizza." In the words of Slats Grobnik, "it ain't."

I consider it an insult to the taste buds and intestinal tracts of Chicagoans to call this thick, heavy slab of dough and topping "Chicago pizza."

To hear them talk, Chicagoans had never tasted pizza until Ike Sewell opened his first place on Rush Street.

Not so.

When I was about 5 years old—which was a few years before Ike Sewell got his idea—my mother regularly visited a lady friend on Taylor Street.

In those Great Depression days, most mothers didn't hire baby-sitters. Unless there was a grandparent or an older sister handy, you dragged the kid along.

So we would ride the streetcars to Halsted and Taylor, then the gateway to one of the biggest Italian neighborhoods in America, and walk to Angela's flat.

After they talked and had coffee, the highlight of the day came. We'd walk down the street to one of the many Italian restaurants and have . . . of course, pizza.

Even now, I can remember what I liked best about it, besides the way it tasted.

You did not need a knife or a fork or any other silverware. You grabbed it with your mitts and chomped.

This, of course, is what has made pizza a national dish. Like the hamburger, the hot dog or fried chicken—the other great American foods—you eat it with your hands.

Being logical little creatures, kids know that anything you can eat with your hands is better than something you have to cut with a knife or stab with a fork.

But we're talking about thin-crust pizza, not the thick slabs that Ike Sewell successfully marketed to the pizza-ignorant.

If you try to pick up a piece of deep-dish pizza, you might get a hernia. Or it could fall on your lap and break your thigh bone.

And the worst part is that it is so thick and heavy, you can eat only a slice or two. And that requires a knife and fork.

Ah, but with good thin-crust pizza, you can pop piece after piece into your mouth, like potato chips, until you are in a happy, satisfied stupor.

That's why about 80 percent of the pizza joints in and around Chicago use thin crusts, which is the true Chicago pizza.

This probably surprises tourists, yuppies and lifelong suburbanites, who have spread the myth that Chicago pizza is the cumbersome creation of Ike Sewell.

They are the same kind of people who put ketchup on a hot dog. And look at you blankly when you tell them that a true Chicago hot dog should receive a dash of celery salt, the barbarians.

And despite what the Boston corporation's publicist says, Ike Sewell didn't even invent deep-dish pizza.

Simple logic requires that we ask how a Texan could come to Chicago and—voila!—decide to create a new form of pizza. We are talking about Texas, where a deep-fried boot is considered gourmet cuisine.

The fact is, Ike Sewell knew a couple of Chicago Italians named Rudy Malnati and Ric Riccardo Sr. These guys knew how to toss spices. They came up with the deep-dish concept, and Ike Sewell marketed it. Both went on to start their own pasta joints.

So if we want to celebrate the 50th anniversary of a real shrewd businessman, who knew how to regularly get the names of his restaurants into gossip columns, that is one thing.

But to call that stuff "Chicago pizza" is an insult to every potbellied glutton in this great city. We burp in shame. ▪

Even a U.S. senator can somehow botch a recipe for success

TUESDAY, NOVEMBER 21, 1995

This simple little quiz is directed at those who love hot dogs. Not any hot dog, but the true, classic Chicago hot dog. The finest hot dog known to man.

Look at the following recipe and see if something is wrong. If so, what?

Chicago hot dog: Vienna beef hot dog, poppyseed bun, dill pickle, jalapenos, relish, mustard, ketchup. Place dog in bun. Cover with jalapenos, relish, mustard and ketchup. Serve with dill pickle.

The flaws are so obvious that by now those with civilized, discriminating Chicago taste buds are snorting and sneering and flinging this shameful recipe to the floor and spitting on it.

It deserves nothing less.

But not merely because it includes ketchup and omits sliced tomatoes, chopped onions and that miraculous dash of celery salt.

No, I won't condemn anyone for putting ketchup on a hot dog. This is the land of the free. And if someone wants to put ketchup on a hot dog and actually eat the awful thing, that is their right.

It is also their right to put mayo or chocolate syrup or toenail clippings or cat hair on a hot dog.

Sure, it would be disgusting and perverted, and they would be shaming themselves and their loved ones. But under our system of government, it is their right to be barbarians.

The crime is in referring to the above abomination as a "Chicago hot dog."

And who did it?

Brace yourselves for a real shocker.

Some time ago, a hot dog recipe book was put together by the American Meat Institute, the National Hot Dog and Sausage Council and other groups that promote the eating of dead animal flesh.

They got their recipes by calling the offices of United States senators. Being publicity freaks, most of the senators responded.

Most of the recipes are ridiculous, since most senators are ridiculous.

And this shameful recipe was contributed by Senator Carol Moseley Braun.

Yes, Sen. Moseley Braun, who claims to be a Chicagoan, actually told them that a Chicago hot dog includes ketchup. And it doesn't require chopped onions or sliced tomatoes or celery salt.

I don't know what could have possessed her to do such a thing. She is a liberal Democrat, so I can understand her deep yearning to seize our money and throw it hither and yon like so much political confetti. That's part of the natural order of Washington creatures.

But to publicly state that you put ketchup on a Chicago hot dog? And overlook celery salt? It is said that power corrupts. I didn't know that it brings on utter madness.

Apparently Sen. Moseley Braun pays little or no attention to my efforts to maintain standards in those things that are unique to Chicago.

If she did, she would have noted a column that appeared here in July of 1993. In it, various hot dog experts said the following about ketchup.

Maurie Berman, who owns Superdawg on Milwaukee at Devon, where I've been eating classic hot dogs for about 40 years: "I see more and more desecrations of the Chicago hot dog. Yes, we provide ketchup, but we have the customer defile it himself.

"We say, 'Sir, the ketchup bottle is on the side. We'll ask you to squirt that yourself.'"

John Miyares, who serves hot dogs at the Irving's near the Loyola campus, says: "No ketchup, no kraut. That's the law. But when you're younger and your mom lets you put ketchup on the hot dog, you get used to it, I guess. The people about 35 and over, they get upset if you mention ketchup, especially if they're born and raised here. And even more if they're South Siders.

"But we get a lot of students from out of town, and they all want ketchup. Except if they're from New York. They want steamed sauerkraut."

Pat Carso, manager of Demon Dogs, 944 Fullerton, said: "You have to ask for it. And more people are asking. I don't know why. Maybe parents think it is better for their kids. But we choose not to put it on. Even if they say 'everything.' In here, that does not include ketchup. We don't even keep ketchup up front. We have a little bottle in the back if people ask for it."

These men are keepers of the flame. They are cultural and culinary descendants of the short Greeks who used to bring their pushcarts into every Chicago neighborhood and would have thumbed the eyeballs of anyone who dared ask for ketchup.

But here we have a United States senator, allegedly representing Chicago and the rest of Illinois—even the Downstate yokels—and she shames herself and the rest of us by displaying her ignorance of what makes a hot dog a true Chicago hot dog.

I'm sure Sen. Moseley Braun has the usual excuse. Someone on her staff did it.

Well, forget it. That only proves that senators hire boobs.

No, the buck and the hot dog stops here.

There is time for Sen. Moseley Braun to mend her ways. But if the election were held today, I'd have to vote for just about anyone running against Sen. Moseley Braun.

Especially someone who knows the difference between ketchup and Shinola. ■

If it tastes bad, fatty, eat it up

FRIDAY, MAY 11, 1984

A fat actor has written the latest best-selling diet book about how he shed excess blubber. If you are overweight, you might be tempted to buy it. Don't waste your money.

Like many of the popular diet books—and there's always one on the best seller lists—it's basically a ripoff.

That's because the author tries to convince tubby people that they can lose weight while still enjoying tasty, delicious, yummy, satisfying meals.

It can't be done. I've read all kinds of diet books because, like most self-indulgent Americans, I've spent much of my adult life overweight.

I've tried the old-drinking-man's diet, the eat-anything-you-want diet, the three-squares-a-day diet, the lotsa-spicy-meatballs diet, the gobble-pasta-till-you-burst diet and all the other enjoy-eating-and-lose-weight diets.

No matter what they claim, there is only one diet that works.

I call it: The-You-Gotta-Suffer Diet.

Having just lost 25 pounds in about 10 weeks, I know it works and I'm willing to share it with you. It's quite simple. You don't have to do a lot of calorie counting, measuring and weighing tiny bits of food or poring over time-consuming recipes.

All you have to do is be miserable, which is fundamental to any successful diet. And you have to remember only one rule, the cornerstone of my diet.

The rule is: If you enjoy it, you can't have it; if you don't like it, you can eat all you want.

This rule derives from the scientifically acknowledged fact that Mother Nature is a nasty, sadistic, mean broad. She made everything that tastes good fattening. And everything that is not fattening tastes terrible.

An example is the Brussels sprout. Under my diet, you can eat all the Brussels sprouts you want. Stuff yourself with them. Shove them in your mouth with both hands. You won't gain an ounce.

That's because Brussels sprouts are awful. Just as lettuce, celery, cabbage, carrots and most vegetables are awful.

The only vegetable that isn't awful is the potato—and only when it is french fried. Or baked and heaped with butter, sour cream and chunks of bacon. Or covered with gooey cheese. Then the potato tastes great. Therefore, you can't eat it.

See how simple it is?

Let's say you go to a German restaurant. There's no big problem in ordering low-calorie foods. You just order the worst thing on the menu.

The menu might have a pork shank with dumplings, which is great cuisine. So, you can't order it.

Instead, you order the broiled white fish, with some sliced tomatoes on the side. It's enough to make me gag.

When the waiter asks you what you will drink, you follow the suffering rule. The best thing to drink would be a liter of German beer. The only thing better would be two liters of German beer. So you can't order it.

Instead, you order the worst thing the bar serves: a diet pop. Or, if you are stupid as well as overweight, Perrier with a twist.

Then comes dessert. You probably want something wonderful, like a big slab of cheesecake or some kind of rich chocolate cake.

Which means you can't have it. Instead, you must suffer and ask if they have any fresh melon. Squirt a bit of lemon juice on it, smile and pretend you are having a fine time, while you are ready to scream and do violence.

Or maybe you choose an Italian restaurant. Once again, the choice is not difficult. The best thing on the menu would probably be a plate of fettuccine Alfredo, or spaghetti carbonara or lasagna. With a bottle or two of red wine. And a snort of anisette with your coffee.

So you order the baked halibut. With Tab.

The rule applies day and night, every meal, every snack.

Breakfast? Don't eat anything good, such as pancakes with sausage, French toast with bacon or hash with eggs. Eat miserable stuff, like a half a bowl of oatmeal and some fruit juice. Achh!

Evening snacks? The best snacks known to civilized man are a big bowl of ice cream or half a pizza or two peanut butter and jelly sandwiches or a giant-sized bag of potato chips and a six-pack of beer. If you are a good American and a decent human being, you love these things.

So you can't have them. Eat some yogurt instead. Ugh.

That's it. When you go shopping, just walk down the supermarket aisle. If something makes you salivate, don't put it in your cart. If something makes you nauseated, take six of them.

Just follow the simple rule of suffering and misery and you'll lose weight. And, possibly, your mind. ∎

Treatment of crabs? Some of us don't have leg to stand on

WEDNESDAY, JANUARY 24, 1996

I felt guilt pangs when I saw a TV news report about animal lovers who are trying to end the practice of boiling live lobsters.

A woman from the People for the Ethical Treatment of Animals said: "No compassionate person would boil an animal alive."

That's something I hadn't thought about before because I have never boiled a lobster and hardly ever eat them.

Although they taste good, they look like giant insects. So do shrimp and crayfish, which I also avoid.

As I once told a Creole friend from New Orleans, where they love to chomp on crayfish and other crawly creatures: "You people eat things that we'd call the Orkin man for."

So why should I feel guilt about lobsters when I don't eat them?

Because it got me thinking about stone crab legs, which rank near the top of my favorite food list.

For years, I've taken vacations in Florida and almost always on the Gulf Coast. That coast not only has fewer New Yorkers but the gulf is where the stone crab legs are harvested.

I don't eat them in restaurants because they cost too much, and it isn't as much fun.

Instead, I go to a small old-time Florida fishing village where local stone crab leg fishermen bring their catch.

I buy a huge sack of the legs, which have been cooked, and the whole family sits around that evening whacking the thick shells with hammers and gorging ourselves on the firm, sweet stone crab meat.

Besides being delicious, stone crab legs don't look at all like big insects. Maybe an entire stone crab does, but I don't know, because I've never seen one. Few people have.

That's because the people who put out the stone crab traps don't keep the entire creature.

What I'm going to say now is not for the faint of heart and the queasy of stomach.

The stone crab fishermen just break off one of the creature's legs and toss the rest of the crab back in the water.

Wait, please. While that might sound cruel and insensitive, it isn't as bad as you might think.

In a miracle of nature, the stone crab doesn't die. To the contrary, it lives on and eventually grows another leg to replace the one that was snapped off by the human creature in the boat.

So someday, that very same stone crab might be caught by the very same human creature and have that new leg snapped off. And again and again.

This means that a stone crab—unlike a lobster or most of the other things we pluck from the sea—can be caught and yet lead a long life.

Why, then, should I feel guilty for having eaten many hundreds of stone crab legs over the years?

Well, I have no idea what goes through the minds of stone crabs. But I have to guess that it must hurt like the dickens to have a leg popped off.

How would you feel?

And I would imagine that if I went to the bottom of the Gulf Coast and wandered around, I would see an awful lot of gimpy stone crabs.

The demand for them is enormous, not only in restaurants all over Florida but in seafood joints throughout the country.

Every day, thousands of stone crab legs are served in Florida restaurants and shipped by air to restaurants in New York, Chicago and other big cities.

So think about that. For every one of those thousands and thousands of crab legs that are being devoured each day, there is a newly disabled stone crab limping around the Florida Gulf Coast.

It must be a terrible sight down there—all those one-legged stone crabs trying to make their way in the ruthless, fish-eat-fish society of the sea.

I once asked an old wrinkle-faced, red-necked stone crab catcher how all the gimpy stone crabs manage to survive. Do they swim in circles? Hop along on one leg? Do they get any help from fortunate able-bodied stone crabs? How does it affect their sex lives? How do they find food?

The old-timer nodded silently as he listened to my questions. Then he said:

"How the heck would I know what the danged things do? I just catch 'em and take their legs. I don't socialize with 'em."

Obviously, he is not a prospective member of People for the Ethical Treatment of Animals.

Despite my feelings of guilt at contributing to such widespread misery and disability, I'll probably go on eating stone crab legs. But I wish there was some way we could reduce the pain, suffering and inconvenience.

Maybe tiny canes? ∎

Shortage of short Greeks ruining us

FRIDAY, DECEMBER 5, 1986

The moment we sat down for lunch, I knew it was a mistake. It was one of those cute new yuppie-poo restaurants with ferns and a menu that listed calories.

I knew it was an even bigger mistake when five minutes passed before the busboy dropped the silverware and napkins in front of us.

About 10 minutes later, I snared a waitress as she was hurrying by and asked: "Is there any chance we can see a menu?"

She flung down a couple of menus and rushed off. About five minutes later, she was back for the orders.

"I'm so sorry," she said. "We're short-handed. One of the girls didn't show up today."

When she finally brought the food it wasn't what I had ordered.

"There are some problems in the kitchen," she said. "We have a new cook."

"Never mind," I said. "I'll eat it, whatever it is. But what about the beer?"

"Oh, I forgot, you wanted a beer," she said. The beer arrived just in time to wash down the last bite of the sandwich.

When she brought the check, which was wrong because she charged me for what I ordered instead of what I got, I asked: "Who runs this place?"

"The manager?" she said. "He's in the end booth having lunch."

On the way out, I stopped at the manager's booth. He was a yuppie in a business suit. He and a clone were leisurely sipping their coffee and looking at a computer printout.

"Nice place you have here," I lied. "Do you own it?"

The young man shook his head. It was owned by one of those big corporations that operates restaurants in far-flung office buildings and health clubs.

He also proudly told me that he had recently left college with a degree in restaurant and hotel management.

That explained it all. His waitresses were short-handed, his cook was goofing up the orders, the customers were fuming, and what was he doing?

He was having lunch. Or, as he'd probably say, he was *doing* lunch.

I don't want to an alarmist, but when this nation collapses, he and those like him will be the cause.

First, we had the MBA—especially the Harvard MBA—who came along after World War II and took over American industry. With his bottom-line approach, the MBA did such a brilliant job that the Japanese might soon buy the whole country and evict us.

But we're told not to worry. Now that we don't manufacture as much as we used to, we'll be saved by the growing service industry.

The problem is that the service industry is being taken over by people like the restaurant manager and his corporation. They go to college and study service. Then they install computers programmed for service. And they have meetings and look at service charts and graphs and talk about service.

But what they don't do is provide service. That's because they are not short Greeks.

You probably wonder what that means. I'll explain.

If that corporation expects the restaurant to succeed, it should fire the young restaurant-hotel degree holder. Or demote him to cleaning washrooms.

It should then go to my friend Sam Sianis, who owns Billy Goat's Tavern, and say: "Do you know a short Greek who wants to manage a restaurant?"

Sam will say: "Shoo. I send you one my cousins. Jus' got here from old country."

Then he'd go to Greek Town and tell his cousin, who works as a waiter, that his big chance had come.

When the next lunch hour rolled around, and a waitress failed to show up for work, Sam's cousin would not sit down to do lunch. He would put on an apron and wait tables himself.

If the cook goofed up orders, Sam's cousin would go in the kitchen, pick up a cleaver and say, "You want I keel you?"

He wouldn't know how to read a computer printout, but he'd get drinks in the glasses, food on the table and money in the cash register.

That simple approach is why restaurants run by short Greeks stay in business and make money. And why restaurants that are run by corporations and managed by young men who are educated beyond their intelligence come and go. And mostly go.

So if you are ever approached by a stockbroker who wants to sell you shares in any of the giant service corporations, tell him not to bother showing you the annual report. Just ask him one question.

"Is it run by short Greeks?"

If he says no, leave your money under the mattress. ∎

CHAPTER 3
Guns and Crimes and Cops

A battlefield view of war on drugs

FRIDAY, SEPTEMBER 15, 1989

John is a white Chicago cop. He doesn't want his full name used because what he has to say might not please his superiors, although many probably agree with him.

"I'm a sergeant and I've worked on the West Side by choice most of my career. So I know something about the problem of drugs. I think I know more about it than some of the people who do a lot of talking about winning the drug war and make the laws and set our national policies, but have never been on the street where everything is happening.

"For years I've been advocating, mostly to my friends, the legalization of drugs and using the billions we'd save from trying to fight the import and sales, to cure those who want to be cured.

"The way things go now, the courts will sentence drug offenders and people who steal to get drug money to rehabilitation as a condition of probation.

"But what happens when they want to go straight and can't get into a program for six months, which is very common? I'll tell you what. They go right back to their friends and habits. So instead of spending all those billions pretending you're doing something, some of the money could be used for rehab, some of it for ad campaigns not to use it, the way it's done with cigarettes and liquor.

"We'd still have laws against the sale to minors. You know, it pains me to see how rich drug laws have made punks and white collar opportunists. But once the profits aren't there, the punks and the others are out of business.

"On the West Side, kids used to complain that we stopped them because they were black and driving a new Cadillac. That was true. Most often the car was stolen and we had to chase them.

"But now that's changed. Now the cars belong to them and they've paid cash. And some of them aren't even old enough to drive.

"Those of us in law enforcement look like fools trying to fight a battle we can't win. And that just breeds contempt for law and order.

"You know, even if we were able to stop the coke from Colombia and Peru, it wouldn't change things. It would come in from somewhere else. And if we stopped that, it still wouldn't change because now they can make this synthetic stuff right here. They're doing it already.

"The problem is the demand. And the only thing for sure is that where there is a demand, it will be satisfied. That's a basic market principle, and that's why all the arguments against legalizing and controlling drugs are nonsense.

"I'll tell you what the biggest change in the last four or five years has been. It's the drug dealers themselves.

"Now we have 13-year-old dealers who make more than me. They go out and sell, then they give some of the money to mom, who maybe lives in the CHA or some dump. She needs it to make ends meet.

"How can President Bush fault someone who lives in a drafty apartment and is wanting for food and has no chance for a decent education or a job for selling drugs?

"How are you going to convince the kids to get back to school so they can be a factory worker, or get a low paying job in a fast food place, or be unemployed, when they can sell drugs for big money.

"Then they're going to have kids and they won't be able to steer them away from drugs or get them to go to school because they can't lead by example. If you're going to have values and morals, they have to come by example. And that's why we have all the casual violence out there, the disregard for life and death.

"The way we're going at this thing reminds me of Vietnam. A quagmire. Lives lost, then we pack up and leave.

"One of the reasons we study history is to learn from our own mistakes. Well, it looks like we didn't learn anything from Prohibition.

"I keep reading that every poll shows that most people are against any kind of legalizing of drugs.

"You know what that tells me? It tells me that most people who get polled don't know what the hell is going on out here."

That's one cop's opinion. But I suspect it is also the opinion of thousands of other cops in Chicago, New York, L.A., and in most cities where the problems are the same.

Since they're the ones who are actually fighting this no-win war, I respect their opinions more than the word-warriors in Washington who have never been any closer to Chicago's West Side, or New York's Bronx, or L.A.'s Watts than their TV sets can get them.

(A personal note to all of my loved ones, friends, relatives and acquaintances. No, I cannot get tickets for any remaining Cub games. If they make the playoffs, no, I cannot get tickets for those games either. And if they make the World Series, no, no, and again, no. So don't ask, don't even hint, or we will stop being friends, loved ones, and I'll deny we are related. Try a scalper. And if you find one, get two for me.) ∎

Let's take revenge on the virus nerds
FRIDAY, MARCH 6, 1992

Millions of computer users are wondering how to protect themselves against the wave of viruses that are threatening their machines. I have a suggestion.

First, they should remember that these viruses don't spring from nature. They are little computer programs created and sent on their way by people who are brainy, malicious and arrogant.

It doesn't seem to bother them that the more destructive of the viruses could take lives if, say, a hospital's computer programs were wiped out. Or that a business, its records suddenly destroyed, could be shut down or ruined.

So the question is, how do you find the creators of the virus programs?

Because they are arrogant, it's likely that they want someone to know what a clever thing they have done. They won't hold a press conference, but chances are they will brag to a trusted friend or acquaintance or fellow hacker.

It is sad, but the world is full of snitches. Look at John Gotti, the nation's biggest Mafia boss. There was a time when it was unthinkable for even the lowest-level Mafia soldier to blab. But now Gotti has to sit in court while his former right-hand man tells about how they had people whacked.

So if Mafia figures can be persuaded to tattle, is there any reason to believe that nerds have a greater sense of honor and loyalty?

Of course not. But how do you get them to do it?

Money. Maybe it doesn't buy happiness, but it will buy information. Cash on the counter has persuaded people to betray their country, their employer and even tell all to The Star tabloid.

The computer industry has tons of money. Some of the fastest growing corporations are those that pump out machines and programs that permit people to make a major project out of a chore they could do just as well with a $5 ledger.

So these companies could use the petty cash fund to place ads in the computer magazines and on the electronic bulletin boards.

The ads could say something like: "A $50,000 reward for information leading to the arrest and conviction of virus authors."

Fifty thousand smackers will buy a lot of floppy disks, DOS, RAM, ROM, megabytes and even gigabytes. As well as a hot sports car, a new wardrobe and a vacation at a Club Med for the pallid nerd who wants to reinvent himself.

A high-powered computer would be needed to keep up with all the tips coming in from the techie bounty hunters.

The next question would be what to do with virus makers once they have been caught. And that's the key to putting an end to the problem: something that could be posted on those electronic bulletin boards that might cause an aspiring virus-maker to go take a brisk walk instead.

A judge would sit and listen to an attorney who would say something like this:

"Your honor, what we have here is an otherwise fine young man from a good family. His father is a brilliant scholar, and the son will someday be the same.

"What he did was no more than an intellectual prank, a cerebral challenge of sorts. Like the man who climbed Mt. Everest because it was there, he created the virus and sent it forth because it was there.

"But he is not a criminal. Until now, the worst thing he ever did was give the family cat a bit of Angel Dust to see if it would run across the ceiling.

"So, your honor, we ask that you consider this lad's future usefulness to society. Why, he has an IQ that qualified him for Mensa. What is to be gained by dimming so bright a light?"

Then, we can hope, the judge might say something like this:

"Yes, I am impressed by the defendant's brain power. And I expected you to ask me to give him a slap on the wrist.

"However, he is not a child. He is an adult. And I would think that so brilliant a grown man would know better than to amuse himself by screwing up the lives of total strangers.

"It's as if he hid inside these businesses and institutions until they were closed and everyone had gone home. Then he came out and went through every file cabinet and drawer and shredded or burned every bit of useful information he could find.

"Now, counselor, what would you and your law partners say if some street mope did that to your law firm—crept in and destroyed every document in your offices? Including the names of clients who owe you money. Hah, you would be in here asking me to hang him from a tree.

"So don't give me that smart kid from a good family routine. He is a self-centered, insensitive, uncaring, arrogant goofball. He didn't give a second thought to the chaos or heartbreak he would cause to an adoption agency, a hard-working businessman or a medical clinic.

"Therefore, I sentence him to the maximum sentence the law allows in the local jailhouse, which is really a terrible place, filled with all sorts of crude, insensitive hulks.

"Bailiff, please get the defendant up off the floor and administer some smelling salts.

"And change his trousers, quickly." ▪

Oh, Pops, you done us proud

WEDNESDAY, FEBRUARY 13, 1985

The cops grabbed "Pops" Panczko the other day. The silly old geezer was messing around with a jewelry salesman's car. Imagine that—at age 66, he's still out there on a cold day stealing. It just shows what pride can do.

That's right, I said pride. Some people probably assume that Pops, who was once Chicago's best-known thief, steals simply for profit.

Well, that's part of it, of course. Everything Pops has stolen in his long career was worth something. The man is, after all, a professional.

But there's been more to it. There was his pride as a steady workman. Since he was a young man growing up near Humboldt Park in the Depression, he has believed in getting up every day, washing his face, shaving and going out into the city to steal something.

On slow days, it might have been only a crate of onions. On better days, it might be a rack of fur coats or a tray of diamond rings.

You don't get yourself pinched more than 1,000 times, by Pops' own estimate, if you are finicky. Nor do you earn enough money to pay lawyers to keep you out on the street working.

And there was pride that went beyond that of the working thief. It was a pride that kept him from going legit when he had the chance.

Yes, Pops once had a chance to become a celebrity, a literary figure, a darling of talk shows. He could have made Donahue. Or at least Kup. But he rejected it.

The chance came about 12 years ago, and this is the story.

I was having a beer with a visiting book editor from New York. He happened to have read a newspaper story about Pops being arrested for stealing a truckload of lawn mowers or something like that. And he asked me about it.

"Oh, that's not unusual," I told him. "Pops' brother Butch was once grabbed for stealing a cement mixer out in the suburbs. He was driving it back to Humboldt Park on the Edens Expressway."

"Did he go to prison?" the book editor asked.

"No, he beat the rap, but I think they got him for driving the cement mixer while under the influence."

"Do they always do things like that?"

"Well, Peanuts, another brother, once did a jewelry heist in Florida and tried to escape by speedboat. But his gang forgot to untie the lines, and they never left the pier."

The New York editor was intrigued. So I told him about the time Pops was caught inside a jewelry store at about 2 in the morning. He told the jury that he had a need to go to the bathroom, and the door of the store was open. The jury was impressed that Pops was too gentlemanly to relieve himself on the street, so they set him free.

Then there was the slugs caper. Pops found that he could use slugs in almost any vending machine. And many of them would give change. But the FBI got him for also using slugs to make long distance calls, and he stood trial.

In a recess in the trial, his lawyer had to phone his office. "You got any change?" he asked Pops. "No," Pops said, offering him a handful of slugs. "But these'll work."

"My goodness," the New York editor said, "the man sounds like a complete incompetent."

"Well, I guess he is in a way. All the Panczkos were. They would plan great heists, then they'd tell everybody in the saloon about them, and somebody would stool to the cops and they'd usually be waiting."

"Do you know Pops?"

"Sure. For years. We came from the same neighborhood."

And so the editor offered the deal. A book contract for Pops' life story. He said it would be a cinch for a movie sale. And maybe a TV spinoff. Pops would make a fortune.

A few days later, I was in the office of Pops' lawyer. He almost salivated when I told him how much the New York publisher was willing to advance Pops.

"It would take him five years to steal that much," the lawyer said.

I told him that was just for the hard-cover book. The paperback rights, the movie deal and the TV deal would bring in much more.

"My God," the lawyer said. "Pops can finally pay me."

When Pops came in, carrying an armload of briefcases he had just lifted from a delivery truck downstairs, I told him about the offer.

"All I have to do is talk to you about my work?" he said.

"That's all. We'll use a tape recorder, and I'll do the rest."

"And I'll get rich?" Pops asked.

"You'll wow 'em in New York and Hollywood."

"I'll do it," Pops said.

We shook on the deal. And Pops pulled up his coat sleeve, showing an arm with a dozen watches, and said: "Here, take one."

But a week later we met, and he said: "I can't do it."

"Why not?"

"My sister doesn't want me to. And I think she's right."

"What did she say?"

"She said it would embarrass the family. It would ruin the name."

So, that's why Pops is still out there, eyeing a salesman's car or a crate of onions.

And the next time you read some movie star's shameless book about her 6 marriages and 138 affairs, think of Pops and his pride.

But remember to lock your car. ∎

In L.A., Sgt. Friday era is over and out

FRIDAY, JULY 12, 1991

Good old Sgt. Joe Friday. Now there was a really decent cop. True, he walked like he had a corncob stuck in his back pocket, but he was always polite, neatly dressed in his crisp Robert Hall outfits and he never violated anybody's legal rights.

He hated the bad guys, but about as mean as he got was when he slapped on the cuffs and gave them a look of disgust.

In his prime on network TV, Joe Friday symbolized to much of the nation what a clean, honest police department was like.

He was totally unlike the Hollywood version of the Southern sheriff, who was always potbellied, scowling, smirking, spitting, wearing dark glasses and picking on the nearest "nigra."

Or Chicago cops, on the take from the Capone mob in the movies. And in real-life, pounding protesters on the head at the 1968 Democratic Convention. Or New York cops—rude, crude and treating that decent Serpico like dirt.

Not Los Angeles, though. Thanks to Sgt. Joe Friday and his sidekick, Frank Smith, the nation knew that the LAPD was different than the rest: Honest, efficient, good, fair and true.

But how times change, and how quickly. Now we've had the famous L.A. video-tape beating, plus more.

The latest disclosures are transcripts of L.A. cops talking to each other on the police radio about their latest adventures, and offering their social insights.

So maybe it is time for Hollywood to resurrect Sgt. Joe Friday and bring him up to date. All they'd have to do is weave in some of the comments from the radio transcripts and the show would be a ratings smash.

"9:35 a.m. Received a call of a woman whose home was burglarized. Hope she has huge set of kazoopers.

"9:40 a.m. Drove down Slausen toward home of complainant. Monkeys in the trees, monkeys in the trees, hi ho dario, monkeys in the trees. Too bad we don't have time for some monkey-slapping. My partner says he wishes he could drive down Slausen with a flame thrower. We could have a barbecue.

"9:45 a.m. Arrived at home of complainant. Asked her, 'Ma'am, did you see the perpetrators?' She said she got a glimpse of two men running through her back yard. Asked her: 'Be's 'dey Naugahyde?' She said: 'What?' I said: 'You know, be's 'dey Negrohide.' She asked if I meant African-Americans. I asked my partner if African-American meant the same as monkeys. He said he believed so. I said: 'Yes, ma'am.' She said: 'No, they did not appear to be African-Americans.' I said, too bad, I was in the mood for some monkey-slapping. Could have gone out on a monkey hunt and questioned a Buckwheat or a Willie Lunch Meat. But she described them as being swarthy. That was a good clue. Meant that we might get some Mexercise. Or maybe they were Indians, the towel-head kind, not the feather kind. Thanked her and left. No sense in staying. Didn't have a huge set of kazoopers.

"11:15 a.m. Arrested an 85-year-old woman for being disorderly. Just slapped her around a bit.

"11:45 a.m. Responded to complaint of wife-beating. Best wife-beating I've ever seen. Looks like a whipped slave.

"12:30 p.m. Got call to do an alley sweep. Drove down alley. I love alley sweeps, especially if they don't want to move. Hammer time. My partner told me he didn't want to hit people. He said: 'I shoot them. My shooting policy is based on nationality and looks.'

"1 p.m. We got a little physical with a suspect. Had to teach him a little respect for the police, ha, ha, ha. We had fun. No stick time, though. But I obviously didn't beat this guy enough. He got right back up and was still being obnoxious. It was fun, but no chance to bust heads. Maybe next time.

"2 p.m. Going to lunch. We's be hungry.

"3 p.m. Pursuit of vehicle. Caught pursuit suspect. Hope he gets ugly, so I can vent my hate. Har, har. Capture him, beat him and treat him like dirt. Sounds like a job for the dynamic duo.

"4 p.m. Finished with suspect. He was crying like a baby. I shoulda shot him. I missed another chance. I'm getting soft. I almost got me a Mexican last night. But he dropped the damn gun. Too quick.

"5 p.m. End of shift. Signing off with motto: 'They give me a stick, they give me a gun, they pay me 50 Gs, to have some fun.'

"And I'm Sgt. Joe Everyday. Only the names have been changed to protect ourselves." ∎

Why O.J. Simpson may well go free

THURSDAY, JANUARY 26, 1995

After hearing the opening statements, my bets would be on O.J. Simpson walking out a free man.

It isn't that the prosecution doesn't have an arsenal of persuasive evidence—trails of blood, DNA samples and a portrait of Simpson as a jealous and violent stalker.

And it's possible that when all the testimony is over, the majority of people watching TV will be persuaded that he is guilty.

But it won't matter what you or I and all the other spectators think. We're just part of the world's biggest gapers' block.

It will take only one person—a member of that California jury—to dig in his or her heels and say: "I don't believe it." And hold to that view. If that happens, it's a hung jury, and the prosecutors will have to decide whether to go through the whole thing again.

Something in Johnnie Cochran's opening pitch makes me believe that he and the defense team will be able to plant enough doubt in at least one juror's mind to prevent a guilty finding.

That something is Mark Fuhrman, the eager-beaver detective who was involved in so much of the early Simpson investigation and seemed to have an uncanny knack for coming across important clues and evidence.

He was also in on one of those past domestic squabbles between O.J. and Nicole.

But most important, the defense believes it has evidence that Fuhrman said things in the past that indicate he is a racist.

If he is, that shouldn't be much of a shock. Many cops are racists. So are many other Americans in other jobs.

But Fuhrman isn't just any cop or any American. And that's why Cochran made a point of mentioning Fuhrman in his opening remarks.

It's a safe guess that Cochran is going to try to put Fuhrman on trial. The goal will be to try to establish that he is a racist cop who didn't like seeing a black man become a big success and marry a gorgeous white woman.

And that Fuhrman's dislike of Simpson was nasty enough to prompt him and possibly others to plant evidence—the bloody glove, for example—to hang Simpson for crimes someone else committed.

Does that sound implausible or even far-fetched? It depends on your background.

If you have lived most of your life in a friendly small town or a quiet comfortable suburb, yes, it might be unthinkable that your nice Officer Friendly would try to railroad an innocent person.

But if you are a black person, you might say: "So what else is new?"

Few blacks, especially in big cities like L.A., would be shocked by the suggestion that a white cop might find it in his heart to try to frame or railroad a black person.

And there are valid reasons for their feeling that way. Blacks have indeed been framed by racist cops and prosecutors. If not framed, then pushed around and deprived of a fair shake. There's nothing new in that. It is part of our legal heritage.

I doubt if there are many adult blacks who haven't had bad experiences with cops. And few who can't talk about someone they knew being given a bad deal in a courtroom or a police station.

We don't know a lot about the 12 Simpson jurors. But we do know that eight are black, and all but one of the others are Hispanic or Native American.

It's possible, I guess, that those eight black jurors are unique, that they have had amazingly carefree lives, somehow sheltered from the tensions and nitty-gritty of a multi-racial society that isn't always friendly and filled with brotherly love.

Sure, it's possible. It's also possible to draw three cards to an inside straight.

It's far more likely that one or more of those eight black jurors already believe that white cops are capable of railroading a black man. If they know that J. Edgar Hoover and his FBI waged a campaign to malign Martin Luther King Jr., why should they have faith in the honesty of some L.A. cop with a possible history of using the N-word?

Yes, all of those jurors promised that they have open minds and would consider only the evidence and testimony. That's what jurors always say.

But no lawyer believes that. To the contrary, a good trial lawyer is looking for jurors who will lean in the direction of his client, whatever the evidence shows. If they wanted someone impartial and influenced only by the evidence, testimony and law, they'd ask for a bench trial and take their chances with the judge.

So Cochran will try to show that there was a bad cop—maybe more than one—out there, trying to nail an innocent man. Such things have happened.

And all it will take is for one juror to believe that it is happening again. Don't bet against it. ▪

Night encounter with city's finest is worst kind

FRIDAY, FEBRUARY 21, 1997

While it was humiliating, painful and shocking, the experience of Richard Velazquez is a good thing.

Before I get into why it was good, let's deal with his experience.

On Tuesday night, Velazquez and a friend were in his car, near Sheridan Road and Loyola Avenue, about to go somewhere to give a lift to another friend.

When they got in the car, Velazquez tried to use the CD player, but it was jammed.

So he began trying to get it unjammed. While he was doing this a squad car pulled up and one of the two cops shone a flashlight in the window and asked what he was doing.

"Right away, I knew what he'd think," says Velazquez. "That we were a couple of Hispanic guys stealing something. So I told him, 'Don't worry, relax, it's my car.'

"I kept saying things like that. And he said: 'You relax, or do you want my foot up your ass?'

"So I got out of the car and started to take out my ID. Then he slammed me against the car."

Velazquez isn't sure what angered the cop. But he was suddenly punched in the nose, which broke.

And the cop—a big guy at about 6 feet and 240 pounds—threw several more punches.

"I tried to move away. I didn't fight back or anything. I just put my arms up to avoid getting hit. Then he hit me on the head with the flashlight.

"And I was sort of sliding along the car, trying to avoid being hit, so he tackled me and we went down on the ground. He was yelling for me to put my hands behind my back, but with him on top of me, I was having a hard time. I kept telling him: 'I'm trying to put my hands behind my back.'

"So he got me in a chokehold and I could hardly breathe. The chokehold increased the pressure on my head, so the blood was really coming out of my nose and the cut on my head.

"I finally got my hands behind my back, and the other officer put the cuffs on me.

"The policeman who hit me looked at the CD player. He saw that it was jammed.

"My friend, Carlos Sanchez, asked him: 'Why did you hit him so much?'

"The policeman said: 'The last time I had something like this, I got my jaw broken.'"

So why did I begin by saying this incident was a good thing?

Because Velazquez, 20, who got the busted nose, and Sanchez, 22, who saw the whole thing, were in the car at that location because it is near the St. Joseph Seminary.

And both men are seminarians at St. Joseph. Velazquez, who will soon be getting a double degree in philosophy and political science, with a minor in theology, was described by Rev. James Presta, rector of St. Joseph, as "just a wonderful young man. They are both fine young men."

So it is always good when someone like Velazquez gets whacked around by an out-of-control cop. He is believable. And his experience tells us that minorities ain't just blowing smoke when they say that some cops treat them like dirt.

It could have happened to a busboy or a gangbanger. But the media and the police Office of Professional Standards might be less inclined to take it seriously.

Back to the story:

"In the squad car," Velazquez says, "I told them I was a seminarian. The policeman who hit me said: 'Oh, maybe you'd like to meet God in an alley.'"

Having grown up in the Back of the Yards neighborhood, Velazquez knew that when dealing with a ham-fisted cop who talks about meeting God in an alley, it's best to say as little as possible.

At the station, the other cop brought him wet paper towels so he could clean the blood off his face. Other police officers took him to Edgewater Hospital, where his nose was treated and four stitches were put in his head.

Word that a seminarian from nearby St. Joseph had been roughed up got around the station fast. While Velazquez was still at the hospital, a considerate police sergeant was there to take his story.

When I spoke to the district commander to confirm that the case is being investigated, he sounded almost devastated. Understandably, since this isn't the kind of thing any decent cop wants happening under his command.

Especially with all the corruption and brutality headlines coming out of the West Side's Austin District.

I'm not going to use the allegedly brutal cop's name for the same reason I sometimes omit names from certain kinds of stories.

I couldn't reach him, and it is possible that he has a wife and kids. There's no reason that they should be publicly humiliated if he is a horse's south end.

Velazquez is pursuing the matter and wants the story made public because, "If that policeman is mentally unstable, a dangerous person, he should not be in that job."

Funny thing is, in a fair fight, the seminarian might have mopped up the cop. In high school at a seminary in Wisconsin, Velazquez was third in the state in wrestling—good enough to be offered college athletic scholarships.

"But I couldn't fight back because he had an advantage—that piece of metal on his chest." ∎

Gun Owner of '83 has ringing in ear

WEDNESDAY, JANUARY 18, 1984

Because I was preoccupied with other matters, I let the end of the year slip by without naming the winner of this column's coveted Gun Owner of the Year Award.

I'm sure this was good news to all my friends at the National Rifle Association, which has never been enthusiastic about this honor.

That's because they believe that the majority of gun owners are decent, law abiding citizens who never hurt anyone with their weapons.

And I agree. What concerns me are the millions of trigger-happy free spirits who regularly shoot up the American landscape. It's from this sizable minority that the contestants for this award are drawn.

So, a couple of weeks late, here are the outstanding contenders from last year's barrage of bullets. And the grand champion.

As usual, we have numerous contestants from the Man or Beast category.

Among them was Jim Dodson, an Oregon hunter who went out to bag an elk one fine day.

He spotted his quarry 60 yards away and fired. Unfortunately, the elk turned out to be Donald Fisher, who was hit in the bellybutton and went to the undertaker instead of the taxidermist. Friends agreed that Fisher, who did not have antlers and walked on two legs, was not known to resemble an elk.

Then there was William Self, who fired a shot up into a tree. Later he swore that he heard something say "gobble gobble," or whatever it is that wild turkeys say in North Carolina.

What came plopping down was the late M.G. Pace, who had been sitting on the limb waiting for something to come by that he could shoot. Those woods do get crowded.

And there were some outstanding entries in the Ain't Love Grand category.

Among my favorites was Daniel Francisco Lopez, of Carlsbad, N.M., who didn't like the dinner his girlfriend served him, so he wounded her in the rear end.

When the cops asked him why he shot her, he said: "Wouldn't you be upset if you had to eat green beans all the time?"

And Jean Rexroat, a Nebraska lady, found it irksome that she couldn't squeeze a carton of milk into the fridge because her boyfriend had stuffed it with beer. She put down the milk, picked up a gun and shot him in the shoulder. I hate to think what she might have done if he had left the cap off the toothpaste.

But the most unusual lovers quarrel involved Quillie Ferguson, 82, and Effie Mae Scott, who would not reveal her age, but is no kid.

Old Effie said something that bugged old Quillie, so he whipped out his old .22, stuck it in Effie's mouth and fired.

Effie didn't even fall down. Instead, she spit out three teeth. Then she spit the bullet into the amazed Quillie's face.

A cop said: "I guess that lady must have flossed her teeth regular."

The outstanding contestant in the Guns are Fun category was a guy named Harry, who went hunting with some pals in Michigan.

While they were in camp, one of Harry's pals went into their portable outhouse and pulled the curtains.

"Let's scare 'im," Harry said, drawing his .44 Magnum revolver and creeping up behind the outhouse. He aimed the gun at the ground and fired.

It got the expected reaction. The man in the outhouse came rushing out with his pants down around his ankles. Harry almost collapsed from laughing.

But then his friend collapsed, too. The bullet had hit a rock, bounced upward and struck the man in his left buttock.

"Be careful you patch up the right one," the poor fellow said to the doctor who made the repairs.

And we had a couple of excellent entries in the Sometimes There Is Justice Category.

One was a Wisconsin man who had a dog that he thought barked too much.

Now, most people who have dogs that bark too much either give the dogs away or take them to some distant spot and kick them out of the car.

But this man decided to take a more direct and final approach.

"I'm gonna kill that dog," he said, leaping from his bed and rushing outside with his rifle.

In a few seconds, his family heard a shot and assumed it was the end of old Spot.

They waited for the head of the house to return. Instead, they heard old Spot give out a few more barks. When they went outside, they found the deceased. In his eagerness to get at his dog, he tripped and put one through his vital parts.

The next candidate should probably be grand champion Gun Owner of the Year.

But he lives in South Africa, and this contest is open only to Americans.

However, he deserves a special mention for his unusual achievement.

He ran a farm on which many blacks worked. White South Africans are not known for their liberal qualities, so one day he was disciplining a black worker. He did this by gripping his shotgun by the barrel and hitting the worker on the head.

The third time he swatted the man's head, the gun discharged and blew half the farmer's head off.

And those ingrate farmhands didn't even sing "Massa's in the cold, cold ground."

Now, finally, the 1983 Gun Owner of the Year. And who else could it be than the now-legendary Willie Moyers of Knoxville.

You might remember Willie. He is one of those people who always sleeps with a gun on their bedstands or under the pillows.

One night the phone rang. Willie, half asleep, reached for it and said hello.

The phone said: "Bang." He had picked up the gun by mistake and shot himself in the ear.

He recovered and he has changed his habits. Now he keeps the phone out of reach when he sleeps.

DECEMBER 26, 1984

Achievement by a Deer Slayer Award goes to a New Hampshire man who saw what he thought was a deer coming over a rise in a road.

He fired, and scored a direct hit. The deer turned out to be a truck, and the driver took a bullet in the shoulder.

Fortunately, the hunter realized his error in time and did not skin the driver or have the truck mounted.

There was also a large number of people in the Man's Best Friend category.

In Rock Island, Ill., a man put his rifle on the ground after shooting a passing bird. As he bent to pick up the bird's carcass, his dog stepped on the shotgun trigger, causing it to fire and wound the bird-slayer.

This confirms the NRA's slogan: "Guns don't shoot people; dogs shoot people."

In Dallas, a man became enraged when his two dogs chewed the wires of his motorcycle. He got a shotgun from his house and began beating the dogs with the butt. As he thrashed them, the gun went off, wounding him in the shoulder.

But the dogs haven't chewed on his motorcycle since.

An even angrier dog owner was a Ft. Lauderdale, Fla., businessman who vowed that if his poodle ever nipped him on the ankles again, he would shoot it.

Sure enough, the poodle nipped. So the man whipped out his .357 Magnum and began blazing away, killing the poodle.

"My wife walked in the damn door at the wrong time," he later told the police, explaining how a bullet bounced off the floor, hitting his wife in the leg. "She's real mad. But I got the dog."

The Build a Better Mousetrap Award goes to a man in Ann Arbor, Mich., who was resting in his back-yard hammock when he saw a rat walking by.

He raised his .22 rifle, took careful aim, fired and shot himself in the foot.

Well, haven't you ever noticed how much a foot looks like a rat?

As the NRA likes to remind us, most gun owners are good family men. So this year's Family Togetherness Award goes to the man in Berkeley, Ill., who was cleaning his pistol while his wife sat nearby, breast-feeding their infant son.

The gun, which was wedged between the man's legs, went off. The bullet went clear through his thigh. It then bounced off the baby's head, causing a slight cut. It kept going and hit the wife in the arm.

They all recovered. But when they get together for more of those quiet family evenings at home, it might be a good idea to let baby wear a helmet.

A special category, the It Could Happen to Anybody Award, is shared by two worthy recipients.

First, there was the country-rock guitarist in Houston who kept a tiny derringer concealed in his cowboy boots.

When he asked his girlfriend to yank off his boots, the gun fell out, hit the floor, went off and got him in the tummy.

He recovered and is reported to be wearing sneakers these days.

And a man in Nebraska was out in the countryside, shooting bottles off a fence, when a bug flew up his nose. He dropped the gun, which discharged and wounded him in the leg.

Things like that never happened to John Wayne.

Finally, our top champion, the Gun Owner of the Year.

The award goes to a guy named Brad, in Cottage Grove, Ore.

Brad was upset over marital problems, so he walked into a tavern, waved a .357 Magnum and told everybody to get the hell out because he was in a foul mood.

Then he started blazing away, shooting whiskey bottles, shattering mirrors and windows.

The police surrounded the place, but Brad kept shooting. Bullets whacked into buildings on the other side of the street. They whacked into buildings on the next street. People all over the neighborhood barricaded doors and windows.

For more than 90 minutes, the bullets flew. Finally Brad walked out, a whiskey bottle in one hand, his gun in the other.

The police asked him to drop the gun. Instead, he aimed it at his own head, fired and collapsed to the ground.

The police rushed forward and found a gaping hole—in the top of Brad's hat. But his head was intact.

"I guess I aimed too high," he said. ∎

Rude awakening for a daydreamer

WEDNESDAY, OCTOBER 15, 1986

I suppose this story falls under the general category of: "In this town, it's every man, woman and child for themselves."

It begins with Rose Ann Morales, 31, a hair stylist, waiting for the traffic light to change. She's listening to her car radio and daydreaming.

So she doesn't notice the young man step off the sidewalk and walk up to her car on the passenger side. Nor does she notice him take a gun from his jacket.

She sees him only when he uses the gun butt to smash her car window and reach in to snatch her purse from the car seat.

This is known as smash-and-grab, a form of theft common to some parts of the inner city.

And where Rose Ann was—at Jackson and Western, in front of a big public housing project—it's more common than kick the can.

Rose Ann screams. The young man strolls into a playlot, stops, turns and stands there looking at her.

Rose Ann looks around. It's broad daylight. Cars are moving along. A few people stand on the sidewalk waiting for a bus. Pedestrians walk by. It's a normal city scene.

Except a man with a gun has just smashed her car window, grabbed her purse and is coolly standing less than 50 feet away.

She rolls down her window and screams. "Help. That man just stole my purse."

A few people glance at her, but nobody responds.

She honks her horn and shouts some more.

A city garbage truck stops and the driver says: "What's wrong?"

"That man in the playlot, he just stole my purse."

"The one standing there?"

"Yes. He smashed my window with a gun."

"You say a gun?"

"Yes."

"I can't help you lady. But I'll see if I can send back some cops."

And he drives on.

In the distance, Rose Ann sees the flashing light of an approaching police car. She thinks: "It's coming to help me."

No, the police car has stopped a speeder.

Rose Ann leans on her horn and waves her arm out the window. The policeman peers at her for a few moments. She blows the horn and waves again. The policeman finally crosses the street to her car.

"That man just smashed my window and took my purse. He has a gun."

"Where?"

"That one, standing in the playlot."

The policeman looks just in time to see the thief disappear into the entrance of the towering project building.

"Can't do anything now," the policeman says.

"You can go catch him," says Rose Ann.

"No, once they get inside there, you can forget it. He could be anywhere in there."

"But he's got to either get on an elevator or go up the stairs. You could catch him."

She looks closer at the policeman. He's no kid and about 50 pounds overweight. She realizes that he's not about to hoof up stairs after a stolen purse.

A teenager walks up and asks what's going on.

"Do you live in there?" Rose Ann asks.

The teenager nods.

"A man stole my purse and went in there. If you can go in and find it, I'll give you a reward."

The teenager gives her a sly look. "If he stole your purse, where you gonna get the money?"

Rose Ann takes cash from the pocket of her slacks. "I never carry money in my purse. But there are personal things in it. I want them back."

Two other teenagers join them and the three discuss the possibility of finding the purse.

"Probably tossed it down the incinerator chute," one of them says. "That's where they always throw them."

"Always?" Rose Ann asks.

"Yeah," one of the kids says. "They do that a lot."

"Get it back and I'll pay you."

"What's it worth to you."

"I'll give you $20."

"Twenty each or just twenty."

The cop says: "Look, kid, twenty bucks split three ways is more than any of you have got."

One of them says: "I could get real dirty messing around that trash."

But his friend says: "Yeah, but I can always wash up and I can use the money."

They go in the building. A few minutes later, they came out and say: "Lady, you're gonna have to tell us what your purse looks like. That thing's loaded with purses. We can't bring 'em all out."

"It's white and brown," she says.

They go back in. When they return, they hand her the purse and she gives them $20.

Her credit cards and checkbook are gone, but her personal papers are intact.

As he leaves, the policeman says: "You did the smart thing."

"What's that?" she asks.

"Not chasing him. He wanted you to chase him. A woman chased one of those guys into the building a few weeks ago. We brought her out on a stretcher."

Later, Rose Ann says: "You know, it was my own fault."

Why was it your fault?

"I shouldn't have been daydreaming."

The observation of a true city dweller. It makes me wonder if we shouldn't drop the old city slogan—City in a Garden—and replace it with something more timely. Something like: "Daydream At Your Own Risk." ∎

Big bang theory of self-defense

TUESDAY, JULY 24, 1990

Those of us who are not crack shots have long been discriminated against by federal regulators. There's nothing new about it and I've complained in the past.

They've done this by making it difficult, if not impossible, for us to buy machine guns and other weapons that unleash a stream of bullets or a barrage of shotgun shells with one pull of the trigger.

And, I might add, land mines, bazookas, war surplus cannons, heat-seeking missiles and other weapons that could be used to defend hearth, home and car stereo system.

My reasons for wanting such weapons should be obvious. I'm a bad shot with pistol and rifle. And I have weak eyes and poor night vision.

Millions of Americans share one or all of these problems, which puts us at a strategic disadvantage if our homes are invaded by fiends or foreign troops.

As an elderly spinster told me: "Plinking away with a pistol, what chance would I have? But if I could plant some land mines among my roses and petunias, as well as my front lawn, and let loose with a fully automatic Uzi, I could get some of the buggers before they get me."

Well put. And her sentiment is one of the reasons I have always supported the right of all law-abiding Americans to buy the weapons of their choice. And to carry them wherever they go.

That's why I have never joined the National Rifle Association. It is too namby-pamby. I once proposed that it not only be legal to carry a weapon in public, but also mandatory that all citizens be armed at all times.

What could be more sensible? A weapon is of no use if it's in your closet while you are walking down a dark, assassin-infested street. The crime rate would plunge if everybody had guns in their belts or purses, or rifles slung over their shoulders. And people would be more polite. They would be less likely to jostle someone on a subway or cut in line at a store if they knew the person they treated rudely was packing a .45.

But I received no support from the NRA on that idea. Nor did they join me in my efforts to legalize the sale and ownership of hand grenades.

I did that when a heavy-drinking acquaintance told me: "Because of my fondness for the grape, my hands shake. So a conventional weapon is useless. But if someone is breaking into my house, I could open an upstairs window and drop a grenade on the villains. That would teach them a good lesson."

And now we have discovered another example of the federal regulators' indifference to the right of the honest citizen to bear suitable arms.

In this case, it is an outright slap at those of us who are kind, considerate and sensitive to the feelings of others.

The government has told several foreign manufacturers of assault weapons that had been banned in this country that it will lift the ban if the guns are modified.

That means the assault rifles can't be rigged to handle bayonets, extra-large magazines, silencers and other combat devices.

The provision that offends me most is the one that prohibits the attaching of silencers. I'll explain why.

Let's say that I am awakened in the night by the sound of a creaking floorboard. I snatch up my assault rifle and creep down the stairs. There I see a homicidal maniac—or several of them—carrying off my new CD player or swinging my cat by her tail.

Naturally, I open fire and zap them all. This is a common occurrence, which is why newspapers are filled with stories about honest citizens using their assault weapons to bag their limit of home invaders.

Ah, but once the smoke clears, what is that I hear? I hear my wife hysterically screaming: "What is happening? What is that terrible din? Am I to be murdered in my bed?" You know how women are.

Even after I explain that the danger has passed, she will be wide awake and won't be able to get back to sleep. And when that happens, she is cranky in the morning. And that makes me cranky and ruins my day.

All because of the federal gun regulators. If I had a silencer, I could handle the matter quietly, discreetly and considerately, and she would not hear a thing.

And in the morning, when she said, "my goodness, what is that awful mess on the floor?" I would tell her that it was nothing worth losing sleep over.

Once again, I expect no support from the NRA. Just as they copped out on land mines, grenades and bazookas, they have been almost silent on silencers.

And I'm sure they'll pussyfoot on heat-seeking missiles for home use. They don't seem to care about the rights of a friend of mine who is an Eskimo. As he told me: "In this climate, if I had just one of those missiles, no blubber thief or hostile polar bear could get within 200 yards of my igloo."

Does the NRA care? Little wonder so few Eskimos join. ∎

She took the law into her own hands
THURSDAY, APRIL 29, 1993

We've had the year of the woman and it is still going on, with females being elected to high office, named to Cabinet posts and the power of Hillary Rodham Clinton.

But what about Curtescine Lloyd? You never heard of her? Well, she is my choice as one of the most amazing and heroic women of recent years.

Ms. Lloyd is a middle-age nurse who lives with an elderly aunt in the rural hamlet of Edwards, Miss., near Jackson.

This is her story, most of it taken from a court transcript.

One night, Ms. Lloyd was awakened by a sound. She thought it was her aunt going to the bathroom.

Suddenly a man stepped into her bedroom. Terrified, she sat up. He shoved her back down and said: "Bitch, you better not turn on a light. You holler, you're dead. You better not breathe loud."

He declared his intentions, which were to rob her and commit sexual assault. Of course he phrased it far more luridly.

Then he took off most of his clothing and jumped into bed.

Here is what happened next, according to court records:

Ms. Lloyd: "I got it. I grabbed it by my right hand. And when I grabbed it I gave it a yank. And when I yanked it, I twisted all at the same time."

(Need I explain what Ms. Lloyd meant by "it"? I think not.)

"He hit me with his right hand a hard blow beside the head, and when he hit me I grabbed hold to his scrotum with my left hand and I was twisting it the opposite way. He started to yell and we fell to the floor and he hit me a couple of more licks, but they were light licks. He was weakening some then."

With Ms. Lloyd still hanging on with both hands, squeezing and twisting the fellow's pride and joy, they somehow struggled into the hallway.

"He was trying to get out, and I'm hanging on to him; and he was throwing me from one side of the hall wall to the other. I was afraid if I let him go, he was going to kill me.

"So I was determined I was not going to turn it loose. So we were going down the hallway, falling from one side to the other, and we got into the living room and we both fell. He brought me down right in front of the couch and he leaned back against the couch, pleading with me.

"He says, 'You've got me, you've got me, please, you've got me.' I said, 'I know damn well I got you.' He said, 'Please, please, you're killing me, you're killing me. . . . I can't do nothing. Call the police, call the police.'

"I said, 'Do you think I'm stupid enough to turn you loose and call the police?' He said, 'Well, what am I gonna do?' I said, 'You're gonna get the hell out of my house.' He said, 'How can I get out of your house if you won't let me go? How can I get out? I can't get out.'

"I said, 'Break out, son-of-a-bitch, you broke in, didn't you?' And I was still holding him.

"He said, 'Oh, you've got me suffering, lady, you've got me suffering.' I said, 'Have you thought about how you were going to have me suffering?' He said, 'Well, I can't do nothing now.' I said, 'Well, that's fine.'"

Ms. Lloyd, still twisting and squeezing, dragged the lout to the front door, which had two locks, and told him to unbolt them.

It was a difficult process because he kept collapsing to the floor and she kept hauling him back to his feet.

When he finally unlocked the doors, he screamed: "I'm out, I'm out."

But Ms. Lloyd, now confident that she had the upper hand (or should I say the lower hands?) and a full grasp of the situation, said: "No, damn it, I'm taking your ass to the end of the porch. And when I turn you loose, I'm going to get my gun and I'm going to blow your [obscenity] brains out, you nasty, stinking, low-down dirty piece of [obscenity], you.

"And when I did that, I gave it a twist, and I turned him loose. And he took a couple of steps and fell off the steps and he jumped up and grabbed his private parts and made a couple of jumps across the back of my aunt's car.

"And I ran into my aunt's room, got her pistol from underneath the nightstand, ran back to the screen door, and I fired two shots down the hill the way I saw him go. And then I ran back in the house and dialed 911."

The police came and examined the man's clothing. Inside the trousers was written the name Dwight Coverson. They found Coverson, 29, at home, in considerable pain and wondering if he could ever be a daddy.

A one-day jury trial was held. As Coverson's court-appointed lawyer put it: "The jury was out 10 minutes. Long enough for two of them to go to the bathroom."

And the judge gave him 25 years in prison.

The defense lawyer also said that Ms. Lloyd was recently on a local Mississippi TV news show and mentioned that she had been contacted about a possible movie of her story.

That is a film I would pay to see.

As for Coverson, if this column should find its way to his prison, I hope the guys in his cellblock don't giggle too much. ∎

Laurie Dann's right to bear arms

THURSDAY, MAY 26, 1988

It was so predictable. After a deranged Laurie Dann went on her shooting spree in Winnetka, the cry arose for gun controls.

State legislators tried but failed to revive some old gun-control proposals. The anti-gun organizations put out the call for action. Angry letters appeared in newspapers. Disc jockeys offered their profound thoughts.

Even a society columnist, horrified that something like this could happen on the *North Shore*, demanded to know when *something* would be done.

And my phone rang with calls from those who wanted to know when I was going to write something about it.

As I explained to those callers, I didn't intend to write anything about gun control.

One of them said: "But you used to always write about it. Don't tell me you've changed your views?"

He was right. I've written about the need for effective gun laws on and off for about 25 years, going back to when it wasn't a fashionable topic. And I haven't changed my views.

But after 25 years, even I know a losing fight when I see one. And if ever there was a loser, it's the campaign to ban handguns or make it impossible for deranged people and criminals to get them.

So a couple of years ago, I decided to stop wasting my time and this space on the subject.

It's not that handguns couldn't be more effectively controlled. They could be. And it's not that the majority of Americans don't favor tighter controls. Numerous polls say they do.

But as much as I loathe the National Rifle Association, the gun lovers' lobbyists, I have to admire their skill at beating back almost every genuine reform of gun laws.

They use a simple but effective tactic: political intimidation. They scare the heck out of politicians, especially those in small towns, rural areas and the southern and western states where the NRA draws its biggest membership.

Any politician from these areas who dares stand up to the NRA faces the threat of mail and phone campaigns and bloc-voting that could drive him or her out of office.

Since the top item on any politician's agenda is to stay in office, few will cross the NRA. So when a proposed law comes up for a vote in Congress or a state legislature or a village council, all it takes is a few turns of the screw from the NRA and the law winds up dying in a committee or being voted down.

Oh, they suffer occasional minor defeats. Here and there, a suburb will ban all guns, more as a symbolic gesture than anything else. Certain high-powered bullets or automatic weapons will be outlawed.

And, as the Wall Street Journal recently pointed out, police groups have finally wised up and are now no longer chummy with the NRA.

But basically, nothing really changes. In the big city ghettos, black and Hispanic gang members are blowing each other away, as well as any innocent bystanders in the line of fire. And some of the gangs are better armed than the cops chasing them.

In some states you can go in one store and buy a fifth of booze, then go next door and pick up a gun. I remember seeing a store's sign in a border town that said "Beer, Wine, Ammo."

And a psycho like Laurie Dann can go into a gun store in a Chicago suburb and buy a Dirty Harry cannon as well as a couple of smaller backup pieces.

Even when the police began worrying that someone like Dann might be dangerous, they had no way of getting the guns away from her. All they could do was ask, and her family said no.

But if you went to the NRA and asked: "Look, do you really think someone like Laurie Dann should be able to just walk in and buy a gun?" the answer would be, yes, she should.

The NRA believes that if you have laws preventing a deranged person from buying a gun in or near a big city, you somehow encroach on the right of a rancher in Wyoming from owning a hunting rifle.

If we try to prevent 15-year-old street gang members from getting Saturday Night Specials, the NRA believes that we are preventing Americans from defending ourselves against an invasion by the Sandinistas.

And my guess is that if the village boards of Winnetka and other North Shore suburbs tried to put in local no-gun laws, there would be a large and vocal opposition saying: "Guns don't go in schools and shoot kids, people do."

Sure. Mentally ill people who need only to plunk down the purchase price and fill out a few meaningless forms.

But why should we be surprised that the NRA keeps on winning?

We have a president who once took a slug from a gun-toting nut. He recovered nicely, but his loyal press aide, Jim Brady, caught a bullet in the head and will be brain-damaged the rest of his life.

And how does this president feel about tougher gun laws? He's still loyal to the NRA.

Sorry about that, Brady, but you should have ducked. ∎

CHAPTER 4
The Beleaguered Little Guy's Best Friend

Pinochle players getting a bum deal

TUESDAY, MARCH 1, 1988

It's a daily ritual for Leo Okopski, who is 79. He yells to his wife that he's going out for awhile. She doesn't hear too good.

Then he heads for the field house in Marquette Park and says hello to Pat. Pat is 83. Dave is usually there, too. He's about 75.

They ease their old bones into chairs around a table provided by the field house and break out the cards.

Their game is pinochle, almost unknown to Yuppies but highly favored by old-timers.

You can play pinochle just for fun, or you can bet a little something on it. If you play it for fun, it's enjoyable. But if you bet a little something, it's even more fun.

So Leo and his cronies spice it up. Not any heavy action, of course, since they're all living on pensions. Leo's comes from a lifetime of working in an electric motor factory.

Nickels and dimes are what they play for. If somebody has a hot day, he might walk away with 95 cents.

A few months ago, this cop started showing up and walking around the room, looking in on the card games. Sometimes there are 25 or 30 old guys whacking their knuckles down on tables when they win a trick. Knuckle-whacking is a lusty part of the game's tradition.

The cop noticed a few coins on Leo's table.

"He warns us that we'd better not be playing for money. I tell him: 'You call this money?' He tells us that we'd better watch out.

"He comes around again and gives us the same routine. One of the other players is a retired cop, and he tells him to lay off.

"I don't know what's bothering the guy. We've been going there for years, getting out of the house. It's something to do.

"It wasn't like we're playing poker. You can lose $5 or $10 in poker. But pinochle, for what we play for? It's not enough to buy a pack of gum.

"Anyway, he keeps coming around. We ask him why he doesn't have something better to do with his time. He says his supervisor told him to do it.

"You buy that? Some supervisor is telling him to go over to the field house and keep an eye on a bunch of guys in their 70s and 80s who are playing pinochle? But that's what he tells us.

"So we don't pay any attention to him. I thought maybe he was coming around because it was warm.

"Then he stopped coming around for a few weeks, and I thought that maybe he got transferred or something and we wouldn't see him again."

Leo was mistaken. Recently, the cop showed up again. He walked over to Leo's table, saw a few coins and asked the players to show him their driver's licenses.

"I'm wondering what he wants my driver's license for. Reckless dealing or something?"

They gave him their ID cards and the cop wrote out tickets, charging Leo and the others with gambling.

"He hands us the tickets. We look at him and don't say nothing. Then he walks out. One of my pals said to me: 'What are we going to do?' I said 'deal the cards.'"

So on Wednesday, Leo and his pals will go to court to appear before a judge for having committed the crime of playing a pinochle game for the price of a newspaper.

There won't be any big time bookies in the courtroom, the guys who drive Lincolns and book hundreds of thousands of dollars in basketball bets every night. Nor will there be any of the juice men, who lend money to the gamblers and crack their shinbones if they don't pay on time.

But Leo and his pals will be there. Leo says he's not hiring a lawyer to defend him. "A lawyer? For what it would cost me, I'd have to win at pinochle every day for 20 years, if I last that long."

Ben Bentley, a spokesman for the Chicago Park District, expressed amazement at the pinch.

"I think it might be the first time in the history of the parks that a policeman did that," he said. "That's a senior citizens group down there. Instead of looking out the window or watching TV, the old guys play pinochle. What's wrong with that?"

When the cop was asked why he nailed the Geezer Gang, he said: "There is an ongoing problem with the senior citizens there."

An ongoing problem with senior citizens? I'm aware that there is an ongoing problem with gun-toting 16-year-olds who are blowing each other away in the streets.

And there's an ongoing problem with drug pushers, child molestors, porch climbers, lock pullers, sex fiends and other urban wildlife.

But I wasn't aware of an ongoing problem with pinochle-playing geezers.

I'll have to start keeping an eye peeled for white-haired guys using canes. ∎

A grave report from Medicare

TUESDAY, SEPTEMBER 17, 1985

It was last February when professor George Blanksten became aware of a very sad event in his life.

He had reason to visit his physician. Nothing serious. But a blood test was required.

The physician sent the bill for the blood test to Medicare, since Blanksten is 68 years old.

A few weeks passed, and Blanksten received a letter from the Social Security Administration, which administers the Medicare program, and it contained shocking news.

"They told me that I was dead," Blanksten says, "and therefore they could not honor the bill."

Obviously Blanksten was surprised. Although he isn't a kid anymore, he feels pretty good—even spry on his better days.

He's alive enough to teach political science, specializing in Latin American politics, at Northwestern University.

Along with the letter—which had been addressed to Blanksten's "estate"—was a form that he could fill out if he wanted his alleged death reviewed.

Naturally he filled it out and sent it in, since he didn't want word getting around that he was dead any sooner than is absolutely necessary.

Soon his estate received another letter. Once again, it was a blank form, the very same form he had already filled out.

So he filled it out again and sent it in.

Apparently he had engaged either a bureaucrat or a computer in some kind of duel.

He would send in the completed form. And it or he or she would respond by sending him another blank form to fill out.

This went on for months, with him filling out the form and them or it sending him the same blank form to fill out. He finally contacted his congressman's office, and somebody there said they would look into it.

And that finally brought him a response from Social Security.

The agency said: "As requested, we have reviewed your entire claim to decide whether our original determination was correct. . . . A specially trained person reviewed the claim. This person did not take part in the original review. . . . And we have found the decision made on this claim was correct. Our reason for this decision is as follows: According to our records, the date of death occurred prior to the date of the service."

In other words, he still was dead. Why, he was dead even before he went in for the blood test. Some doctor.

Even worse, he doesn't know when he died or what it was that did him in.

"That part really gets me. I asked them for the date and circumstances of my death, and they won't tell me."

Hoping that a face-to-face meeting might help, the professor went to the Social Security office in Glenview. He took a number, a seat on a bench and waited to be called.

When his number came up, he tried to explain to a female bureaucrat that he was not dead.

"That's what you say," she said, leading him to believe that they must get a lot of dead people posing as the living. And she gave him more of the forms he had already filled out.

But he hopes that there still remains a chance that he might be allowed to return to life.

The last letter—the one that in which he was declared dead by an impartial, "specially trained person"—did hold out one slim hope.

It said, "If you do not agree with our findings, you can request a fair hearing within six months of this date."

So he sent them a letter, asking for a fair hearing.

"I haven't heard anything from them yet, but I'm hoping for a fair chance to convince them that I am alive."

He hasn't decided what he'll do at a hearing to show them he isn't a cadaver. Possibly a soft shoe dance or, if the hearing officer is a female, a lascivious grin or even a pinch on her bottom.

In the meantime, he is thinking of taking legal action under the Freedom of Information Act.

"It bothers me that they won't tell me anything about the circumstances of my death. So I might take action on that.

"The least I should be able to do is visit my own grave." ▪

Adding insult to a tragedy
WEDNESDAY, JUNE 26, 1985

After a tragedy, somebody has to pick up the pieces. Funeral arrangements. Legal documents. Personal effects. These things have to be taken care of.

So on June 14, Ocer Smith got in his tow truck and drove to 82nd and May to get his dead stepson's car.

His stepson, Dimitric Grant, 18, had been killed. It was another of those stupid, pointless deaths that happen so often on the city streets.

Grant was just sitting in his car. A gang member shot him, though Grant wasn't involved in gangs. Just the opposite: He worked regularly and coached a Little League team.

When Smith, in his truck, got to the car, the detectives were still there. They told him he couldn't have it yet. They had to examine it for evidence: fingerprints, ballistics and such.

They said they'd need it for about five days. Then he could take it away.

The five days passed. The funeral was held, the family and friends wept and prayed and the young man was buried.

Then Smith called the Police Department and asked whether he could come and get the car. Somebody told him to call the police auto pound, which is where cars are towed.

He called the pound.

"The fella on the phone, he says that, yeah, the car is there and I can come and get it and it'll cost me $80.

"I asked him what the $80 was for. He says that was $50 for towing and $5 a day for six days of storage.

"I told him what happened, that our boy had been murdered and that I had come for the car but that they told me they had to keep it for evidence.

"But he says to me, 'That'll be $80 if you want the car.'

"Now, isn't that something? He gets murdered, and now we have to pay them $80 to get his car back. It's almost like paying a tax for being murdered."

That did seem peculiar. It's one thing for a car to be abandoned on the street and towed in as a nuisance.

But young Grant didn't abandon his car. He happened to die in it. And his stepfather had been willing to tow it away.

Nor does the word storage seem appropriate for an object that was being studied for evidence in a crime. If a murder had been committed in somebody's kitchen, and they wanted to study a coffeepot for fingerprints, would the victim's family have to pay a storage fee for the coffeepot?

We called the Police Department to find out why Smith had to pay a fee. The answer varied, depending on who we talked to.

One man said he might not have to pay the fee. Another said he might have to pay for the tow but not for the storage. Another said he would have to pay the whole thing. And somebody else said he wasn't sure whether Smith could have the car at all, because they weren't sure who the car belonged to now that young Grant was dead.

Meanwhile, another day passed. And when Smith called again, he was told that, yes, he could come and get the car but the fee had gone up to $85. Another day, another $5.

"But at least they said I could come and take the car," Smith said. "But they said that I should be sure and bring the death certificate with me."

Since they had arrested somebody in the killing, you would think that they wouldn't need a document to tell them that Grant was indeed dead.

But Smith got the death certificate and put $85 in his wallet and went to get the car.

A little later he phoned and said: "I got here, but I can't have the car yet. They said that there was a hold put on it by some detectives. They want to keep it for evidence for a while.

"I don't know how long that's gonna be. But I guess it'll keep costing me $5 a day."

Smith then said: "I got to get away from all this. I'm going up north and go fishing for a while. I have to get all these things off my mind."

He'd better not stay away fishing too long. Those murder taxes can start mounting up. ∎

Easy to become dad, harder to be father

TUESDAY, MARCH 7, 1995

If you think about it, one of the easiest things a male can do is become a biological father.

By the time we're 12 years old, most of us are not only physically capable of this deed, but eager to give it a try. Actually, the end result—fatherhood—is not foremost in our minds, but the process is.

It can take as little as a few seconds in bed, on a sofa, in the back seat of a car, on a beach, in a hallway, a bush, a tent or an igloo. Just about any place on the face of the Earth will do, as today's movie scripts demonstrate. When a guy puts his mind to becoming a biological father, he's not fussy about where. The big question is always when?

You can have the IQ of a frog and become a biological father. And why not? Frogs do.

To show how easy it can be, one of the most productive biological fathers on record was Emperor Moulay (The Bloody) Ismael of Morocco, who had 525 sons and 342 daughters by numerous wives by the time he was 30.

Actually, that's a meaningless record. Any able-glanded man could become a biological father thousands of times if he knew enough cooperative females. Fortunately, most women aren't eager to share in such records. For them, a roll in the hay is the beginning of a long, arduous process. The male, on the other hand, is merely along for the ride.

And as the deadbeat rates for child support indicate, the ride is often over almost before it begins.

It's so easy to become a biological father that you really don't need a willing partner. Even a rapist can do it, and some have, which shows that old Mother Nature isn't much of a feminist.

Which leads me to Otakar (Otto) Kirchner, who has had more than his 15 minutes of fame by being the biological father of Baby Richard, the child caught in the nightmarish legal tug of war.

It appears that Kirchner has the law on his side and, unless something unexpected happens, will get possession of his biological son, who doesn't know that Kirchner exists.

That's the law, but it doesn't mean that the law is right. Common sense tells us that it isn't; that Baby Richard should remain with the adoptive parents who brought him home from the hospital and have raised him as their own child.

The higher courts are impressed by Kirchner's claims as the biological father. But what is it that he did, besides hop in the sack with a very good-looking woman?

Did the prospect of becoming a father impress him so much that he rushed her to the altar as soon as it was known that his seed was effective?

Nah, he couldn't make up his mind. He was still in love with his longtime sweetie, Maria. Then he was in love with the pregnant Daniela. Then with Maria. Then with Daniela. Maybe both at the same time. Some guys aren't sure where they're going to have breakfast.

As most mothers will agree, the place for a father to be nine months after he does his thing is right there in the maternity ward. If he can't share the pain, the least a man can do is show up to express curiosity and throw in a few reassuring hand squeezes.

But where was Otto when his biological child came into the world? Pacing in the hospital's waiting room? Asking a nurse how it's going?

No, while Daniela spent nine hours grunting and groaning to make Otto a biological father, the biological daddy was visiting relatives in Europe, reportedly with the always-reliable Maria.

Most women would take that as kind of a snub. But most judges are not women.

So the evidence indicates that about all Otto did to establish himself as a biological father was what most young men would do if a good-looking blond said: "You want to come up for a drink?"

Does that make him a father? The law says, yes. So do blood tests, DNA tests and the rest of it.

But common sense says that after four years, the true father is the man who has been raising Baby Richard since birth. And, according to all reports, doing a fine job of it. All Otto did was enjoy getting lucky, as the saying goes.

And if Daniela had just said, "No, I have a splitting headache," maybe Otto would still be running around Europe with Maria. ∎

ASCAP 'hit' gives geezers the blues

FRIDAY, FEBRUARY 17, 1984

If you happen to walk into Lois and Pete's Tavern on a weekend night, you'll probably hear some old geezer squeezing an accordion and singing "The Beer Barrel Polka." If he is in more of a hip mood, it might be "Poor Butterfly."

On a real lively night, there might be another geezer flailing at a piano, another geezer whacking a set of drums and maybe even a tuba or a guitar going.

And when she's in the mood, Lois Szalacha, the owner and bartender, might belt out an old Tin Pan Alley song in her gravelly, whiskey voice.

When the song ends, the people at the bar and tables—mostly little white-haired ladies and bald, wrinkled gents—will give a wheezing cheer. If their pension checks just came, they might even buy the accordion player a drink.

It's not exactly Rick's Cafe or George's, but the regulars enjoy it. Most of them are of pension age and live within walking distance of the tavern, which is at 2916 W. Irving Park Rd.

So are the musicians. They play just for the fun of it and an occasional free beer.

"It started right after I opened the place," said Lois, who at 59 is one of the kids in the crowd. "A guy named Carmen came in and saw I had an old accordion. I used to play. He took it home, got it tuned and came in the next weekend and started playing.

"So I started buying old instruments. The piano, drums, a guitar—and some of the customers who knew how to play would get up and do some songs.

"It got to be so much fun that some people even went to the field house at Horner Park and took lessons. We got a trumpet player that way and even a guy who plays the tuba. They aren't real great, and sometimes you can't be sure what song they're playing, but it's something for them to do and it's fun."

Naturally, a city inspector showed up one day and told Lois she needed a city music license, which costs $219 a year. She grumbled but paid. In the tavern business you're used to buying licenses: city liquor, $1,338 a year; state licenses, $150; even a $25 potato chip license.

Then one evening a couple of strangers came in. They sat at a table, listened to the music, took some notes and left.

A few weeks later, a letter came. It was from the American Society of Composers, Authors and Publishers [ASCAP] and it said that Lois had to send them $240 a year for a license to perform songs copyrighted by their members.

Lois showed the letter to her customers and said: "Can you beat that? They say we got to pay to sing songs."

The customers pondered the letter. Then they reached a legal opinion. As the accordion player put it: "They can't mean us. We're just amateurs and most of us don't even know all the words. Forget it."

So Lois forgot it.

But ASCAP didn't. Notices kept coming in the mail. Lois would show them to the old-timers and they'd say: "Ya' can't make amateurs pay to play some music."

"So I started just throwing their stuff in the garbage can. It went on for years. I didn't even read most of it. I don't know anything about legal stuff."

So she didn't even know that ASCAP went into federal court last June and sued her for copyright infringement, asking for $10,000 in damages.

She was served with notice of the suit, but she tossed that away, too. "I thought it was just more of their nonsense."

So she didn't even show up in court and a federal judge socked her for $3,000 in damages and gave ASCAP permission to grab the money from her bank account.

That's when she discovered what had happened—when she went to her bank and found that her $1,200 in savings was frozen. So she called a lawyer, who told her to pay up and forget it—his legal fees would be more than she could save by fighting it.

"So now I can't even pay my bills. It's so stupid. This is just a little neighborhood tavern with a few old people trying to have a little fun. And they make a federal case out of it."

The court record shows that the songs that the ASCAP snoops heard performed included "Poor Butterfly," "Tea for Two," "Pennies from Heaven," "With a Song in My Heart," "Where or When" and others.

And the plaintiffs were heirs to the estates of composers like Vincent Youmans, Richard Rodgers and Lorenz Hart and Warner Bros. Studio.

"Can you imagine," Lois says, "a Polish saloon keeper like me being sued by Rodgers and Hart?"

Will Lois pay? "Hell no," she says. "Now their fee is up to $324 a year. I'm already paying the city for a music license. Do they think I'm running some nightclub with Frank Sinatra singing? If I get 15 or 20 people in here on a Saturday, it's a big night. I'd rather close up and go to work somewhere as a barmaid. I'd earn more."

She may have to do that because ASCAP says it won't give in.

"Payment is required wherever there is a public performance," a spokesman said. "They are paying for drinks, so she is making money."

To which Lois says: "Let that guy try to live on what I make."

Lois has one other tactic that she is considering.

"Maybe we'll do nothing but Polish songs. Let those snoops write down *those* titles." ▪

City bureaucrats do the java jive

WEDNESDAY, JANUARY 25, 1984

Most people mistakenly think of bureaucrats as being plodding and unimaginative. They don't appreciate the creativity of the bureaucratic mind.

It takes creativity to find problems where none exist, to take a simple situation and turn it into confusion.

Consider Dick Peterson's coffee urn.

The coffee urn stands in his store, Peterson's Foods, at 5423 Devon Ave.

It's a friendly supermarket that the Peterson family has run for 43 years. It has faithful customers and friendly employees.

It's the kind of store where the checkout clerks and butchers greet customers by their first names, and you don't have to take a lie detector test to cash a check.

As part of the friendly atmosphere, the coffee urn is always there so you can have a cup while you wait for the meat cutter to fill your order, or while you just chat with a neighbor.

But now the coffee urn is unplugged. It's been turned off since Friday, when a city inspector showed up for a routine inspection.

The inspector browsed around, then went up to Peterson and asked, "Do you have your license for the coffee table?"

"I have all my licenses," Peterson said.

"Do you have a limited food dispensing license?" she asked.

"For what?"

"For the coffee."

"But I don't sell the coffee; I give it away."

"That doesn't make any difference. If you are serving coffee, you have to have a license."

"But everybody gives free coffee. Banks, beauty parlors, barber shops. They give it away free just like me."

"Makes no difference. Whether you give it away or charge for it, you're still vending a product. You have to have a license."

"I can't believe this. How much is the license?"

"It's $150."

With that, Peterson pulled the plug on his faithful coffee urn.

Now there is a sign on the urn that says:

"Sorry—due to the fact that the City of Chicago is making me buy a 'food dispensing' license to *give away* coffee, I cannot *give away* coffee until the license is in place. [The license will cost $150 *to give away coffee*.] Thank you. Dick Peterson."

Customers have been chuckling at the sign, but Peterson says:

"Can you believe that? They want me to pay $150 to give something away free?"

Well, are you going to do it?

"Hell no! It's ludicrous. Look, that coffee costs me about $15 a week. That's about $500 a year. Why should I have to spend another $150 a year for the privilege of giving away $500 worth of coffee?

"And it's not like I don't need licenses to operate. I don't think people realize how many licenses you need in this business."

He dug into his desk.

"Here—my normal food purveyor's license. That costs $180.

"Then there are the cigarette licenses. You need one for every checkout counter. Eighty bucks each. That costs me $320.

"If you sell can openers or anything else that can be considered hardware, that's another license—$24.

"We sell Easter lilies and poinsettias. So I have a florist license for $120.

"I don't exactly know how much they are, but I've got a license for that Coke machine, and I even have a license for the gumball machine.

"But if they think I'm going to buy a license to give my customers a free cup of coffee, they're nuts. Never."

That doesn't seem to make much sense. Especially since thousands of businesses give away free coffee.

So we called the city's Department of Consumer Services, which is where the inspector was from, and asked why Peterson couldn't keep his urn going.

Naive soul that I am, I kind of thought someone in charge would say something sensible like: "Oh, gosh, it must be an overzealous inspector. Of course we don't want to stop people from giving away a friendly cup of coffee."

But after years of dealing with bureaucrats, I should have known better.

The department's deputy commissioner, Jesse Blackmon, said, "There is a law against it," and cited chapter whatsis of the Municipal Code.

Yeah, but does the law really intend to deprive us of the pleasure of offering somebody a neighborly cup of java?

"What if somebody gets sick from that coffee?" he said. "Then they will be asking why the city allows this."

So you have been warned. If you are giving away free coffee, you could be in trouble.

Maybe Big Brother isn't watching us, but a lot of his idiot cousins are. ▪

Abused baby 1, system a big 0

THURSDAY, NOVEMBER 14, 1985

I suppose I should take satisfaction out of the fact that Lashaunda, the battered baby I've been writing about, is finally going to be placed in a foster home where it's unlikely that she'll have any more broken legs, concussions, burns, internal injuries and other miseries.

Judge Ronald Davis finally made that decision Wednesday after a lot of ridiculous delays by the public defender, who represented Lashaunda's mother. Until the very end, the public defender was trying to portray the doctor who blew the whistle on this case as the villain.

It also can be considered good news that Judge Davis, who initially botched this case by refusing to take the baby out of a dangerous environment, is being whisked away from Juvenile Court to another assignment, where he can ponder such things as contracts or parking tickets. Things that don't bleed and cry out in pain.

And it's encouraging that the last thing Judge Davis did before ending his stint in Juvenile Court was to put Lashaunda's 3-year-old brother in temporary custody of the state, pending an investigation to see if he too should be put in a foster home.

But there's really not much reason to feel more than a passing satisfaction from the way this case turned out.

Oh, it's fine that this one baby, and maybe her brother, is being protected from potential harm.

But what it amounts to is nothing more than a Band-Aid for a massive hemorrhage.

If I learned anything from this case, it's that the legal system that has been set up to protect children like Lashaunda is a frustrating, disastrous failure.

Sure, Lashaunda is now safe. But not because of the system. She's safe because one doctor had the courage to speak out and because stories about the case aroused public anger. Despite what judges say about being above outside influence, their ears can quiver when the public raises hell.

If the system had followed its course, with lawyers going through the motions of doing something while actually doing nothing, Lashaunda would still be home. Or maybe she'd be in a tiny coffin.

So there can't be any satisfaction when there are hundreds and hundreds of other Lashaundas out there that we don't know about—and the system hasn't protected.

And that it isn't capable of protecting.

What's the problem? There are lots of them.

For one thing, there is a state agency, the Department of Children and Family Services, that is supposed to be responsible for checking on cases of child abuse.

You think the CIA is secretive? You should try dealing with this outfit.

Throughout this entire case, every time I tried to get even a speck of information from Family Services, all I heard was the whiny response: "Oh, we're not permitted to discuss these matters."

If somebody was known to be eating babies on a sesame roll with mustard and onions, their response would be: "Oh, we're not permitted to discuss these matters."

We're supposed to take it on faith that this agency does its job. But if there's anything I've learned during 30 years in this business, it's that you can have as much faith in bureaucrats doing their job as you can in the warranty offered by the guy selling jewelry out of a shopping bag in a gangway.

Then we have court hearings being run on an adversary basis, like a personal injury case or a murder trial.

The result was that the mother's court-appointed lawyer tried to put the doctor on trial, suggesting that the doctor who diagnosed the injuries wasn't qualified, even implying that maybe the doctor was somehow responsible for the kid being mauled and maimed.

And that led to a two-week delay so that the imaginative public defender could find a doctor who could testify to . . . damned if I know to what. That the kid broke her own legs? That some clumsy nurse dropped her a dozen times? That, as Mom suggested, the baby inherited broken legs, concussions, burns, etc.?

After the two-week delay, the public defender couldn't find a doctor, or even a Gypsy fortuneteller, to be her expert rebuttal witness.

All that legal jockeying is to be expected in courtrooms where the fates of dope peddlers, throat cutters, jackrollers and porch climbers are decided. But in this case, there were only two questions: Had the baby been bashed around? And should she be returned to the place where it obviously happened?

(I say "obviously" because most 1-year-old kids don't sneak out of their cribs and toddle down to the street corner for a brawl.)

Those questions could have been answered in a day, if that long.

Then there is the judge. Not just this particular judge, but any judge in Juvenile Court. The question might sound silly, but why is the final decision left to a lawyer who, through political connections, happens to be wearing black robes?

I'm sure that his legal training has made him a whiz at contracts, writs, motions and knowing when to overrule an objection. But how does that background qualify him as an expert in the field of child abuse?

Why not, instead of a judge—or in addition to a judge—a panel that might include a doctor, a psychologist and a streetwise social worker.

I'm not an expert in this field, just as I'm not an expert in automobile engines. But I don't have to be an expert to know that when you turn on the car engine and it sputters, spits, howls and clunks along, something is wrong.

And the whole juvenile protective system needs more than a tune-up. ▪

A restaurant where charity isn't served

WEDNESDAY, OCTOBER 14, 1992

Frank Barwacz, 75, comes downtown almost every day to go to church and stroll or to play chess in the park. It's seldom that he doesn't run into a street person asking for a handout.

Barwacz has a soft spot for the down and out. He can't walk by a panhandler without helping.

But he isn't a soft touch. He won't give cash because he doesn't want it spent on booze.

"If they tell me they are hungry, I tell them: 'Come with me, I'll buy you some food.'"

And he takes them to a fast-food place for a bite to eat.

He's not rich. There's a pension and Social Security. But he lives simply and frugally and has something left over.

So for the past eight years, he has spent about $20 a day buying hamburgers, fries or the Colonel's chicken for street people.

It's become part of his everyday routine—church, chess and taking some shaggy character into a McDonald's or a Hardee's for a fast meal.

Some babble crazily. A few want money or nothing else. But most are grateful for this act of kindness.

"I do this because I know what it is to be hungry, to have bad times," Barwacz says. Indeed he does, but more about that later.

You would think that a simple humane act—buying a burger for a street person—wouldn't get complicated. But what can't become complicated today?

One chilly day last spring, Barwacz took a man into the McDonald's at 730 N. Michigan Ave., ordered food, then went out to buy a paper.

When he came back, the man was gone.

"He was chased out by the people who run the McDonald's," Barwacz said. "They didn't want him in there.

"I went outside to leave. Then a woman asked me for help. She was shivering. I asked her if she was hungry. She said she was very hungry. I took her back to the McDonald's. The woman, she stood by me while I bought the food.

"The girl who served the food, she said: 'You cannot eat inside here. Take the food and go out.' But I took her to a table to sit down. She was so hungry. She was eating and asked if she could have a milkshake. I went to get it. Then the police came in."

The police had been called by the restaurant manager, Barwacz says. He didn't want street people eating inside. It might offend other patrons.

The police listened to the manager and Barwacz, then left. There really wasn't anyone for them to arrest, since feeding a hungry, shivering woman isn't against the law.

Then, Barwacz said, the manager lectured him. "I wrote what he said on a napkin. He said, one, I will not be served there anymore and, two, he doesn't want me to come in there anymore."

Barwacz left. But it wasn't over. That McDonald's manager didn't know it, but he had messed with a very tough old man. And there is a tattoo, the number 95398, on Barwacz's arm that proves how tough he is.

It was put there by Nazis when they rounded up slave labor in Poland. Barwacz, American-born, had been taken back to Poland by his parents. He was a student in Krakow when the Nazis took him to a concentration camp.

Before the war ended, he had been in four camps: Auschwitz-Birkenau, Buchenwald, Dora and Bergen-Belsen. He saw and endured unspeakable cruelty and suffering. He survived, was freed, made it back to this country and worked in a food factory until retirement.

Those horrible years are why he is sensitive to street people. "I do this because I know what it is to be hungry. I went through hell on earth. And I would pray to God. I said, 'God, please help me and I will help others.'

"So I am keeping my word to God when I help these people. Sometimes we talk. Some of them are crazy, but some understand. And if I tell them about where I have been and show them my tattoo, some take my arm and hold it to them and cry.

"So this manager, this big fat man, he doesn't know what it is to be hungry. He doesn't know what it is to be beaten down, to be tortured. And he has the nerve to do this to me? To tell me I can't come in there and buy food for people? He thinks he can do that? We'll see."

Barwacz began knocking on doors. He told his story to the ACLU, NAACP, the Illinois Department of Human Relations, Operation PUSH, ministers and lawyers.

Finally he found someone who would do something more than cluck sympathetically.

Ed Voci, a lawyer with the Leadership Council, helped Barwacz file a complaint with the Chicago Commission on Human Relations against that McDonald's franchise.

"You can't discriminate on the basis of your source of income," Voci says.

So the complaint alleges that the restaurant discriminated against people who accept charitable contributions.

It seeks damages for Barwacz, although he isn't looking to get rich, and donations to homeless shelters.

And it wants an order forbidding McDonald's giving the bum's rush to Barwacz and his dining guests.

Maybe we have too many lawsuits in this country. But in this case, I think there's room for one more. ∎

EEOC is lacking in wisdom teeth

WEDNESDAY, JUNE 29, 1994

A Chicago corporation recently received an ominous letter from the Equal Employment Opportunity Commission.

The letter said: "You are hereby notified that a charge of employment discrimination has been filed against your organization under the Americans With Disabilities Act."

It told the corporation to submit "a statement of your position with respect to the allegation contained in this charge, with copies of any supporting documentation. This material will be made a part of the file and will be considered at the time that we investigate this charge. Your prompt response to this request will make it easier to conduct and conclude our investigation of this charge."

Then came the specific allegation, which was made by a woman:

"On or about April 28, 1994, I applied for the position of Benefits Representative at the above referenced Respondent. On or about April 28, 1994, I was interviewed by the Respondent for the position.

"During the interview, I advised the Respondent that I have a microchip embedded in one of my molars and it speaks to me and others.

"I believe I have been discriminated against because of my disability in violation of the Americans with Disabilities Act of 1990, in that I am qualified for the position.

"After explaining to the Respondent that I have a microchip embedded in my molar, I was not hired."

Now, imagine for a moment that you are a federal bureaucrat at the Chicago office of the EEOC, and someone comes in and says something like this:

"I just applied for a job and I was turned down because of discrimination."

You would probably ask what form the discrimination took.

"I have a microchip embedded in one of my molars."

Ah, a microchip in your molar.

"Yes, the microchip speaks to me and to others."

Ah, the microchip in your molar speaks to you.

"Yes, and that is why they didn't hire me."

I see. They didn't hire you because a microchip in your molar speaks to you. Well, well. An interesting problem.

Assuming you are a reasonable person, how would you respond to such a complaint?

Well, you might ask the woman to go and get a statement from a physician or dentist verifying that she has a microchip in her molar that talks to her.

Or you might suggest that she ask her dentist to remove the microchip from her molar.

You might even ask her how and why the microchip found its way into her molar and what it talks to her about?

Actually, I've had considerable experience in such matters. Anyone who works on a newspaper long enough—especially the night shift—will eventually talk to people who receive personal messages through fillings in their teeth, bed springs, light bulbs, their TV sets or voices that ride the winds.

So do desk sergeants in police stations and those who answer 911 calls.

Sometimes the strange messages come from outer space, fiendish neighbors, a nasty relative, Elvis or the president.

But when a caller says she is getting messages through fillings or microchips in her teeth, the cops don't send out a detective to peer into her mouth. Newspapers don't assign a reporter to press an ear against the molar to listen in on the messages.

Yet, here we have a federal agency that takes a talking molar seriously.

Some EEOC investigator actually took down the information and guided the woman through the complaint procedure.

Then the appropriate forms were filled out, a higher-up signed the complaint and the file and investigation were officially opened.

Now an official at the accused corporation is required to formally respond to the federal complaint, supplying "any supporting documentation" as to why the corporation wouldn't hire a woman who said she had a microchip embedded in her molar that talked to her.

I don't know what the corporation's response will be. How do you answer a charge of this sort?

Maybe you could say: "Our company policy forbids employees receiving personal calls through microchips embedded in their molars on company time."

Or maybe: "At this time, we did not have a need for someone with a talking microchip embedded in her molar. However, should such a position open . . ."

The most appropriate response would be to dash off a note saying: "Hey, do you bureaucrats have microchips embedded in your heads? Is this what we're paying taxes for? Bug off."

But that wouldn't be smart. If offended, the EEOC might very well order the company to make amends by hiring a dozen people who receive messages through their teeth. Nothing the EEOC does would surprise me. Or any of the businesses they torment.

We asked a spokesperson for the EEOC whether the laws require the agency to investigate any and all discrimination complaints—even those from people who claim to have microchips in their molars.

No, the law doesn't require it, the spokesperson said. It is an office policy.

"You have to remember," she said, "what's crazy to you might not be crazy to someone else. . . . Besides, you're always calling us heartless bureaucrats. Do you really want us heartless bureaucrats making the decision about what cases to take?"

I'll have to think about that question. Or maybe I'll get the answer through one of my teeth. ∎

Criminal's death was a crime

TUESDAY, OCTOBER 8, 1985

It's a widely held belief that our society's legal system coddles criminals. But that's not always so. Society can be pretty tough on some wrongdoers.

Just consider the case of Kathryn Ann Entress, who recently got in trouble with the law.

At first glance, you wouldn't think that Miss Entress, 37, was capable of committing a crime. Or at second and third glance.

Only 5 feet tall and barely weighing 100 pounds, she seemed more frail than a bird.

And her tiny body was often racked by terrible fits of asthmatic gasping, wheezing and coughing.

But looks can be deceiving. It appears that beneath this pathetic exterior was a criminal. A thief, to be precise.

She wasn't always a criminal. At one time she was a postal worker. But her chronic breathing problems kept her from working regularly, so she was given a small disability pension.

That's when she wound up living in a drab trailer park outside Ft. Lauderdale, Fla. Just she and her cat, whose name is unknown, in the sparsely furnished trailer.

There are a lot of people like her in Florida. The vegetation and many of the residents don't have deep roots.

It was in the trailer park that Miss Entress turned to crime and got in trouble with the law.

In fairness, she wasn't trying to get rich fast, as some criminals do.

Her motive was thirst. And a desire for personal hygiene.

Because she was of modest means, to say the least, Miss Entress sometimes had trouble making ends meet. She didn't live high, but by the time she paid her rent, bought the groceries and a few scraps for her cat, she didn't have much spendable income.

So sometimes she couldn't cover all the bills. And one bill she fell behind on was water. When she fell far enough behind, her water was cut off.

Water is something most of us take for granted. Like air. But when you don't have enough of either of them, life can be hard.

And that was what happened to Miss Entress. When her water was cut off, she began taking jugs to the trailer park's laundry room, filling them and carrying them back to her trailer.

Because of her asthma, her air would sometimes be cut off. So she would have to stop, put the jugs down and use an inhaler to get her breathing again.

She finally couldn't take it anymore, all that hauling of the heavy water jugs, especially in Florida's summer heat. So she found a way to turn the water on in her trailer.

And that made her a criminal. She was stealing water, because she wasn't paying for it.

Eventually her crime was detected. The investigation was made, the papers were filled out and the cops came to get her.

Her bond was set at $250. That's not a fortune, but to somebody who has to steal water, it's more than walking-around money.

She couldn't make bond, so she was taken to the Broward County Jail and put alone in a cell in the women's section.

I'm not sure what the penalty is for stealing water in Broward County, Fla. But I do know what Miss Entress' punishment was.

When she was jailed, her inhaler was taken away from her. It's the policy in most jails that inmates be stripped of all personal possessions.

And though an inhaler is a harmless enough device—you can buy them in any drugstore—the rules are the rules are the rules.

So sometime during her second night in jail, Miss Entress had an asthma attack. Nobody heard her wheezing, coughing and gasping for breath.

When somebody finally looked in her cell, she was dead.

The coroner's physician, who examined her body, said that if she had an inhaler, she probably would be alive.

So don't tell me we're easy on criminals. Maybe some of them. But even the most skeptical law-and-order zealots will have to admit that death by choking is a pretty severe penalty for filching some water.

I don't know what happened to her cat. ∎

CHAPTER 5
Sports and the Creatures Who Do It

3 ex-Cubs assure spurning of Atlanta

The experts have spoken. The Atlanta Braves are the best of the playoff teams. The bookies have made them the favorites to get to the World Series and win it. Some sports pundits already talk of them as one of the great teams of all time.

The experts just never learn.

As always, they ignore that strange, mysterious and almost-always fatal malady known as the Ex-Cubs Factor.

Regular readers of this column know about the Ex-Cubs Factor. But bear with me as I explain it to newcomers.

Twelve years ago, a Chicago sports nut named Ron Berler stumbled across an amazing statistic.

Since 1946, 13 teams had entered the World Series with three or more ex-Cubs on their roster.

Twelve of these 13 teams lost.

Berler theorized that it was a virus. Three or more ex-Cubs could infect an entire team with the will to lose, no matter how skillful that team might appear.

When Berler revealed his findings, the sports experts sneered and scoffed. Stupid and meaningless, they snickered. No scientific basis, they hooted.

Then came 1990, and they were still sneering, scoffing and making their mindless predictions.

That was the year about 99 percent of the experts declared that the Oakland A's could not possibly lose the World Series.

Even before the games began, they hailed the A's as one of the greatest teams—maybe the greatest—in the history of the game.

As the Washington Post's resident baseball genius put it: "Let's make this short and sweet. The baseball season is over. Nobody's going to beat the Oakland A's."

As Ben Bentley, the Chicago sports savant, said: "Could the Oakland Athletics be the greatest in baseball history?"

Yes, cried the experts: the greatest, a dynasty, a team of immortals. They could win while yawning.

But out there were two lonely voices: Berler and this writer.

We warned of the Ex-Cub Factor. We pointed out that the A's had foolishly defied the terrible virus by signing a third ex-Cub. And before that World Series began, Berler publicly stated: "As good as they are, they will lose. And they can blame their own arrogance for ignoring history."

So what happened? Not only did the A's lose, it was world class humiliation. Four straight defeats. One of sports' all-time flopperoos.

That made it 13 out of 14 teams with three or more ex-Cubs to collapse in the World Series since WWII.

The A's haven't been the same since. Once it struck, the ex-Cub virus burrowed into the fiber of the franchise. In only three years they have gone from a dynasty to limping mediocrity. Sources say their hot dogs don't even taste as good as they once did.

Have the experts learned anything? Of course not. As the late Mayor Richard J. Daley once said: "Duh experts—what do dey know?"

The sports experts are now hailing the Atlanta Braves as the super-team of this era.

On Sunday, Dave Kindred, columnist for the Sporting News, wrote: ". . . Atlanta has become baseball's best team since the Yankees of Mickey Mantle and Yogi Berra . . . the NL's best team since the Brooklyn Dodgers of Duke Snider, Gil Hodges and Pee Wee Reese . . ."

He may be right. They have thunderous hitters, overwhelming pitchers and a seamless defense.

But they also have the dreaded virus. Of the four teams in the playoffs, only the Braves are afflicted by the Ex-Cub Factor. Only the Braves have three former Cubs.

They are Greg Maddux, the superb pitcher, Damon Berryhill, the reliable catcher and . . .

Even a bleacher creature would be hard-pressed to name the third ex-Cub.

But Berler, the virus discoverer, knows. "I have it all in my computer," he says.

A relief pitcher named Jay Howell. Although he has been in the major leagues for 14 years, he's not a big name, not a big star, no flashy stats. A solid journeyman. Probably good to his family, a nice neighbor, a patriot and he doesn't kick little dogs.

But he is one of the three skeletons in the Atlanta closet. He has a sordid past.

For a brief time in 1981, when he was a mere lad, he was a Cub. He pitched in only 10 games, a total of 22 innings, and wasn't very good.

But as Berler says: "That is all it takes. He is a genuine, bona fide, star-crossed ex-Cub, the poor guy. He is a carrier. It always comes back to your roots. Once a Cub, always a Cub."

Berler, who is a free-lance writer and teacher, recently interviewed Maddux, who chose to become an Atlanta Braves multimillionaire, rather than a Chicago Cubs multimillionaire, because he wanted to play on a winning team.

"I told him: 'You think you're leaving a loser? Ha! You are a loser. And you're going to infect your 24 teammates.'"

He explained the ex-Cub Factor to Maddux. And the star pitcher responded by shouting: "I don't believe it, I don't believe it, I don't believe it!"

So if the Braves defeat the Phillies and make it to the World Series, bet on the Braves at your own peril.

But this puts a Chicagoan such as myself—a devout Cubs fan—in a difficult position.

Those who are true fans of the White Sox or Cubs loathe the other team. This crosstown rivalry takes precedent over civic pride. So if the Sox play the Braves, I must root for the Braves. It is the only decent thing a Cubs fan can do. Sox fans, being dedicated haters, will understand.

It will be the first time I will be cheering for a virus. ∎

Big bucks sink joys of fishing

FRIDAY, SEPTEMBER 28, 1984

The first time I saw one of them, I was sitting in a small tin boat, anchored in a quiet cove on a sprawling lake in Arkansas.

A friend and I were fishing. That means we were half asleep in the shade of a tree, with a couple of lines dangling worms in the water. Every so often, one of us would snap open a can of beer, study the puffy clouds drifting across the blue sky, check the worm's health, then doze off again.

Suddenly, we heard the terrible howl of a big piston engine. And into our quiet cove roared a low, sleek boat doing about 60 miles an hour. It bounced across the water, did a sharp turn, and the motor went silent.

It was unlike any fishing boat I had ever seen. It seemed to be covered with sparkledust and was equipped with all sorts of electronic equipment. It had the names of fishing-equipment makers written all over the side.

In it were two men wearing jump suits and long-billed caps. No sooner had the engine been turned off than they began whipping casts near the shoreline. They would cast and furiously crank the reel. Over and over, they cast and cranked.

After a few minutes, they started the engine and went roaring away. But a little later, we heard a distant sound that became louder and louder, and another boat barreled into our cove. Once again, the two occupants flailed the water with dozens of rapid-fire casts before speeding away.

"What the heck is going on?" I asked my fishing partner.

"I don't know," he said, "but they must be nuts. That's no way to fish. They don't even have time for a can of beer."

Later, we discovered that what we were seeing was a professional bass fishing tournament. All over the lake that day were high-powered bass boats, equipped with everything from depth sounders to cigarette lighters.

Dozens of good old boys named Billy Bob and Willie Joe were trying to catch enough bass to grab a hunk of the $50,000 prize money.

And they were fishing in a way I had never seen anybody fish. Instead of doing the sensible thing, which is to anchor in a restful spot, toss a worm or minnow over the side, sip a can of beer, admire the sky, observe a circling hawk and catch a few winks, they were rushing about in a frenzy.

They'd stay in a spot for only a few minutes, hammering the shoreline with casts. Then they'd speed away to another spot.

At the end of the day, they'd roar into the marina and turn in their fish, which would be weighed. And the guy with the heaviest catch would be the winner.

That was about 15 years ago. Since then, professional bass fishing has become a big-time sport. Tournaments are held all over the South and Southwest. Professional bass fishermen trailer their boats from one lake to another. And all over the country, ordinary fishermen emulate them by buying powerful boats, with swivel chairs, electronic equipment and sophisticated rods and reels.

But I still think my friend was right when he said that was no way to fish. Certain pastimes lend themselves to professional competition. Fishing isn't one of them. If there is any sport that is meant to be done slowly and relaxed, it is fishing. Huck Finn and Tom Sawyer knew how to fish. Feet up, eyes closed. Lazy. No competition.

And no greed.

I mention greed because it turns out that the world of professional bass fishing now has a big scandal. Some of the fishermen worked out a scheme to give them the edge in catching the fattest bass.

They would go to Florida, where the biggest bass are found, catch some, keep them alive in fish tanks and take them to the Louisiana or Texas lake where the next tournament was to be held. Then they would sneak the fish into the water of some cove or inlet and return to that spot when the tournament was being held. The fish, being dumb creatures of habit, would still be hanging around. And, being dumb, they would let themselves be caught again.

Various federal agencies are investigating. One former champion apparently killed himself after he was called to testify before a grand jury. There are reports of death threats against witnesses. And now, nobody knows which fish to trust.

It's hard to believe that an act as simple as catching a fish could wind up being the object of a grand jury investigation.

I'll stay with the old cane pole. And pass the beer cooler, please. ∎

Baseball justice just a swing away

WEDNESDAY, AUGUST 5, 1987

While I was watching a baseball game, an incident occurred that made me question why this sport, above all others, is considered the great American pastime.

In this particular game, the pitcher was obviously agitated because things hadn't been going too well. It was his own fault, of course, since he was an incompetent.

So he reared back, let fly and the ball sped toward the batter's head.

The batter sprawled in the dirt and the ball missed conking him by only a matter of inches.

When he got up, he shouted a few obscenities at the pitcher. Then he took one step forward, as if thinking about going out to the mound and wrestling a bit.

The umpire stepped forward, waggled a finger at the batter and warned him not to do any such thing. And the game resumed.

It was an example of pure injustice.

Here you had a batter, doing what the rules and his paycheck require him to do: Trying to hit a ball thrown by the pitcher.

The pitcher's job is to try to make the batter swing and miss the ball or hit it to one of the fielders.

Instead, the pitcher threw the ball in the general direction of the batter's brain.

Now, the rules don't say the pitcher should throw the ball at the batter's brain. That's not how you get the batter out. That's how you kill someone. Even worse, if struck in the head, the batter could be permanently impaired and become a sports broadcaster.

But who had a finger of authority waggled at him? Who was warned by the enforcer of the rules to restrain himself and be nonviolent?

Not the pitcher, who was the assailant in this incident, but the batter, who was the intended victim.

What kind of system of justice is that?

In no other sport does such unfairness exist. In football or boxing or hockey, if somebody tries to knock you down, you or your teammates are allowed to knock them down. In most sports, if somebody does something sneaky and unsportsmanlike, the offender is punished—not the victim.

But in baseball, it's just the opposite. Recently, a cowardly cur from the San Diego Padres threw a ball that hit Andre Dawson of the Cubs in the face.

For several long moments, the spectators weren't sure if Dawson were alive or dead. When he finally regained consciousness, his reaction was perfectly normal and justified. He got up and went looking for the guy who had bloodied his face.

Naturally, the lotus-eater ran away and hid in the locker room.

And when order was restored, who was punished? The person who had flung a deadly missile at someone else's head?

Not at all. It was announced that the sneak had left the playing field by his own choice or that of his manager.

But for the crime of trying to retaliate in a manly way, Dawson was officially ejected from the game by the umpire.

Some of the philosophers who broadcast baseball games try to justify this inequity by saying that the "brushback pitch" is part of baseball. That is what they call a ball thrown 90 miles an hour in the general direction of someone's nose—a "brushback pitch."

But I've looked through the rules of baseball. There is nothing that says it is the pitcher's right or duty to use a ball as a deadly weapon.

I also asked a prosecutor how the law would react if someone was walking down the street and someone else threw a hard object that hit him in the face and spilled his blood.

He said: "We'd go after him for assault, a felony, which can carry with it a prison sentence."

I also asked what the law would say if the victim, dripping blood, pummeled his assailant.

"He would be perfectly justified," the prosecutor said.

So it's clear that the rules of baseball should be changed to conform with those of an occasionally civilized society.

I suggest something I call The Cavarretta Response.

Some of you may recall Phil Cavarretta, a native Chicagoan who was once a Cub star.

One day, I was at a game when a pitcher threw the ball at Cavarretta's head. He ducked and survived.

But on the next pitch, he swung. The bat somehow slipped from his hands and whirled right at the pitcher's head. The pitcher dived to the ground, narrowly avoiding decapitation. The pitcher didn't throw at anybody's head again that day.

This response should be made part of baseball's official rules: "If a pitcher throws a ball that forces a batter to fall down to avoid being struck in the head, the batter may, during the course of the game, fling his bat at the pitcher's head."

It would not only be fair, but it would make the sport more entertaining.

But as it stands now, there might be something in what the Russians say about their having invented the game. ∎

City has hope that 2nd coming is near

FRIDAY, MARCH 10, 1995

It's 2:30 on Thursday afternoon and the rumors are flying across a great city like flocks of crazed birds.

In the Tribune newsroom, the phones are ringing with calls from reporters' wives, husbands, friends and news sources, all asking: "What have you heard? Has he said anything? Can it be true?"

That's what happens in any newsroom when a really big story starts breaking or even leaking.

In years past, the reporters and editors would have been clustered around the clattering teletype machines that brought in the wire service bulletins.

Now they punch up the stories on their computer monitors. The technology changes, but the excitement is the same.

Down in Billy Goat's Tavern, the Simpson trial is on the TV and Detective Mark Fuhrman has been on the stand. This is supposed to be one of the key moments in the O.J. show. But the excited murmuring is about something else. A beer drinker nervously says, "I'm not going to get my hopes up. What will be will be. But, gosh, wouldn't it be great?"

There was even a typical Chicago cynic who said, "That's why Jerry Reinsdorf caused the baseball strike. If they wiped out the season, then Jordan would have to quit baseball and come back to the Bulls."

And fans were calling ticket brokers to get suddenly-hot Bulls tickets.

Having covered many of them, it's still hard to think of any big Chicago news event that could be compared with the return of Michael Jordan to the Bulls.

We've seen many big stories of far greater significance than a basketball star coming out of early retirement.

Off the top of my head, I'd include the sudden deaths of Richard J. Daley and Harold Washington, which left the city stunned and saddened.

There was the brawling 1968 Democratic Convention; the now-forgotten Summerdale police scandals; the great blizzards; and murders such as the Degnan and the Grimes cases.

But like most big stories, they were about tragedy, scandal, disaster or conflict. That's the grim nature of so much of what we call news.

What made even the possibility of a return by Jordan unique is that it would be major news that is also happy news—something that can grab and exhilarate an entire city.

Yes, other stories, most of them in sports, have done that. But they were not quite the same.

The Bears winning the Super Bowl? Sure, it made Chicago bounce. But they were so dominant a team that the win wasn't a nail-biting surprise.

Cubs fans were ecstatic when their team made the playoffs. But Sox fans just sneered. And when the Sox won the pennant, most Cub fans smiled politely and yawned.

But only the most devout sports-haters could say that they were indifferent to a rumored return by Michael the Great.

If you think about it, the whole thing is kind of silly. Why should a city of 3 million and a metropolitan sprawl twice that, start high-fiving at the prospect of a wealthy athlete deciding that, on second thought, he would enjoy flipping balls through a hoop?

Does it put any money in your pocket? Does it lower your cholesterol or grow hair on your bald spot? Does it make you any more appealing to the opposite sex (or even the same one)? Does it make your marriage happier, your children less goofy or your mortgage smaller? Does it get rid of your chronic slice or hook and permit you to break 90 or 80 once in your life?

No, but so what? What's wrong with getting excited about something just because it's plain fun? There is more to life and to news than Newt's revolution, the plight of this or that miserable group or individual, the ups and downs of the dollar or the yen or the peso, the price of Sugar Pops and what Detective Fuhrman really thinks of his fellow man.

In a nutshell, watching Michael Jordan play basketball is a special kick because he is that rare talent—someone who is so good at what he does that nobody is even close. That's what it must have been like listening to Caruso sing or watching Babe Ruth hit.

And the reaction of Chicago to all of Thursday's rumors shows what a remarkable impact someone that talented and likable can have.

The last time we had this much excitement was when Jordan abruptly announced that he was quitting. That was probably the biggest sports story in Chicago's history.

And the most depressing Chicago story of that year.

So maybe he owes us one. ■

Cub fans, let's be careful out there

MONDAY, AUGUST 8, 1988

As fans of old horror movies know, when the sun goes down and the moon comes out, spooky things can happen.

Bela Lugosi used to rise from his coffin, a gleam in his eye, and go into the night to give young ladies some really unsightly hickies.

And when the moon was full, Lon Chaney Jr., a nice fellow during the day, would sprout fur on his face and feet, let out a howl and chew the first rustic he met.

It was always after dark that Jack the Ripper, blade in hand, prowled foggy London in search of a helpless doxy.

In fact and fiction, night is scarier than day. Things go bump in the dark. Shadows take on strange shapes. Who knows what menace lurks in those dark corners?

That's why ancient tribes huddled near their fires. And modern tribes huddle near their Mitsubishi.

As T.B. Aldrich wrote: "Night is a stealthy, evil raven, wrapt to the eyes in his black wings."

And tonight in Chicago we're going to begin finding the answer to a fascinating psychological question that concerns the debilitating effect of night on the human mind:

Does the coming of darkness cause otherwise decent, polite, hygienic Cub fans to have a fiendish compulsion to make wee-wee on a stranger's lawn?

This, of course, is a specter that has haunted many North Side Chicagoans since it was decided that night games would be played in Wrigley Field. They have visions of beer-bloated Cub fans rushing from the ballpark to the nearest patch of yuppie-owned grass.

Then jostling each other for space while shouting: "Lemme through, I get first shot at that lawn."

"Okay, then I get the tulips."

"What about me?"

"You can take the hedge."

And other cries of: "Downwind, you fool, always aim downwind."

The coming of night baseball has created a few lesser issues, too. Parking, traffic congestion and noise. And a magazine even raised the frightening prospect of Cub fans, depressed by defeat or high on victory, storming into nearby gay bars to harm winsome young men.

But the single greatest fear I've heard expressed has been from those who have said: "I know it's going to happen. Somebody's going to do it on my lawn."

I've heard it so often that I'm starting to have my own visions of people in the Wrigleyville neighborhood rowing boats down their flooded streets. And National Guard troops stacking sandbags along Waveland Avenue.

I can see Bill Kurtis in hip boots, standing on Waveland Avenue and saying to the camera: "I'm here with Nadine Yuppwife, whose home is one of those that have been flooded by the bladders of Cub fans. Mrs. Yuppwife, what is the extent of the damage to your property?"

"We lost everything. Even our beloved BMW has floated away with my husband in it."

Should this happen, there is a price the city will pay beyond the abused lawns, the splattered porches, the soaked sidewalks.

Because the eyes of the nation will be on us, the entire city will be humiliated. Most of America will be laughing at us.

That's because hundreds of reporters, TV crews and other professional gawkers have flocked to Chicago for the novelty of our first Cubs night game. You would think Tom Edison himself was going to pull the light switch.

And if the fears of the neighborhood are realized, we will turn on our TV sets and hear David Letterman singing: "Chicago, Chicago, that tinkling town."

On the other hand, the presence of so many media creatures might have a beneficial effect. Besides the newspeople, there will be almost 200 cops. And there will be the residents of the neighborhood out in force, once they've finished covering their homes and loved ones with plastic sheeting.

There will be so many watchful eyes that if anyone reaches for a zipper or even hitches up his trousers, he'll promptly be surrounded by all three networks, Cable News, USA Today and three members of the Police Department's Special Wee-Wee Strike Force.

This alone should discourage any wanton spraying of lawns, gardens or small individuals.

And if that isn't enough, then as an elder Cub fan I am making a personal plea to my fellow Cub fans:

Don't give the Wrigleyville yuppies a chance to say: "I told you so." Conduct yourselves properly. Don't give in to the temptation presented by that patch of grass. Let us all try to project an image of decency and propriety.

In other words, be a gentleman. Do it in the alley. ∎

Rodman just a Bull, not the 4 horsemen of the apocalypse

TUESDAY, OCTOBER 10, 1995

Now Chicagoans have some idea what it must have been like when the armies of Attila the Hun or Genghis Khan came thundering down on terrified and unsuspecting villages.

Until last week, life here was as normal and ho-hum as it ever gets. Not too hot, not too cold. Some clouds, some sunshine. People went about their daily business of getting on with their lives, as the media philosophers would say.

Then suddenly it happened. The city was caught in the grip of confusion, shock and fright.

Oh, my, oh, my, goodness, gracious, for gosh sake's, Dennis Rodman is coming!

All right, that's probably a slight exaggeration. The entire city and suburbs weren't terrified and confused. It just seemed that way when you read the sports pages and listened to the sports radio and TV babblers.

Then you might have asked yourself: Is this really one of this nation's major population centers, a world-class city that has more Fortune 500 companies than any city except New York, great universities, hospitals and cultural temples? A sophisticated city that knows you put a dash of celery salt and never ketchup on a hot dog?

How could it be in such a dither at being invaded by one very tall and eccentric basketball player?

After my initial media-induced panic, I came out from under my bed and tried to understand why the man was causing so much emotional trauma.

But I'm still not sure. I've checked Rodman's record and have found nothing concerning drugs, rape, murder or other acts of mischief that aren't unknown in the sports society.

One writer referred to Rodman's "depravity."

As a Bulls fan, I'd rather not have to cheer for someone who is depraved. But in Rodman's case, I'm not sure what that means.

True, he colors his hair red, green and other bright colors. But so what? Thousands of outwardly respectable Chicago men color their hair brown, black or blond without causing terror in the streets. Others buy thatches of someone else's hair and tape it to their own heads and no one gasps.

Rodman paints his fingernails and tattoos his skin and wears earrings on his ears and other body parts. That might not be considered fashionable by any mayor named Daley or the guys in your bowling league, but it isn't uncommon on much of Chicago's North Side. What the heck, most of the time he wears what appears to be a form of men's clothing.

Many commentators expressed grave concern that his presence would spread discord and unhappiness among his Bulls teammates. But from time to time, long before Rodman, I've heard morose Bulls players express their unhappiness at being mere multimillionaires instead of deserving billionaires.

One of the more urgent questions raised on the sports talk shows and in other scholarly circles is: Will Scottie Pippen talk to Rodman and will Rodman talk to Scottie Pippen?

It appears that nobody knows. As they say on the TV news shows: We'll have to take a wait-and-see attitude.

But if Scottie doesn't talk to Dennis and Dennis doesn't talk to Scottie, will it matter? There are millions of people to whom Scottie has never spoken. Just about all those reading this paper will go to their graves without being talked to or glanced at by either Scottie, Dennis, Michael or even Luc Longley. Do you feel that your life is any less meaningful?

My guess is that eventually they will talk. Scottie will probably say something like: "Next time, throw me the ball." And Dennis will say something like: "OK." Basketball players are always saying things like that.

But even if Scottie doesn't say it, Dennis will probably throw the ball to him anyway. And why not? That's what he is paid to do.

Besides, the ball is too big to wear as an earring. ∎

Fox going into hall and going out of the limelight

FRIDAY, MARCH 7, 1997

Poor Nellie Fox, the spunky little hero of White Sox fans. He's been gone awhile, so he doesn't know about the bad thing that was just done to him. Or maybe he does.

They have voted Fox into baseball's Hall of Fame. In the sporting press, this means that he has become an "immortal"—a word tossed around more freely by sportswriters than clergymen.

But what it really means is that Fox will now be forgotten.

Until this week, Fox was part of a long tradition of lucky baseball stars who were thought to be unfairly overlooked in the Hall of Fame voting.

I call it the Hack Wilson Syndrome.

If you consider yourself a baseball fan—especially of the Cubs affliction—quick, tell me about Hack Wilson. Stats, career, personality, legends and so on.

Chances are you can't. So ask yourself, when was the last time you heard the name Hack Wilson?

See? But for many years after he stopped playing and after he died, Hack Wilson had an enviable measure of fame in Chicago.

Every year, that would be what amounted to Protest the Injustice Done to Hack Wilson Festival.

Sports columnists would thunder about why the Hall of Fame voters could be so thickheaded as to once again deny good old Hack entry into the sacred hall of immortals.

They would rehash how he once struck 56 home runs in a season, still the National League record. How he drove in 190 runs in one season, a major-league record.

Yes, they would concede, good old Hack had been known to take a few dozen drinks too many once in a while. But who didn't? And was that common human weakness any reason to deny an otherwise decent fellow the immortality that he had earned?

White-haired sports fans in bars would recall being in the stands when good old Hack hit a couple out. Those, they would say, were the glory days of the Cubs when Hack led them to a league championship. Of course, they still lost in the World Series.

And some would retell the story of the time a Cub manager tried to persuade good old Hack to cut down on his drinking. The manager held up a glass of whiskey, then dropped a live worm in it. The worm promptly died.

"What does this tell you?" the manager supposedly asked.

"It tells me," Hack said, "that if I keep drinking, I'll never have worms."

Probably not true, but it was a good story.

And they would toast the memory of good old Hack and curse the damn fools who didn't appreciate what a great player he was, despite his fondness for whiskey.

Some would talk about the rumors that there were other reasons besides his drinking that deprived good old Hack of his rightful immortality. It was thought by some that he was what we now call a gay, although he had remained in the clubhouse closet.

After many years, Hack was finally voted in. And from that day on, the only people who took notice of him were those who visited the Hall of Fame in Cooperstown, N.Y., and glanced at his plaque on the wall.

There isn't even a shotglass with a worm in it as part of his display.

The sportswriters now ignore him, and the fans have forgotten him. Some honor. Some immortality.

And now they have done it to Nellie Fox.

In recent years, we've had an annual outburst of sports-page indignation about Little Nellie being deprived of his rightful place in the hall.

They've written with considerable emotion about his spunk, the many hits, his nimble feet, his iron-man durability and, of course, how he always hustled.

But now you can forget about Nellie. He's in the great baseball tourist attraction, and that's the last we'll hear about him.

So who will be next as the topic of annual indignation?

I figure it will be Ron Santo, and he will be a fine choice since he is still a relatively young man and should have many good years of being snubbed ahead of him.

What a lucky guy. Once it starts, he can look forward to an annual ego boost from reading about all the home runs he swatted, the many runs he drove in and the fearless way he guarded the hot corner.

Some of the more insightful baseball scholars might even make note of how many tons of home plate dirt he scooped up and rubbed into his hands and forearms. Or the time he heroically slugged an abusive fan, a hit for which he received the praise of a Chicago judge who hadn't even been bribed.

And there will be angry commentary about Santo being deprived of his rightful immortality because of the stupidity of East Coast baseball writers who would surely vote him into the sacred hall if he had been a New York Yankee rather than a lowly Cub.

Eventually, Ron will make it. And a few days later, someone will wave to him on the street and say: "Hi, Don." ∎

Brits' scorn for McEnroe a riot

FRIDAY, MAY 31, 1985

In the past, many Americans have felt embarrassed by the rude behavior of John McEnroe when he has played tennis at Wimbledon in England.

He has used foul language, abused the officials, made obscene gestures at the fans, kicked the grass, pouted and shouted. Once he even swatted a ball at a line judge, hitting the bloke's bald spot.

Although he's done the same things in this country, it seemed much worse in England. That's because the English have an image of being so, well, so civilized, so sensitive to unsportsmanlike behavior.

And they have reacted with dyspeptic indignation. The English press has described McEnroe as nothing less than a thug, a barbarian and—even worse—as a cheeky sort of fellow. English government officials harrumphed that he not be permitted to play at the hallowed Wimbledon tournament.

Their tennis officials have fined him thousands of dollars. They even went so far as to deny him membership in the All England Lawn Tennis Club, the first singles champion in 104 years to be snubbed.

In this country, many Americans shook their heads and felt sheepish. That's because many of us feel superior to the English—at least in the social graces.

They have this precise, yet languid way of speaking. They never seem to lose their poise. Even if you're a head taller, they manage to look down their thin, patrician noses at you. And they *do* take high tea.

Well, I say to hell with them and their haughty airs. And I hope that the next time John McEnroe plays at Wimbledon, he demands an apology for the past criticism.

If he doesn't get it, he should go to center court, drop his whites and moon the entire stadium.

Where, I ask, do the English get off berating a kid from New York for a few cuss words, an extended middle finger and a bit of spouting and pouting?

As a rude lad, he's just a piker, a twit, a mere nuisance.

For world-class unsportsmanlike behavior, I offer you the murderous British soccer fans.

When they get upset, nobody tallies up the swear words. Instead, there's a body count. And at last count in Belgium, the number of dead—trampled when the Brit fans attacked the Italian fans—was 38.

And the amazing thing is that there's no reason to be surprised. Horrified and disgusted, sure. But surprised? Not at all. On a less grand scale, this has become standard conduct for English soccer fans.

Whenever there is a big match in England—or an English team plays on the continent—it is usually preceded by a full-blown riot in the streets.

Then, during the actual game, there is maiming and mauling in the stands.

And, after the game, win or lose, there is another full-blown riot in the streets.

Now, I'm not talking about the kind of rowdiness that occurs in this country after a World Series. In comparison, we are mere pussycats.

An English judge recently sent 25 fans to prison for showing their displeasure with another fan's loyalties. They slashed his throat with a broken bottle and then mauled a cop who tried to interfere.

At another match, the fans bashed each other about the streets. Before the festivities ended, 80 were hurt. Almost 100 cops were hurt. And the fans managed to knock down a brick wall that fell on a 15-year-old bystander and crushed his brain beyond repair.

In this country, fans entering a stadium might be asked to show the contents of a bag to make sure they aren't bringing in their own booze. But in England, they frisk them for knives, razor blades, railroad spikes, lead pipes, brass knuckles, whips and chains. I guess waving a team banner is too tame for them.

And these are the same people who sneer at John McEnroe for conking a line judge with a rubber ball.

Next time, John, spit in his eye. The one without the monocle. ∎

Opening Day—like it used to be

FRIDAY, APRIL 10, 1992

I'll probably leave the office at about 12:30 today and take a cab to Cubs Park. Then I'll meet my host in our reserved seats, which will have a fine, unobstructed view of the playing field.

I'm not sure what I'll choose for lunch. As at most of today's ballparks, the food menu has become extensive.

When the game is over, we might pause in the private club and have a drink. Then, after the crowd subsides, another cab home.

A very nice way to spend the day at the ballpark, you must agree.

But it isn't the best way to do it. Not nearly.

The best way was to get up early, yell for the pal down the street to come on out and start walking at about 7 a.m.

It was about 3 miles down Armitage Avenue, then north about 2 more miles to Addison. Five miles wasn't that much if you could save the 10 cents streetcar fare and use it later for a hot dog.

At the end of the walk, there it was: the eighth wonder of the world in the eyes of a 12-year-old.

The idea was to get there early to be near the front of the crowd of other kids at the "seat gate." At least that's what we called it.

After a while, a guy would come out and point to us, one after another. "You, you, you . . . and you, yeah, you. . . ."

I don't know how he made his selection. Maybe size. Or maybe the most pleading, yearning looks in the eyes.

But when you became one of the youse, you dashed inside. No ticket: free, on the house. Of course, it wasn't charity. Strictly business.

In those days, the box seats—those that were truly box seats—had folding chairs. And the stacks of chairs had to be unfolded and put in place before the gates opened and the box-seat swells arrived.

So that's what we did, setting up a few thousand seats. And we thought it was a swell deal, which it was. Of course, it was a swell deal for P.K. Wrigley. For about $10 worth of freebies, he got what a union would probably sock him $2,000 for today.

By the time the seats were in place, and we were up in the grandstands, the players had started drifting out on the field. Loosening up, playing the pepper game, clowning around, spitting, scratching. Coaches hitting fungo flies to the outfielders. The more ambitious pitchers doing a few wind sprints in the outfield grass.

Then came the best part of the day. No, not the game. Batting practice.

This was when you could study this year's prize rookie phenom to see if he hit the long ball as long here as he did in the minors. And when you would watch in terror as the visiting team's cleanup hitter drove shot after shot onto the street.

And if the Andy Frain ushers were nice guys, as many were, you could sneak down the box seat aisles and coax an autograph out of one of the Cubs. Free, of course. The $20 signature wasn't even a science fiction concept.

Why do I cherish Andy Pafko? Because the Kid from Boyceville, as he was known to our world, took a few seconds away from the batting cage to sign a scrap of paper. And he even smiled. I hear that a smile costs an extra 10-spot today.

Infield practice. The strong arms of the hot corner guardian and the keystone combo whipping blue darts across the diamond. (Sportswriters don't write that way anymore, but I like it.)

Then the grounds crew, who I thought had the best jobs in America, raked and patted the infield, put down the chalk lines, and old Pat, the field announcer, said in that dust-dry voice: "Have your pencils and scorecards ready, and I will give you the correct lineup for today's ball game. Batting first, and playing second base. . . ."

The game was on. And what made it so good was that there was nothing else. Only the game.

We didn't know what anyone on the field earned. And if we had known, we wouldn't have cared. We thought in terms of dimes and quarters, which could buy hot dogs and a pop.

But we knew the batting averages. We knew how much Bill Nicholson's bat weighed to the ounce and that he would almost always pull the ball and that he had once smashed one almost to the concession stand in the center field bleachers. We knew that Philabuck always made contact and hit to all fields and would move the runner up. We knew that Clyde McCullough had a terrible hitch in his swing, a habit we should avoid at all costs.

We didn't know if this player was moodily yearning to be traded or if that player hated the manager. We assumed that they were all happy. And how could they not be happy? They were Cubs and playing baseball in one of the most beautiful spots on the face of the earth.

We didn't know about front office executives, marketing, TV revenue, salary arbitration, agents, contract extensions, incentive clauses or urine tests. We knew nothing of bond issues, expansion cities or congressional inquiries into the role of superstations.

But we knew that it was not a good idea to get behind in the count to Stan the Man and that our outfielders had to hustle on shots in the gap because Enos Slaughter would always take the extra base.

In other words, we knew all that really mattered. And when the last out was made, and we trudged the 5 miles back to the neighborhood, we had the scrupulously maintained scorecard to prove it.

I think they ought to change the rules for who goes to Opening Day. Only ages 12 to 15 admitted. They know the score. ∎

Dad's Cubs quizzes were always reader favorites, and I've appended some additional Q&As from the following year. —D.R.

Time to test Cub quotient

WEDNESDAY, APRIL 10, 1985

"How do you think the Cubbies are going to do this year?" the Yuppie man brightly asked Slats Grobnik.

That was all Slats had to hear. He set his beer down and stared contemptuously at the creature.

Then he said, "Answer a simple question for me: What high school did Phil Cavarretta attend?"

Quick as a flash, the young man answered, "Phil who?"

"That's what I thought." Slats snarled. "You are not a true Cub fan. A true Cub fan never says Cubbies. You are one of these parasitic, bandwagon-hopping, trend-following, glory-seeking, know-nothing bubble heads who showed up last year for the sole purpose of standing in front of a TV camera in a sports-theme bar while holding a finger in the air and babbling that you are No. 1. Any true Cub fan knows what high school Phil Cavarretta attended."

"New Trier?" the young man asked.

"Get out of my sight, you boob."

As the young man slunk away, Slats said to me, "I think it is time."

I agreed. It's time for my annual Cub quiz. There has never been a greater need for it. Because of last season's excitement, the city—the entire nation, in fact—is swarming with nouveaux fans of the kind described by Slats.

The Cub quiz will weed them out, since only a true fan with a sense of history can answer even half the questions.

So when you hear somebody chirping about the "Cubbies," just whip the quiz out and demolish him with questions.

Q—This question will surely cause excited tittering around Broadway and Diversey. Which immortal Cub outfielder was known as "Swish"?

A—The immortal Bill Nicholson. They called him that because of the way he waved the bat over the plate, not because he blew kisses at his teammates.

Q—Which immortal Cub outfielder once hit four home runs in a doubleheader against the New York Giants?

A—The immortal Swish Nicholson. And the Giants walked him intentionally with the bases loaded his last time up, the cowards.

Q—In May, 1960, the immortal Don Cardwell pitched a no-hitter in his first start after being traded to the Cubs. Name the Cub outfielder who saved the no-hitter with a diving, tumbling catch for the final out.

A—The immortal Moose Moryn, who enjoyed diving and tumbling so much that he later opened his own saloon.

Q—Name at least one Cub pitcher in the 1950s who wore a golden earring.

A—The immortal Fernando Pedro Rodriguez. And in 1956, his rookie year, he didn't lose even one game. On the other hand, he didn't win one either.

Q—The Cubs once had a rookie pitcher who was 36 years old. Name this phenom.

A—The immortal Fernando Pedro Rodriguez, dummy, the guy with the earring.

Q—Which Cub batboy went on to fame as a TV news anchor creature?

A—The immortal Skippy Jacobson. He said the worst part of the job was that Harry Chiti and Dee Fondy used to throw their athletic supporters at him. I don't know why that bothered him. Jacobson could have turned one of them into a hammock.

Q—Speaking of throwing things, when the immortal Hank Sauer hit a home run, the fans in the left field bleachers used to throw packages of his favorite delicacy at him. What was in the packages?

A—If you live around Lincoln Avenue, you probably said quiche, but it was chewing tobacco. You'd think that when Ron "The Penguin" Cey hits a home run, his fans would toss him a dead fish.

Q—Which of these two Cubs always had sore feet: the immortal Heinz Becker or the immortal Dominic "Dim-Dom" Dallessandro?

A—Becker had the sore feet. Little Dominic had tiny feet. It took him 20 jumps to get out of the dugout.

Q—What Chicago shortstop hit an astonishing .388 in 1936? Careful, careful.

A—The immortal Luke Appling. Sure, he was with the White Sox, but I told you to be careful.

Q—In 1969, Ron Santo shouted so much at the Cub center-fielder that he made the poor fellow cry. Name this wretch.

A—The immortal Don Young. He hit .239 that year, and if he were around here today, I'd yell at him too.

Q—The Cubs once had a rookie second baseman who crossed himself every time he came to bat. Name this devout fellow and his batting average as a rookie.

A—The immortal Tony Taylor, who hit .235 and made the atheists in the stands snicker.

Q—Which Cub pitcher was born in Ozanna, Poland?

A—The immortal Moe Drabowsky, who is still considered the greatest pitcher Ozanna ever produced.

Q—Which Cub third baseman used to do TV commercials for a wig maker?

A—The immortal Steve Ontiveros. But his mustache was real.

Q—Which Cub once made a Herculean throw from the outfield that went into the dugout, through an open door and into a toilet bowl?

A—The immortal Dave "Ding-Dong" Kingman. If he's ever voted into the Hall of Fame, they should put the toilet bowl there too.

AUGUST 25, 1986

Q—Which Cub great holds the record for most dirt rubbed into his hands during a career?

A—The immortal Ron Santo. His hands got so dirty that he used to wash them before he went into the men's room.

Q—In 1953, a Cub player used to amuse himself by stuffing chewing tobacco into the mouth of a bat boy and making him chew it. Name the player and the bat boy.

A—The bat boy was the immortal "Skippy" Jacobson, who grew up to be the TV philosopher, Walter Jacobson. Walter recalls: "Harry Chiti stuffed tobacco into my mouth and made me chew it. Ick. It was yucky." Walter no longer chews tobacco, having developed a taste for his thumb.

Q—During spring training in 1975, a Cub player said he was unable to sleep because a cricket had hidden in his room and was keeping him awake. He said he probably couldn't play on opening day because he was exhausted. Who was this strangely tormented athlete?

A—It was the immortal Jose Cardenal. But he overcame adversity and stepped into the opening day lineup. How could the Cubs have traded a man with that kind of courage?

Q—In 1966, Cub rookie Lee Meyer, 19, married statuesque actress Mamie Van Doren, 33, who said: "He is very mature. He shaves." How many games did Meyer win that year?

A—None. He did not last beyond spring training. Maybe a cricket kept him awake.

Q—In what year did the immortal Jack Brickhouse first utter the immortal words: "Hey, hey"?

A—Jack recalls that the first time he shouted "Hey, hey" was in 1952, when Hank Sauer hit a home run and he was overwhelmed by joy. He says he doesn't know why he shouted "Hey, hey." He could just as easily have shouted "Yum, yum" or "Bebop, bebop." But "Hey, hey" is what popped out, and he has been shouting it ever since. Over his career, he has shouted "Hey, hey" more than 3,350 times, not counting instant replays and the 10 o'clock news, which would bring the figure to more than 10,000 "Hey, heys." That is the record for most "Hey, heys" in a career. Meanwhile, Lou Boudreau holds the record for most lifetime "Kiss it good-byes." Doesn't that make you proud to be a Chicagoan?

Q—The Cubs once had a pitcher who said he could hypnotize his arm by talking to it. Who was the pitcher, and what did he say to his arm?

A—It was the immortal Bill Faul. And what did he say to his arm? Maybe he said: "Hi, arm." Or, "Do your stuff, arm." Or, "Are you happy, arm?" How do I know what he said to his arm. Anybody who would talk to his arm is a nut. I only talk to my feet. "Hi, foot." ∎

Rite of spring now another fish story

FRIDAY, MARCH 24, 1995

This is the true story of how I almost became part-owner of the Chicago Cubs and why I am so happy I didn't.

It was 14 years ago and I was sitting at a corner table in Billy Goat's Tavern with Charley Finley.

Finley was the former owner of the great Oakland A's teams that won three World Series in the 1970s. We occasionally had a few beers and talked baseball.

That night we chatted about rumors that the Wrigley family might have to sell the team because P.K. Wrigley had died and left a whopping inheritance tax bill.

Finley said he thought the chronically mismanaged franchise could be had for about $21 million. If he was right, it would be a bargain, especially if the team fell into the hands of owners brilliant enough to develop a winner.

We agreed that we possessed the necessary brilliance. But we lacked $21 million.

Actually, Finley, a successful businessman, might have had the millions. But he didn't have enough to compete with wild spenders like George Steinbrenner or Gene Autry. That's why he had sold the A's.

And even if he wanted to buy the Cubs, he couldn't because the other owners hated him for being smarter than they were.

Ah, but I knew someone who had enough money to buy the team, fix up the ballpark and sign good players.

He was my boss, Marshall Field, who owned the Sun-Times, where I worked.

With his distinguished Chicago name the owners couldn't possibly object.

Finley and I hatched our plan. I would persuade Field to buy the team because it made good business sense. And he would bring Finley in as a 5 percent owner and general manager. I would mortgage and borrow and buy a small sliver, which would permit me to be on the board of directors and cadge free beer.

So we flipped for the tab and set out to make baseball history.

By chance, I was going on a fishing trip with Field soon after that evening. So he and I and two of his executives would be in a North Woods cabin or a boat for three days. Unless he jammed his fingers in his ears, he'd have to listen to my pitch.

He did, but at first he wasn't enthusiastic.

"I don't like baseball," he said.

I told him that he didn't have to like baseball. Finley and I liked baseball enough for all of us. He liked money and he would make money.

The two executives snickered and said it would be a foolish deal. But I persisted.

First, I said, we would yank the Cubs off Channel 9, which was owned by the rival Tribune Company. We'd see if they had enough old Charlie Chan films to fill those empty afternoons.

And we'd put the Cubs on Channel 32, which Field owned.

Meanwhile, the shrewd Finley would build a winner. The sappy but loyal Cubs fans would flock to the ballpark.

Fans would be so grateful to Field for giving them a good team, they would buy more of our newspapers.

Finally, I said, we could rename the ballpark after the new owner. We would call it Field Field. Catchy and easy to remember.

By the time the fishing trip ended and we were back in Chicago, Field had agreed. Probably out of exhaustion.

He met with Finley and said he would buy 51 percent of the franchise if Finley would put together a group of investors to buy the rest.

That would be easy, Finley said, and he set about doing it.

Then the tarpon began running off the coast of Florida. What have tarpon to do with it? Field is an avid world-class fisherman, so when the tarpon run, he runs, that's what.

Finley kept phoning and asking when Field would return so we could make the offer.

Soon, I said. The tarpon would tire of running and Field had to get tired of running after them.

And we waited.

On June 16, 1981, a sports reporter loped over to my desk and said: "Hear 'bout the Cubs?"

What about them?

"They were just sold to the Trib."

I kicked the wall so hard that I limped for a month.

Every spring since I have thought about what might have been. I would be a part-owner at the training camp, saying: "Shawon, lay off the outside pitches this year. And Sammy, no law says you can't let the pitcher walk you, kid." Of course, Finley would tell me to shut up and go sell beer.

But now the regrets are gone. What might have been would be that today I would be a baseball owner. I'd have to growl about how stupid the players are, which they are, without admitting how stupid I am, which I would be by default.

Instead, I can yawn at baseball while watching Michael soar.

If I ever catch a tarpon, I'll give it a kiss. ∎

Joe has 'yo'-down on baseball strike

THURSDAY, AUGUST 4, 1994

There's only one way to appreciate the full impact of a baseball strike on the true fan. And that is to catch the popular 24-hour sports call-in show on WBAM, hosted by Billy Babble and Jake Jamoke. So let's listen in:

"Yo, we got Joe from Stickney out there on his car phone. Yo, how you doin', Stickney Joe, yo?"

"Hey, Billy and Jake, you know, you guys are doing a great job, there, hey, hey?"

"Yo, thanks there, Stickney Joe, so what's up, what's doin', what ya say, what ya know, hey, Joe, yo, yo?"

"Hey, hold on, I got some hot coffee in my cup holder that's sloshing around, you know, hey?"

"Yo, sure, coffee, how you doin' coffee, coffee, yo?"

"Hey, guys, it's OK now, and did I say what a great job you guys do, hey?"

"Yo, gotcha, Stickney Joe, and we think you're doin' a great job, too, Joe, yo, what ya know?"

"Hey, tell ya the truth, I ain't got no job, that's why I ride around in my car all day callin' the sports shows and talkin' to youse guys, hey?"

"Yo, that's what we're here for, and that's what you're there for, you know, Joe, yo?"

"Hey, gotcha. So what's goin' on?"

"Yo, you called us, Joe, you know?"

"Hey, that's right, I did call youse guys. So's I got a question, hey?"

"Yo, gotcha. So what's the question, Stickney Joe, yo?"

"Hey, the question, that's right, I got a question. Lemme remember. Hey, I got it. What about this baseball strike stuff, hey?"

"Yo, you got it, Joe, that's right, what about this strike stuff, yo?"

"Hey, I been thinking about it and I think I got it figured out, what this strike stuff is all about, hey?"

"Yo, way to go, Stickney Joe, so tell us moe, Joe, what's it all about, yo?"

"Hey, you know, the way I figure it, the players, they want to get paid more, right, hey?"

"Yo, gotcha, Joe, way to go, yo?"

"Hey, and then there's the owners. The way I figure it, the owners, they want to make more profit, hey?"

"Yo, could be, Joe, you might got something there, yo?"

"Hey, so I figure that if the players are looking to get paid more, and the owners are trying to make more, than there's only one thing that this is all about, hey?"

"Yo, I think you might really got something there, Joe, you know? So the players want to get paid more, and the owners want to make more. So what's it all about, Joe, yo?"

"Hey, I think it's one of those money deals, you know, hey?"

"Yo, you mean it's one of those old dough-rey-me deals, yo, Joe?"

"Hey, that's the way I figure it. Like it ain't the dinger or the round-tripper or the ribbie that really counts with these guys. Or hikin' the ol' battin' average and lowering the ol' ERA. It's the ol' money deal, so what ya think, hey?"

"Yo, so you're sayin' you think it's one of these what's-in-it-for-me deals, where everybody is trying to make a buck and lookin' out for No. 1, Joe, yo?"

"Hey, I'm startin' to have my suspicions, you know, hey?"

"Yo, that's heavy stuff, Joe, a very serious charge, if you know what I mean, Joe, yo?"

"Hey, yeah, that's why I called youse guys when I thought about it because youse guys tell it like it is, or like it was, or like it will be, even if it ain't yet, you get my drift?"

"Yo, got the drift, Joe, yo."

"Hey, and I figure that if there's a strike, the season will be gone forever, like it didn't happen, and what are we gonna put in its place, which can't be done, hey?"

"Yo, that's real heavy stuff, Joe, you know, yo?"

"Hey, yeah, and I got it figured out how the players don't have to strike and they'll still make more money and the owners will make more profit, and then we won't miss a season and there won't be no hole in history."

"Yo, gotcha, Joe, so how do we do it, yo?"

"Hey, the president, whatsis name?"

"Yo, you mean Clinton, yo?"

"Hey, that's him, yeah. So, what President Clinton gotta do is pass a law so the players don't pay no income tax. That way, the owners don't have to pay them more, but the players get to keep more 'cuz they don't pay no tax. And when the owners don't have to pay them more, the owners get to make more profit, you know, hey?"

"Yo, gotcha, Joe, and what you say makes sense, yo?"

"Hey, thanks, guys. And when you think about it, they shouldn't have to pay no taxes because playing baseball ain't like a real job. I mean, when I played baseball, I didn't have to pay no taxes, right, hey?"

"Yo, gotcha, Stickney Joe, you hit the head with the nail. You do a great job, yo?"

"Hey, that's what bein' a real fan is all about."

"Yo." ∎

For it's 1, 2, 3 Maalox at the . . .

TUESDAY, APRIL 8, 1986

I didn't need a calendar to know it was Opening Day. All I had to hear was Wally the Worrier telling the bartender to put two Maalox pills in his martini.

When he saw me, he posed the question that is tormenting all Cub fans. It is being asked in the home, the work place, the school, the bars, the sports pages and, for all I know, from the pulpit.

"Do you think," Wally said in a somber voice, "that Ron Cey is too old?"

I told him that only Mrs. Cey could answer that question.

"That's not what I mean," said Wally. "Can he still hit the ball?"

Only time will tell, I said, quoting any number of profound TV commentators. It's a long season. When it is over, we will have the answer.

Wally moaned. "By then it will be too late."

Too late for what?

"I don't know. Just too late."

Look, why don't you relax and enjoy the grand spectacle of it all. The crack of the bat against the old horsehide, the diving catches, the mad dash toward home plate, the chant of the crowd for a strikeout, the roar for a home run, the pudgy coaches mouthing obscenities at umpires, the batters spitting and adjusting their athletic supporters for the cameras. Relax. It is but a game.

"How can I relax? What about Matthews? Do you think that the Sarge is too old?"

If he is too old, we'll soon see the telltale signs. His hair and teeth will fall out, he'll snore with his mouth open and he'll cackle and offer candy to girls in the stands. Until then, don't worry.

"Don't worry? We need healthy pitchers. What about Sanderson's aching back?"

What about my aching back?

"Who cares about your back?"

Well, I do. I'll bet my back is in worse shape than Sanderson's back. It's in worse shape than Quasimodo's.

"Who's he with?"

Used to be with Notre Dame.

"Never mind that. What about the kid at shortstop, Dunston. He looked good at the end of last year, but the pressure was off by then. Do you think he's for real?"

What is reality? What is truth or beauty? What is the meaning of life? As that Greek philosopher, Hophead Gus, once said: You gotta go with the flow.

"Well, if Dunston can't handle shortstop, we're in real trouble."

I'm not in any trouble. I've paid my taxes and parking tickets. They don't have a thing on me, see.

"And I worry about 'Bull' Durham, too. He's always getting hurt."

Then don't worry about him. The Tribune Company has excellent medical benefits. He and his loved ones will be well taken care of.

"But there are so many question marks on that team."

Life is a big question mark. And the answer is often written on the page that has been torn out.

"What does that mean?"

I'm not sure. But it's something to think about.

"Well, I'm thinking that we've got to have big years out of Dernier and the Zonk and Jody."

The bigger the year, the better, I always say.

"That's right. Remember, as great as he is, Ryno can't do it all by himself."

No man is an island. No woman is an island, either. For that matter, no island is a man or a woman.

"Yeah, but what about our middle relief? Oh, what a headache that is. We got starters, if they stay healthy. And we got a stopper in big Lee. But what do we do about the middle?"

I hear sit-ups are good for the middle, if you can stand the pain and don't have a hernia.

"Well, one thing I'm sure of is that this year the Cubs got a great bench."

As well as an excellent water cooler, a more-than-adequate latrine and hot water in the showers. Who could ask for anything more?

"But I worry about the weather. What if the wind blows in a lot this year. Does it help us or hurt us?"

It depends on which way you're facing.

"Sometimes I think it's not worth it all, being a fan I mean. The season lasts so long. There's so much pain. Even if they have a great year, they lose a third of their games and I have to suffer every time. Sometimes I wish I could just go to sleep after Opening Day and wake up for the last game."

That's possible. Bartender, another martini.

"Dry. With a triple Maalox." ▪

Why America was left out in the cold

WEDNESDAY, FEBRUARY 17, 1988

Many Americans are disappointed and depressed by our poor showing in the Winter Olympics. As a patriotic friend told me: "It seems like everybody who wins a medal has a name that sounds like a brand of vodka."

But if you think about it, there's no reason to feel that way. There are two valid reasons why we're losing, and we don't have to apologize for either.

First, and most obvious, our best athletes aren't involved in these games. They're not dummies. Why waste time learning to steer a sled with their feet while lying on their backs when they can make millions of dollars hitting a baseball, dunking a basketball or catching a football?

Beyond that, though, is the fact that the Winter Olympics are rigged against the United States. And I don't just mean the figure-skating judges, some of whom are kinkier than any Chicago judge.

It's the sports themselves. These are not the winter pastimes in which Americans participate on a regular basis. Who do you know that rides a luge or a bobsled or jumps 300 feet on a pair of wooden slats?

True, many Americans go to ski resorts, but most of their time is spent in the lodge bar looking for someone with whom to have safe sex.

Some of us ice skate, but we're not obsessed with it the way the various scandihoovians are. If Hans Brinker had been an American youth in need of transportation, he wouldn't have been puffing around on a pair of skates. He'd have gone out and stolen a car.

If the Olympics were fair, they'd include our cold-weather pastimes, and we would walk away with a sack of medals.

For example, there should be a snowblower event, or several of them. The short competition would be for sidewalks. The longer, more grueling event would be for sidewalks, driveways, alleys and side entrances.

The scores would be based not only on speed but on displaying proper form, which would include how much of your snow you flung onto your neighbor's property.

Another event would be snowmobiling. Once again, there would be two categories—straight-line snowmobiling and Northern Wisconsin snowmobiling.

The second part of this event—the Northern Wisconsin slalom—would be the most challenging because it would require that the snowmobile drivers consume a pint and a half of Monarch Brandy and six beer chasers before racing in the dark of night over hill and dale, between utility poles and trees, in and out of ditches, through patios and back yards and under wire fences before reaching the finish line with their heads still attached to their shoulders and being able to walk unaided from their machine without falling down or throwing up.

Another exciting event would be battery-cable jumping, which is tremendously popular in northern inner-city neighborhoods. We could send a crack team made up entirely of men who are somebody's brothers-in-law. I don't know why, but throughout the history of battery-jumping, the top cable jumpers have always been somebody's brothers-in-law. You never hear somebody say: "My battery is dead. I'll call my cousin (or uncle or father or neighbor), because he's got cables." It's always "I'll call my brother-in-law." Sociologists should study this.

And there could be an event called Marathon Subzero Bus Stop Waiting, which could be dominated by Chicagoans. The contestants would be judged on how long they can wait without freezing to death, as well as on their form. The form points would be given for style shown when stepping off the curb and peering hopelessly into the distance, and for obscene muttering.

Another event—which would draw contestants from neighborhoods in such icy cities as Milwaukee, Chicago, Detroit and Buffalo—could be called Staggering Home. Instead of a starting gun, the race would begin with someone with an apron shouting "Closing time, last call," and the contestants staggering out into the cold and making their way over a slalom course consisting of ice patches, snowbanks, slush puddles and abandoned cars, all the while being pelted with sleet, hail and blinding snow while searching their pockets to see whether they can find their house keys so as not to awaken the little lady. Style points would be awarded for how well they negotiate the front steps on all fours.

The best part of my Olympic proposals is that reporters would not only be able to cover the competition, many of us could also take part. And win. ▪

Factor made A's the world chumps

MONDAY, OCTOBER 22, 1990

"*Let's make this short and sweet. The baseball season is over. Nobody's going to beat the Oakland A's, whether we like it or not.*" Thomas Boswell, Washington Post.

"*Sure as the sunrise, taxes and death, the Oakland Athletics will repeat as World Series champs.*" Michael Collier, Oakland Tribune.

"*It should take the Athletics as many as five games to win the World Series.*" Allan Malamud, Los Angeles Times.

"*A's in six.*" Joe Goddard, Dave van Dyck, Brian Hewitt, Chicago Sun-Times.

"*Could the Oakland Athletics be the greatest team in baseball history?*" Ben Bentley, moderator, "Sports Writers" television show.

Oh, I could go on and on, filling this entire page and the next with the addled predictions of alleged sports experts. All we heard before the Series began was how the awesome Oakland A's would maul, maim and mutilate anyone who dared set foot on the field with them.

As it was put by the above-mentioned Thomas Boswell, considered the leading intellectual among baseball writers, which is sort of like being the tallest midget in the circus:

"The Cincinnati Reds are a good team, but they [will] wilt in the Series. How [can] they look the A's in the eye? Everything the Reds do well, the A's do better."

How silly. The Reds didn't look the A's in the eye. They looked at the ball and hit it, which is far more effective than eye contact.

But is it really the fault of the nation's sportswriters and broadcasters that about 99 percent of them were so embarrassingly wrong?

Yes, it is their fault, the boobs.

Once again they chose to ignore the Ex-Cub Factor. They scoffed at the scientific findings of Ron Berler, the discoverer of the amazing factor.

Berler is the Chicago teacher, writer and baseball nut who revealed in 1981 that it is almost impossible for any team with three or more ex-Cubs on its roster to win the World Series. It's like a curse or a powerful virus. Three ex-Cubs can make an entire team look like . . . well, like genuine Cubs. Since 1946, 13 teams afflicted with three ex-Cubs had entered the Series. Twelve of them lost.

Now the A's have made it 13 out of 14.

This should not be any surprise to readers of this column. Before the Series began, I quoted Berler as saying:

"No matter who Oakland plays, they will be the overwhelming favorite to win. Oakland is already being hailed as the dominant team of this era—a dynasty team.

"But as good as they are, they will lose. And they can blame their own arrogance.

"They had the arrogance to defy the Ex-Cub Factor. Last year (when the A's won the Series) they had only two ex-Cubs, so they were safe. But they couldn't leave well enough alone.

"They went out and got Scott Sanderson, a pitcher they didn't need, but who became the fatal third ex-Cub. He will be their undoing. Even if he doesn't play, just by being there, he will do it.

"Tony La Russa [the A's manager] is also an ex-Cub himself. And I think he is trying to overcome that sad episode in his life, that curse, by challenging the Ex-Cub Factor. And that's why the tormented fool went and got Sanderson. He thinks that if he can overcome the Factor, he will somehow erase his own shameful stain. How foolish and how sad."

That was more than 10 days ago. Now the Series is over, and Berler, the prophet, says:

"This was the greatest challenge the Ex-Cub Factor ever faced. Intuitively, The Factor itself knew it was being challenged. So what did it do? It humiliated this A's team as no team has been humiliated in baseball history.

"Who can doubt it anymore?

"The only thing I was afraid of was that CBS would be so worried about their ratings and profits that they'd go to Oakland just before the Series began and demand that they get rid of one of their ex-Cubs."

Although Cub fans can take some satisfaction in knowing that their former heroes were instrumental in the outcome of the Series, there is a negative side to it.

If they are to become a good team, the Cubs must get better players. And one of the ways they hope to do this is by making some shrewd trades. So their general manager will be calling around to interest other teams in swaps.

But throughout the world of baseball, the question will be: "Would you buy a used Cub from this man?" ▪

Pete Rose on way to folk-hero status

TUESDAY, FEBRUARY 5, 1991

Pete Rose doesn't realize what a neat break he got by being effectively barred from baseball's Hall of Fame.

He's now assured of not being ignored or forgotten. Or as the sports page theologians put it, he will be an "immortal."

That's because Rose will benefit from something I call the Hack Wilson Syndrome.

Hack Wilson. When was the last time you heard that name? Not lately, I'd wager, even if you are an old-time Cub fan. And for many sports fans, the name might not ring a bell.

In his day, Hack Wilson was quite a player. In 1930, he hit 56 homers and drove in 190 runs, still records.

He was also quite a boozer. That's why his career wasn't as long as it might have been and why he keeled over dead at age 48.

That's also why he wasn't in the Hall of Fame when he died, and didn't get in until he had been in his grave for more than 30 years.

The sports writers who vote players in wouldn't come right out and say it, but they didn't think that someone who spent most of his career loaded, half-loaded or hung over was worthy of the great honor of having his face on a plaque in a tourist attraction in a small town in New York.

So year after year, the writers would vote and Hack Wilson would come up short.

This always infuriated my father, who had seen Wilson in his prime. He used to say: "They ought to give him twice as much credit because he was a drunk. It's hard enough to hit a home run when you're feeling good. But I saw him hit them when he had the shakes and his tongue was hanging out. Anybody who can do that is a great athlete."

There was a certain logic there. It was said that Ted Williams had such keen eyesight he could see the seams on the ball as it whizzed toward the plate. That's impressive. But there were days when Wilson could see the seams on two balls and he had only a fraction of a second to decide which of them to hit.

But for 31 years after Wilson died, the sports writers were unforgiving and pitiless in denying him his "immortality."

And, as it turned out, that was just fine because every year the sports columnists on Chicago's four newspapers would have raging debates about whether he should or should not be officially designated as immortal.

They would sputter and fume, as sports columnists are still inclined to do, about whether it was fair or unfair to treat old Hack that way. And that would inflame sports fans to heated barroom debate.

Wilson didn't care, of course, since he was quietly pushing up daisies.

So as a result of being kept out of the Hall of Fame, Wilson received his annual sports page and barroom immortality.

Then in 1979 it happened. After the sexual revolution, the flower child drug revolution, the gays leaping out of their closets, athletes sniffing and snorting and being forgiven and other American moral codes being tossed upside down and hither and yon, Hack Wilson's boozing didn't seem like that big a character flaw anymore. So they voted him in.

And what happened? We haven't heard another word about Hack Wilson since. He's gone, forgotten, just another poor likeness on a brass plaque in baseball's tourist trap.

So that's why Pete Rose is lucky. Baseball's commissioner has banned him from baseball. And the stiffs who run the Hall of Fame have slipped in a new rule that anybody who is banned can't get in, which means Rose. (They will let in coke heads and pitchers who spit on the ball, which is a form of cheating, so they aren't totally lacking heart.)

I'm sure Rose is feeling sad about the whole thing, but that's because he's kind of dumb.

He should be elated. This means that every year, when the writers vote, the debate will begin anew: shouldn't Pete Rose, who had more hits than anyone in the game's history, be forgiven? The commissioner will have to issue a statement, the keepers of the sacred Hall will have to sound pious and the writers will ponder deep moral issues.

And since Rose is a relatively young man, and his vices are slow horses and fast bookies, rather than 86 proof skull popper, he's going to be around for a long time to enjoy his unique fame.

Meanwhile, those who have made it into the Hall will be going to sports celebrity golf outings and saying: "Remember me? I used to be . . . ."

See? There's a certain justice in this injustice. Or maybe it's the other way around. ∎

In general, Dad didn't think much of his colleagues' "farewell" columns, and he had no intention of writing one when he retired. His plan was to add a brief paragraph as an addendum to whatever column he'd written for that day, announcing that he was all done. He never got that chance. After writing this column, Dad left for a Florida vacation, never to return to the job he'd done for a third of a century. Nobody, including Dad, knew that it would be his last. I truly believe that, given the chance, he would have scripted it that way. —D.R.

It was Wrigley, not some goat, who cursed Cubs

FRIDAY, MARCH 21, 1997

I t's about time that we stopped blaming the failings of the Cubs on a poor, dumb creature that is a billy goat.

This has been going on for years, and it has reached the point where some people actually believe it.

Now a beer company, the Cubs and Sam Sianis, who owns Billy Goat's Tavern and the accused goat, have banded together to lift the alleged curse that was supposedly placed on the Cubs in 1945—the last time they were in the World Series.

As the story goes, the late Bill Sianis, founder of the old tavern, tried to bring his pet goat into Wrigley Field and was turned away because the goat smelled.

That's when the curse was placed on the Cubs, and they haven't been in a World Series since.

It's an entertaining story, but is only partly true.

Yes, blame for many of the Cubs' failings since 1945 can be placed on a dumb creature. Not a poor, dumb creature but a rich one.

I'm talking about P.K. Wrigley, head of the chewing gum company and the owner of the Cubs until he died in 1977.

In many ways, Wrigley was a nice man—shy, modest and very good at selling chewing gum. He was a lucky man, inheriting the thriving gum company and a fine baseball team from his more aggressive father.

In baseball, what P.K. Wrigley was best known for was preserving day baseball long after all other franchises were playing most of their games at night.

A myth grew that Wrigley believed baseball was meant to be played in sunshine and, as a matter of principle, kept lights out of his park.

The truth was that he planned on lights very early. But when World War II began, materials needed for lights were needed in the war effort. So he shelved plans for the lights, and when the war ended, he didn't bother.

The only other baseball feat he was known for was running the worst franchise in baseball.

And a big part of that can be blamed on racism. If not Wrigley's, then that of the stiffs he hired to run his baseball operation.

After World War II ended, the best players available were being discharged from the military and returning to the teams they had starred in for a few years earlier.

But Wrigley had a unique manpower problem. His best players had remained home during the war because they were 4F for one physical defect or another or too old to have served.

So as other teams quickly got better, all the Cubs' 4F team did was get older and more enfeebled.

Because he had a second-rate minor-league system, there were few good young prospects moving up.

But all of that could have been overcome in 1947—two years after the Cubs' last World Series and the end of the war.

That was when Branch Rickey of the Brooklyn Dodgers knocked down the racial wall in baseball by signing ex-Army officer Jackie Robinson.

Although he went on to a fabulous career, Robinson was not nearly the best available black ballplayer at the time. Rickey chose him because Robinson had the education and character to endure the racial abuse heaped on him by fans, press, some of his own teammates and opposing players.

The old Negro League was loaded with outstanding players. When they played off-season exhibition games against white all-star teams, the blacks won as often as they lost.

By 1947, the year Robinson broke in, the Cubs were already pathetic doormats.

Had Wrigley followed Rickey's lead, he could instantly have had a competitive team. And depending on how many black players he could have tolerated, maybe a great team.

He didn't. His players had made their feelings clear, voting not to play if the other teams boycotted Robinson. And his team's front office wouldn't listen to those who urged them to sign black players.

It wasn't a momentary hesitation. It was not until September 1953—nearly seven full seasons after Robinson arrived—that Wrigley signed two black players.

By then, the Dodgers, with Robinson, Roy Campanella, Junior Gilliam, Don Newcombe and Joe Black, and the New York Giants, with the amazing Willie Mays and clutch-hitting Monte Irvin, had become dominant teams.

Who did Wrigley ignore? Besides some of the names above, there was Larry Doby, who became an American League home run leader; slugger Luke Easter; Minnie Minoso; the great Satchel Paige; and Hank Aaron, who broke Babe Ruth's lifetime home run record. During the years Wrigley snubbed black players, the black players who were in their late 20s or early 30s when Robinson broke in had aged past their primes.

By the time Cubs management got over their racial fears, the black league was getting ready to fold. Fewer players were available and better teams competed for them. Other sports, college and pro, began going after black athletes.

So what might have been wasn't. It had nothing to do with a goat's curse. Not unless the goat wore a gabardine suit and sat behind a desk in an executive suite.

Yes, I know, so don't grab your phone: The corporation that owns this paper has owned the Cubs since 1981. So why, you ask, haven't they made it to the World Series?

Because they haven't been good enough. But I do know that if they thought a three-legged green creature from another planet could hit home runs or throw a 95-m.p.h. fastball, they'd sign it. And we'd cheer. ∎

CHAPTER 6
Politics and the Creatures Who Play It

Make my day; tell a little lie

THURSDAY, MARCH 15, 1984

In 20 years, I've never once asked anything of the readers. I don't ask you to give money to worthy causes, help needy families, donate your vital organs for transplants or take part in any outer journalistic do-good endeavors.

But this one time, I'm asking all of you to join me in a noble cause. It's something that will make you feel wonderful, and—if enough of you do it—will win national respect and admiration for Chicago, Cook County and the State of Illinois.

I'm asking you to lie.

Not a big lie. Not a bad lie. Not something that will later cause you to run to your clergyman, psychiatrist or bartender to get your guilt eased.

This is a good lie, a worthwhile lie, a lie that will put bounce in your step and a giggle in your voice and make you feel wonderful. Let me explain:

Next Tuesday, many of you will be voting in the Illinois Democratic primary. The eyes of the nation will be upon us, as the anchormen love to say.

Some of you will come out of your polling places and be grabbed by exit-pollsters working for one of the networks.

They will ask you who you voted for and why.

Be polite. Talk to them. But lie. Don't give them one honest answer.

If you voted for Mondale, say you voted for Hart. If you voted for Hart, say you voted for Mondale. Or if Glenn is still in the race, say you voted for him.

When they ask you why you voted for Hart, say it is because he is so mature and serious that he reminds you of your grandfather.

Or say you voted for Mondale because he reminds you of Johnny Travolta.

What will this accomplish? You probably know the answer, but I'll tell you anyway.

The pollsters will take your answers and feed them to a computer, which will chew on them, digest them and finally burp a sheet of paper. The networks' high priests of politics will stare at the numbers, then announce: "I project the winner as . . . "

Even before the polls close and one vote has been counted, the TV anchors will be on the air telling the world how Illinois voted.

And one minute after the polls close, before 1 percent of the vote has been counted, they will be on the air "declaring" the winner of the Illinois primary. Then they'll sit there, looking smug and waiting for the results to confirm their infallibility.

But if enough of you lie, the entire nation will be treated to one of the finest evenings of television viewing since the tube was unleashed.

As the evening wears on and the actual votes are counted, we will see Dan become more and more wild-eyed. We'll see Peter hyperventilating. And even David will look like he is fully awake. And they'll all be stammering about how "goodness, something seems to have gone wrong."

Or maybe they'll scream that the votes should be thrown out on the grounds that they disagree with the exit polls.

There will be chaos in the newsrooms, network executives will try to cut their wrists and anchormen will have nervous breakdowns before our eyes.

Don't doubt that it can be done. I once saw it happen on a smaller scale.

A few years ago, I was asked to spend an election night at a Chicago TV station talking about the results.

One hour before the polls closed, a meeting was held and one of the polling gurus came in and announced the result of the state's attorney race.

He said: "Bernard Carey has won with 63 percent of the vote. But there is a margin of error, so we are calling it at 57 percent."

All the TV newsmen nodded their heads. I said: "You aren't going to say that on the air, are you?"

"Of course," they said.

"You're nuts," I said. "He not only won't get 63 percent or 57 percent, he might lose."

The polling guru looked at me as if I were something that had come out from under a rock. And a TV whizbang said: "They're never wrong."

So before any votes were counted, they went on the air and declared Carey the winner, as did another station.

And I went on the air and declared that they were all nuts.

By midnight, when the real votes had been counted, the polling guru looked suicidal, the TV whizbangs were sweating through their pancake makeup and Carey lost with 49 percent of the vote.

"How did you know?" a whizbang asked me.

I explained that because of Chicago's unique political atmosphere, many Chicagoans would not dream of telling a stranger how they voted in an important local election. They have a deep sense of privacy. They also fear a brick through their windows.

Many Chicagoans had simply lied to a stranger that day.

Unfortunately, Chicago, like the rest of the nation, has now become accustomed to exit polling. Some people probably believe that they are required by law to answer.

So it will take a conscious effort in and beyond Chicago to turn the networks' projections on their ears.

But it can be done. Illinois can be the toast of the nation's TV viewers.

All you have to do is tell a little fib. Then go home, sit back, relax and watch the anchormen slowly swallow their tongues. ▪

Come on, Arabs, Israel's a runt

WEDNESDAY, AUGUST 9, 1989

When I look at a world map, I sometimes wonder what the insane fuss in the Middle East is all about.

Sure, I listen to the experts, the pundits and even Henry Kissinger. But then I look at the map and it still makes no sense.

If I look closely and squint my eyes, I can find a country that has about 8000 square miles. That's Israel.

To give you an idea how small that is, you could take about 40 Israels and put them together and the whole thing would still be smaller than Texas. There may be counties, even ranches, in Texas that are bigger.

Little New Hampshire, where just about everybody gets a handshake from a politician during presidential primaries, is bigger than Israel. So is Vermont. In fact, we have only four states that are smaller.

Then consider the population: about 4.4 million. There are many cities that have more people. New York is much bigger. So are London, Istanbul, Bombay and Tokyo. You could put three times the population of Israel in Mexico City. And Chicago, if you include the suburbs, is almost twice as populous.

So we're talking about a mere speck on the map.

In acreage, Israel isn't as big as Belize, Burundi, Djibouti, and is only slightly larger than Fiji, but a little smaller than Haiti.

People sometimes refer to Japan as being small. But it's almost 20 times as big as Israel, with 30 times as many people.

So when it comes to land size and population, we're really talking dinky. Why, during any really cold winter you can find more Jews in southern Florida (seven times as big).

But if you want to talk big, just unsquint your eyes and look at some of the countries near Israel—those that have been trying to squash their tiny neighbor for the last 41 years.

Syria, nine times as big with three times as many people; Iraq, 20 times as big with 17 million people; Iran, 80 times bigger, with almost 50 million people.

Put that part of the world together and there are millions of square miles with a population bigger than that of the United States.

And most of them, at one time or another, in one way or another, with guns, tanks, terrorists or oil money, have tried to squash a country that isn't as big as Vermont.

You would think that with more than 3 million square miles of land—probably more, but I'm not that good at math—and 200 million-plus people, they wouldn't make such a fuss about what amounts to a tiny sliver of real estate and fewer people than live in many of their cities.

But instead, they've spent the last 40 years making themselves look like idiots by unsuccessfully trying to wage war on this itsy-bitsy country.

They didn't wait long. The day after Israel was first established as a state, the Arabs invaded. They expected little trouble overrunning so few victims, only 800,000 at the time.

Instead Israel beat them back, making the Arabs look like some of the most incompetent warriors in history.

But they kept trying. Again in 1956, 1967 and 1973. And as Winston Churchill might have said, never have so many had their butts kicked by so few.

Looking back, the Arabs would have been wise to let Israel alone—to let them irrigate, turn arid land into something green, make greasy chicken soup and start some small industries. Who knows, if the Arabs hadn't been so warlike, Israel could have turned its energies to peaceful pursuits. And today, instead of watching a Sony, we might be looking at a 36-inch Goldberg.

Now the Arabs are irate because Israel has expanded its borders. Of course it has. It wised up. When the Arabs kept attacking and Israel chased them away, the Israelis decided that if they have to keep going through all that trouble, they might as well keep a few acres. Besides, if somebody is using nearby hills to lob shells at you, you'd be silly not to kick them off the hills.

The way the Arabs act, you would think Israel treated them the way our ancestors treated the Indians. (Actually, my ancestors can't take much credit, not being WASPs.) We came here, stomped every which way, conned, cheated and slaughtered, until the whole thing was ours, from sea to oil-slicked sea.

In contrast, the land Israel has seized doesn't amount to much more than Coney Island.

But we keep hearing that the Palestinians must have their homeland. You'd think that with millions of square miles of vacant land, the Arabs could find them a homeland, the cheapskates. Jordan is right next door to Israel. It would make a fine homeland. That was the idea of creating Jordan in the first place. Lots of vacant land. Same climate. If they'd stop spending their oil money on bumbling wars, they could probably turn Jordan into something that looks like Palm Springs.

Instead, we have these vast, and in some cases, wealthy countries now entering their fifth decade of trying to take over a place you can barely find on the map.

It makes no sense. I mean, Israel doesn't even have one really good golf course. ∎

All that money down the drain!

FRIDAY, MARCH 2, 1984

A fascinating tidbit about Washington high society caught my eye the other day. It had to do with a spectacular weekend of fancy balls, black tie dinners, parties and a fashion show luncheon that were attended by the Reagans, top people in government and hundreds of wealthy industrialists, tycoons and movie stars. Sort of a Republican rainbow coalition.

Some of them wore such heavy gold objects that they set the Secret Service's metal detectors to howling.

They paid $5,000 a person to attend all the events, less if they wanted to be choosy. But it went to a worthy cause—the Princess Grace Foundation, which will provide arts scholarships.

Actually, this is routine recreation for rich Washington Republicans. They don't go in much for Saturday Night Bingo.

But one fact struck me as unusual. It was tucked down in a story in the Washington Post.

It said that at the fashion luncheon, carnations were sprinkled in the toilet bowls in the ladies' room.

When the ladies came in and used the toilet bowls and flushed them, a maid [presumably a Democrat] would scatter more carnations in the toilet bowl.

Naturally, this item set my social conscience to quivering with thoughts of poverty, the jobless, homeless, foodless and cutbacks in social programs.

In the midst of this suffering, there were all these Republican ladies having flowers scattered, not at their feet as is traditional, but at their . . . Well, you know.

And what Republican ladies. The guest list included Mr. and Mrs. James Baker, of the White House, Mrs. Alfred Bloomingdale of the New York store, Clare Booth Luce, Mr. and Mrs. Caspar Weinberger, Margaret Heckler, secretary of Health and Human Services [flowers in the can are *some* human service] and about 120 others.

So I decided to track down the full story and find out why they put carnations in the toilets. I mean, I entertain, too, and I've always thought that Ty-D-Bol, that blue stuff, is pretty classy. And much cheaper. Carnations go for a buck each. And with that many people at the luncheon, if they had weak kidneys it could deplete an entire floral nursery.

Well, it turns out that things are not always as they appear.

A call to the Princess Grace Foundation brought a response from a spokeswoman who was almost trembling with indignation.

She said: "Neither the foundation nor the White House had anything to do with the carnations being put in the toilet bowls."

Then who did it? A volunteer?

"No. It was the hotel's idea. They thought it was a gracious thing to do. But the Washington Post didn't mention *that*. Oh, I could kill the reporter who wrote about the carnations. But that's off the record, of course."

Of course. By the way, have you any idea how many carnations were used?

"How would I know that? You'll have to ask the hotel."

The manager of the Loews L'Enfant Plaza Hotel, where the luncheon was held, was also oozing indignation.

When he was asked about the flowers, he said: "You mean my *overkill*? Hmmmph. *That's* what the reporter for the Washington Post called it.

"They were also inaccurate. They said we put chopped carnations in the toilet bowls. They were not chopped. We used only the petals. We pulled the petals off and dropped them in."

Good grief, that really is irresponsible journalism. But what was the idea in the first place? What's wrong with Ty-D-Bol?

"It is not new. It is a practice we have used for VIPs long before this. We have been doing this for four years. We did it for a reception for the mayor of Washington and for many others."

He was also miffed that the Post mentioned that the hotel answered their phones by saying "bonjour" and "bonsoir."

"This hotel has been here for 14 years, and we have always answered the phones by saying bonjour before 5 p.m. and bonsoir after 5 p.m."

Of course. Who doesn't? But to get back to the flowers. How many carnations did you use?

"Oh, I doubt if we used any more than a dozen for that event."

The luncheon lasted three hours, so those Republican ladies must have the bladders of camels.

"By the way," he added, "we normally use roses. But carnations were Princess Grace's favorite, so we used them instead."

What a beautiful tribute.

So that's the story. Flowers in toilet bowls are definitely not a regular part of gracious living among Washington Republicans.

But even at one hotel, it does raise a question about sexual discrimination.

If you are going to sprinkle carnation petals in the ladies' toilets, in the spirit of fairness and equality, should there also be something put in the men's urinals?

The trouble is, I can't think of anything appropriate for a man's urinal.

Well, maybe there is something. For all those rich Republicans, how about a $5 cigar? ∎

Brief gift looks like brilliant deduction

THURSDAY, AUGUST 5, 1993

While getting dressed this morning, I pulled a pair of underwear from a drawer. I noticed that the elastic was frayed, which would cause the shorts to sag.

I pointed this out to the blond, who said: "Throw them away."

A predictable response from someone who is not known for her fiscal shrewdness.

No, I told her, I am not going to throw my old underwear away. I am going to put them in a box along with any other old underwear I come across.

"Out of nostalgia or as a weird hobby?" she asked.

Neither. A sly financial move. I will make money off my old underwear.

She said: "I doubt if even your most faithful readers—if there are any—would buy them as souvenirs."

That isn't my plan, I explained. I intend to use my old underwear to reduce our tax burden.

"Where did you get that nutty idea?" she asked.

Nutty? Not at all. I had simply been following the example of our commander in chief.

And I explained how the old underwear trick works.

Recently, a Washington-based magazine—the American Spectator—looked into records listing the charitable contributions made by the Clintons when Bill was governor of Arkansas.

They discovered that every year the Clintons would bundle up their used clothing and donate it to the Salvation Army or the Goodwill stores, which sell second-hand items.

Besides being good-hearted, the Clintons had a keen eye for a tax break. So they would write off the value of the garments they bestowed.

And for tax purposes they would estimate the value of Clinton's used underwear at $4 a skivvy.

Reading that, I was filled with admiration for their financial savvy. Of course, they attended Yale Law School, where one would expect to gain such knowledge.

And I slapped my forehead in disgust at the memory of all the underwear I have thrown away over the years and all the tax benefits I had stupidly overlooked.

But I vowed that I, too, would turn my old underwear into a tax break.

Shaking her head, the blond said: "I don't see how you could value your underwear at $4 for tax purposes when you didn't even pay $4 for it new."

She had a point. I buy my underwear at big discount stores, where they cost about $3.75. Even less in the three-pack bundles.

But then how could the Clintons have placed a $4 value on Governor Bill's briefs?

"Well, maybe he wore silk underwear. You can spend $50 or $60 for a pair if they are silk."

I doubted that. Maybe if he had been the governor of California or New York, or mayor of San Francisco. But Arkansas? I question if he could even buy silk underwear in Arkansas, where many of the rustics prefer a sturdy burlap.

Of course, it's possible that because of the size of his underwear, the Salvation Army might have converted them to bed sheets or even a hammock, which would rate higher prices.

"Or if they were silk," the blond said, "they could have been turned into parachutes."

Possibly. But I still doubt that Clinton would have donned silk undies. He is too politically astute. If word had leaked out, the backlash in the Ozarks would have been disastrous. On the other hand, he attended Oxford University in England, and one never knows what odd quirks a person can pick up in a dapper place like that.

Out of curiosity, I called some Salvation Army and Goodwill outlets in Chicago and asked for the going price of used underwear.

About 75 cents, they said.

Then I called a few outlets in Little Rock, Ark. One said underwear goes for about 50 cents. Another said 25 cents.

"Only 25 cents?" I said. "Up here in Chicago, they get three times that much."

"Mebbee you got classier underwear," he said. "Or a higher cost of living."

If that is so, how could Clinton have valued his briefs at $4?

"Don't know," the Arkansas clerk said. "Never seen his underwear and I wouldn't know 'em if I did."

Then I phoned the tax accountant who helps me out each year and told him of my new-found dodge.

"I strongly recommend that you forget it. Just throw your underwear away. If you start placing a $4 value on shorts for which you paid $3.75, an Internal Revenue computer will probably spot it and go off like a fire alarm. Then we will have a full-blown audit, which can lead to nothing but misery and grief."

But the Clintons are reported to have done it. And what is good enough for my prez ought to be good enough for me.

"Maybe the tax offices in Arkansas don't have computers. Believe me, $4 a pair would be a rather aggressive interpretation of the tax laws. I suppose Julia Roberts or Michelle Pfeiffer could get away with it, but not you."

He's kind of conservative. Maybe I should hire myself a Yale man.

But it makes you wonder: If Clinton's old underwear was worth $4 as governor of a small state, what is it worth now that he is the leader of the last superpower?

And I wouldn't even try to make a guess about his jogging shorts. ∎

Heaven knows why God is a GOP issue

TUESDAY, AUGUST 25, 1992

"You think that maybe God is a Republican?" Slats Grobnik asked.

I don't know. My guess is that he's non-partisan. Why do you ask?

"Well, listening to some of the Republicans, they talk like God is an honorary chairman of their party. Even President Bush slammed the Democrats for not mentioning God in their party platform. You think God really cares if he's in a party platform that hardly anybody reads anyway?"

I've never heard a theologian express that view.

"From what I can tell, most party platforms are a lot of baloney. So I figure God would probably say: 'Hey, if you're going to make a lot of phony promises, don't do it in my name, OK?'"

I'm not sure he'd phrase it that way, but that could be his sentiment.

"And what about his son?"

What about him?

"He was Jewish, right?"

On his mother's side, yes.

"And he was kind of liberal, right?"

In some ways, I suppose.

"Well, he said the poor are blessed. And so are the merciful. And that the meek are going to inherit the earth. You didn't hear nobody at the Republican convention putting in good words for the poor or the merciful or the meek. Pat Buchanan sounded like he'd like to hang 'em from a tree. And what about the rich Republican fat cats?"

What about them?

"Didn't God's son put the whammy on the rich? He said something like woe to them. And that a rich guy has about as much chance of getting to heaven as a camel has in getting through the eye of a needle. Boy, put that in the Republican platform and see what happens to contributions."

Yes, he frequently made harsh statements about the rich. Especially those who were tightwads. He was in favor of giving your riches away.

"See? If that ain't a liberal, I don't know what is. And I think he was in favor of taxes too."

I'm not sure about that.

"Sure. When some guys came to him and tried to con him into bum-rapping the taxes, he pointed at the coin that had Caesar's mug on it and said that they should give Caesar what he has coming. Which meant not beefing about paying taxes. You don't find that in the Republican platform, either. And what about the hooker?"

What hooker?

"That Mary Magdalene. He said she's going to heaven, but all the rich fats ain't. Now, if that ain't liberal, I don't know what is. And the thief too."

What thief?

"Remember, the one on the other cross. I mean, the guy was a criminal, which is why they nailed him up there. But he gets an ironclad promise that he's going to the kingdom. Hah, all the fat cats are still trying to get through the eye of a needle, and some crook walks right through the pearly gates. Hey, if he showed up today, you think he could get into one of those fancy private country clubs a lot of the Republicans belong to?"

Jesus in a country club?

"Yeah. If he goes in and applies, and says that his mother was Jewish, the old blackball would come out, right?"

At some clubs, I suppose they would exclude him on that basis.

"Imagine that, some membership chairman saying: 'Sorry, Jesus, we believe in you and all that, but right now our membership list seems to be filled up.'"

Well, he could apply at one of the predominantly Jewish country clubs.

"Yeah, but he couldn't get in there either. There ain't no way they'd let a carpenter in. No status. And he couldn't afford the downstroke or the dues. Besides, he'd probably want to carry the bag for the caddy, which would embarrass everybody."

Well, this is all mere conjecture. In answer to your original question, we have no way of knowing if God is a Republican, a Democrat, an independent or if he even takes an interest in such matters.

"Then the Republicans ought to stop acting like he's one of them. And if they keep doing it, the Democrats ought to say: 'Hey, if God is a Republican, how come his son was a Jewish liberal?'"

Because we don't know that, either.

"Come on. What about turning the other cheek when someone whacks you? And loving your enemies. And giving hell to the money changers. Hah! Put a blast on the money changers in the Republican platform and the Dow Jones would drop 3,000 points."

Well, I don't think God should be an issue in the political campaign.

"Me, either. And I bet God doesn't think so too. So I wish he'd send down a sign to the Republicans to lay off."

What kind of sign?

"One Republican speech writer and one bolt of lightning, and that would be the end of it."

That would do it.

"And if Dan Quayle is smart, he'll get off the course when it gets cloudy." ∎

Duke's fans give hate a bad name

TUESDAY, NOVEMBER 19, 1991

The supporters of David Duke, in Louisiana and elsewhere, are owed an apology from me and others.

When his campaign for governor began, I wrote that it would serve as sort of a Hate-O-Meter.

But I have since been assured that it was nothing of the sort. Hatred and racial and religious bigotry had nothing to do with their feelings.

As one Duke supporter, Jim Means of Denton, Texas, poignantly wrote: "No, the vast majority of people that supports Duke hates no more than those in other groups. These are average Americans who simply want their country back. A return to traditional values. Even a man with a past as suspect as Duke's provides hope for millions."

Yes, a return to traditional values. A yearning for things as they used to be. And a sense that government no longer cares about the average middle-class guy or gal. No hatred. Just a feeling that something has gone wrong.

Here are some other letters that reflect this non-hateful yearning. They are typical of at least 90 percent of the pro-Duke mail I received in recent weeks.

"I can see people like Carl Rowan and Vernon Jarrett speaking out against David Duke because they are black bigots," says Walter Kennard of Northlake.

"But when people like you stab David Duke in the back, you become nothing but a white traitor that is lower than snail s—. Back in the South, they had what they called field niggers who never came in from the cotton field. What happened to you? Maybe a corn field?"

Tony Franco of Las Vegas poured out his humanity too. "What Hitler did to the Jews, I could never do. Still, Hitler did not kill all those Jews himself. He had plenty of people willing to help because people in Germany had grown mad over money practices of the Jews.

"All the David Duke backers do not live in Louisiana. Hopefully you and other writers will tell the Jesse Jacksons and Al Sharptons that the days of race riots are growing near and the niggers with all their guns are not plentiful enough to win."

And from R.N. Tarrell of Portland, Ore., another seeker of traditional values: "This guy David Duke really has the commies in this country running scared. There must be something good about him after all. I'm sure that's how Hitler made it big—people could size him up by what they read in the Jewish-controlled press."

A desire for social fairness was expressed by Dan Sliviar of Orlando: "There are Americans who feel Duke may be correct and are not bigots or racists.

"It appears to me every time I read the paper or listen to TV it is black gangs, Hispanic gangs and Asian gangs.

"Where are the white gangs? All we have is a mass murderer now and then."

And this expression of solid middle-class values from Robert Obergfell of Long Beach, Calif.: "If David Duke loves Hitler, why does that make him any worse than you who fawn over Mao, Lenin, Stalin, Tito, Ho Chi Minh, Castro, Ortega and every other Red tyrant?

"Hatred is not dead. It burns brightly in the hearts of the liberals. They have given countless billions to the Red tyrants in the past, and you ain't seen nothing yet. Russia's $300 billion will come out of my pocket.

"The man who shot Lincoln did it right and said it right: 'Death to all tyrants.' Our country would be a kinder and gentler place if Lincoln, McKinley, Wilson, Roosevelt, Truman, Kennedy and Johnson had never been born."

This upbeat message came from Ms. Randi Scott of Northbrook: "Even though your column is against David Duke, I figure it's good because Duke is getting publicity in a major paper.

"Besides being a nigger lover, you also love Jews."

And Joe Smith, which may or may not be his real name, of West Palm Beach, Fla., offered his version of the game "Jeopardy."

"Answer: They greatly influence and partially control the Democratic Party, the United States Congress, several state governments, American Civil Liberties Union (also known as the American Communist Liberal Union) and script writers for movies, TV and the Media. They are only 2½ percent of the entire United States population.

"Question: Who are the Jews?"

There are many more. But how many cries of middle-class frustration can we hear before we burst into tears?

Or grab the passport and run? ∎

GOP sets its sights on Hillary Clinton

THURSDAY, AUGUST 13, 1992

Just in the nick of time, with their convention about to begin, the Republicans have found their new Willie Horton.

You can bet that all next week, the name of this dangerous person will be thrown around the convention hall by Republican orators.

Hillary Clinton: Public Enemy Number One of the traditional American family.

Actually, it's already started. I've heard right-wingers describe her as a Nazi, a pinko, a baby-snatcher and a vicious, ambitious, grasping man-hater. At least they give her credit for versatility.

Just this week, Rich Bond, the Republican national chairman, made a speech in which Hillary Clinton seemed to be a bigger target than her husband the candidate.

To hear Bond tell it, Hillary thinks that as an institution, marriage is a modern-day Devil's Island.

Most of this seems to stem from her feminist activities and long-standing belief that children have legal rights and are not merely living, breathing hunks of parental property.

But to hear the Republicans describe her, you get the impression that her goal—should Bill Clinton become president—is to rip every child in America out of its momma's arms and shove it into a government-run youth camp.

Or to trot children into court to sue their parents because they've been deprived of the latest Nintendo game or were grounded for the weekend and told to stay off the phone.

Which shows a certain desperation on the part of the Republicans. Using Willie Horton as a campaign tool might have been unfair, but at least he was a genuine rapist and thug. But Hillary Clinton is not a baby-snatcher.

If she is, then so am I, because I share some of Hillary Clinton's concerns.

As some readers of this column may have noticed, nothing gets my blood pressure soaring like child abuse cases. Especially those in which some social agency or judge treats it like a parking ticket.

I've written about kids who have been beaten, scalded, sexually abused, only to be returned to the same parent or parents who did these terrible things.

And I've written about these same kids after it happened again and they ended up dead.

I've had the satisfaction of forcing some indifferent or incompetent officials out of Family Court. But after the kid is dead, that's a hollow victory.

I have a physician friend who specializes in treating abused children. And she tells me that for every damaged child that is rescued from abusive parents, hundreds more are returned to the same misfits.

That's because it is the policy of social agencies in most states that their top priority is keeping families together.

Mom has a dope-sniffing boyfriend who can't stand crying infants? The boyfriend punches the child? Or shoves it into a tub of scalding-hot water? Mom sits there glassy-eyed and does nothing? The boyfriend also likes to have sex with another little daughter? Mom snores through it?

This is a true story. And what was the social agency's solution, approved by the judge? Why, just teach mom that it is her responsibility to prevent her boyfriend from trying to murder and/or rape her kids. Then give the kids back to her.

Is that nuts or is that nuts?

The reality is that there are countless children who are, through no fault of their own, in the clutches of parents who are stupidly cruel and dangerous. They suffer. Many of them die. They belong in foster homes or with adoptive parents.

It isn't merely a social problem. It is a national crisis. But it's a crisis that legislatures, social agencies, law enforcement and the courts haven't been able to handle.

And it's a crisis that the Republican chairman, a professional wise guy, hasn't said anything about, except to make smart-aleck remarks about Hillary Clinton wanting to break up families.

Maybe he thinks that a family life in which an infant winds up with about 20 fractures (another case I wrote about) is better than no family life at all.

They'll also pounce on Hillary Clinton's belief that children should have access to the courts.

And they'll probably mention a case in Florida in which an adolescent boy sued his parents "for divorce," as the headline writers put it.

But they'll leave out the specifics. Yes, the boy's foster parents went to court in his behalf. But it wasn't a frivolous suit. The boy's father was an abusive drunk. The divorced mother had a long history of neglect. And the state agency hadn't done much besides get forms filled out.

So the boy said, enough, he wanted to remain in the stable home provided by the foster parents. The judge agreed.

If that's baby-snatching, then we need more of it.

Now, if the Republicans really believe what they've been saying about Hillary Clinton and children, maybe they ought to include something about it in their platform.

That would be the first time a political party came out in favor of child abuse. ∎

Non-voters are good at casting aspersions
THURSDAY, MARCH 17, 1994

One of the first calls Wednesday morning was from a woman who was furious about the way she was being treated in Divorce Court.

The judge, she said, was an indifferent, insensitive fool. She also suspected that he was a male chauvinist. And he seemed to treat her estranged husband's lawyer with greater respect than he did her lawyer.

Worst of all, the case had been dragging on and on. That, too, she blamed on the judge. She thought he might be moping along to permit the lawyers to run up bigger fees.

When she finished her long list of grievances, I asked a question: "Do you have your stub from yesterday?"

She said: "Stub? What are you talking about? What stub?"

I told her I was talking about the stub you get after you vote. You hand the ballot to a person who tears off the stub and gives it to you. Sort of like a store receipt.

"What do you want to know that for?" she asked.

"I'll get to that in a minute. But do you have your voting stub?"

She hesitated for a few seconds, then said: "No."

"Why not?"

Sounding irritated, she said: "Because I didn't vote, that's why."

(I give her credit for honesty; she could have said she lost it or threw it away.)

"Why are you asking me about that anyway?" she asked.

So I told her an outrageous lie.

"I ask you that because it is our policy to investigate complaints about government only when they are made by someone who has voted.

"You are complaining about a judge. Yesterday, there were all sorts of judicial candidates on the ballot, but you didn't bother to cast your vote.

"It is unfortunate. If you had your stub, I would assign a team of crack investigative reporters to your case. But now? I'm sorry, but you are disqualified for reasons of civic non-participation."

I can't repeat what she yelled before slamming down her phone, but it was not at all ladylike. It's understandable that she and her husband might have had a turbulent relationship.

As I said, I lied about the stub and voting. There is no such policy. And I can't assign anyone to do anything. Back when newspapers had copy boys, I could assign one to go out and get me a sandwich. But computers have made copy boys extinct.

Even if she had voted, I wouldn't poke around her divorce suit. Years of covering the courts taught me that there are more lies told by combatants in divorce cases than in most murder trials.

Asking her about the stub was just a whim. At the moment she phoned, I had been looking at the results of Tuesday's voting.

The turnout was really puny. About 70 percent of those who could have voted didn't bother. The weather was decent, the polls were open from dawn to well after sundown.

True, many of the races were yawners or no-contests. But many of them do matter. They can have an impact on schools, taxes, the environment, crime and who sits there in a black robe and sorts out the hysterical fibs in a divorce case.

Yet, the vast majority of registered voters couldn't drag themselves a few blocks to a polling place. But they will grouse, as that woman did. As a nation, we lead the world in many things. Among them is grousing. Also among them is not bothering to vote.

So now that I think about it, maybe a "stub rule" wouldn't be a bad idea.

A day doesn't pass without someone calling to beef about inept government service, lack of service, injustice or offense. We look into many of the complaints. Some are true, some aren't. Some become stories, most don't. But even in cases that don't make the paper, the problems are often rectified because our inquiries serve as a wakeup call to a bureaucrat or politician.

It stands to reason that if 70 percent of the eligible voters skipped Tuesday's primaries, all of the grousing can't be coming from the 30 percent who showed up.

And a look at the statistics makes it clear that the most lethargic non-voters are in those parts of Chicago and the suburbs that depend the most on government and complain the loudest about its failings.

It doesn't say much for a metropolitan area when a million people will turn out in zero weather to cheer a Super Bowl winner but only a small slice of that number will vote on deciding what kind of society their kids will live in.

The fans who recently booed the Bulls were criticized in some circles.

But at least they bought tickets and know who the players are. Most of the grousers about government don't know the players, don't want a scorecard when it is offered and don't even have a stub.

So they get what they pay for. ∎

Bush needs liberal doses of history

WEDNESDAY, MAY 6, 1992

Looking back on Selma, Ala., in 1965, I'm trying to remember how many liberals I saw smashing the heads of peaceful civil rights marchers. I can't remember a single one. The only liberals I saw were attached to the cracked heads.

That was the case at most of the confrontations I saw. Those swinging the clubs or shooting from ambush could probably be described as social conservatives. Those on the receiving end tended to be of the liberal persuasion.

This applied to the politics of that era. Any legislation thought to be beneficial to blacks—voting rights, access to public places, job opportunities—was opposed by most Republicans, especially the far right.

Laws that finally were passed had been pushed by gutsy politicians like Sen. Paul Douglas, of Illinois, an unabashed liberal.

It isn't hard to make the argument that if it had been up to the Republican party of the 1960s, there would be far fewer black office-holders, school teachers, policemen, firemen, lawyers, doctors, executives, bank tellers, reporters, businessmen and other members of the black middle-class.

And it isn't hard to make the argument that if it hadn't been for Democrats, especially those who were liberal and progressive, we would have an even worse racial mess in this country than we have today.

So I'm not sure what President Bush is talking about when he blames the Los Angeles riots on Democratic policies that he says began in the 1960s.

Is he talking about Operation Head Start? Yes, Democrats pushed that through. The idea was to start educating black kids as early as possible.

Pre-school education isn't a radical concept in the suburbs where most of Mr. Bush's friends, relatives and political associates raised their children. But it wasn't widely available in the slums of Chicago, Detroit or New York.

The only thing wrong with that program is it wasn't big enough. But even with limited funding, it was one of the most successful educational programs ever launched in this country. And it would have even greater impact if it hadn't been opposed by so many of Mr. Bush's political allies.

Is he talking about laws that were intended to prevent discrimination in hiring and promoting? Sure, in some cases the laws were abused. And we've all heard the complaints about reverse discrimination, some valid, some sour grapes.

But I didn't notice Mr. Bush's party putting forth any bright ideas about job opportunity, other than to whine about what a hardship it was for businesses if they couldn't be selective, another way of saying that they wanted their rights as bigots preserved.

Just who does President Preppie think he is kidding? Since 1968, when Richard Nixon was elected president, the White House has been controlled by the Republicans for all but four years. We've had Nixon, Gerald Ford, Ronald Reagan and George Bush, with only one term for Jimmy Carter.

If there is anything that the 20 years of Republican presidents shared, it was an indifference, almost a disdain, for big cities—especially those big cities that have large black populations.

High-tech weapons for foreign dictators? There were always a few billion dollars to spare. Subsidies for tobacco farmers? Just ask. Huge contracts for military industries? Stop by anytime, the check is ready. Billions for S&L crooks? Just print some more money.

But at the bottom of the list were Chicago's West Side, New York's Bronx, L.A.'s Watts and the other big, multi-racial cities. If all these Republican presidents had an urban policy, it was this: to hell with them; they're Democratic voters anyway.

Now, after decades of indifference and neglect, a Republican president says it's all the fault of Democrats. However, he hides behind a press secretary and doesn't say just what it is that the Democrats did to cause the riots.

If I had to guess, I'd say he was falling back on that old favorite of Republicans such as Vice President Spiro Agnew and President Reagan.

Agnew and Reagan helped create that legendary urban folk-figure, the welfare mother who travels in a Cadillac, wears mink and fills her shopping cart with lobster, filet mignon and fine burgundy.

That was the contribution to racial harmony of Agnew, a convicted crook, now sunning his corrupt hide in Palm Springs, and Reagan, the upholder of family values, whose own kids now bum-rap him as an indifferent father. Agnew had the gall to sneer at some woman raising three kids on $300 a month, while he was stuffing his pocket with graft. Reagan did the same while on the mooch from big corporations.

Now President Preppie says it's all the fault of Democratic policies. Tune in tomorrow. He'll probably say he saw Willie Horton looting a shoe store. ▪

Fond memories of '68 convention

FRIDAY, JUNE 24, 1988

We're closing in on the 20th anniversary of the 1968 Democratic convention in Chicago. That means newspapers, magazines and TV stations are going to look back and ponder the historic significance of that wild week in Chicago.

Just about everybody who was there will be telling their stories—the politicians, anti-war protesters, policemen and news people.

One former high-ranking policeman told me: "I've already been interviewed four times. And I didn't even hit anybody on the head."

We'll see flashbacks of protesters taunting cops and cops chasing protesters. We'll see Sen. Abe Ribicoff scolding Mayor Daley and Daley bellowing at Ribicoff. There will be paddy wagons, tear gas, bandaged heads, the National Guard and shaggy poets chanting their mantras in Grant Park.

The long-haired Yippies, who have become short-haired yuppies, will talk about their idealistic anti-war sentiments. The retired cops will ask why idealists thought they could end a war by lobbing bags of do-do at them.

Some political historians will say that because Daley was bullheaded, the convention became a riot and that put Richard Nixon, instead of Hubert Humphrey, in the White House. And aging Chicago politicians will say that if it hadn't been for Daley, Abbie Hoffman and his dope-ridden pals would have carried off Chicago's womenfolk and eaten babies.

Me? I'll probably write something or other when the time comes. But right now, when I think about that crazy, turbulent, violent, crazy week, all I feel is nostalgia. I get so sentimental, my eyes are teary.

How can I feel sentimental and nostalgic about a week that has been described as one of the most disgraceful in Chicago's history, if not in the history of American politics?

That's easy. It was the last political convention that was fun, that wasn't carefully orchestrated and a big bore.

I'm speaking selfishly, of course. To those who had their hairy heads cracked or their political careers disrupted, it wasn't a big hoot. But, hey, every four years I have to cover these things. And given a choice between long, droning speeches or rioting in the streets, I'll take tear gas any time.

In 1972, both parties went to Miami. You try sweating out Miami in August, while listening to George McGovern, a personality kid, put a nation to sleep. Or watch a thousand Republicans in white shoes gaze reverentially at Richard Nixon and Spiro Agnew.

Spend a week in New York just to watch Jimmy Carter floss his teeth. Or go all the way to Kansas City to see if Jerry Ford will stumble off the stage.

I have to admit that 1980 in Detroit had its bright side. A lot of the small-town

Republicans genuinely feared that Detroit's black population might cook them in pots.

And next month we're going to Atlanta, where it will be 102 and humid, and thousands of news people will spend a week asking each other: "Do we know what Jesse wants yet?"

After that, it will be New Orleans, where it will be 105 and humid, with Republicans hoping for a miracle: George Bush stepping before the cameras to make his acceptance squeaks, but instead ripping off his coat and shirt and suddenly becoming Rambo.

If the television networks were smart, they wouldn't bother to show any of it. They'd just get out all the old film clips of 1968 in Chicago. Wouldn't you rather watch a fat cop chasing Abbie Hoffman and Jerry Rubin? Wouldn't you like to see, just one more time, Dick Gregory being lifted bodily into a paddy wagon?

Five years ago, a big California politician told me that Chicago would never get another convention because of the bitter memories of 1968. Instead, he said, they would hold the '84 convention in San Francisco because it is so civilized a city and would help the Democrats' image.

So they did. And on the first day of the convention, a big, burly guy named Erma came around the press rooms to announce that there would be an ejaculation contest that afternoon. Some image.

One of these years, they're going to wise up and come back to Chicago where we know how to show them a good time. I'm sure we have a few canisters left over. ∎

Read my lips, no quota for court

TUESDAY, JULY 2, 1991

President George Bush a closet liberal? That has to be the biggest political shocker in modern times. But it appears to be true.

Despite everything he has said, it's now clear that Bush believes in racial quotas and affirmative action, which are almost obscene words to most of his fellow Republicans.

It has to be assumed that he believes in these measures because he has just practiced affirmative action and observed a racial quota.

As you surely know, he has nominated Clarence Thomas, 43, to replace Thurgood Marshall on the Supreme Court.

Why Clarence Thomas? Does he possess the finest legal mind in the land, the keenest intellect, the broadest vision? Is he the best qualified lawyer in the United States to sit on our highest court? So far, nobody has accused him of these qualities.

He's been a federal appellate judge for a little more than one year. In sports terms, he's just finishing his rookie season.

Also in sports terms, he hasn't been rookie of the year. Those who follow the courts say he has written no significant opinions.

A distinguished legal career? A reputation as a great trial lawyer, a renowned law professor, a brilliant state judge? Not really. His major career accomplishment was being a bureaucrat in the Reagan administration.

As one acquaintance put it: "He may not be the brightest bulb on the bench, but he's not the dimmest."

Not the brightest and not the dimmest. Sort of somewhere between. It's not what you would want on your tombstone.

So why did Bush choose Thomas?

The only apparent reason is that Thomas is black. Marshall, who is retiring, is black, and Bush decided to replace one black man with another black man.

If that isn't following a quota, I don't know what it would be called. A coincidence maybe? Forget it.

And since Thomas' career hasn't been nearly as distinguished as countless judges and other lawyers who are available, his appointment could be considered affirmative action, at least by Republican standards.

Ask any Republican why he objects to affirmative action hiring programs, educational admission policies and other measures that are designed to help minorities and he'll probably say: "Because the best qualified person might be passed over, and that isn't fair."

Even Thomas dislikes quotas and affirmative action programs. In fact, that's what he is best known for.

He is that rare creature, a conservative, Republican black man.

And when he was in the Reagan administration, he achieved a certain degree of fame for his stern opposition to affirmative action policies that were designed to help blacks, Hispanics, women and others who had been the victims of discrimination.

His attitude was that nobody should be given favorable or unfavorable treatment because of race, sex or ethnic background.

In other words, may the best man or woman win.

Now he is the beneficiary of a quota mindset and an affirmative action appointment.

Before he goes on the Supreme Court, he's going to be grilled by members of the Senate, which must approve the appointment. That should be entertaining.

A senator might ask: "Judge Thomas, you are on record as opposing affirmative action programs that give a member of any group an advantage. Now, do you believe that you would have been nominated for the Supreme Court if you were a blond, blue-eyed honky?"

Or: "Judge Thomas, based on your disdain for affirmative action programs and quotas, wouldn't you have been justified in telling President Bush that you could not, in good conscience, accept this nomination because people would be saying that you don't practice what you preach?"

And maybe: "Judge Thomas, doesn't this situation make you feel just a little bit foolish?"

But Thomas could snap back: "Look, senator, it happens that I was born a poor black child in Georgia and I managed to get myself a good education and become a lawyer. Maybe not one of the best known legal minds in America, but I'm pretty good.

"If I had been born in some upper-class suburbs with wealthy parents, hell, I might have wound up in a big, fancy law firm, made a big legal name for myself and you would be sitting there thinking what a fine choice I am.

"But the fact is, by the accident of birth and the history of racism in this country, I did about as well as I could under the circumstances. So, yes, I think I am qualified to be a Supreme Court justice."

Which might be true. But if he says something like that, then it would mean that he believes in affirmative action and quotas.

Of course, he might just say: "Hey, guys, those things I used to say, I was just kidding."

And why not? It appears that President Bush was kidding us, too—the liberal scamp. ■

Hey face it, judge, Hill passed the test

MONDAY, OCTOBER 14, 1991

It has been said over and over and over again that one of them is lying. It's a standoff. So whom are we to believe? It's her word against his word, so how can there be a tiebreaker?

Everyone is free to weigh all of the evidence and make up their own minds. Or simply to follow their political biases and sexual hangups, as most people are doing.

But Professor Anita Hill settled the question for me on Sunday when she took and apparently passed a lie detector test.

The polygraph test was administered by what has been described as a highly reputable and independent Washington-area security firm that reportedly has trained FBI polygraph operators.

And Professor Hill is said to have answered a series of yes-no questions that show that she has been telling the truth.

The president of the security firm said: "It's thereafter my opinion Ms. Hill is truthful."

Only minutes after the test results were announced, there were angry cries from supporters of Judge Clarence Thomas that Professor Hill was grandstanding and engaging in dirty tricks and foul play.

Naturally, they would say that. Some of them have been implying that Professor Hill is some sort of "Fatal Attraction" psycho, a spurned female seeking revenge. Or that she is in cahoots with various anti-Thomas groups.

After hearing herself described as possibly being a kook, a fantasizer, a viper and a liar, she apparently decided to shove their words down their throats.

And by taking and passing a lie detector test, she did exactly that.

Yes, polygraph results are not admissible in most courts of law. But judges have used them to screen witnesses; government uses them; law enforcement agencies use them. And so does private industry.

Now Anita Hill has used the test to give her credibility a big edge over Judge Thomas and to get the old stomach acids churning in his supporters.

She now has the clear edge. She has taken and passed a lie detector test, and he hasn't. All he has is his capacity for righteous indignation, which is considerable. He has turned questions of sexual harassment and lying into a racial "lynching." He has described himself as having been "killed." He's portrayed the affair as a dark day for truth, justice and the American way.

No, the hearings aren't a lynching. And the Senate hearings aren't going to cause earthquakes, volcanic explosions and the collapse of our society. The hearings are a valid effort to find out what kind of guy is a roll-call vote away from going on the U.S. Supreme Court for life. The process might be an unpleasant spectacle. It might be painful, embarrassing and at times nasty, but as Harry Truman said, "If you can't stand the heat, get out of the kitchen."

If Judge Thomas is willing to lie under oath to the Senate Judiciary Committee about what he said or didn't say to Professor Hill, we ought to know about it. That doesn't mean that he isn't qualified to be on the Supreme Court. I'm sure many people, especially middle-aged men, might say that smutty remarks to a female employee are no big deal, and what's a fellow supposed to do—admit it all?

On the other hand, if he sat there and lied about what he did or didn't say to Professor Hill, leading many people to conclude that she is deranged or the agent of shadowy but powerful political forces, is there anything wrong with the public knowing that he lied? They still might want him on the Supreme Court. But at least they will know what they're getting. Sort of truth in political packaging, which we seldom see.

So we have the results of a lie detector test. Now what?

Well, I'm sure the Senate Judiciary Committee will try to ignore it. They'll pretend it doesn't exist, unless some senator is bold enough to say: "Hey, let's cut the bunk; this is reality."

And the White House will scoff and say that a lie detector test has no place in the process.

But it's there. It happened. And by now, everyone who has been following the hearings knows that it's there. If the White House and the Senate want to play make-believe and say it's unimportant, that's OK. I'm not sure what else they can say when a soft-spoken law professor flings their nastiness back in their faces.

So until Judge Thomas wants to take the same kind of test, which he won't, since he can say it is beneath his dignity, a tennis term can be used to describe the score: Advantage, Hill. ▪

GOP tries to keep old liberal in closet

FRIDAY, OCTOBER 28, 1988

Slats Grobnik looked puzzled as he asked: "What ever happened to Abe Lincoln?"

Lincoln? He's still on Mt. Rushmore. Why do you ask?

"Well, has he kind of fallen into disgrace or something? You know, like in Russia, where they kick old leaders out of the history books and take down their statues."

Of course not. Honest Abe is revered, one of the two or three greatest presidents in our history.

"That's what I always thought. But something funny is going on."

Such as?

"Like this news story I just read where President Reagan makes a speech about what a great guy Harry Truman was."

I read that.

"And isn't he always talking about what a great guy Franklin Roosevelt was?"

Oh, he's very fond of FDR.

"And I read where Danny Quayle said something good about Truman. And so did Bush. And I think Bush said something nice about FDR, too."

Yes, they've spoken highly of them.

"Well, maybe I missed something, but I thought Truman and Roosevelt were Democrats."

Of course they were.

"Then how come all these Republicans keep dropping their names? Why don't they talk about Republican presidents?"

Now that you mention it, that is curious.

"I mean, I can see why they don't want to talk about Nixon, because he got kicked out of office. Or about Hoover, because he started the Great Depression. Or Coolidge, because most people don't know who the heck he was. But wasn't Abe Lincoln the father of their party?"

That he was.

"Then why don't they ever mention him?"

It's probably just an oversight.

"I don't think so. Nowadays, with all those sharpies who run campaigns, there's a reason for everything. And there's gotta be a reason why Honest Abe is getting the silent treatment."

I can't think of any.

"Come on, let's figure it out. Like Sherlock Holmes and Watson. Let's look for clues."

All right, what are the clues?

"Well, what was Lincoln most famous for?"

He preserved the Union by winning the Civil War.

"Hah! Now we're getting somewhere?"

I don't understand.

"It's elementary, my stupid Watson. The Republicans want to win the South, don't they?"

Of course. It's essential to their battle plan.

"So what happens if Bush or Reagan or Quayle go down to Georgia to make a speech and they say: 'Remember, my fellow Americans, we are the Party of Lincoln?'"

There might be a certain coolness.

"A coolness? Hey, the audience is going to jump up and yell: 'You damn Yankee carpetbagger, don't you know that Lincoln sent General Sherman through here and burned up my great-grandpa's house in Atlanta.'"

That's quite possible.

"You bet it is. You go down South and start talking about Lincoln and guys named Bubba are gonna grab their shotguns and set their hounds on you. You ever notice who they name streets and highways after down there?"

Who?

"Not Lincoln or President Grant, I'll tell you that. Everywhere you go, it's Jefferson Davis Boulevard, Jefferson Davis Highway. He's still their guy."

You may have something.

"Okay, what else is Lincoln famous for?"

Everybody knows that. He freed the slaves.

"Right. So you think Reagan and Bush and Quayle want to remind white voters about that?"

But it was one of Lincoln's noblest achievements.

"Sure, but it's not something they want to mention in a 1988 campaign. If Bush gets up and says: 'My friends, we are the Party of Lincoln, the great man who freed the slaves,' you know what some white Southerner is gonna say, or some white guy in a bungalow in Chicago or Cleveland?"

What?

"They're gonna say: 'Oh, yeah? Then Lincoln's worse than Dukakis. Dukakis only let that Willie Horton out on furlough. Lincoln turned the whole mess of them loose and now they're moving into my neighborhood.'"

I suppose it's possible that some might react that way.

"Possible. Lemme tell ya, if the Republicans went around saying: 'Fellow Americans, vote for us because we are the Party of Lincoln, the man who won the Civil War and freed the slaves,' you know what would happen? Dukakis would get 70 percent of the vote. Even Lincoln's first name would hurt them."

His first name?

"Yeah, Abe. Some people would think he was Jewish, and they'd lose the anti-Semite vote."

An interesting analysis. I wonder what Lincoln would say if he came back to life today?

"I don't know what Lincoln would say, but I know what Reagan and Bush and Quayle would say."

What?

"They'd say: 'Look, another liberal.'" ∎

Rest easy, world, there's rent-a-cop

FRIDAY, NOVEMBER 23, 1990

Many Americans, concerned about the Middle East situation, have been asking: "Why should this country try to be the world's policemen?"

There's been no satisfactory answer to that question. Depending on who you believe, we're doing it because we don't like naked aggression, or even fully clothed aggression; or we're doing it because of oil; or we're doing it because we want to prevent Israel from blowing Baghdad away.

Whatever the reasons, we do appear to have become the world's policemen. We've been at it for much of this century, with mixed results: World War I, World War II, Korea, Vietnam, Granada, Panama and now in the desert.

So maybe the question should be: "If we are going to be the world's policemen, why don't we do it on a business basis and show a profit?"

Within this country, the private-security industry has boomed in recent years. Businesses, communities and individuals now hire rent-a-cops to protect their property and persons. The security agencies provide a full range of police services and send a monthly bill.

Since that's what we're now doing as a country, maybe we should follow the example of the security industry.

President Bush has been hopping around the world, trying to round up support for a military adventure against Iraq. He hasn't found much enthusiasm, so that could mean we've been taking the wrong approach all along.

Maybe it would be better if Bush walked into the offices of these timid heads of state and said:

"Good afternoon, Sheik Babbadabbado, I'm George Bush, and I represent U.S. World Wide Security Inc. I'd like to explain our full range of services to you."

"Ah, yes, Mr. Bush, but I have my own in-house security coverage and we've found that adequate."

"I understand. But are you covered against massive naked aggression, fully-garbed aggression or invasion by power-mad tyrants?"

"Well, no, but I don't anticipate such problems."

"Ha-ha, nobody anticipates such problems, Sheik Babbadabbado, but they have a way of happening. Let's face it, it's a jungle out there. Studies have shown that the naked aggression rate among power-mad tyrants is rising and will do so indefinitely. One can't afford to take chances, can one?"

"You may be right. So what can you do for me?"

"As I said, we have a full range of services. Professionally licensed Army, Navy, Marines and Air Force, plus a part-time manpower pool of reserve personnel who can be called in for special events. And we offer the very latest in state of the art anti-tyrant technology."

"Missiles?"

"You name it, we've got it. Little ones, big ones. Everything from your basic heat seekers to full scale ICBMs. We can guarantee the most boom for your buck or your money back."

"Submarines?"

"The very latest in nuclear-powered. And so quiet that they can be in your swimming pool without you knowing it. Here, glance at this brochure and you'll get an idea of what we have to offer."

"Yes, very impressive. Everything from supersonic bombers to fully armed choppers."

"Well, Sheik, we didn't get to be the biggest and the best by playing with sling shots."

"I see here that you also offer intelligence services?"

"One of our specialties. We've got round-the-clock spy satellite service. Not to brag, but right now I could punch up my computer here and in minutes have a closeup photo of what your wife is doing at this very moment."

"What about my mistress?"

"No problem. It's all part of the basic package. Now, I'm sure you know what it would cost you to put up your own spy satellite? If you've priced it out, you know that it would be far more cost-effective to use our service."

"How long does it take to install your system?"

"Our technicians are the best, and it can be done in almost no time. You'll have this key pad. When you go to bed at night, you punch the 'Border Secure' button. That means that if any power-mad tyrant crosses your borders it alerts our main dispatch office in the Pentagon and our security forces are dispatched to apprehend the perpetrators."

"What's the cost?"

"It depends on the client's size and needs. In your case, it would be about a billion a month, payable on the first."

"I can live with that. But one other question. What happens if I aspire to become a power-mad tyrant and to engage in naked aggression against a neighbor?"

"That would depend on whether your neighbor and intended victim is also a client of ours."

"And if he is?"

"I'm sure we can work something out. Business is business." ∎

To this day, the Jerry Brown Moonbeam moniker still appears in the media. —D.R.

Time to eclipse 'Moonbeam' label

WEDNESDAY, SEPTEMBER 4, 1991

Over coffee last week, Jerry Brown was musing about the possibility of his running for president.

His thoughts about a campaign theme were intriguing. Politics has become a corrupt, big-money game that has made millions of Americans cynical.

It's no longer a question of what a candidate has to say, but how many millions can he raise from special-interest groups. And how those millions are spent by the hired media wizards who create the slick commercials, buzzwords and sound bites.

The ordinary person feels powerless and left out because he truly is powerless and left out. And that's why they don't vote. They believe their vote means nothing.

Near the end of our chat, Brown was weighing his long-shot chances. And like any Democrat, he would be a long shot. But unlike other Democrats, he has an added handicap.

Looking me in the eye, he said: "I'd have to deal with the, uh . . . the . . ."

He paused. I said: "The moonbeam factor?"

He nodded while I mentally squirmed.

If you follow politics, you may recall that when Brown was governor of California, someone thought he was a bit eccentric and slapped him with the label, "Governor Moonbeam."

And the tag stuck. Oh, did it ever. The disc jockeys, his political enemies and every editorial wise guy in California picked it up. And from then on, he was Governor Moonbeam.

But as I told him last week, that was a long time ago. By now, the label had surely faded away. Especially since he is obviously a serious man and every bit as normal as the next candidate, if not more so.

He shook his head. "No, it's still there."

What a guilt trip. You see, I have the dubious distinction of being the author of the phrase "Governor Moonbeam."

Even worse, I don't even remember when I wrote it or in what context. But I do know that that column appeared in several California papers and, to my amazement, "Governor Moonbeam" became part of the political vocabulary.

During the 1980 Democratic convention, Brown made a speech that was far more sensible than any of the other babblings at that grim gathering. So I wrote a column renouncing the Moonbeam label. I not only renounced it, I denounced it, rejected it and declared it unfair, inappropriate and outdated.

I mean, as the author I should have that right, right?

Anyway, when we finished our coffee and parted, I again assured Brown that the media would not be so lacking in imagination, so wedded to the past, that it would grasp at an obsolete and discredited phrase to spice up a story.

He said he hoped so, but he didn't appear convinced.

Shows what I know. Two days later, I picked up this paper and saw a column item that Brown had been in Chicago talking to acquaintances about the possibility of his running for president.

And there it was: "Moonbeam."

Then the latest Newsweek magazine came out. He was in it. And so was Moonbeam.

He is now a declared candidate. So Tuesday I read a story by the Cox wire service. The first paragraph said:

"WASHINGTON—Former California Gov. Jerry Brown, whose unorthodox lifestyle and political leadership earned him the nickname 'Governor Moonbeam,' began running for president Tuesday."

Hold on, there. His "unorthodox lifestyle and political leadership" did not earn him that nickname.

He got that nickname because a guy in Chicago was stringing some words together one evening to earn his day's pay and tossed in what he thought was an amusing phrase. And if he had it to do over again, he sure as hell wouldn't.

The fact is, Brown's lifestyle wasn't all that "unorthodox." He didn't get boozed up, zonked out or hop from bed to bed. If anything, he pondered questions that most politicians are afraid to think about, much less mention. But because the media like to demand original thinking, while declaring that any original thinker is zany, it decided Brown was "unorthodox."

Of course, if it hadn't been for that idiotic, damn-fool, meaningless, throwaway line, the rap that he was a bit unorthodox wouldn't have mattered or lingered.

Would somebody today have written: "Former California Gov. Jerry Brown, who was once thought by some to have an unorthodox lifestyle and approach to political leadership, began running for president Tuesday."

Of course not. Ah, but toss in the "Moonbeam" tag and the reader has a vision of some weird, wild-eyed California oddball.

Which he isn't. There's nothing strange about him, unless you consider it strange to recognize that Washington is filled with career hustlers who live from one campaign bundle to another; that hundreds of millions are poured by fat-cat contributors into media blitzes that appeal to fear and bigotry; that genuine concerns and issues are buried under Madison Avenue buzzwords. If that's strange, then the majority of Americans are strange because they believe it and it's true.

So enough of this "Moonbeam" stuff. As the creator of this monster, I declare it null, void and deceased.

And to America's political pundits, gossip columnists and other opinion-warpers, I say this: Create your own stupid labels and leave my stupid label alone. Bunch of moonbeams. ▪

Democrats just got a boost from GOP without even trying

FRIDAY, NOVEMBER 10, 1995

It seems like only yesterday that the Democratic Party had one foot in the grave and was being given its last rites.

Those bright young Republican clones of Newt had seized Congress and launched their yappy-yuppie revolution.

Sure, the Democrats still had the White House. But Newt's lads were almost laughing in the face of President Clinton, who couldn't seem to get anything right. And when he happened to, he'd change his mind the next day and get it all wrong.

So the question wasn't whether Clinton could be re-elected. That thought was laughable.

The only question was who the Republicans would choose to evict Clinton and finally and mercifully put an end to the suffering of the Democratic Party.

The pundits saw it that way. Newt's lads did too. So did all of those weary Democrats in Congress who decided the end of political life was near, and they didn't want to run again.

We were about to enter the greatest era in Republican history. By the new century, liberal Democrats would be as rare as conservative war veterans.

Except that we forgot that Republicans have as great a talent for goofing up as the Democrats.

And boy, oh boy, did they do it.

A few days ago, they had a potential candidate who would have peeled Clinton as easily as a tangerine.

Yes, I'm talking about Colin Powell. Distinguished military man, but not a chest-thumping bully. Mature, yet still youthful. Articulate, but not a bull-shooter. An intellectual, but not dogmatic or superior. Quiet but not weak. Confident but not arrogant. Of humble origins, but without sullen resentments.

Just about as perfect a candidate as either party could imagine. And to boot, he is of African-American ancestry although he doesn't make a big deal out of it.

You would think that every sensible Republican in the country would have said: "We haven't had anyone like him since Ike. Patriot, hero, statesman, charmer. He will not only get our votes, but he will bring us the young, since they are not saddled with our racial bigotry; he will bring us the growing middle-class black vote; he will bring us rootless liberals and independents. And he has no soiled political baggage. Poor Clinton—all he'll get is the afternoon-rate motel vote."

Yes, the Republicans could have grabbed it all. Instead, they chose to assure us the survival of the two-party system.

Just when it appeared that Powell would declare his candidacy, the right wing of the Republican Party rose up in all of its nastiness.

It appeared that Powell didn't pass all of its knee-jerk, right-wing litmus tests on gun control, abortion and affirmative action. His views reflected those of the majority of Americans.

But after more than 30 years in the Army, he was viewed by Republican right-wingers as some kind of dangerous liberal.

They started whispering about his military record. One wax-faced, non-elected spokesman for the rigid right went on TV to question Powell's military record. He said Powell was merely a "milicrat"—a uniformed desk-bound bureaucrat—instead of a true battlefield warrior.

That from someone who—like most of the right wing's leaders—wangled one campus deferment after another during the Vietnam War. They are probably the toughest-talking draft dodgers in our history.

They also managed to leak into print and broadcast the fact that Powell's wife takes medication to control depression. That gives her something in common with about 50 million other adult Americans.

It's assumed that her depression is caused by an imbalance in body chemistry. Or maybe it has to do with her husband becoming a Republican and having to associate with klutzes.

They should have been kissing his shoes. Instead, one after another, the spokesmen for the rigid right made it clear that while they wouldn't mind Powell becoming a Republican and helping them win elections, he wasn't their idea of a presidential candidate.

So he took the hint and got out and they were happy.

But they got up the next day and looked around, and those who aren't too stupid or dogmatic saw what they had done.

They left themselves with as motley a collection of candidates as either party has had.

Sen. Robert Dole is now the front-runner. I admire him, but he's over 70, comes off as a grouch and his time has passed. Sen. Phil Gramm sounds like

Lyndon Johnson's dim-witted kid brother. The others? You can't name them and this time next year you still won't.

Now they're even talking about Newt as their candidate. They apparently hope the average American voter is as indiscriminate in his choice of heroes as Congress babblers are.

By chasing off Powell, the Republican rigid right did something the Democrats couldn't do—they clinched a second term for Bill Clinton.

Those people are even more dangerous than they realize. ▪

2nd thought on that invite: Oh, forget it

WEDNESDAY, JUNE 8, 1994

The morning stress began with a call from a women expressing outrage at what she called "the most arrogant piece of journalistic tripe I have ever read."

"I cannot believe you could write anything this stupid," she said.

Well, if it is on Page 3 with my lopped-head picture, the stupidity must be mine.

"You should be ashamed of yourself," she said. "The president of the United States invites you to dinner, and you treat it as a joke.

"Don't you realize what an honor that invitation is? The average American would be thrilled just to shake a president's hand. You are typical of today's media arrogance. Shame on you."

It was an impressive tirade, and I thanked her and said I would reread what I had written and reconsider my arrogant position.

Which I have done. And now I realize that she has a point. The fault was mine for not having explained more clearly why I turned down a dinner invitation at the White House.

Stated as simply as possible: Politicians are enormously charming.

I've been talking to, reporting on and writing about politicians for almost 40 years.

And I have to admit, I have never met a politician I didn't like.

That might sound odd, coming from someone who has made a cottage industry out of bashing politicians.

But it's true. From Chicago aldermen—the lowest of the political food chain—on up to presidents and ex-presidents, I've pummeled them: Democrats, Republicans, liberals, conservatives, independents, the brilliant and the harebrained.

And I have yet to meet a politician who didn't have some redeeming qualities.

I like politicians because they put it on the line. In a society of salesmen and pitchmen, they are the ultimate hustlers. To succeed, they need approval of 50.01 percent of the customers. That is one tough sales rate.

They do it with charm. In my lifetime, FDR had it in excess. Truman in a spunky way. Ike the hero, by being bigger than life. Kennedy was the ultimate youth-vigor symbol. Nixon because he was Every Man, the mope who somehow makes it. Carter because he was so decent. Reagan, who had it all. And Clinton . . . Clinton?

I don't doubt that Clinton has a brilliant mind and that his wife exceeds him. You don't get to be president of the United States unless you are smarter than about 99 percent of the people who voted for or against you.

And you don't get to be president, governor, mayor, senator, congressman or even a schnook alderman in Chicago unless you can ooze charm and shake a hand like you love the other end of that appendage.

So that's the main reason I declined the invitation to dine at the White House.

There is no doubt that if I spent the evening with Bill and Hillary, they would charm me out of my shoes. And I would be inhibited every time I decided to write something mean about them. And if I can't be mean, what the heck good am I?

Journalists are human. At least some of us older ones. So if I sit down for dinner with a president, I feel like an "in-person." I am no longer some guy who grew up along Milwaukee Avenue. I am a VIP, big heat, or why else would a prez invite me to chow down at the White House?

Which is ridiculous. If I was my friend Big John, an expert on the printing industry and many other things, or my friend Danny, who went from laying bricks to running his own construction company, I wouldn't be invited to the White House.

I was invited because by dumb luck, an editor's folly and my willingness to work cheap, I ended up writing a newspaper column.

And that is why President Clinton or one of his flunkies decided to invite me to dine in that great transient home in our capital. It ain't me, it's my job.

But if I went, I would be charmed. Hillary would smile and I would melt. Bill would give me that stiff lower-lip grin and I would be saluting.

That's why I have had my own rule of journalistic ethics: Don't get chummy with pols because you will like them, and when that happens, you can't beat them up.

It's why my favorite politician was the late Richard J. Daley, mayor of Chicago from 1955 until his death in 1976. He was the last of America's great municipal politicians.

I wrote countless columns and a best-selling book about him. But any time he was asked about something I wrote, he would put on a stone face and say: "Who's he?"

That was his way of saying that he didn't care what some goof with a typewriter wrote. He had the votes, and that's what counted. I admired him for it then, and I do so even more today.

So as much as I like politicians, I keep my distance. It's the only way I can keep whatever scruffy integrity I have.

And any politician who feels the same way—and many do—has my respect. I wouldn't have me over for dinner, either. ∎

CHAPTER 7
Music, Film, TV, Art and the Creatures
Who Make It

'Mairzy Doats'—that's real music

Here it is, only June, and I've already taken care of most of my Christmas shopping.

It happened by chance, when I flipped through an obscure magazine in a doctor's waiting room.

A full-page ad happened to catch my eye. The big black headline said:

"'Mairzy Doats' plus 43 More Wacky Hits from the Fun '40s. The Original Hits! The Original Stars!"

"Mairzy Doats"? It had been many decades since I last heard the stupid lyrics to that song, one of the jukebox hits of my childhood.

I am cursed with the kind of mind that never completely forgets a really stupid song. I have trouble remembering my own phone number, my children's birthdays and the names of people I've met a dozen times.

But all I had to do was see those words—"Mairzy Doats,"—and out of some long dormant cells in a dark corner of my brain, the rest of the lyrics erupted and the incredibly stupid song began racing through my mind:

"Mairzy Doats and Dozee Doats and Little Lamsydivy, akiddleetivytoo, wouldn't you, hoo, akiddleetivytoo, wouldn't you?"

(That might not be the precise spelling, but it is the way I remember it sounding.)

Just then the nurse sent me in to the white-haired doctor's office, where he took my blood pressure.

"It is kind of high," he said.

"Of course it is high," I said. "I am agitated because I just spotted the words 'Mairzy Doats' and now the lyrics are stuck in my mind. 'Mairzy Doats and Dozee Doats. . . .'"

"Stop!" he cried, covering his ears. "Now it will be running through my mind."

169

"Well, don't blame me; it's your waiting room magazine."

Then I resumed singing: "If the words sound queer/ and funny to your ear/ a little bit jumbled and jivy/ sing 'Mares eat oats, and does eat oats, and little lambs eat ivy'/ Mairzy Doats and Dozee Doats. . . .'"

When I left, the doctor was twitching and grinding his teeth.

I snatched the magazine on my way out, thinking I might bring a lawsuit against the record company for disrupting my mental processes.

But when I had a chance to study the ad further, I realized that I had come across a remarkable musical collection.

Someone had put together some of the most amazingly idiotic songs in the history of recorded pop music.

The collection includes:

- "Civilization" ("Bongo, bongo, bongo/ I don't wanna leave the Congo/ no, no, no, no, no.")
- "Three Little Fishes" ("In an itty-bitty brook. . . .")
- "Too Fat Polka" ("I don't wanna her/ you can have her/ she's too fat for me/ hey/ she's too fat for me. . . .")
- "All I Want For Christmas Is My Two Front Teeth"
- "Rag Mop" ("Rag Mop, do-dee-do-dow-dee-dowdy.")
- "Cement Mixer" ("Cement Mixer, puttee-puttee.")

And many more than I can list here: "Aba Daba Honeymoon," "Chickery Chick," "Woody Woodpecker," "The Thing." "Open the Door, Richard," "I'm a Lonely Little Petunia in an Onion Patch," "The Maharajah of Magador."

I cursed my brain cells because I could remember some, or all, of the lyrics to these tunes. Not my very own ZIP code, but "Open the Door, Richard."

Why, I thought, would anyone want to do this? These are songs that should be buried in a concrete time capsule, to be opened in 200 years when people want to study ancient and goofy cultures.

So I called the Good Music Record Co., in Katonah, N.Y.

Ed Shanaphy, the owner, said: "We started selling the 'Mairzy Doats' collection about four years ago."

But why?

"My philosophy is that people like to remember when they were silly, when songs were silly. There was a time when nobody was afraid to do a pratfall. It's all like comedy, really. These songs are like comedy routines. People need some silliness in their lives.

"At first, I just called it 'Fun Hits of the '40s,' and it didn't go anywhere. Then I changed the name to 'Mairzy Doats,' and we've sold 125,000 sets of the collection. It's one of our biggest winners. I guess 'Mairzy Doats' says it all."

This is one of those companies that doesn't sell in stores. It depends on a huge customer database and ads in magazines that appeal to the elderly.

"We go for the mature audience," Shanaphy said. "Our customers are retired, primarily living in retirement, with discretionary income. We've also released a D-Day collection and another one called 'Stage Door Canteen,' with WWII songs. That sold 300,000 copies already. We just keep putting different handles on the '40s hits, and they sell."

Why didn't I think of that? I could be rich. And like Ryne Sandberg, I could blink away my tears and retire to my home fitness center.

But I will do the next best thing. I'm ordering a stack of these songs and will give them to all of my friends and relatives, young and old.

Then all I will have to do is hum "Mairzy Doats and Dozee Doats and Little Lamsydivy," and watch the panic sweep across their faces as the song infects their minds.

Actually, it is a fair swap. I have been trying to understand contemporary rock music for years, and most of the time I can't understand a nasal word that is being shrieked.

And much of modern hippity-hop and rappity-rap music contains f-words and m-words I prefer not to understand.

So while there may be little social significance in "Cement Mixer, puttee-puttee," you can sing it in a schoolyard and you won't be arrested. Nor do you need a gold ring through your nose. ∎

Alderman's brain is a museum piece

TUESDAY, MAY 17, 1988

You may remember Ald. Ernie Jones. He's the statesman who recently said female cops take too many days off because of their "minister periods."

I'm not sure who was more confused and offended—the lady cops or their ministers.

Now Jones has turned his pea-sized intellect to other pursuits—art criticism and constitutional law.

Jones was one of the City Hall hysterics who took it upon themselves to yank a painting out of the School of the Art Institute because it offended them.

By now, most Chicagoans know the story. A student-artist thought it clever to draw the late Mayor Harold Washington in women's undergarments.

Why did he do this? Who knows? Why did Warhol love Campbell Soup cans? Why did Van Gogh cut off his ear? History tells us that many artists are kind of weird.

This young man's painting was exhibited at a private—I repeat, private—display at the school. It was part of a showing of works by graduating seniors.

Someone called a black alderman or two and they spread the word among their colleagues and everybody went berserk. Several rushed to the Art Institute—probably for the first time—to seize the painting.

But fearing that the students might splatter them with white paint, they backed down and had the police confiscate the painting for them.

The police justified the seizure by saying that a painting of Harold in female undies might incite black citizens to riot.

Actually, if anyone was inciting to riot, it was this handful of alderboobs. Only the students and faculty knew about the foolish painting until the alderboobs started yelping about it.

There certainly were no reports of blacks milling about the Taylor Homes, Cabrini-Green or West Side streets, saying: "My man, have you heard about the offensive portrait of Harold at a private showing in the School of the Art Institute? Shall we show our displeasure by going there and trashing a Monet or two?"

As I said, one of the aldermen who took part in this art-raid was Jones. I single him out because I find certain parallels between that painting and this alderman.

Jones says the painting was offensive, and I agree with him.

However, many policewomen told me they found Jones offensive for saying they stay home for their "minister periods," and I agree with them, too.

Jones clearly believes that if a painting is offensive to a segment of the population, it can and should be taken to jail.

Then why wasn't Jones taken to jail when he offended a segment of the city's population?

If anything, I find a painting far less offensive than an alderman. A painting is nothing more than an inanimate object. You just hang it on a wall and it stays there. Some aldermen are inanimate, too, but you can't hang an alderman that way, although it would be fun.

Name me one painting that has ever taken a kickback. Has a painting ever upped your taxes? Has a painting ever put its idiot cousin on the city payroll?

So here you have this alderboob Jones, sitting in the legislative branch of one of the great cities of the world, and what does he babble about? The "minister periods" of policewomen.

The least one might expect is that he go to the dictionary and find the correct word. (In fairness to Jones, some observers insist that he said the women missed work because of their "minstrel periods." I doubt that. It's been decades since minstrel shows have been seen in Chicago.)

But I digress. My point is that it is not the job of aldermen to go around snatching paintings, as offensive as they might be.

The aldermen should be content with their traditional role of snatching votes, or seizing gratuities for city contracts, zoning changes and license fixes. If they would work at their own art more diligently, they wouldn't always be getting caught by the feds.

Some civil libertarians fear that the picture-snatching might lead to other forms of illegal censorship by the alderboobs. As a concerned liberal said: "What is to stop them from going in bookstores and libraries and seizing books they don't like?"

That's possible. But it would take more effort than seizing a painting. They'd have to find someone to read the books to them. ∎

Calling Mr. Silver: America needs you

TUESDAY, OCTOBER 15, 1991

Seka's phone has been ringing almost constantly for the past two days. She's talked so much that her voice is hoarse when she says: "I've lost track. Let's see, People magazine called. And there's 'Entertainment Tonight.' And this show and that show. Everybody's trying to find him."

By "him," she was referring to a person known as Long Dong Silver, whose name emerged during Professor Anita Hill's testimony at the Senate Judiciary Committee.

Mr. Silver (I'll call him that for reasons of propriety) is a one-time porn movie actor known for his manly attributes. Professor Hill testified that Judge Clarence Thomas found Mr. Silver's dramatic performances interesting.

Naturally, elements of the news media have been trying to track down Mr. Silver to see what he thinks of his new-found fame.

So they've been calling Seka, who was a porn star herself and has been involved in the production of X-rated movies.

"Yes, I knew him," said Seka, who lives in Chicago. "In fact, I made one movie with him."

Uh, was he how shall I put it, a skillful performer?

"Well, it wasn't a hard-core movie. It was R-rated. We made it in England. I really didn't know him well. I believe he was English. I called him L.D. for short. That's no pun, by the way.

"As far as I know, he only made a few movies. I'm not sure how many. They were all called 'Electric Blue.' They were numbered. That was about 8 or 10 years ago. I don't know what happened to him."

The fact that Seka and others in the porn industry have been deluged with calls about Mr. Silver shows how deep the media interest has been in the solemn process of confirming a Supreme Court justice.

And this reflects the effort of millions of Americans to be better informed citizens.

Only a few weeks ago, when the hearings on Judge Thomas' confirmation were being televised on cable TV, the audience was relatively small. That's when Judge Thomas was being asked about his views on natural law, past Supreme Court decisions and other weighty matters.

Then came Professor Hill's testimony. America became aware of the existence of Mr. Silver. Suddenly the viewing and reading public couldn't get enough information on the Senate's confirmation process.

Some of the networks, realizing that the Senate hearings were of great civic importance, provided live coverage. Even the baseball playoffs were aced out in the ratings.

Now the hearings are over, and after one more day of senatorial bluster and chest-thumping, Judge Thomas will be confirmed. I'm certain of that because senators are men of principle, conscience and avid students of public opinion polls.

Judge Thomas will go on the Supreme Court and live happily ever after. Professor Hill has returned to her classroom in Oklahoma and will shock the nation by not making a fortune as a public speaker, not writing a best-selling book and not selling the movie rights to her life story. People will wonder what her angle is.

So that leaves Mr. Silver as the one loose end in the Senate drama.

America wants to know about Mr. Silver. Well, maybe not all Americans, but a heckuva lot of them. Video stores all over the country have been getting calls from people trying to rent his movies.

"I never heard of the guy before," says Al Zwick, who runs Video Shmideo, a Chicago video outlet. "I wouldn't know him if he walked in here. At least, not with his pants on. But my phone started ringing from people asking me about him as soon as the professor testified.

"So I called my West Coast distributor. They told me he's dropped out of porn movies, as far as they know. He was in those 'Electric Blue' movies about 10 years ago, but hasn't been doing anything since. Maybe my distributor can tell you more."

So I called the West Coast film distributor and asked him if he knew the whereabouts of Mr. Silver, of Senate Judiciary Committee fame.

"I don't know if he's dead or alive," the distributor said. "He was never that big in films anyway. He was better known for the magazines. You see, he had a problem making movies. Kind of an interesting problem."

The distributor explained Mr. Silver's problem quite bluntly. However, I will have to paraphrase it.

It seems that when the studio lights were on and the director yelled "action" and the cameras began rolling, Mr. Silver became inhibited. Or maybe he didn't take the proper vitamin pills.

Whatever the reason, he was unable to display his talents in their full glory. And he faded away, no pun intended.

But now civic-minded Americans are clamoring for Mr. Silver's films. So if he's out there and happens to read this: Mr. Silver, call People magazine and "Entertainment Tonight." You will be contributing to the public's right to know, you know? ∎

Construction din is music to his ears

WEDNESDAY, JULY 3, 1991

For many weeks, I've spent my working days in what may be the noisiest part of Chicago.

Construction crews have been tearing up Michigan Avenue, just outside my window.

Giant machines have slammed the pavement, drilling, pulverizing, crushing concrete.

There have been entire days when it sounded like King Kong was outside my window, playing the world's biggest bongo drum.

And because half the street lanes remain open, there's the usual honking of taxi horns, the hissing and squealing of CTA buses, the clanging of the Tribune's musical bells, the wailing of ambulances and the chanting of angry Croatian protesters.

Visitors are in my office only a minute or two when, in order to be heard, they yell: "This is terrible. How can you stand it? How do you concentrate?"

They're amazed when I say that I not only can tolerate it, but I like it.

In fact, it's possible that I'm the only male person working or living in this part of town who enjoys the construction project.

Many females have enjoyed it for other reasons. In a word, hunks. Yes, I've seen them giving sidelong glances—some even straight ahead lustful gazes—at the tanned, muscular, young construction workers.

I happened to have an after-work beer with a couple of the workers and asked if they noticed that they were being ogled.

One grinned and said: "It's more than ogling. There's this good-looking blond from an ad agency. And after she came around a couple of times and watched, I took a break and we got to talking, and a couple of nights later . . ."

Ah, but that is another story, and not something I should write in a newspaper that can be read by the young and impressionable, other than as a career lesson: You don't have to be a chief executive officer to get surprisingly good perks in your job.

To get back to the constant roaring and thumping and why it doesn't bother me.

It's simple enough. The noise is so loud that it has driven away the Dreaded Saxophone Man.

I don't remember exactly when the Dreaded Saxophone Man first appeared. Two years, maybe three years ago.

He stationed himself on the other side of Michigan Avenue, usually about noon when people go to lunch, dropped his hat on the sidewalk and began tooting his horn. And he stayed and played, taking a break now and then, until the evening commuters had gone home.

At first I thought that, as street musicians go, he wasn't bad. He did an acceptable version of "Misty" and a few other standards.

But after a few days, I noticed something about his music. He played about a dozen or so songs. Then he would play them again. And again.

And something even worse. He played them exactly the same every time. He didn't change a note. He didn't improvise. If he drew out a particular note for 7 seconds the first time he played a song, he would draw it out for 7 seconds the next time, and every time.

After a couple of months, I began to hate the Dreaded Saxophone Man. That made me feel guilty because I am a music lover. I like just about every musical form: classical, jazz, folk, blues, country, marching band, small combo, drum and bugle. Even those styles of rock in which a quivering adenoid is not the lead instrument.

And I felt more guilt because I've always believed in the right of street musicians to earn a living. After all, if Madonna can make millions by appearing on stage in what appears to be my granny's girdle, a harmonica player ought to be able to hustle rent money on a subway platform.

But the Dreaded Saxophone Man exceeded reasonable limits of street musicianship. Because the buildings on Michigan Avenue form what amounts to an echo chamber, he might as well have been sitting across the desk from me.

I couldn't just walk by, drop a coin in his hat and in a minute or two be out of range. Or listen for a couple of minutes, then get on a subway and be gone.

For most of the afternoon, I was his musical prisoner. And hearing the same songs over and over began to warp my thinking.

I would be in chipper mood, preparing to write about what a fine young man Dan Quayle had become, his intellect broadened, his grasp of world affairs—nay, galactic issues—exceeding those of Abe Lincoln and Albert Einstein. Honest.

Then I would hear the notes of "Misty." The same "Misty" I had heard a thousand times. My nerve endings would buzz. My cheerful nature would turn to bile. And I'd smash my fingers on the keyboard and write a snide Quayle remark unworthy of Jay Leno.

It finally reached a point where I asked my assistant to tour nearby buildings and ask people if they would contribute to a fund to import a Mafia hit man from Sicily to shoot the saxophone. Not the Dreaded Saxophone Man himself. But I figured that one blast from a stubby shotgun into his horn would be a hint that he should move on.

My assistant refused, saying her job description didn't include such chores. It's hard to find good help these days.

So I was about to take the matter into my own hands. The plan: a ski mask, a dash across the street, a few squirts of Log Cabin syrup into his horn and a quick escape. If caught, I could plead that I was a deranged prankster.

Then came the roar of the heavy equipment and the crumbling of concrete, and the Dreaded Saxophone Man was gone. Peace and thunderous noise at last.

But one of these days, the job will be over. So I make this personal plea to Mayor Daley:

To hell with the cost; tear it up again. ∎

Hollywood should learn from Garbo

WEDNESDAY, APRIL 18, 1990

When I was a kid, and it's been awhile, Greta Garbo was already a legend. Her famous line, "I vant to be alone," was part of the language.

In fact, that was all I knew about her, since I had not seen even one of the movies she made before retiring from the screen in 1941. She appeared in romantic stories, and my tastes ran more toward sword-fighting pirates, gun-slinging cowboys, the Wolfman, Dracula and Abbott and Costello.

But there was something intriguing about someone who would walk away from so much fame and just drop out.

The ladies in the neighborhood talked about it and swapped theories. I remember some of them.

"She got fat . . . somebody broke her heart . . . she got fat as a cow . . . she was a German spy . . . she had an illegitimate baby . . . she got fatter than me . . . she turned into a drunk . . . she's so fat she can't stand up. . . . "

You must understand that this was before People Magazine, the National Enquirer, Oprah, Geraldo and "Entertainment Tonight," so the ladies in my neighborhood didn't have much material to work with.

As the years passed, you might have expected Garbo to be forgotten. But she wasn't. If anything, the legend grew. And not because her movies were shown that frequently on TV. They weren't. In the early days of TV, the Cisco Kid got far more air time. And as the years passed, old movies that featured aging, living stars had priority. If you wanted to see Greta Garbo, you had to go to an old film revival or wait up until 2 a.m.

Her legend grew because she did something that is unthinkable in modern times. When she said she wanted to be left alone, she wasn't being coy. She actually meant that she wanted to be left alone.

She refused to be interviewed, ducked photographers, traveled with the secrecy of a KGB agent, and when she came out of her New York apartment to stroll or shop, she wore big floppy hats to shield her face from gawkers or camera pests.

If her name made it into the gossip columns, I didn't notice it. Apparently her friends were loyal enough not to call with tidbits about where they had lunch, or to disclose that Greta made a quip. Garbo may be the most famous person in show business to have never been quoted as quipping in a restaurant.

But every few months, there would be a picture of her, on the street or ducking in or out of her building. The photos were usually fuzzy and her face barely visible because she was so good at evading the photographers, even the pepperonis, or whatever they call those European camera fleas.

That's really what built her legend, even more so than her old movies. She was the great star who walked away, dropped out and stayed out for almost 50 years. Even her funeral was private. And through all those years, the question was *why*?

One story contained a hint of an answer. One of her friends said she was basically a self-centered, selfish person who, when off-camera, really didn't have much to say or offer.

If that's true, I consider her a heroic figure. She should be held forth as a role model for others who manage to become specks in the public's eye.

Think of what a wonderful society we would have if every well-known person who had nothing to say would realize they had nothing to say and would not say it.

No more: "Uh, see, Johnny, one day I woke up and saw all those empty vodka bottles on my bed and it was 1990, and I didn't remember anything since 1979, and I asked my agent how my latest record was doing, and my agent turned out to be a lamp, so I thought I'd better cool it, see, and that's when I became a follower of the Raja Daja, and I meditate, and now I'm performing on a 50-city tour, and . . ."

Or: "Bubba, congratulations on your new $10 million contract. You must be very happy."

"Are you kidding? That was two days ago. If they don't renegotiate, I'm gone."

How much gentler and kinder a society we would have if we could read this exchange:

"Donald, there are reports circulating that you are involved romantically with a Miss Moolah and your wife is seeking half your fortune. Would you comment?"

"Of course I won't comment on my private life. And if you don't leave my doorstep I will set the hounds on you."

"Ivana, would you tell us what your feelings are about Donald?"

"My feelings are none of your damned business, you prying floozy."

Let's see, Madonna is sleeping with Warren Beatty. You knew that, didn't you? Of course you did. It's been widely babbled.

But who did Garbo sleep with? Nobody knows if she even napped with her cat.

Elizabeth Taylor has been hospitalized with a nasal infection. You knew that, too, didn't you? If that woman gets even a zit, it is widely babbled.

But if Garbo's nose fell off, we wouldn't have known.

With tens of thousands of publicity addicts crawling over each other for their TV bite or column squib, Garbo is one of that rare handful who said, in effect, who needs it? Fred Astaire was another. In sports, I can think of only Ben Hogan. Joe DiMaggio dropped off my list when he started selling coffee.

In honor of Ms. Garbo, Hollywood should announce that it is going to hold a big tribute to her on TV. And all the great stars should come.

Then they should just sit there and not say a word. ▪

'Superstars' lack glow of years ago
WEDNESDAY, NOVEMBER 29, 1989

In an excited voice, the TV announcer urged us to stay tuned for the news show because we would be treated to a live interview by Gene Siskel with "superstar Michael J. Fox."

Suddenly my mind was a blank. I couldn't place someone named Michael J. Fox. So I asked the blond if she could refresh my memory as to the identity of this superstar. I rely on her in such matters because she occasionally reads People Magazine.

"He's a young actor," she said.

To my embarrassment, that information didn't help. I still drew a mental blank. So I asked if we had ever seen superstar Michael J. Fox perform.

"Sure," she said, "he was in 'Back to the Future.'"

Ah, yes, now I remembered. It was a silly but entertaining movie, although I don't remember if he was going forward or backward.

"A sequel to that just came out," she said. "And he is in some Pepsi commercials."

And that's why he is a superstar?

"I guess so. He used to be in a sitcom, and now he's on the cover of People."

How about that? Michael J. Fox, Superstar, and I didn't even know. I'll have to pick up more supermarket newspapers.

Not to take anything away from a young man who has been back to the future twice, and is in soda-pop commercials, but it seems to me that bestowing the title of "superstar" on him may be premature.

I'm not sure what the precise guidelines are to become a "superstar," but when I hear that word, some show business names come to mind: Fred Astaire, Humphrey Bogart, Katharine Hepburn, Spencer Tracy, Clark Gable, Marilyn Monroe, Marlon Brando, Bette Davis, John Wayne, Cary Grant, Gary Cooper, Paul Newman, Robert Redford, Frank Sinatra, Robert De Niro, Bob Hope, Bing Crosby and Bill Cosby.

Some of them have been dead for many years. But just about everyone still recognizes their names and talents.

So if Michael J. Fox is suddenly a "superstar," what do we call Sinatra, who has been a world famous singer-actor since the 1940s? A super-dooper-star? A galaxy-star?

Actually, most of them were never called "superstars." They were simply "stars." You were either a star, which meant you were very famous, or you were just him or her, whosis or whatchamacallit.

I'm not sure when the title of "superstar" came along, or who decides when someone goes from being a "star" to a "superstar." Siskel and Ebert? People Magazine? Is it based on how many Oscars you win or how much money your agent can demand?

Maybe the measure is how many times your name appears in the nation's gossip columns or you are invited on the Johnny Carson show. If that's the case, Zsa Zsa Gabor is a superstar but Laurence Olivier wasn't.

It might have started in sports, possibly when what used to be known simply as the professional football championship game became the super-inflated Super Bowl.

That always struck me as presumptuous of football. Baseball, our national pastime, doesn't call its championship the Super Series. Basketball doesn't call it the Super Hoop. In fairness, the bowling championship would be more justified in calling itself the Super Bowl, since that's what the sport does. Football should call its big game the Super Foot.

My guess is that the "superstar" designation was originated by sports announcers, earth's most excitable creatures.

There was a time when an athlete had to be of Hall of Fame stature to be known as a mere "star." Anyone else was called a "good player."

This last baseball season, Will Clark had a year that would have made Babe Ruth consider retirement, caused Ted Williams to check into the Mayo Clinic for observation and humiliated Hank Aaron. But Clark was elevated to "superstar" status by the broadcasting hysterics.

Or could it be that it's a side effect of inflation, that in those decades when new cars jumped from $2,000 to $20,000, a .240 hitter was inflated from mope to star, and .280 hitters were promoted from being "good players" to superstars.

And now a young actor who does a TV sitcom, a couple of silly but commercially successful movies and a Pepsi commercial becomes a superstar.

Can this be part of the decline of our once great nation? Does history show that mediocre chariot drivers and cowardly gladiators were hailed as "superstars" before the fall of the Roman Empire?

If so, to prevent further decline, we should create some national standards for superstardom. We must clearly establish the difference between a superstar and a star, and a star and a whosis or whatsis.

I would not take on the job, myself. It should be done by a panel of experts—possibly the nation's gossip columnists, disc jockeys, sports babblers, gate-crashers, talk-show hosts and champion couch potatoes.

Until this is done, though, I have my own standard.

If I have to ask my wife who a superstar is, he's still a whosis. ∎

Get the picture? Not at this price

MONDAY, FEBRUARY 16, 1987

W e were looking for something to fill blank space on the living room wall, which is how I found myself standing uncomfortably in an art gallery on a recent Saturday afternoon.

Art galleries are not my usual hangouts because—and I'm not embarrassed to admit it—I have little appreciation of visual art.

Some people are tone-deaf. To them, Beethoven's music sounds like a construction crew at work.

That's the way I am with paintings. My only reaction to the Mona Lisa is the thought that if she went into a singles bar, she'd spend the entire evening buying her own drinks. When I visited the Sistine Chapel, I looked at the ceiling and thought: "Boy, lying on that scaffold, I bet he got a stiff neck and a lot of paint in his eyes."

But, as I said, we have this empty space on the wall. And the female person who shares the living room said that we had to find something to hang there.

I suggested a calendar, the kind that has a different picture for every month. But she said that the smart set doesn't hang calendars on the living room wall.

She also rejected the suggestion that we put up a shelf and display my collection of old saloon-league softball trophies. She said they're not chic.

That's one of the things that confuses me about art. Recently, a famous artist made the cover of Time magazine when it was revealed that he had spent many years drawing his cleaning lady while she was naked. That is considered chic. But I ask—would you rather be known for persuading your cleaning lady to remove her skivvies or for hitting a home run to defeat Wally & Helen's Tavern?

Anyway, that's how I found myself in this art gallery, trying to blend in with the yuppies by cocking my head to one side, grasping my chin with my thumb and forefinger, peering at a painting and mumbling: "Hmmmm, interesting."

My act must have been convincing, because a woman who sold the paintings veered toward us and said: "Do you like that?"

"Yes," I said, and it was almost true. The painting appeared to be a long, thin, multicolored bird, and it wasn't bad. Actually, if a bird looking like that ever flew overhead, I'd probably dive under a porch. But at least I thought that I knew what it was, which is the first step in art appreciation. Even more important, it seemed to be just the correct size to cover the blank space on the living room wall, which is the second step in art appreciation.

The gallery lady said: "And one of the nice things about this is that you can hang it this way or that way." And to demonstrate, she turned it so that it was hanging sideways. Then she turned it again, so it was upside down. Or maybe it was right side up.

"You see?" she asked.

That's why I'm embarrassed by my ignorance of art. If I decided to put a picture of my uncle Chester on the wall, I wouldn't think of hanging it upside down. In his prime, Uncle Chester wasn't much to look at, but the sight of him with his mouth above his eyes would turn a child's hair white.

Still faking it, I told the gallery lady: "Ah, very interesting. Either a diving or soaring effect, hey?"

Then she told me about the artist, a South American lady who now paints in New York and has been commissioned to do some posters. From her tone, I gathered that doing the posters was significant, although I don't know why. I've seen posters in Chicago that say "Elect Albert (Al) Zbygniewski Alderman, He Hates Crooks," and I wouldn't want them in my living room. Maybe the garage, though.

She also told how the South American lady worked. "She says she just gets up in the morning, throws the paint on the canvas and shifts it around until she gets the effect she wants."

My grandfather was a house painter, and if he had taken that approach, my grandmother would have wound up as a bag lady.

"It's reduced during our sale," the gallery lady said. Then she peered around the side of the frame, where they had stashed the price tag.

"It's reduced 40 percent," she said. "So you can have it for $4,800."

"Ahhh," I said. Or maybe it was more like, "Huhhhh?"

The fact is, it wasn't a bad deal, considering that I could point a thing that might be a bird in any direction, up, down, north or south. In an earthquake, it would always look good.

But I told her that we would have to think about it and would drop back sometime.

We probably won't, though. Next Saturday, I'm going to browse around some calendar stores. ∎

If only the Acorn could play it again

TUESDAY, AUGUST 28, 1990

There are bars and there are bars. Some are just fast-drink emporiums where you grab one before hopping a commuter train. Some are places where you can sit, sip a beer and actually talk to other bipeds. There are mean joints where one cross word gets you a facial scar, and friendly joints where you might meet the girl/boy/mutant of your dreams.

I know a lot about bars. More, I'm sure, than is good for my health. It was my family's business in the long-gone days when the neighborhood tavern was the working class equivalent of the country club. The corner tavern was—as the theme song of the TV series, "Cheers," puts it—"where everybody knows your name."

So I must take a moment to mourn the closing of one of the best gin mills in Chicago. Which is saying something. I doubt that any other city has a bar called

"Stop and Drink." Here, a shot is a shot, a beer is a beer and a corporate lawyer and a tuckpointer can belly up as equals.

The "Acorn." Or more formally, "The Acorn on Oak." Or, as some of us called it: "Buddy's."

It's closed down. Damn progress. Damn real estate prices and rentals. Damn the changing drinking habits of the American public. We have lost one fine bar.

A minute or two after 11 o'clock. Not a.m. If you're a morning person, the Acorn wasn't for you.

Buddy Charles would shake a few hands along the front-door bar, let go with his boisterous laugh and slide onto the bench in front of his upright piano.

A bar wrapped around Buddy's piano, and it seated maybe 15 or 20. I never counted. All that mattered was the rule: When Buddy played, you shut up.

The first time I went in there, many years ago, I was skeptical. I'd heard a lot of piano-bar players banging out junk, second-rate Liberaces grabbing for the conventioneer's tip.

Then Buddy smiled across the piano. Only one smile like it. With his lean face and sharp-pointed beard, he was the Devil incarnate. Except he wasn't. The man actually teaches Sunday school.

"Anything special you'd like to hear?" he said.

I threw him the curve. I've whipped it by piano-bar players from one coast to the next. They always expect that you'll ask for "Send in the Clowns," or some toned-down Beatles banality.

"Yeah, play 'Black and Blue.'"

He grinned. "Don't get many requests for that."

Then wham, his fingers raced in a flourish from low E to high E, he leaned back, his eyes half-closed, a devilish grin, and his piercing tenor froze the place:

"Cold empty bed/springs hard as lead/pains in my head/feel like Ol' Ned/ hey, what did I do/to feel so black and blue."

And that was the beginning of a very fine friendship. During my bleakest years, before I met and married the blond, I spent many a night listening to Buddy. He made them less bleak.

Name the song and he played it. And it wasn't just the playing. He gave it style. When he played Cole Porter or Irving Berlin, I could imagine them sitting there saying: "Exactly as I intended."

Some of you reading this have been there. Midnight, 1 o'clock, 3 o'clock. You know what it's like when you're feeling low, lonely, miserable, and you want to go somewhere where the dark hours start throwing sparks.

That's what the Acorn on Oak was. Or, as we regulars called it, "Buddy's."

I did a TV show some years ago. Interviewed celebrities and all that nonsense. I twisted the arm of the TV producer—a classic nonentity of his craft—to end the show with a performance and chat with Buddy.

Buddy talked about the kind of people who come into late-night bars to have one or two pops and listen to a piano player. He talked about widows and widowers and the kind of music they liked. Good music. And when the show ended, he slid into "One for My Baby, and One More for the Road."

We didn't do another show. The producer said it was too depressing. Being a TV creature, he paid no heed to our rating—highest in our time slot—or more importantly, Buddy's unique style. He suggested that I replace Buddy with a one-man band—thumping a drum, banging a multi-purpose keyboard. I suggested things that are unprintable.

So the Acorn is closed. The post-midnight gang feels homeless.

What to do? I don't know. I've been writing for a living a long time. Maybe I'll open a joint. Let me know. Is there anybody out there who appreciates the world's best rendition of "Black and Blue"? ■

Harvard art class has a bone to pick

FRIDAY, NOVEMBER 13, 1987

I hesitate to comment on contemporary art because when I've done it in the past, art experts have called me a boor and a philistine, which hurt my feelings.

For example, I once became curious about an art exhibit at a Chicago gallery. It consisted of the artist lying motionless between sheets of glass for several days. By doing this, he became the art object.

It created considerable enthusiasm among art lovers. But what interested me was how the artist could remain in that position for so long without going to the men's room, and I asked the gallery about it.

They told me that it wasn't relevant to the artistic message he was conveying, which I didn't understand either.

I finally got them to admit that the artist solved the problem I asked about by just wetting his pants. When I reported this, the art community said I was crude and insensitive.

They were probably right, but at least my pants were dry.

Now I've come across another contemporary art story, which I've been trying to understand.

An art lecturer at Harvard has assigned her students to make sculptures from chicken bones.

This, in itself, isn't unusual. Artists use all kinds of strange materials—beer cans, old cars, peanut butter, contraceptives—to create sculptures. The advantage of these materials is that nobody can tell what the sculpture is supposed to represent, which means the work is an artistic triumph.

But the Harvard art teacher added a new dimension to this assignment. She gave each of the students in her Fundamentals of Sculpture Class a live chicken and told them to take it home and keep it around as a pet for one day. Then they were to take it to a slaughterhouse, watch it being killed and processed and have it for dinner.

And after picking the bones clean, they were to use them to create a work of art.

The teacher explained that her goal is to bring the artist and the object closer together.

As she said: "Because they will have eaten the chickens, the chickens will be part of their bodies. This experience will expand their imagination and understanding."

However, several of the students disagreed. They said "yucky," or words to that effect, and took their chickens to an animal shelter.

And some animal-protection groups said the project sounded disgusting.

But most of the students approved. As one Ivy League lad said, after seeing his chicken separated from its head: "It's a very interesting process. It's something you usually don't see."

That probably explains why so few Harvard grads run poultry stores.

Another student said that having the live chicken stay overnight in her dormitory was an enlightening experience. As she put it: "It's better to eat something that you had a relationship with because you respect the fact that it was alive."

I hadn't thought of relationships that way, but there is some logic in what she said. And it's a heck of a lot cheaper than going through divorce court, especially if you don't get caught.

Although I am in no position to judge the merits of the chicken-bone sculptures the students will create, I think this story illustrates why the wealthy and influential are eager to send their offspring to Harvard. It's obvious that they get educational opportunities that aren't available elsewhere.

I'm sure that if I were a Harvard parent, I'd be pleased if my kid phoned and said:

"Guess what I did for my art class today?"

"What did you do? Paint a naked lady?"

"No, I took a chicken in to have it beheaded."

It would make those hefty tuition payments seem worthwhile.

Because I want to shed my philistine and boorish attitudes, I'm going to try to learn something from this approach to the creative process.

The next time I chomp through a bucket of the Colonel's chicken and look at the stack of bones, I'll feel a sense of artistic kinsmanship with the chickens I just ate.

And when I burp, I'll tell my wife: "That ain't crude—that's art." ■

Now, ACLU debate puts Flynt movie in different light

TUESDAY, FEBRUARY 4, 1997

I have to express my gratitude to the National Organization for Women and the American Civil Liberties Union.

They are having a silly but very serious spat over the merits of the movie "The People vs. Larry Flynt."

The ladies at NOW, as well as Gloria Steinem and other prominent feminists, despise Flynt because they say that his magazine, Hustler, exploits and glorifies cruelty to women.

So they are upset that the movie shows him in what can be considered a favorable light.

And while they can't prevent people from seeing the movie, just as they can't stop clunks from reading his magazine while their lips move, they have launched a lobbying campaign to prevent the movie from winning any Oscars.

On the other side is the ACLU, which considers Flynt—a self-described scumbag—as something of a hero because of his successful legal battles to defend the rights of free speech.

And the ACLU believes that NOW misses the point of the movie and is misguided in trying to discourage people from seeing it.

I'm grateful to both for having this public debate because it hadn't occurred to me to see the movie until I heard about their squabble.

Flynt has never been one of my favorite American folk characters. As for his magazine, I've always exercised my right to ignore it.

Except twice. Early in his publishing career, I looked at his magazine, saw something remarkably offensive (I have forgotten what it was) and wrote a nasty column about him.

Flynt, born and reared a poor hillbilly, never lost his belligerent roots and is not one to turn the other cheek. So he counterpunched by making me his magazine's [anal orifice] of the month, a designation he hands out to people who bug him.

But his presence and alleged influence in our society has never bothered me. As Flynt himself has often said, his single worst offense is being guilty of "bad taste."

And if we start censoring bad taste, we'd have to shut down most of the TV stations in America. And I don't doubt that some of the stuff that appears in this space would soon vanish.

But when Steinem and NOW get in a spitting match with the ACLU and other liberals, I have to find out what it is that has them all so worked up.

So I slipped into an almost empty movie theater to take in "The People vs. Larry Flynt."

And I agree with the movie critics, most of whom gave it rave reviews.

It is one heck of a good movie: intelligent, well acted, funny, sad and in a crude way, touchingly romantic.

Also, it has no car chase scenes, helicopter crashes, explosions, kung fu, gun battles, earthquakes, dismembered bodies or graphic sexual acts.

What it does is tell the story of a crude and unread young guy who came out of a dirt-poor background but manages to goofily luck his way into starting a really cruddy magazine and using his canny intelligence and instincts to build it into the foundation of a publishing empire and enormous personal wealth.

In other words, it is an American rags-to-riches business success story.

It also has a surprisingly moving love story about Flynt and his fourth wife, an ex-stripper who died at age 33.

But the main thrust of the movie is about Flynt as an unlikely hero and defender of his and our right to free speech.

Every movie plot needs conflict. And that's the tension in the Flynt story—his battles with anti-porn crusaders and the justice systems in several states that tried to shut his magazine down and put him in prison.

The movie treats that side of him as somewhat heroic, although he has always admitted he didn't start out as a 1st Amendment defender. He was just trying to get rich and have a good time.

But the movie isn't dishonest when tossing honors Flynt's way. There are constitutional experts who agree that as unworthy a guy as Flynt might be, his successful court battles were important defenses of our free speech rights.

And since when do we demand the purest of backgrounds and motives of those who do something special?

I recall writing about a man who had won the Medal of Honor for single-handedly taking on and defeating a slew of German tanks and soldiers. Sometime later, I bumped into that hero's closest boyhood friend, and he said:

"You missed one important thing about that battle. The night before, his platoon bunked down in a house that had a stash of cognac in the cellar. So when he did all those things, he was drunk as a hoot owl."

What surely bugs Steinem and the people at NOW most is that the script and Woody Harrelson's portrayal of Flynt let him come off as kind of a tragic figure and, in many ways, a likable guy.

If that's what they fear, I think they're right.

I walked out of the theater with a regard for Flynt that I hadn't had before.

Which might be further proof that I still deserve the dubious honor Flynt once gave me. ∎

Movie critics' view from isolation booth

FRIDAY, SEPTEMBER 23, 1994

I'm disappointed to learn that I blindly missed a defining moment in American history.

This has come to my attention in the many gushing reviews of a new movie called "Quiz Show."

The movie is loosely based on the true story of how a popular TV quiz show from the 1950s called "Twenty-One" was rigged to heighten suspense and increase ratings and profits.

Most of the critics say the movie is of great significance because the quiz-show scandal marked the loss of our national innocence.

Americans were supposedly stunned to discover that they couldn't believe everything they saw on their rabbit-eared TV sets. They were shattered by the revelation that Charles Van Doren, a bright, young college teacher and a member of a prominent literary family, had been slipped the correct answers and really wasn't as brilliant as he appeared.

And that is when we lost our national innocence, which is a serious loss, indeed.

It just shows how alert you have to be if you don't want to miss defining moments.

I owned a TV during much of the 1950s, and I vaguely recall watching a few segments of that tainted quiz show. I also vaguely remember the scandal.

But I stupidly failed to recognize its great significance—namely the loss of my innocence and that of my fellow Americans.

Shortly after the quiz-show scandal, I forgot about it completely. In fact, I didn't think much about it even when the scandal was unfolding. And I haven't given one thought to Van Doren, the scandal and the rest of it until I read the scholarly movie critiques.

That's because I was a Chicagoan. As such, I was familiar with aldermen, bagmen, juice men, hit men and other exotic urban wildlife. I had a naturally suspicious nature and assumed most public activities weren't on the legit.

As for the honesty of TV, by the late 1940s our family tavern had one of the city's early sets. Those were the days when pro wrestling was one of the biggest hits, and everyone knew those outrageous matches were fixed.

In fact, the wise men of the tavern agreed that just about everything they saw on the tube was a fake. When bowling became popular, fat Eddie would say: "They oil the lanes for higher scores." When roller derby became a hit, skinny Chisel said: "If it wasn't rigged, they'd all get killed." When somebody read the news, Birdie said: "Hey, what's he know, sitting in front of a camera?"

But that is no excuse for any alert person missing so significant a defining moment as the loss of our national innocence.

My only excuse is that it is difficult for any American to keep track of defining moments.

If anyone did a computer search of the phrase "defining moment" in the general press, we would find that it has been used an estimated 1,286,543 times in the last year or two.

In modern journalism's socio-jargon, the only phrase even approaching "defining moment" might be "sea change."

I'm not completely clear on the difference between "defining moment" and "sea change." I suppose that if you have a sex-change operation, that is a "sea change" in your life. Of course, it might also be a "defining moment," if not for you, at least for the other guys on your softball team. So I'm still confused.

If the forgettable Charles Van Doren punctured America's faith in TV, why do millions of Americans tune in every day to watch talk shows on which transvestite mothers-in-law describe their affairs with their sons-in-law?

While I would never argue with profound movie critics about defining moments or the precise time we lost our national innocence, these are debatable points.

Some might say that we lost our national innocence during the terrible slaughter and hardship of our Civil War. Or when tens of thousands of young men went off to die in World War I. And were there any innocents left after the Great Depression, World War II and the dropping of the A-bomb on Japanese civilians?

There are national shrinks who say we lost our national innocence when the 1919 White Sox threw the World Series for gambling bribes. Cub fans might respond that they lost their innocence in the fall of 1969.

Others will argue that national virginity was violated by the Korean War ending our winning streak. Or it was plucked when John F. Kennedy, Martin Luther King and Bobby Kennedy were assassinated. Or the debacle of Vietnam.

And what about Watergate? If I had a dollar for every time someone said that scandal shattered our national innocence, I could afford a nose job.

That's the tough thing about being an American. In most countries, defining moments and loss of innocence are the result of the collapse of governments, invasions or revolutions.

But in our society, defining moments are defined by movie and TV scripts. And the loss of national innocence is that poignant moment when a movie critic twitches.

By the way, I went to see "Quiz Show." I fell asleep. It was not one of my defining moments. ■

Work the bugs out, Channel 11

TUESDAY, MARCH 26, 1985

A friend of mine asked if I had seen some wonderful television show recently presented on Channel 11.

When I told him that I hardly ever watch that channel, he looked amazed.

"You don't watch Channel 11?" he said. "But that's the only station that shows anything of *quality*."

That's what everybody always says. If you want to see thoughtful drama or fine music or shows with deep social significance, you are supposed to watch Channel 11.

Well, maybe they have such shows, but they're never there when I turn my set on.

No matter when I turn my set on, all I ever see on Channel 11 is one of four shows:

1. Insects making love. Or maybe they are murdering each other. With insects, it's hard to tell the difference. But after a day's work, my idea of fun isn't watching a couple of bugs with six furry legs and one eye trying to give each other hickies.

2. A lion walking along with a dead antelope in its jaws. I don't know how many times I've seen that same mangy lion dragging that poor antelope into a bush. The tourist bureau in Africa must bring him out every time a TV crew shows up. But the question is, why do they keep showing it? Does somebody at Channel 11 think that we must be taught that lions don't eat pizza?

3. Some spiffily dressed, elderly Englishman sitting in tall-backed chair in a room that is paneled in dark wood. He is speaking to a younger Englishman who wears a World War I uniform and stands before a crackling fire. The older bloke says things like: "Well, Ralph, see you're back from the front. Jolly good luck that you weren't killed. Sorry to hear about your brother. Bloody bad luck, that. Shell took his head clean off. Oh, well, we must go on. Will you be joining us for dinner?" And the younger man says: "Thank you, Father."

4. Marty Robinson, talking about what great shows they have on Channel 11. The last time I tuned in, Robinson was talking about how great the next show was going to be. He talked about it for so long that I dozed off. When I awoke, he was talking about how great the show had been. Before I could get to the dial, two insects started making love again.

That's it. That's all I ever see on Channel 11.

Wait, I forgot. There are a couple of others.

Some skinny, bearded, squeaky-voiced, wimpy guy from Seattle does a cooking show. I have never seen a grown man get so excited about sautéing a Chinese pea pod. He even jiggles the pan so that the pea pod flips in the air. I guess he does that to prove he's macho.

And there's a show in which an intellectual carpenter clumps around somebody's old house, and they talk about refinishing the woodwork. The last time I happened to tune in, the intellectual carpenter and a Yuppie couple were standing in the upstairs john and the young woman was talking about improvements she was considering for her old toilet.

Now, let's say you've driven on the crowded expressways to and from your stress-filled job. You've finally made it home, had a couple of beers to calm your nerves, eaten dinner and you sit down to watch some TV.

And there is this woman pointing at her toilet bowl and saying, "We are now working on the problem of the loud gurgle."

That's entertainment?

When I explained this to my cultured friend, he said, "What kind of *trash* do you prefer?"

The very best kind of trash, as a matter of fact. And I have found it on a show called "Lifestyles of the Rich and Famous."

Recently, they had Lana Turner on, showing off her face lift and talking about how she was mysteriously drawn to visit Egypt because she is convinced that in another existence, many centuries ago, she lived there.

And I don't doubt her. Maybe in the good old days, Lana was a camel.

Regardless of what she was, it was better than hearing some Joan Baez lookalike talking about her gurgling toilet.

On another segment, the rich and famous were shown at a big party, wolfing down pounds of beluga caviar and quarts of $50 champagne. Sure, it was disgusting conspicuous consumption. But I'd rather watch that than that damn lion conspicuously consuming the dead antelope.

And if there is a starlet in a bikini who has been overlooked by the rich and famous cameras, she must be hiding.

"Ah, that's what you're interested in," sneered my cultured friend. "It's the T and A."

Well, it beats watching those insects going at it. With the starlets, I can tell which end is up. ▪

New film on Jesus causes holy mess

FRIDAY, AUGUST 12, 1988

"What'ya think?" Slats Grobnik asked. "Should we go see it?"

See what?

"You know, that movie about Jesus that's got everybody foaming at the mouth."

Ah, you mean "The Last Temptation of Christ."

"That's it. You wanna go?"

Well, it would be interesting to see what the flap is all about. Do you want to go?

"I dunno. I like happy endings, but from what I read, it sounds like a downer."

Well, it's hard to have a happy ending with a crucifixion.

"No, it can be done. I saw a Bible movie on the late show that finished okay. Victor Mature was a gladiator. He started out as a mean guy, but after the crucifixion he turned into a good guy, although he still looked like a mope, but that's the way Victor Mature always looked. I was falling asleep near the end, but I think he turned in his sword and armor for a burlap wardrobe and that made him holy. Hey, why is it that if you're going to be holy, you got to wear clothes that itch?"

I don't know, but that was your standard Hollywood Bible film. I gather that "The Last Temptation of Christ" is something quite different.

"Yeah, I don't remember any Catholic cardinals or Jerry Falwell or anybody getting mad about Victor Mature. Or any of those other old movies where there would be a lot of clouds and lightning jumping around the sky and then you hear God talking. Except it wasn't God, it was some guy with a deep radio announcer voice. Why didn't they get mad when some guy who did soap commercials played God?"

Because in "The Last Temptation of Christ," Jesus is portrayed as someone with human frailties, subject to the same temptations as the rest of us.

"Like what? They didn't have racetracks in those days."

Well, there is a scene in which He has a dream that He gets married.

"He dreams about it? What's wrong with that? It's only if you actually get married when you're wide awake that you have troubles."

Yes, but in the movie He also dreams about having sex and some of it is shown on the screen.

"Huh. At my age, I dream about having sex, too, but to be honest, I wouldn't want to see myself doing it on a movie screen."

The point is, Jesus is portrayed as having self-doubts, character flaws, not being sure of his own divinity.

"Sort of like a split personality?"

From what I've read, yes.

"I can see where that could be a problem. In those days, they didn't have shrinks. And even if they had one, he probably couldn't have afforded it on a carpenter's paycheck. Especially before they got union scale. So, are we going to go see it?"

I don't know. There will probably be pickets at the theater. People are really angry. Fundamentalists, Catholics, the whole range of Christianity is up in arms.

"That don't make sense. It's just a movie, some pictures on a screen with a sound track. If they don't like it, they should just stay home, read their Bible and not go to see it."

No, they believe it is blasphemous, an insult to Christ, morally unacceptable. And that it could undermine the faith of those who do see it.

"I don't understand that kind of thinking. If the movie is so terrible, then why didn't God hit the studio with a bolt of lightning. He used to do stuff like that, turning somebody into salt, flooding the whole world, getting a guy swallowed by a big fish. So if He let them make the movie, He can't be too upset about it, right? I mean, it wouldn't have even taken a lightning bolt to stop them. A stagehand strike would have done it."

Only the theologians can answer your questions, and I'm not sure about them, since they can't agree on the movie.

"Well, I don't get it. Why didn't all those people get mad when George Burns played God. I mean, if they don't like Jesus having weird dreams, what about God smoking a cigar and doing parlor tricks?"

George Burns playing God was meant to be funny.

"It was?"

Sure, that was the whole idea—God as a standup comic.

"Well, they fooled me. Considering the shape the world is in, I thought it was a documentary." ∎

Fred Astaire was a class act to end

TUESDAY, JUNE 23, 1987

When a Fred Astaire movie came to the Congress Theatre, we all groaned. It meant that on Saturday afternoon—movie time in the neighborhood—we had to go up Milwaukee Avenue to the fancy Harding, which cost more. Or down the street to the grimy Oak, which ran nothing but the worst B-films.

But anything was better than sitting through a Fred Astaire movie, with their sappy stories, mushy love songs and dance after dance after dance.

His movies were the worst, the pits. No Errol Flynn boldly sword-fighting with pirates. No rib-busting jokes from Abbott and Costello or Curly, Larry and Moe. No monsters like Boris or Bela or Lon. Or John Wayne facing down the bad guys. Or Bogart snarling. Sissy movies is what they were.

And Astaire himself. What a geek. Skinny, homely, always strutting about in his fancy clothes and singing in a frail voice. He was a star? Don't make me laugh.

Only Slats Grobnik had the slightest appreciation of Astaire. As Slats said: "If a guy who looks that goofy can wind up with Ginger Rogers, I got to have a chance with Theresa Gabinski, if her fodder don't come out on the porch and catch us."

I don't remember precisely when it happened. Sometime after I started shaving regularly. But I was looking up at a movie screen when it dawned on me that I was watching just about the sharpest, hippest, coolest guy in the world. In my social circle, we didn't use words like debonaire or sophisticated, but that's what I meant.

And one of the most talented. I didn't know that Balanchine, the dance genius, had said Astaire was the greatest dancer in the world. It wouldn't have mattered because I didn't know who Balanchine was. But I'd figured that much out myself. If anybody danced better, he'd need an extra leg.

From that point on, I saw every Astaire movie ever made—the new ones when they came out, the old ones when they were on TV or, more recently, in video cassettes.

I still think most of the plots were sappy. In fact, I have trouble remembering the names of the films, or which Astaire movie was which.

But the names and plots aren't important. What mattered was the music, written by the best composers, and Fred Astaire dancing and singing or just looking debonaire. He could stroll across a room with more style than most dancers can dance.

As the years went on, I found something else about him that I admired tremendously. It was that I knew very little about him, other than what I saw on the screen.

I didn't read about his love life or about his punching somebody in a nightclub. I didn't read about him storming off a set, feuding with a director, fighting with the press or babbling about what he liked to eat, what he liked to drink, snort or smoke.

In other words, he did his work, went home, closed the door and said: "That's it, world. You get my performance. The rest belongs to me."

These days, any mediocrity who gets his mug in People magazine is considered a "star." If they don't fade into oblivion after two years, they are declared "superstars."

So if Michael Jackson is a "superstar," what do we call Fred Astaire—a constellation?

Monday the guy who, in my boyhood eyes was a skinny geek, died. He went privately and quietly—a class act right up to the end.

So when I finish writing this, I'll go home, have dinner, then get out my video cassette of "That's Entertainment." I'll fast-forward to the part where Gene Kelly tells us about Fred Astaire and his remarkable talents.

For about the 20th time since I've had that cassette, my wife is going to have to sit and listen to me say: "Will you look at that? He's dancing with a coat rack . . . on the ceiling . . . look at that move . . . look at that timing . . . you know, he's an incredible athlete . . . fantastic."

But when Astaire finishes gliding through "Dancing in the Dark" with Cyd Charisse in Central Park, and they almost float into a carriage, I won't say a word. I never can. ▪

CHAPTER 8:

Come On In, Meet the Family, Her Father Probably Won't Bite

In his younger days, for a variety of reasons, Dad rarely referenced the immediate family—Mom, me or my brother Rob. He guarded his, and our, privacy—which was protective, since he had so many enemies of all kinds. Also, his public persona wasn't exactly that of a family man. But as he grew older and, especially, after Mom died and he started his second family with Judy that produced son Sam and daughter Kate, he wove them into his columns much more frequently. In fact, Judy appeared countless times, often as "the blond." Dad was older, more comfortable with sharing that side of himself with readers and had, I believe, a deepened appreciation of what he had. This is a handful of my favorites, beginning with one about Sam. —D.R.

It can be pretty silly when you dance with a Putty

MARCH 21, 1995

I now have a distinction that, I believe, no other columnist in the country or the world can claim. Maybe in the history of the world.

But first, the background.

The other evening, I went to the Rosemont Horizon, an arena, to see a live performance of the Mighty Morphin Power Rangers.

There were two reasons for my going to the show:

1. As an observer of our society's pop culture, I wanted to see firsthand why America's children have made this their favorite show.
2. My 7-year-old son had begged me to take him and his buddy to see it.

Walking through the parking lot, which seemed to be filled with minivans, I was briefed by both kids on what to expect.

"See, there are these bad space invaders who try to take over Earth."

Oh, them again.

"The leader is Lord Zedd. He's real ugly. And Lumitar. He's ugly, too. And Rita Repulsa. She's funny."

Zedd ugly. Rita funny. Got it.

"And the Putties. The Putty Patrol. They are Lord Zedd's soldiers and are weird. The Putties are made out of putty."

That makes sense to me.

"And the Power Rangers are good and fight with Lord Zedd's invaders."

Well, a man's got to do what a man's got to do.

"Some of the Rangers are girls."

A girl's got to do it, too.

And we found our seats, which happened to be in the front row, smack-dab center.

This prompted a woman behind me to say: "I was the second person in line when the tickets for this show went on sale in February. And the man ahead of me was first in line. But we're in the second row. How come you have front-row tickets?"

Just lucky, I guess. Besides, nobody said life is fair.

To the shrieks of thousands of tiny voices, the show began.

I'm not really qualified to review it as a professional critic would.

There were sensational visual effects: laser-like lights, billowing smoke, fountains of flame, bomb-like explosions, blinding flashes and ear-splitting rock music. Those who didn't want to watch the live action on stage could follow it on two giant TV screens.

The evil and ugly Lord Zedd was supported by a small army of wild and crazy space aliens whom you wouldn't want landing in your back yard at night.

And the Power Rangers—athletic and trim in their Spandex costumes—were brave and noble, although their pansy karate kicks and punches would have got them killed if they messed with Chuck Norris, much less Bruce Lee.

As for the plot, the woman in the second row summed it up when she said:

"I haven't an idea what is going on, and I don't understand what anyone is saying. Do you?"

No, but that didn't mean it was bad, because I can say the same thing about a few operas.

But most of the children seemed to enjoy it, although I think the Mutant Ninja Turtles have more wit and style and kick the enemy's heads more realistically.

And I had an experience that I will never forget and few of my friends will believe.

There came a point when several of the Putties—silent, gray creatures with bloblike heads—came down off the stage and prowled right in front of us.

One of them crouched and peered at me with the sort of curiosity a space creature might have upon seeing someone who looks like me.

He or it came closer and pawed my arm. Then he yanked me out of my seat and—

The creature began dancing a wild twist. And he motioned for me to join him.

I tried to maintain my dignity, especially in a stadium with thousands of people watching.

On the other hand, I didn't want to offend a thing with a blob of putty for a head.

So I, too, began dancing wildly. I improvised, flapping my arms like a chicken gone berserk, while letting my feet perform sort of a modern, free-form polka.

Judging by the cheers, the bulb-headed Putty and I must have made a striking couple.

Then the Putty flung its arms around me in a bearhug, and, I believe, tried to engage in close dancing. Possibly a fox trot.

At that point, I said, "I happen to be a happily married man" and freed myself. The Putty waved and bounced away.

When the show ended, I said to my son:

"Well, I guess you're the only kid in school who can say his dad danced with a Putty."

And he said: "Is the hot dog stand still open?" ∎

A true story about my brother Rob opens this column. The soundtrack to the movie "Zorba the Greek" was one of the records Dad would blast early Sunday mornings, a sort of family's alarm clock. (Beethoven's "Eroica" symphony and Sousa marches were also on heavy rotation.) Robby and I loved it, and would spin around during "Zorba's Dance" until we fell over with dizziness. And we didn't just absorb the music, but the snippets of dialogue as well. —D.R.

Young artists have plenty to learn

FRIDAY, MARCH 17, 1989

When one of my sons was in kindergarten many years ago, the class did something called "Show and Tell."

The kids would have to bring something to school and talk about it. Put on a performance of some sort.

One day, without our knowing it, my boy took one of my records to school with him. He was going to play a few songs from it and join in on the words.

It was a fine piece of music, the score from the movie "Zorba the Greek." The movie was one of my favorites and I frequently played the record. I played it so often that apparently my son was familiar with every song and every word.

So he put on an excellent performance. However, it was cut short. The teacher gave him the hook. Later, she called my wife and was quite upset.

If you've ever heard this record, you know that almost all the songs are instrumental Greek music. There is little singing.

But there are words. Before each song, you hear Anthony Quinn speaking some of the more memorable lines from the movie.

As the teacher explained it, my son got through two of them before she sat him down and switched off the turntable.

The first one went something like: "You ask me why I love women so. How can I not love them? They are such weak creatures, and they give you all they've got."

But it was the next one that ended the show. That's when my son, shoulders back, speaking in a loud voice, joined in with Zorba as he said something like:

"There is only one sin God will not forgive. When a woman asks a man to her bed, and he does not go. I know that, because an old Turk told me."

The teacher was understandably upset. That was rather risque stuff for a kindergarten class. Or even a 5th grade class. And she asked that if our son brought any more music to Show and Tell, it be something less advanced.

So the next time my boy did a Show and Tell, it was with the music from "Mary Poppins."

At the time, I agreed with the teacher's judgment. But now I wonder if I had made a mistake by not standing up for my son's right to express himself creatively.

The reason I've had second thoughts after all these years is because of the fracas that has just ended at the Art Institute of Chicago.

As everybody in Chicago, and much of America, now knows, a student at the institute's school has achieved great notoriety simply by spreading an American flag on the floor.

His creation, part of a minority student exhibit, was called: "What is the Proper Way to Display a U.S. Flag?"

The exhibit included a couple of ledgers on a shelf in which people could write their responses. Spectators had the option of walking around the flag or walking on it to get to the ledgers.

This has enraged veterans, who have marched and protested, and given politicians a chance to voice their patriotism and get on TV.

It's also delighted the student, who says he is a revolutionary communist and considers this the most terrible, oppressive country in the world.

Despite all the protests and threats to cut off tax grants, the people who run the Art Institute have stood firm in defending the student's right to express himself. So have most of the city's intellectuals, civil libertarians and, of course, artists.

So I wonder if I did the right thing many years ago, when I didn't stand up for my student-son's right to chant along with Zorba.

Think about it: If a student can toss a flag on the floor and call it art, ain't Zorba art?

At the time, however, I was under the impression that students do not have 100 percent freedom of expression. Being students, I thought, they had to abide by rules of taste and judgment.

For example, if I was the dean of a journalism school and someone came to me and said: "In the next issue of our student paper, George, our columnist, is going to write a piece about how he would like to have sex with little boys. And he is going to describe the acts he would like to perform," how would I react?

My first response would be to say: "No, he's not. I'm going to toss that piece into the waste basket. If George wants to express those weird thoughts, he should find a mimeograph machine and go stand on a street corner and hand them out like a self-respecting nut. But we're not printing them in this institution's paper."

But maybe that would be wrong. If I follow the example of the Art Institute, I would be suppressing this student's need to express himself.

Or if I were running a medical school and a student wanted to perform brain surgery on a patient, would I be right in saying: "Young fellow, you are not a physician, you are only a student. Just watch and listen. When you are qualified, you can do such things. Not yet."

Would I be doing the right thing? You bet I would be.

And maybe one of these days the people who run the Art Institute's school are going to say:

"Look, kid, you are not an artist yet. You are only a student. And what you have created is trash. Now, when you are an artist, you can display your trash in a gallery, if they will have you, or on your front lawn. But while you are a student in this institution, you are going to have to conform to standards of quality and decency and judgment."

My kid's kindergarten teacher was right. If she's still around, the Art Institute might consider hiring her. It appears that they have students in her grade level. ∎

Except for changing Clifford's name to Zeke, it's all true as Dad wrote it. Uncle Clifford was married to Dad's sister Dorothy. —D.R.

A slap in the face of all dads is recanted

WEDNESDAY, SEPTEMBER 4, 1996

Finally, there is justice for John Jerkins, whom I would nominate for the title of America's Father of the Year.

You may have read or heard about Jerkins, a police sergeant in Stillwater, Okla.

Earlier this year, Jerkins awoke during the night, went downstairs to his living room and was shocked to find his daughter and her boyfriend, both 17, on the couch, apparently engaging or about to engage in "it."

The young man sprang to his feet and, while still wearing little more than a condom, walked toward Jerkins.

Jerkins hauled off and gave the lad a sharp openhanded slap in the face.

The boyfriend went home and told his parents about being slapped but lied about why Jerkins did it. The parents reported it to the police.

And because Jerkins is a police sergeant, it became a much bigger deal than it should have been.

Although the local prosecutor decided not to pursue the case, reasoning that it would be impossible to find a jury that wouldn't consider the slap in the face deserved, Jerkins' superiors thought otherwise.

They demoted him from sergeant to patrolman and gave him a paper-shuffling desk job.

The demotion cost him $700 a month in pay and meant that he would lose about $4,000 a year in pension benefits when he retired.

They said the demotion was justified because he would not admit that slapping the young man had been wrong, while they insisted he didn't have the right to smack someone else's kid, regardless of the circumstances.

And they said they could not tolerate a policeman justifying what they considered to be an improper use of force against someone else's child. Even one wearing a condom in the policeman's parlor.

That was last spring, and Jerkins has since refused to back down. He also showed admirable restraint in declining invitations to share his story with Oprah, Sally Raphael, "Good Morning America," "The Today Show" and other peddlers of mass silliness.

He's also received countless letters of support from strangers, and the governor of Oklahoma said that if he had been in Jerkins' house slippers, he would have given the young fellow more than a slap.

This week, the Stillwater city administration finally stopped looking at rule books and law books and decided to get back to the real world.

So it restored Jerkins to the rank of sergeant and his job in the criminal investigations division, although it would still like to suspend him for a week.

Jerkins' experience is another example of how difficult it is to be a parent in these changing times. Especially when you have daughters.

Not only do you get stuck with paying for their weddings. But, if you have any traditional values, you must be concerned with their "honor."

As one whose parental experience has been mostly with sons, I've always been less concerned with their honor than with how noisily they banged on their drums and guitars or with the possibility that they might bring friends home to deplete the beer supply and throw up on the front lawn.

Jerkins' story brings to mind the tale of one of my in-laws, Zeke the city fireman, and his two daughters.

Zeke is an old-fashioned fellow. Rode the rails seeking work during the Depression, a paratrooper infantryman in WWII, a ladder-climbing smoke-eater in civilian life.

As the father of two very lovely girls, he insisted on certain formalities. When they got to high school and began dating, he required that the young men come to his house so he could meet and approve of them.

The ritual went like this. The boy would arrive to pick up his date. He would be introduced to Zeke, who would offer them a soft drink and say: "Are you interested in trains?" Most weren't. Then Zeke would say: "I collect model trains. Let me show them to you."

Then they would go down to Zeke's basement, where he kept his big train layouts.

One evening, Zeke's wife walked by the basement door, which was slightly ajar. And she heard Zeke's voice. She lingered there and listened. This was what she heard:

Zeke was saying: "Listen, kid, I was a young guy once myself. And I know what young guys think about when it comes to girls. I know that you've got one thing on your mind.

"So let me tell you what I'll do if you try any funny stuff with my daughter. I'll hurt you real bad. I mean, you'll feel terrible pain. Maybe I'll even kill you. Yeah, I'll probably kill you."

I should explain also that Zeke was built something like an NFL middle line-backer—a neck as thick as a fire plug and forearms like 5-pound hams. And all his life he wore a military crewcut. So when someone like that says he will hurt or kill you, it has a sincere ring and makes an impression.

That is when his wife knew why her two daughters were beginning to have doubts about their femininity and desirability.

They had told her that the young men who asked them for dates inevitably turned out to be shy and reserved.

Not one had ever tried to hold their hands at the movies or steal a good night peck when they took them to the door. Always well before midnight.

They wondered if it had anything to do with their deodorants or mouthwash.

Now the two daughters knew the reason for all the uncommon shyness—it is difficult for even a colt-like young man to display affection when he thinks that the slightest touch or leer might cause a hulk in a crewcut to leap out of the shadows to inflict torture, pain or even an early grave.

I'm sure that there are permissive parents who will say that Sgt. Jerkins over-reacted and that Zeke was too protective.

But as Zeke put it: "I raised very good girls. And I helped their dates be very good boys."

And the boys survived, without even a slap in the face. Maybe Sgt. Jerkins should have developed a little basement lecture of his own. ▪

Another one about Sam. —D.R.

Horrors of the past are G-rated today

FRIDAY, FEBRUARY 24, 1995

While walking through the video store, the 7-year-old boy stopped and gawked at a display of movie tapes.

"Wow," he said, "what are those?"

His father said: "Never mind. You don't want to watch those movies."

"Why not?"

"They are old horror movies. And they'll scare you, give you nightmares."

The boy began reading the titles of the video boxes aloud. "'The Wolf Man.'

Wow. 'Frankenstein.' 'Dracula.' Wow. 'Frankenstein Meets the Wolf Man.' 'The Mummy's Tomb.' Wow, what's a mummy?"

The father explained, "A mummy is a very scary guy. They are all very scary."

"Did you ever see them?" the boy asked.

"Yes, all of them, a long time ago when I was a kid."

"Did they scare you?"

"I was so scared that I crawled under the seat in the movie theater and hid. People in the audience screamed and fainted."

"Cool, let's rent one."

"I told you. They are just too scary. You won't be able to sleep. And you might be the only kid in your class with gray hair."

"C'mon, please. Pleeeese."

They discussed it for a while, as modern families do, and finally negotiated a deal. The boy agreed that if he became too terrified, and closing his eyes and putting his head under a sofa cushion didn't protect his psyche, the father could switch the film off.

They walked out with three tapes—"Dracula," for Friday night; "Frankenstein," for Saturday night; and "Frankenstein Meets the Wolf Man," for Sunday night.

"Can't we get that mummy movie too?" the boy asked.

"Your mother will kill me as it is," the father said.

He wasn't far off. "Are you crazy?" she said. "Those three movies over the weekend? By the time he gets back to school Monday, he'll be afraid to go to the bathroom alone."

"Don't worry. If it's too much for him, I'll hit the zapper."

"Why are you doing this?" she asked. "It's sadistic."

"No, it was his idea. Maybe he'll learn a lesson, that you should be careful about what you ask for."

That night they watched "Dracula."

When the ship carrying the vampire's coffin arrived in England, and all the crew members were mysteriously dead, the boy asked: "What killed them?"

"Count Dracula. He got their blood."

"Why didn't we see that?"

"They didn't show stuff like that."

"Oh."

Later, a leering Dracula leaned slowly toward a sleeping woman's throat. But the scene ended.

"What happened?" the boy asked.

"Dracula bit her on the neck and got some of her blood."

"Why didn't they show it."

"Because they didn't show that kind of stuff."

"Huh."

When the movie ended, the boy said: "Hey, what happened to Dracula?"

"Professor Van Helsing found the coffin where he sleeps and pounded a stake through his heart and killed him."

"When?"

"Just before the end."

"I didn't see that."

"No, they didn't show it."

"Why not?"

"I guess it's too scary."

A few minutes later, he heard the boy say to his mother: "It was kind of boring."

The next evening, they watched "Frankenstein."

It reached the memorable scene when the monster has croaked the nasty hunchback, escaped from the castle and tossed a girl into a stream.

"What happened to her?" the boy asked.

"She drowned."

"Couldn't she swim? She was only a few feet from the shore and it didn't look very deep."

"I guess not."

"Huh. Anybody can do the dog paddle."

The angry villagers were finally marching, torches aloft, to find the monster.

The man glanced at the boy. He was sleeping soundly.

In the morning, the boy said: "What happened to the monster?"

"He died."

"Yeah, I figured that would happen."

The mini-festival ended Sunday night with "Frankenstein Meets the Wolf Man."

"How come there's never any color in these movies," the boy asked.

"Because it is scarier in black and white."

"Oh."

When Larry Talbot (Lon Chaney Jr.) grimaces at the full moon and slowly turns into a hairy-face, the boy said: "Hey, cool."

But a few minutes later, he said: "What happened there?"

"He kills people by biting them on the neck."

"Why didn't they show that?"

"I told you, they didn't show graphic stuff like that."

The movie abruptly ended with a dam bursting and the floodwaters sweeping both creatures to wherever wet monsters and werewolves go.

The boy yawned and said: "Too bad. That Wolf Man was really a nice guy."

Then he said: "When you were a kid, you didn't really crawl under the seat in the movie theater, did you?"

"Uh, no, not really, unless I was looking for a lost glove."

"Yeah, I knew you were kidding."

"Yeah, sure I was." ▪

I could have been named Bronko, and Robby, Rocco Ricco. Thanks, Mom. —D.R.

What's in a name? Let me tell you . . .

THURSDAY, JUNE 4, 1987

A young couple I know has been trying to choose a name for their first child, which will arrive soon, and it hasn't been easy.

They don't want to name it after a relative, a famous person or themselves. They want a name that's distinctive but not unusual.

So they asked if I had any suggestions, since I went through the same thing a couple of times.

"If it is a boy," I said, "name him Bronko or Bruno. Better yet, name him Bronko and give him Bruno as his middle name."

The woman was appalled and said: "Why would I want to name a tiny child Bronko? Or Bruno?"

Because it's a tough world, and with a name like Bronko Bruno, he won't grow up to be a wimp.

"Then why didn't you name your sons Bronko or Bruno?" she asked.

The fact is, I tried. When my first son was born, and I saw how big he was, I wanted to name him Bronko. I figured that with a name like Bronko or Bruno Royko, he would probably end up as a tight end or maybe a linebacker, get through college free, maybe turn pro, make a lot of money, and I could cash in for 10 percent as his agent.

As it turned out, I was half right. He grew big enough not only to be a tight end but maybe a goal post.

But I was overruled on his name. Instead of Bronko, he was tagged with David.

David is a fine name, but it doesn't have any mud or soot or coal dust on it. It's a clean, refined, sensitive name.

So what happened? There he stands today, about 6½ feet high, huge arms, strong back, and not once in his life has he ever knocked anybody unconscious. Instead, he's a shrink, a musician and a scholar. Try to get 10 percent out of that parlay.

And as I explained to that couple, it was his name that helped shape his career. Who'd go to a shrink named Bronko?

I wanted to name my second son Rocco Rico Royko. I figured that he could wind up as alderman of the 1st Ward, or maybe a jukebox distributor. But I was vetoed on that, too.

"But if I have a son," the prospective mother said, "I'm not particularly interested in his becoming tough or macho. We just want something nice but distinctive, whether it is a girl or a boy."

Then they showed me one of those books that contain thousands of names to help parents make a choice.

"We've been looking in this," the husband said. "It even has a list of the most popular names today and the least popular. And it also has a list of the names that were popular years ago, when you were a kid."

I looked at the list and wasn't surprised by what is now popular. Everybody I know has a kid with a trendy name.

Girls are being named Heather, Jennifer, Erin, Jessica, Kimberly, Kelly, Allison, Melissa or Stacy.

Boys are Christopher, Brian, Joshua, Scott, Jason, Mark, Kevin and Jeffrey.

When I was a kid, I didn't know anybody named Heather or Joshua. In my neighborhood, boys had solid, workmanlike names: Stanley, Chester, Walter, Norbert, Albert, Henry or Joe. Girls had in-the-kitchen names like Bertha, Dorothy, Helen, Mildred, Eleanor, Mary, Lucille and Gertrude.

But today, it's not unusual to find people with monickers like Heather Potkowski, Kevin Bongorino or Danielle Goldberg. No wonder young people grow up confused about who they are.

So I suggested that they go for an old-fashioned name, maybe Gertrude, so they could call her Gert.

"I'm not going to name my daughter Gert," the woman said. "That's awful."

I suggested Phoebe, too, but they didn't like that any better than Gert.

"If it's a girl," the husband said, "I'm kind of leaning toward Lisa."

I made a retching sound and warned them that by the year 2000, one out of every five young females in America would be named Lisa. And they would all marry guys named Mark. Far better to name her Pearl. There will be few Pearls, so she'll stand out. And if it's a boy, Elmer.

"Elmer," she cried. "That's horrible."

Which shows how little she knows. There used to be a very popular song called "Elmer's Tune." Have you ever heard of a song called "Jason's Tune" or "Kevin's Tune?"

When I left, they were pondering Samantha as a possibility. The wife said: "We could call her Sam. That's cute."

I told them that if they wanted to give her a man's name, why not just call her Horace and be done with it.

But a name choice is a serious matter, and many people have been embarrassed by the label they're stuck with.

I'm sure many people remember the famous case of the man named Joe Crapp who went to court to get his name changed.

The judge said: "I don't blame you for wanting a new name, Joe. What name have you chosen?"

And Joe Crapp responded: "I want my name changed to John Crapp. I'm tired of people always saying: 'What'ya know, Joe?'" ∎

Not about family, but a close friend, Les Lubash. I met him once as a kid, on a trip to California. —D.R.

In many ways, he earned his wings

WEDNESDAY, SEPTEMBER 6, 1995

The two young Air Force recruits were riding a public bus in a Southern city. They had just spent their first day away from the base after several weeks of training.

It had been a good day, talking to pretty girls in a lovely park, lunch and dinner in a Mexican restaurant, with more than a few cold beers to wash down the unfamiliar spicy food.

Now, they were returning to the base.

Being from Chicago, they knew about racism. But the bus ride was their first exposure to the more structured Southern style.

Blacks rode in the back of the bus. If the rear seats were filled, they stood. They could not sit in whites-only seats in the rest of the bus.

An elderly black couple stood in the back, although there were several empty seats near the front.

The two young airmen began talking about the unfair seating arrangements, loudly and sarcastically.

A white man glared at them and said: "Why don't you boys just shut up?"

One of the airmen responded: "You ever hear of freedom of speech? That's one of the reasons we're wearing these uniforms, to defend freedom of speech. You against that?"

The man didn't answer, and the airman went on:

"We're going to ship out pretty soon, and we might go to Korea. There's a war there. Have you heard about it?"

By now, everyone on the bus was looking and listening.

The airman continued. "I might get killed over there. And I want you to know something. If I get killed, it won't be for you because you don't deserve it. You aren't nice people or good Americans. If I get killed, it will be for the people in the back of the bus because they're better than you. How do you like that?"

He went on in that vein, and it was quite a speech. But nobody applauded. When the bus reached the base entrance, he waved and said: "God bless the rest of America."

The young airman's name was Leslie Q. Lubash. He was 19 at the time, which was 1952, and was from the blue-collar bungalow neighborhood around Montrose and Cicero.

Fortunately, he wasn't killed in the Korean War. The Air Force turned him into an officer and—on paper—a gentleman.

He became a navigator on the giant planes that refueled Strategic Air Command bombers in the air, usually over the cold north end of the planet where the Russians might show up.

He was good at his work, but when a colonel asked him to re-enlist, he surprised the man by saying: "No, thanks. I'm deathly afraid of airplanes."

But he ended up flying anyway. He moved to Europe and navigated for a one-plane charter service that would go anywhere with anything. He flew refugees, elephants, guns and other cargo in and out of every continent and just about every country—sometimes with bullets flying as the plane took off from a bumpy airstrip. In one belly-flop landing, he busted both ankles.

Later, he went legit and became one of the last Braniff navigators on transcontinental flights.

But when computers replaced live navigators, his profession died and he was out of a job.

For a while, he owned a restaurant in Berkeley, Calif., that pioneered the eclectic menu—serving hamburgers and quiche, malted milks and fine wines.

He also was an artist whose lopsided style some critics found promising. And a photographer with a keen eye.

He took time out to work in Bobby Kennedy's California campaign and was devastated by the assassination.

After a lifetime of roaming the world and doing some of this and some of that, he drifted back to Chicago and the Northwest Side neighborhood where he grew up and where members of the big Lubash family still lived.

Despite health problems—severe manic depression was one—he built a successful career in Chicago as a free-lance photographer.

He died a few days ago in his sleep. He was 63, but he had crammed at least 100 years of adventure into his life. Not bad for a Wright Junior College dropout.

There were no obits for Les, but he rated one, if for no other reason than the speech he gave on that Southern bus many years ago.

I once asked him what we would have done if the people on the bus had decided to stomp us.

He shrugged, laughed and said: "We would have defeated them. The good guys always win, don't they?"

He is survived by a whole lot of Lubashes. And a very sad old buddy. ∎

This one is bittersweet for me. Dad and Sam were, like most Chicagoans, unabashed fans of Michael Jordan, so when an opportunity came to get something autographed for Sam, Dad succumbed to the desire to make Sam's dream come true. It also wouldn't hurt for Dad to interact with M.J. himself. Dad hoped he wouldn't mind and maybe even have an idea of who he was, since Dad had written about him from time to time. But he was wrong. And reading between the lines of the column, it stung. —D.R.

Oh, the humiliation a dad must endure

TUESDAY, JUNE 13, 1995

Standing by the golf course pond with a fishing rod in his hand, the man felt foolish and nervous.

Not that there is anything foolish about dangling a nightcrawler in a golf course pond. It's more relaxing and less costly than hacking a ball into the water, and you can eat what you catch. Who eats a score card?

But catching fish wasn't his real reason for being there.

He was engaged in what detectives, spies or journalists would call a stakeout.

In other words, while he appeared to be spending some quiet time in the shade of an old oak tree, pulling out an occasional bluegill or small bass, he was really furtively watching and waiting for a certain person to walk by.

When that person appeared, the man would do something that he had never done in his entire life and never thought he would do. He would ask a celebrity for an autograph.

The prospect filled him with shame. He would have preferred to dive into the pond or run to his car and roar away with his pride intact.

But he couldn't. The reason was standing next to him and holding a fishing pole—his 8-year-old son.

The boy was dressed in his Sunday best, his Monday best, Tuesday best and 24-hour-a-day best.

Deep red Chicago Bulls shorts. The very latest in black basketball shoes fashion. And a Bulls jersey with the number 45 on the back.

A few days earlier, the man had been tipped off that the world's greatest basketball player and a few friends might be playing golf that morning on that golf course.

The course and clubhouse would be closed that day for weekly maintenance with only a few workers there.

The basketball star and his group would have something rare and precious—total privacy. No gawkers, intruders and no autograph hounds.

The man had casually mentioned this to his wife, and the boy had overheard them talk.

From that moment on, it was, "Dad, can we? Can we, Dad? Mom, ask Dad, please? Dad, Mom says it's up to you. Dad, puleeze?"

There are things a parent must do. Cheerfully change fragrant diapers. Smile happily while burping a child who drools milk down your shirt collar. Sit through musical assemblies.

And that's what had the man squirming more than the worms he put on the hooks. He was asked to barge in on a privacy-seeking celebrity, to be the gawker, the intruder, the autograph hound.

But how do you say no to a kid who, since he was 3, has been chanting along with the team introductions: "And from . . . North Carolina . . ."?

So there the man stood, already feeling like an ass, while hopefully telling himself: "Maybe when he sees the fishing rods, he'll ask how we're doing. People always ask fishermen how they're doing. And that will be the conversational ice-breaker and . . ."

Suddenly they were there, teeing off, then walking briskly down a path near the pond, not 10 feet from the man and his son.

The man blurted, "Good morning." Surely they'd pause and ask how they're biting.

Not a word. Not a glance. Eyes squinting, long strides, the Great One nodded once he was past them. It was something he's had to learn to do instinctively, or he'd never get where he was going. Even on a near-deserted golf course, there was some bozo coming out from under a tree with a felt-tip marker in his hand.

The man took a deep breath and said, "Michael?" The Great One stopped, turned and gave him a cold look that might have been taken to mean: "Person, just what is it that you want?"

"Uh, Michael, could I have a second of your time?"

Without hesitating, he said: "You've already had a second."

It wasn't exactly a slap in the face. More like a little poke in the eye.

The man had an urge to back off and grab a fellow worm.

But the smiling, wide-eyed boy was looking up, as if at a god. So the man stammered: "Look, he hasn't worn anything else since you came back. He sleeps in that outfit. Could you maybe just initial. . . ?"

A slight hesitation, then he stepped forward, took the marker and made a long squiggle on the jersey. A celebrity signature is not expected to be legible. I suppose that the touch and the moment are what matter.

With a slight smile, he said: "There you go, my little man. Nice uniform." Then he shook the boy's hand, turned and headed up the fairway.

The boy looked down at his jersey, then looked up with a huge smile and moist eyes. "I'll never wash this. I'll never wash my hand. Dad, let me have the marker. I'll never let anyone write with it. Wow, Dad, wow."

Later, in the car, the man told his wife: "He said, 'There you go, my little man.'"

"Why, that's really nice," she said.

"Yeah. But I wonder if he was talking to me." ∎

Yes, this one is harsh. Maybe too harsh. But Dad's description of my grandfather Fred Duckman is spot on, and his point, whether you agree or not, is worth considering— as usual with Dad. His daughter that died was my mother. Gramps died later that year at age 83. —D.R.

When a 'tragedy' is only vanity

THURSDAY, MARCH 19, 1987

I've received my first phone call from a teenager who indicated that she was contemplating suicide.

Actually, she didn't call to tell me that. Not at first. She opened the conversation by asking if I knew the phone number of any suicide hot lines.

I told her I didn't, but suggested she call information to see what they had listed under "suicide."

She said: "I have to talk to someone."

I said: "Why? Are you thinking of killing yourself?"

She said: "I don't know. Maybe. I've been feeling depressed."

"About what?" I asked.

"Oh, things. Just things."

I said: "That's too bad. Try the information operator."

Her voice, which had sounded flat and dull, suddenly became shrill, and she said: "You don't care. You really don't care, do you?"

"If you kill yourself? Yeah, I don't think you should do it. It's kind of a dumb thing to do. But if you insist on doing it, it's not going to affect me one way or the other. That's about all I can tell you."

"Well thanks a lot," she snapped, and hung up the phone.

Now I feel bad. Not because I didn't sound deeply concerned about what she might do, because I'm not. But I should have taken the time to tell her why I wasn't deeply concerned.

There is this old man I know. When I first met him, many years ago, he was tall and handsome and proud. He worked hard in his electrician job, had a sweet and intelligent wife, a tall son and a beautiful daughter. They were a close, loving family.

When his wife was in her late 30s, she was stricken with multiple sclerosis and spent the rest of her life in a wheelchair. A tough break for both of them. But they made the best of it. I never once heard either of them complain.

I saw this man's grief when his only son, at 46, was buried after a heart attack. I was with him at the funeral of his daughter who died at only 44 of a stroke. And I was there when his wife could no longer keep up her brave fight against the ravages of her disease.

The old man suffered and wept. But he never once said pity me, oh please, feel sorry for me.

He didn't say it during those terrible times and he didn't say it when diabetes caught up with him and the doctors had to cut off one leg above the knee. Then the other leg. What he said to one of his grandsons was: "Well, now I guess you're the tallest in the family and I'm the shortest."

Now he spends his days and nights in a bed in a nursing home. And if I've ever known anyone who would be justified in taking a handful of pills and swallowing them, it's that old man.

But he hasn't done it, because if he did, he would not see his grandsons any-more. For all he's lost, he still has them. And they, as well as his courage and many wonderful memories, are enough to keep him going.

So I'm sorry, but I can't get weepy when those who are 17 and healthy say they can't go on after being jilted by a boyfriend: Life is too painful. Or they aren't popular enough in school: Life is too painful. Or their parents don't listen when they talk: Life is too painful. Or they are depressed because their best friend is depressed: Oh, life is too painful.

Don't tell me that pain is relative. Like hell it is. There's a big difference between a pinprick in the finger and a knife to the gut.

However, if someone out there insists on going into a garage, turning on the car and fading into oblivion, don't kid yourself about what you're doing.

You probably fancy yourself a tragic figure and believe that others will, too.

Forget it. Few people will care. They have their own troubles. Just check out the obit pages or the hospitals.

Oh, some strangers will glance at the TV or newspaper and wonder why you did it. A few alleged experts and TV babblers will even say we have a national crisis, which is nonsense.

But most people will give your dramatic gesture about five seconds of thought—if that much—then forget it.

Your friends at school? Sure, they'll spend a day or two striking melancholy postures. Then they'll get on with their own lives and you'll fade. Just someone they knew once. One of many kids they knew once.

And this might sound harsh, but that's really all you'll deserve because what you'll have done is nothing more than an act of vanity, selfishness and weakness. As well as stupidity.

Of course, you'll cause considerable grief for your parents, sisters and brothers, which might be your motive. But you could stick around and do that.

So that's why I didn't spend much time trying to soothe the young woman who called me. Most of us, except for saints, have only so much compassion stored away.

I prefer to dole mine out to the truly deserving. ∎

This one is among those that fans still mention to me as one of their favorites. What nobody knows is that it is a true story about Mom and Dad. Except for describing Mom as "kind of pretty" for the purpose of the tale (she was a knock-out), this is exactly the way I'd heard the tale when I was a kid. —D.R.

A lovely couple, bound with love

TUESDAY, DECEMBER 24, 1985

The conversation at the bar got around to Christmas trees. Somebody had mentioned how much they cost today and what a pain in the neck it is to go out in the bitter cold and shop around for a good one.

"Nah," said Slats Grobnik. "There's nothing to it; not if you know what you're doing."

What makes you an expert?

"I used to work in a tree lot when I was a young guy," said Slats. "My uncle used to sell them in the. vacant lot next to his tavern. And that's when I learned the secret."

What secret?

"The secret of having the most beautiful tree you ever saw."

That's easy. The secret is to go out with a pocket full of money and spend what it takes to buy the best tree.

Slats shook his head. "Uh-uh. Money's not the secret."

So, tell us the secret.

"Awright. It was a long time ago, maybe 30 years. I was in the lot and it was the night before Christmas Eve, about a half hour before I was going to close up. I hadn't seen a customer in two hours.

"I had maybe a couple dozen trees left, and most of 'em weren't much to look at. By the time you get that close to Christmas, they've been picked over pretty good.

"So I'm standing by the kerosene heater when this young couple comes in and starts looking at the trees.

"I don't know 'em by name, but I know they live down the street in the basement of one of the dumpiest three-flats in the neighborhood.

"He's a skinny young guy with a big Adam's apple and a small chin. Not much to look at. She's kind of pretty, but they're both wearing clothes that look like they came out of the bottom bin at the Salvation Army store.

"It's cold as a witch's toes, but neither of them have got on gloves or heavy shoes. So it's easy to see that they're having hard times with the paychecks.

"Well, they start lifting the trees up and looking at 'em and walking around 'em, the way people do. They finally find one that was pretty decent. Not a great tree. But it wasn't bad. And they ask me the price.

"It was about $8 or $9. They don't say anything. They just put it down.

"They keep looking. They must have looked at every tree in the lot. Like I said, there weren't many that were any good. But every time I gave the price on a decent one, they just shook their heads.

"Finally, they thank me and walk away. But when they get out on the sidewalk she says something and they stand there talking for a while. Then he shrugs and they come back.

"I figure they're going to take one of the good trees after all.

"But they go over to this one tree that had to be the most pathetic tree we had. It was a Scotch pine that was OK on one side, but the other side was missing about half the branches.

"They ask me how much that one was. I told them that they'd have a hard time making it look good, no matter how much tinsel they put on it. But they could have it for a couple of bucks.

"Then they picked up another one that was damned near as pathetic. Same thing—full on one side, but scraggly on the other.

"They asked how much for that one. I told them that it was a deuce, too. So then she whispers something to him and he asks me if I'll take $3 for the two of them.

"Well, what am I going to do? Nobody's going to buy those trees anyway, so I told them they had a deal. But I tell them, what do you want with two trees? Spend a few dollars more and get yourself a nice tree.

"She just smiled and said they wanted to try something. So they gave me the $3 and he carried one of them and she took the other.

"The next night, I happen to be walking past their building. I look down at the window and I can see a tree. I couldn't see it all, but what there was looked good.

"The lights are on, so I figure, what the heck. I knock on the door. They open it and I tell them I noticed the tree and I was just curious.

"They let me in. And I almost fell over. There in this tiny parlor was the most beautiful tree I ever saw. It was so thick it was almost like a bush. You couldn't see the trunk.

"They told me how they did it. They took the two trees and worked the trunks close together so they touched where the branches were thin.

"Then they tied the trunks together with wire. But when the branches overlapped and came together, it formed a tree so thick you couldn't see the wire. It was like a tiny forest of its own.

"The two of them looked so happy with it that it made me feel good the rest of the week.

"And thinking of those two orphan trees, which would have been tossed out if they hadn't come along, made me feel good, too.

"So that's the secret. You take two trees that aren't perfect, that have flaws, that might even be homely, that maybe nobody else would want."

But if you put them together just right, you can come up with something really beautiful.

"Like two people, I guess." ∎

CHAPTER 9
Sonny, Back in MY Day . . .

The coups that changed mankind

MONDAY, APRIL 13, 1987

The world of science is delirious with excitement over the discovery of new, efficient ways to get electricity from here to there. Or there to here, I suppose.

It's said that these recent discoveries will have an enormous impact on the economy and our lifestyles and make possible all sorts of wondrous technological advances.

One scientist was quoted in this newspaper as saying about the rapid development and potential of the new electrical conductors: "Nothing like this has ever happened in science before."

Another said: "Superconductivity developments are the most exciting new breakthroughs of our lives. It will change the way we live."

With all respect for the scientists, I have my doubts about that. Changing the way we live, I mean.

For example, nothing I've read has said that this amazing breakthrough will lead to the elimination of some of the most terrible curses known to modern man—the rush-hour traffic jam, flavorless tomatoes, devious politicians or goofs who talk during movies.

Every few years, scientists insist on telling us that something new and amazing will change our lives. But what happens? The military uses the new development to refine the methods we might use to blow up the world. And the rest of us wake up with the same problems, bills, aches and pains.

Consider the transistor, which replaced the vacuum tube and was hailed as one of the great inventions of the ages. What did it give us? A sub-race of zombies who shuffle or jog through life with Walkman radios attached to their heads.

That's why I'm skeptical about most scientific breakthroughs. I've seen few of them lead to a genuine improvement in the way we live. Have any of them eliminated the hangover?

And that has led me to compile a list of what I consider to be some of the most important inventions of my lifetime. It isn't a comprehensive list, of course, and others may have their own choices. If so, you might send them to me and I'll add them to the list.

In no particular order, here are my choices.

The automatic car wash, especially the kind that lets you shove a slug in a slot and squirt hot wax on your car. The automatic car wash has freed millions of men from the weekend ritual of slopping soap on their sneakers and has permitted them to do more important things, such as nothing.

The disposable diaper. Only those who had children before it was available can appreciate how much less offensive it is to be a young parent. As Slats Grobnik once said: "Everybody says babies are so sweet. But if a grown man did the things a kid does, he'd be run out of every saloon in town."

The cut-proof golf ball. Scientists have estimated that this amazing advancement has eliminated so much stress that the average golfer's life has been extended by 2½ years. I made that up, but it's probably true anyway.

The remote-control channel changer. The world would have been better off if TV had never been invented. What would we have missed—Sam Donaldson? But as long as we're stuck with it, it's nice to be able to flip through the channels effortlessly to see if there's anything lewd going on.

The automatic ice cube maker. I can't imagine what life is like in societies that don't have this device. It's little wonder that there is so much discontent in the Third World.

The one-size-fits-all men's stocking. Until we had this, we never knew whether a stocking would be too big or too little when we bought it. So most of us had toes that were either scrunched or pinched. As Plato said: A person cannot be truly happy with painful toes.

The phone answering machine. It's been maligned and ridiculed. But it's permitted me to at last be honest with those who phone my home. Before I had one, I had to say, "Hello. Oh, hi, how are you. Uh-huh, that's interesting. No kidding. Well, maybe we can get together and do that." Now, my recorded message states a simple truth: "I'm here, but I don't want to talk to you. At the beep, just go away. Thank you for listening."

As I said, others may have their favorites. Venetian blinds, for example, which admit light but discourage peeping toms; automatic windshield washers; and any garment made of polyester.

But we have a long way to go. We can put a man on the moon, make electricity move more efficiently.

When will science develop a martini that is good for you? ■

A tale of two smut merchants

WEDNESDAY, AUGUST 1, 1984

In simpler times, there lived a neighborhood photographer near Armitage and Milwaukee on the Northwest Side.

He was self-employed, working weddings, anniversaries, graduations and other family events.

But he also padded his income with a line of goods he didn't advertise in the neighborhood paper. He sold nude photos, the kind that used to be called dirty pictures.

His model was usually his wife, an empty-faced woman who tended their second-floor flat and two small kids and did what her husband told her to do.

Other than having a big chest, there wasn't much to recommend her as a model, except that she was willing to take off her clothes and pose in embarrassingly re-vealing positions—usually with her tongue hanging out, which was supposed to lend an erotic effect.

The photographer would sell stacks of the wallet-size photos to guys he knew in factories and taverns, and they in turn would sell them to guys they knew. That's the way such things circulated in the days before porn stores and national smut magazines.

The people in the neighborhood didn't know about his dirty picture business because he went outside the neighborhood to sell them.

But then he made the mistake of asking a teenage girl from the next block if she would be interested in making some money as a model.

When he told her exactly what he had in mind, she told her mother. The mother told the father, who owned a corner tavern. And the father and his large son, carrying baseball bats, went to the photog's home and banged on the door.

Not being a dummy, he wouldn't open the door. So the father yelled that if he ever came near that girl again, they'd kill him. He yelled back that it was all a mistake. And they yelled that one more mistake would get him dropped into sewer.

A few weeks later, the local grammar school had its June graduation. The gym was filled with proud parents and grandparents and uncles and aunts.

The tavern keeper was there for the graduation of one of his other children.

During the ceremony, the tavern keeper glanced around and saw the photog-rapher with a camera in his hand.

"What's that creep doing here?" he said.

It turned out that the creep was there as the official photographer of the graduation.

"He ain't taking my kid's picture," said the tavern keeper. And he got up and bashed the creep in the jaw.

"What are you doing?" the principal shrieked.

"He's a creep," the tavern keeper explained, knocking the photog to the floor.

"Stop," the principal cried.

"I'm almost done," he said, giving him a couple of kicks that sent him fleeing from the school.

The tavern keeper then explained to the other parents that he had driven a degenerate from their midst, so someone else was called to make the class picture.

And within two days, the photog had moved from the neighborhood and was never again seen.

I thought of that incident while watching Bob Guccione, owner of Penthouse magazine, being interviewed on a network news show about the Miss America photos.

It occurred to me what remarkable changes have occurred in only a few decades.

That neighborhood pornographer was punched around and had to move away in disgrace.

In contrast, Guccione, a multimillionaire, wears gold chains, has corporate offices, travels the world in jets and is invited to the best parties in New York.

If the photog tried to explain why he did what he did, nobody would have cared. They would have just punched him some more.

But Guccione appears on network shows to speak with great seriousness about the journalistic necessity of publishing photos of two young women in lesbian poses in his magazine.

And there are people who take him seriously.

Actually, there's little difference between that neighborhood pornographer and Guccione the magazine publisher, other than financial success. The only significant difference is that the neighborhood photog knew what he was.

Some might say that the neighborhood photog was born before his time.

Maybe. But I prefer to think that it was the tavern keeper, unfortunately, who was born before his time. ∎

Lincoln's speech doesn't compute

THURSDAY, MARCH 8, 1990

The ad caught my eye and intrigued me. It was for a computer program and it said: "Write better in 30 days or your money back!"

I'm not a computer nut, but I'm familiar with computer programs that correct spelling and have built-in dictionaries.

But the ad for this program said that it would correct "stylistic errors." Style. That's a big part of what writing is about.

So I decided to check it out. I stopped by the computer store to give it a test run. I wanted to see what the program would say about the style of a short piece of writing that has always been one of my favorites.

I typed it into the computer just as the author is said to have written and delivered it.

Then the computer printed out its critique. Here's the final product, with the computer's comments in parentheses.

Fourscore and seven years ago our fathers brought forth on this continent, a new nation, conceived in Liberty, and dedicated to the proposition that all men are created equal. (#Long sentences can be difficult to read and understand. Consider revising so that no more than one complete thought is expressed in each sentence. #Passive voice: "are created." Consider revising, using active. See Help for more information. #Usually a paragraph should have more than one sentence.)

Now we are engaged (#Passive voice: "are engaged." Consider revising using active voice. See Help for more information.) *in a great civil war, testing whether that nation or any nation so conceived and so dedicated can long endure. We are met* (#Passive voice: "are met." Consider revising using active voice. See Help for more information.) *on a great battlefield of that war. We have come to dedicate a portion of that field, as a final resting place for those who here gave their lives that that* (#Delete doubled word or punctuation mark.) *nation might live. It is altogether fitting and proper that we should do this.*

But, (#Use "But" sparingly to start a sentence.) *in a larger sense, we cannot dedicate—we cannot consecrate—we cannot hallow—this ground. The brave men, living and dead, who struggled here, have consecrated it far above our poor power to add or detract. The world will little note nor long remember* (#An adjective "long" is usually not followed by a verb "remember." You may need to use an adverbial form of "long" [e.g. "quickly" instead of "quick"), or you may need a comma before "remember."] *what we say here, but it can never forget what they did here. It is for us, the living, rather* (#This word usually adds little and should be omitted.) *to be dedicated here to the unfinished work which* (#"That" is almost always preferred to "which" in this situation. If you really mean "which," then it usually needs to be preceded by a comma. See Help key for more information.) *they who fought here have thus far so nobly advanced.* (#Long sentences can be difficult to read and understand. Consider revising so that no more than one complete thought is expressed in each sentence.) *It is rather* (#This word usually adds little and should be omitted.) *for us to be here dedicated to the great task remaining before us—that from these honored dead we take increased devotion to that cause for which they gave the last full measure of devotion; that we here highly resolve that these dead* (#Usually "these" should be followed by a plural noun.) *shall not have died in vain; that this nation, under God, shall have a new birth of freedom; and that government of the people, by the people, for the people, shall not perish from the earth.*

(Problems marked/detected: $^{13}/_{13}$)

That's something. As often as I've read this speech, getting a lump in my throat every time, I didn't detect even one stylistic problem, much less 13. Shows how little I know.

But I suppose we really shouldn't expect anything better from someone who grew up in a log cabin, hoofed to a one-room schoolhouse and never made it to college.

We might remember, though, that Abe Lincoln was at a stylistic disadvantage when he wrote what has become known as his Gettysburg Address. The poor guy didn't have a "Help Key" to push.

And even with his 13 stylistic flaws, we can say one thing in Abe's behalf: he sure as hell wasn't a computer nerd. So run that through your program and spit it out. ■

To tell the truth, a good deal of lying is often needed

TUESDAY, JANUARY 16, 1996

The practice of lying has been getting a bad rap lately, mostly because of Hillary Clinton.

A columnist for The New York Times called her a "congenital liar," which touched off a nationwide journalistic tizzy about whether Hillary speaks with forked tongue.

I don't understand this. Although she holds no office, Hillary is a politician, and all politicians tell lies at one time or another.

If they didn't lie, most would never be elected because they'd have to declare their candidacies by saying:

"I seek this office because I have an enormous ego. I love power and wheeling and dealing; crave admiration, recognition and approval; am infinitely more intelligent than the rest of you; have an insatiable need to impose my will on others; and I'm bored stiff with my present station in life. Incidentally, I think I can do some good if elected, but, hey, only time will tell."

So they tell us lies about what they will do for us, rather than what they will do to us, and we vote for the candidates whose lies appeal to our noblest instinct or lowest prejudice. Or those who have the coolest TV commercials.

This is as it must be. We would have chaos if politicians told us only the truth.

How would you feel if a president pre-empted your favorite sitcom for a State of the Union Message and said:

"My fellow Americans. Boy, oh, boy, you wouldn't believe what a mess we're in right now. And I don't have the faintest idea what to do about it. Thank you and good night."

Some may remember a presidential hopeful named George Romney, who blurted out the truth one day and destroyed his political career.

It was during the Vietnam years, and he declared that he had been "brainwashed" by the White House and the Pentagon into believing that the war was going well.

Well, everyone hooted and sneered and giggled and said: "Ho, ho, Romney wants to be president, but he was brainwashed. What a goofy guy."

As we later learned, most of us were being brainwashed about the war. But it was the end for Romney, which served him right for truth mongering.

No, we can't have our leaders telling us nothing but the truth or we'd be nervous wrecks and the country would be run by people who are honest but dumb.

And if truth mongering ever becomes the norm in all our everyday dealings with each other, civility would collapse and our society would suffer from a national nervous twitch.

Every day, billions of lies are told—little, medium and big. Which is good. Without them, we'd have chaos, rioting and the economy might collapse.

Who would buy stocks if a broker said: "To tell you the truth, I don't know if the market is going to go up or down and if that company will thrive or go into bankruptcy. So, how many shares do you want?"

Our legal system would not survive if lawyers suddenly began telling juries: "My client has entered a plea of not guilty, and I'll go along with that, although I'm certain he committed the foul deed. But I will do my best during this trial to bewilder you 12 gullible boobs into enough silly doubts to let the loathsome creature off the hook."

And if you read the financial pages, how many times have you seen stories saying that some big-name executive has left a corporation to "pursue other interests."

Hah! If he was so eager to quit and pursue other interests, how come he came out of the CEO's office as pale as milk, hands trembling and rushing toward the nearest martini?

Our national divorce rate is already too high. But think of what it would be like if husbands and wives told each other nothing but the truth.

"So, how did things go at the company convention?"

"Oh, the meetings were kind of dull. But I met a cute little bimbo from marketing in the hotel bar, we got half-loaded and ended up in the sack. So how are the kids and what's for dinner?"

Consider how many times each day a chirpy waiter or waitress stops at a restaurant table and says: "How's everything? OK?"

And 99.9 percent of the time, people say: "Oh, fine, yes, fine."

What if people were truthful and said: "No, as a matter of fact this grub is barely mediocre, the service is sloppy, the coffee is weak and I wish you would stop interrupting us with that dumb question"?

Would that improve the food or service? No, we would just have a lot of depressed waiters and waitresses and things would get worse.

We all do it. During my recent vacation, I found myself thrown into a round of golf with three strangers, including a New York yuppie.

When we finished, we all shook hands and said: "Nice playing with you. Enjoyed it." That's what golfers always say under the circumstances.

Had I been truthful, I would have said to the New Yorker: "I have never heard anyone whine and moan so much over bad shots, which is all you hit. And your endless dirty jokes were not only tasteless but old. And you babble when others are hitting. You don't deserve to live. But whoever said death was fair?"

But then he might have thought that I, too, was rude.

So let us give lying the respect it deserves.

By the way, it is real nice to be back at work.

See? I did it again. ∎

Kids always have a prayer in school

THURSDAY, AUGUST 20, 1992

Every day I learn something new about "traditional family values," one of this year's trendiest political issues.

My latest lesson came from Charles Black, a senior adviser to the Bush campaign.

He told a gathering at the Republican convention that family values include the right of children to have voluntary prayer in public schools.

This surprised me, since I thought that children already had that right. And that they have always had it.

When I was a lad in public schools, it was not uncommon for some of us to sit and offer up silent prayers that Mrs. Purvis would not call on us to answer questions about the reading assignment because we hadn't read it.

I know for a fact that Slats Grobnik prayed all the way through high school that he would have a carnal experience before he reached the age of 30.

So when school begins next month, millions of public school children will be praying. Some will pray that they don't get pimples. Others that they will pass an algebra test.

True, under our laws, the teachers can't lead the children in formal, organized prayer or set aside time for this purpose. But why should they? For all a parent knows, that teacher might be a member of a secret cult that worships parking meters or some such false idol. Is that the kind of person they want giving their child religious guidance?

And it is especially difficult at a time when churches of all faiths have fallen upon hard times, with collections and donations down because of the recession and the flighty nature of today's young people. Are Republicans in favor of churches shutting down and preachers being put out of work because of unfair competition from the schools?

Besides, any theologian will tell you that for a prayer to be valid, it isn't necessary for it to be uttered aloud at a given time or place, including the schools.

I recently discussed this with Dr. I.M. Kookie, a noted expert on a lot of stuff, including religion.

He said: "No, you don't have to pray out loud. In fact, it is better if you don't."

Why is that?

"Well, what if you are praying that the teacher will let you go to the bathroom so you can sneak a smoke? You wouldn't want her to hear you say that, would you?"

I suppose not. But what about the proper demeanor while praying. Is it necessary for your head to be bowed, your hands clasped and the prayer whispered or muttered?

"Not at all. You can pray while looking at the ceiling with your eyes crossed. Or while you are hanging upside down on the monkey bars in the school yard. The Lord won't mind."

How do you know he won't mind?

"Because he hasn't said she minds. And until he sends word, it must be OK. And if she minded, why did he make some people cross-eyed and create monkey bars?"

That's true. But I notice you refer to the Lord as he and as she. Can you explain that?

"Sure. We are created in his image, right?"

So it is said.

"Well, that can mean a lot of things. Maybe he looks like you, bald, a little overweight, a big beak, beady eyes with bags under them."

I'd be flattered.

"Or maybe the Lord looks like Jane Fonda."

An interesting thought.

"Or a New York bag lady."

An even more interesting thought.

"How about a midget?"

Possibly, but I can't picture the Lord as a midget, especially if he is wielding his mighty and swift sword.

"It could be a little sword. But for the sake of this discussion, let us assume that the Lord looks like Ronald Reagan."

That would please Republicans.

"OK, a nice-guy Lord, and he is sitting up there in his heavenly quarters, a California-style mansion with a good view of the universe. And one of his aides comes in and drops a stack of prayer memos on his desk for him to answer. He picks up the top memo and looks at it. It is from a kid who is praying that the school lunch is not the same old bland macaroni and cheese. But the prayer memo says that the kid was picking his nose when he silently made it. Now, what do you think the Lord is going to say?"

Use a handkerchief, I would imagine.

"Nah, what kind of understanding is that? He would know that kids can be disgusting little buggers because he made them that way. So if it is a Ronald Reagan kind of Lord, he gives a little chuckle and says: 'I don't like bland macaroni and cheese myself. Switch that kid's lunch to pizza.'"

Do you really believe that?

"Why not? Unless the Lord is black, in which case he might make it fried chicken. Of course, if the Lord is a black Democratic liberal, that would mean he believes in political correctness and would not order up fried chicken because that is a stereotype, even though it tastes better than macaroni and cheese. But there are other possibilities."

Such as?

"Maybe he or she isn't listening. So it wouldn't matter if the kid prays silently or if the whole class jumps up and down and yells hallelujah. They're stuck with the macaroni and cheese, which might explain why school lunches taste the way they do."

Do you think that is possible that he isn't listening?

"Well, they start off these political convention sessions with a prayer, don't they?"

I believe so.

"And what do they pray for?"

Wisdom. Yes, wisdom has always been in demand.

"I think that answers your question." ∎

Lincolnshire makes lunch a real hassle

THURSDAY, JUNE 23, 1994

Kevin Perkins, 28, is starting to feel like one of those characters featured on TV shows about America's most wanted fugitives.

The first time it happened was last summer. He took his lunch break at his technician's job at MDA Scientific Inc., which is in the prosperous northwest suburb of Lincolnshire.

"I went over to the bank to use the cash station. I got some money, and as I walked out of the bank a police car pulled up.

"The officer told me to step over to his vehicle. He had his arms at his side like he was ready to draw his gun.

"I asked him, 'What's the problem, officer.' He said: 'The bank called and said there was a suspicious character.'

"That shocked me because I had been going to the bank for more than a year and the tellers all know me."

But, Perkins said, the Lincolnshire cop put him in the back seat of the squad car, radioed in his name and other personal information, discovered that Perkins was not a wanted felon and let him go.

Then it was January. Once again, Perkins took his lunch break, walked to the bank and a Lincolnshire cop yelled: "Can I help you?"

"I ignored him and went in the bank. He followed through the door and said: 'Can I help you?' I said: 'Can you help me with what?' He asked me if maybe I needed a ride somewhere. I told him, no, I didn't. Then he asked to see some ID. So I gave him my driver's license.

"Then another policeman came through the door. And they took my driver's license and read stuff off it into his radio. And he again offered me a ride. I told him, no, I don't need your help. So I left and went back to my job."

Now it was last Thursday, and again lunch time.

"I'm walking to Italian Connection, a fast-food restaurant. About a half mile from where I work.

"All of a sudden a police car pulls up and the officer says: 'Where are you going?'

"I said: 'Why do you want to know?'

"He said: 'Perhaps I can take you there.'

"So I told him I didn't need him to take me nowhere. And he gets out of the car and tells me to put my hands on the car and to 'spread 'em.'

"I asked him: 'What did I do?' He pushed me against the car. He asked me for my name on my driver's license, but I told him I wasn't going to tell him anything until he told me why he was doing what he was doing.

"So he put handcuffs on me and put me in the back of his squad car and asked if I had any warrants or felonies he should know about.

"I told him I wasn't going to tell him anything until he told me what I had done wrong.

"So we exchanged some words. He said I was 'copping an attitude.' And I told him, yes, I was having an attitude because I was tired of being stopped by the police for no reason.

"Then he radioed in and the dispatcher told him: 'He works for MDA. You have to let him go.'

"So he let me out of the squad car and took the handcuffs off. Then two plainclothes detectives pulled up and he talked to them and they started hassling me for having used obscenities to an officer. I guess I did say something about this being a lot of bull—.

"So we exchanged words and I told them that if they were going to arrest me, do it. Or else I was going to have lunch and go back to my job.

"When I got back to work, I was kind of steaming and I told our personnel department. And the next thing I knew, the president of the company heard what happened. And he went to the police station with me to make an official complaint. I couldn't believe it. The president of the company doing that for me.

"When we got there, the desk sergeant who took the complaint said to me: 'Hey, don't you remember me? I stopped you too.'

The president of MDA, which services toxic-gas detectors, confirmed Perkins' story.

John McAlear described Perkins as a model employee—well educated, dedicated to his job, a fine work ethic. "You give him the work, he gets it done. What else can you ask for."

He's so dedicated, in fact, that he commutes by public transportation more than two hours each way from his Chicago home.

"I have people who live two minutes away and Kevin is at work before they are," said his supervisor, Frank Gambino.

So why is he always being arrested by the Lincolnshire cops? At this point, he has already been questioned by about one-third of the town's entire police department.

Seeking an answer, we called the police chief, but he was on vacation. An assistant said the matter was being reviewed and he had no comment.

Then we called the village manager and asked if he had any idea why Perkins had so much difficulty in going to lunch without being stopped by the Lincolnshire police.

The village manager said he didn't know, but the matter was being investigated.

"Could the fact that Mr. Perkins is black have anything to do with it?" we asked.

The village manager said he could not comment on that.

Well, even if he can't comment, he might think about it. It's what you might call a clue. ∎

Some cars make dumb statements
TUESDAY, OCTOBER 25, 1988

Although I've never met Frederick J. Schwab, I must assume that he's a big heat in his line of work.

His stationery says he is senior executive vice president of Porsche Cars North America Inc.

I know this because he has sent me a personal invitation to drive one of his Porsche cars. And maybe buy one.

In a burst of enthusiasm, he wrote:

"Imagine yourself behind the wheel of one of the most powerful and exciting automotive machines in the world—a new Porsche 928 S4."

I did as he suggested. I closed my eyes and imagined myself behind the wheel of a Porsche 928 S4.

The imaginary vision didn't do much for me. I could hear my wife saying, as she always does: "Do you mind not smoking in the car?"

Then I saw myself pulling onto the madness of the Kennedy Expressway, being wedged between a giant truck and a '69 Pontiac belching black fumes, and everybody slowing to 5 miles an hour to gape at a family of 12, who share 20 teeth, standing on the shoulder of the road pondering a flat tire on their pickup truck.

As fantasies go, it wasn't much fun, so I opened my eyes and went on with Vice President Schwab's letter.

"We've got one with your name on it, and I want to personally invite you to your local Porsche dealer for a complimentary test drive.

"Come and experience the incomparable handling, the smooth power, the pure excitement of driving this exceptional automobile. Sit behind the wheel and surround yourself with the sleek styling that made Porsche famous.

"However, one word of caution: After you drive a new Porsche 928 S4, you may be compelled to own one."

No, Mr. Schwab, you're mistaken. I will not be compelled to own one.

After receiving your invitation, I called a Porsche dealer and asked how much your 928 S4 doodad costs. He said between $74,000 and $80,000 depending on what accessories I wanted in it.

I told him that for $75,000 to $80,000, the least I would expect to find in it would be a couple of gorgeous blond kraut dollies. The stiff said those were not the kinds of accessories they dealt in. Well, if they did, Mr. Schwab wouldn't have to resort to sending letters to the likes of me.

In any case, he couldn't have picked a less likely prospect.

Not that I'm cheap, but I consider $75,000 to $80,000 a bit steep for a car— even one with "incomparable handling" and "smooth power."

How much incomparable handling and smooth power does one need to get around Chicago? The secrets of survival are to get out of the way of interstate trucks, remember that Friday is drunk-driving night on the expressways and never give the finger to someone with a tattoo on his arm who is driving a clunker that looks uninsurable.

And while I don't want to criticize Mr. Schwab's product, frankly I don't see where they get off charging $80,000 for something that small.

If I was going to throw that kind of money around, I would want something long and flashy—an old-time, fat, bloated, Detroit gas-guzzler. Then, with a big cigar clenched between my teeth and a pinky ring on my finger, I could pass for an alderman or a Mafia elder and get some respect.

But in a Porsche, people would justifiably assume that I was a yuppie who trades pork bellies or soybean futures, since those are the sort of people who buy Porsches. Who needs that kind of humiliation?

As students of the auto industry tell us, once you pass a certain prudent, sensible limit in car buying, you are no longer just buying transportation.

You are making a statement.

My cars have always made a statement. They are covered with bird droppings, soot, grime, salt. The inside is littered with ashes, grimy coffee cups, old newspapers, crumpled candy wrappers and letters I forgot to drop at the corner mailbox.

The statement my cars make is: "Modern life requires that I own one of these things, but I don't have to like it."

But if I bought one of Mr. Schwab's trinkets, I would be making an entirely different statement.

I would be telling the world: "Look, everybody, I have paid $80,000 for a small car that is capable of going 150 miles an hour, although the speed limit is 55 where I do most of my driving. And if I leave it unattended on a city street for more than two minutes, the car thieves will have a tag team match over who gets to steal it. Therefore, the statement I am making with this car is: 'I am a real jerk.'"

Finally, Mr. Schwab, I have to tell you that I cannot buy your car because it is not made in this country. I don't buy cars made in Germany or Japan.

I'm not spiteful, and I believe in letting bygones be bygones. But I have a personal policy of waiting 100 years between wars before doing business.

Write me again in 2045. ∎

At age 350, you can expect senility

WEDNESDAY, SEPTEMBER 3, 1986

Harvard is celebrating its 350th year, and many newspapers and magazines are doing stories about its distinguished history and the great Americans who studied there. Young men who became presidents, senators, scholars and giants of finance, law and literature.

All of this has brought back memories of the first Harvard man I ever met.

I was about 25 at the time and working as editor of the midnight shift at a local news service in Chicago.

One day the boss hired a new reporter fresh out of Harvard. Although he was inexperienced, he had a quality the boss admired—a wealthy and socially prominent father.

Most of us were intrigued by having someone from that school in our midst, since the closest we had been to Harvard was when we covered a fire at 63rd and Harvard.

After a few weeks on days, tagging along with experienced reporters to learn some fundamentals, Charles was assigned to my shift to fill in for a police reporter who was on vacation.

At our first meeting, I was impressed. He wore a genuine Brooks Brothers suit with a vest. Most underpaid young reporters looked like they shopped at Goodwill outlets.

Charles turned out to be a pleasant young man, stout and prematurely balding, with a jovial manner and a tendency to refer to people as "chaps." And he assured me that he could handle any news assignment. I think he said it would be a "cup of tea."

The second night he was on my shift, midnight came but Charles didn't. At 1 a.m., he wasn't there. At 2 a.m., still no Charles.

Then the city desk phone rang and the absent Charles cheerfully said: "The most unusual thing has happened."

Yes, you're about three hours late for work.

"Right. You see, I went to my club for a late dinner."

That in itself was unusual. Most young reporters carried late dinners in a brown bag.

"So after dinner," Charles explained, "I went into one of the reading rooms and ordered a brandy and was sitting in a chair reading a paper.

"I must have dropped off to sleep, and when I awoke the place was closed. Everything was dark. And I had to find the night watchman to let me out.

"You know, the evening manager of my club is a complete idiot for failing to notice me sleeping in that chair."

A complete idiot, I agreed.

"Well, I didn't want you too concerned. I'll be along in a while."

I thanked him for easing my worries.

A few days later, Charles was assigned to spend the night at police headquarters.

About 3 a.m., I received a phone call from a detective who asked me if Charles was one of our reporters.

When I admitted to this fact, the detective said: "We have him in custody."

For what?

"Suspicion of auto theft?"

What? Charles, our Harvard man, a car thief? There must be a mistake.

I sent another reporter to police headquarters to find out what had happened.

It turned out that the detective, who specialized in auto theft, had noticed an expensive new sports car illegally parked in front of police headquarters.

The color and model jogged his memory. He checked the license plate against his current hot sheet. Sure enough, the car had been stolen the previous day.

He looked at the windshield and saw a press parking card with Charles' name on it.

He went up to the press room and asked if Charles was around.

"Pleased to meet you," said Charles, giving the detective a firm handshake.

"You're under arrest," said the cop.

Fortunately, Charles had an explanation. It was, he said, a perfectly understandable mistake.

It seemed that Charles' father rented a fleet of those sports cars for his wife, children and himself.

Charles' car had started making a pinging sound. So Charles took it to the dealer who provided the cars and told a mechanic to tune it up.

"Then," Charles said, "I took another car as a loaner."

Did you tell them that you were taking it?

"I don't think so. I assumed they'd know that I needed a replacement and took one. Can you imagine? The idiots reported it stolen."

Complete idiots, I agreed.

A few days later, Charles left my shift, and within weeks, resigned his job. On his last day, he gave me a firm handshake and said: "This has been fun, but I've decided on law school."

Harvard again? I asked.

"Yes," he said.

Good choice.

That was the last I saw of Charles. But I later heard that he had joined a respectable law firm that had many respectable clients.

So wherever he is, I offer him a distant toast on the 350th birthday of his alma mater and to all of its distinguished alumni.

And after he has the drink, I hope the manager of the club wakes Charles up. ▪

Astaire dances all over Jackson

FRIDAY, FEBRUARY 5, 1993

Having seen every Fred Astaire movie, I'm qualified to say that not once did Fred Astaire grab his crotch. It's possible that he grabbed his crotch in the privacy of his home or dressing room. But that would be of no concern to the public.

I mention this because Michael Jackson, the alleged super-duper star of show biz, has been described by many dance critics as being the Fred Astaire of his generation.

While I'm no expert on dancing, I watched Jackson perform during halftime of the Super Bowl, and I saw little that reminded me of Astaire, other than being skinny.

Their dance styles are not alike. Astaire was always smooth, no matter how fast the dance. But Jackson appears to be suffering from a severe spastic disorder.

Astaire had a bony face that bordered on the homely, but when you looked at that face, there was no doubt he was of the male persuasion.

But when the camera zoomed in on Jackson, I tried to figure out what he looked like. Then it came to me: He looks like an aging female movie star who has had too many face lifts.

That's not a bad way for an aging female movie star to look, but it's unusual for a 34-year-old man. Especially since he selected that look. Either that or his plastic surgeons were goofing around.

The single biggest difference, though, is that Jackson grabs his crotch. As I said, that's something Astaire never did. And from what I've read about Astaire, he wouldn't have grabbed his crotch even if the movie director gave him a direct order. He was not that kind of guy.

Nor did Gene Kelly. Nor did Donald O'Connor, Bill "Bojangles" Robinson, "Peg Leg" Bates nor any of the other legendary dancers. "Peg Leg" Bates never even grabbed his peg.

I watched the Super Bowl with several friends, and the first time Jackson grabbed his crotch, Harry said: "Why did he do that?"

"Maybe the poor kid has got the crabs," Tony said.

When he did it again, Hank said: "Boy, if he's got them, it must be a bad case."

But Harry said: "No, it can't be the crabs because he's not scratching, which one normally does when so afflicted. He's just grabbing, which does little to ease the discomfort brought on by those little beasties."

"Then it must be something else," Tony said. "Maybe he has to go to the john real bad."

We thought about that for a while, then Mitch said: "No, if he had to go to the john real bad, he would cross his legs. But he's bouncing up and down and twitching and flapping his arms like a duck. You don't do that when you have to go to the john real bad. It would just make the situation worse. So maybe he is reassuring himself that it is still there."

"What is still there?" Tony asked.

"His crotch," Mitch said.

"That does not make sense," Harry said. "A crotch is not something you misplace or lose like your wallet or car keys. If his crotch was suddenly gone, he would know it. Such a loss would surely cause considerable pain."

"As well as embarrassment," Mitch said.

"I think I understand why he is doing it," Hank said. "He has a worldwide audience at the moment, so he is using this opportunity to send a message. He is making a social statement."

"Ah, of course," Harry said. "But what statement is he making?"

"I'm not sure," Hank said. "He could be saying: 'Look, world, I have a crotch. Or in philosophical terms: 'I grab, therefore it is.'"

"Could be," Mitch said. "Or is he rebelling against traditional sexual inhibitions by saying, through that gesture, that it is OK to grab your crotch in public."

"Actually," Tony said, "if you did that around a school yard or on a street corner, you'd get arrested. If you did it in my favorite bar, you'd be tossed out the door. And if you did it in front of my wife, I would hammer you in the chops."

"Yes," Harry said, "but maybe that is his point. It is a victimless crime. Nobody is harmed by his grabbing his crotch."

"Neither is sticking your finger in your nose," Mitch said, "but I wouldn't go on TV in front of a billion people and stick my finger in my nose."

Just then, we were joined by Shawn. As you can tell from his name, he is a member of the Baby Boom generation. Thus, he is attuned to popular art and culture.

So we asked him for insights on Jackson's crotch-grabbing.

"Oh, that's quite common, the thing to do," he said. "If you watch MTV, the odds are that someone will be grabbing their crotch. And Michael Jackson isn't the first. Rock performers have been grabbing their crotches for a long time. Nor is Michael Jackson the most renowned crotch-grabber. Madonna is much more widely hailed for that art form. And the audiences are thrilled. Just listen to the roar when Jackson or Madonna grab their crotches. It might be the highlight of their shows."

We pondered that for a while, then Tony said: "We live in a strange world when the most popular male star and the most popular female star get their biggest cheers for grabbing their crotches."

And Mitch said: "I guess it's true—there's no business like show business. So maybe I will stick my finger in my nose." ▪

After the heroics, hustlers take over

FRIDAY, MARCH 25, 1988

How about this as a plot for a thriller TV movie?

There's this sweet little girl, only 18 months old, playing outside her home in a Texas town.

Suddenly, terror. She falls into a hole. It is a deep and narrow abandoned well.

She's alive. The challenge is to get her out of the well, which is not much wider than a drainpipe. There's no way an adult can squeeze in and get to her. And if they try to widen it by digging, she will be smothered.

The rescuers work out a plan and go to work. For three days, they frantically drill another shaft next to the one the girl is in.

Reporters and TV crews flock to the scene. The whole country watches and waits, filled with dread. Will they reach her in time? Will she live or die?

At last, the second shaft is finished, and they tunnel to her and bring her up. She is cold and injured, but alive.

Her parents rejoice. The rescuers hug each other. Much of the nation weeps.

Sounds familiar? Of course. It's the dramatic true story of baby Jessica McClure, who held the attention of the whole country about six months ago.

And the dramatic story goes on, but in a different way.

In a fascinating account this week, the New York Times described how the Jessica story has evolved into something tacky.

The movie people have swooped down on Midland, Tex., with their contracts, deals, money offers and proposed scripts.

They're competing to buy the rights to the story from those who lived the story, the rescuers and Jessica's parents.

And human nature being what it is, the rescuers are now fighting among themselves.

They've split into two groups. One is made up of the official rescuers: the police, firefighters and other public employees. The other group is made up of the volunteers.

Each group is claiming to have the rights to the story. Each group has hired lawyers. And each group is accusing the other of greed while claiming only pure motives for itself.

The Hollywood people are, of course, acting as they always do. Which means that compared to them, a used car dealer is a living saint.

Some want to spice up the story by making the marriage of Jessica's parents shaky. Then, of course, the child's peril and rescue bring them back together, get it?

Others want to create one heroic figure among the 400 people who took part in the rescue. Got to have a star, right?

And while the Hollywood hustlers are making their pitch, the two competing rescue groups are squabbling over who gets what if a deal is made.

Having dealt with Hollywood dealmakers, I know how sleazy they can be. And I also know how lacking in creativity most of them are. Consider what they produce. Without car crashes, naked bodies, blood squirting from severed heads and everybody saying "s—," 9 out of 10 movies wouldn't be made.

So I'm not surprised that they've overlooked a far superior movie plot than the one they've been chasing in Texas.

Let's face it, we all know what happened to little Jessica. That means we all know how a movie about her will end. Do we want to sit through almost two hours of guys digging a shaft when we know the outcome?

Not me. But here's a plot that would be a grabber:

The movie opens with a little girl playing in her yard in a Texas town. She falls into an old narrow well. She's trapped. The rescuers frantically dig a parallel shaft. They tunnel to her and bring her up—cold, injured, but alive. Her parents rejoice, everybody hugs and the nation weeps and sighs with relief.

Right. Same plot. But we do all that in the first 15 or 20 minutes, which is really all it takes to tell that part of the story.

Then the rest of the movie develops. In come the Hollywood hustlers with their contracts, their deals, their big money offers.

And we watch as greed sets in, envy and distrust. All those good old boy rescuers are suddenly in warring camps. Pals who hugged are now ready to duke it out. Everybody is saying: "Where's mine? How big is the pie? Is there enough for everybody?"

The Hollywood hustlers are tripping over each other trying to nail down a deal. And deals are made—but quickly unmade when somebody's agent says they ought to have a bigger piece of the action.

Every so often, we can cut to Jessica's parents warily peering through their curtains at the dealmakers camped in the front yard while Jessica asks: "When can I go out and play again?"

How would my script end? I have the perfect closer.

One of the dealmakers finally gets the names of the rescuers he needs on a contract. Then he persuades Jessica's folks to sign.

He rushes from Jessica's house, triumphantly waving the contract over his head.

And he falls in an old well.

Trust me, it'll work. Everybody loves a happy ending. ∎

Arrghh! Disney walks the plank for politically correct

FRIDAY, JANUARY 10, 1997

A heated debate has taken place in Southern California over whether political correctness has stuck its pointy nose into one of the oldest and most popular features of Disneyland.

It was decided recently that a change had to be made in the sexist behavior of the mechanized creatures who provide the entertainment in the Pirates of the Caribbean exhibit.

Those who have seen this display in either the California or Florida Disney parks know that pirates from a big sailing ship have shelled and overrun a town and are behaving as we have been conditioned to believe pirates did in their heyday.

They are boisterously looting, drinking, eating, singing, swaggering and chasing the town's womenfolk.

But there has long been a subtle difference in the Florida and California shows.

At Orlando's Disney World, the women being chased are carrying food. Those who are inclined to give pirates the benefit of the doubt could believe that the buccaneers are after a hearty meal rather than a roll in the hay.

But at California's Disneyland, the fleeing women don't have food. So a spectator who analyzes the scene might conclude that the pirates are intent on doing "it."

This is apparently the conclusion that was drawn by some spectators, presumably of the feminist persuasion. And they brought their views to the people who run the Disney park.

So it was decided that while the pirates exhibit was closed for renovation, a change would be made.

The fleeing ladies would be equipped with platters of food, making them appear to be waitresses, barmaids, cooks or something of the sort.

Then the pirates might be assumed to be after the food rather than the female bods.

The change was greeted with cheers by feminists and sneers by those who are less sensitive.

Although I have been in both Disney parks more than once—the fate of those of us who can't stop rearing kids—I have to admit that I never noticed whether the fleeing women were carrying food.

If I had thought about it, which I don't recall doing, I would have assumed that the pirates were pursuing the women because they had sex on their minds.

After all, they were low sorts—thieves and cutthroats—who had been cooped up with other men on a ship for who knows how long.

Let us be honest. We all know what pirates were like when it came to women. And accountants, lawyers, carpenters, tree-trimmers and journalists, too.

So what we were seeing in the Disney exhibit were a bunch of scruffy criminals with—let us not mince words—sexual assault on their minds. If they had minds. But of course, being mechanical creatures, they didn't.

I'm sure that Walt Disney, a square sort, wasn't thinking about rape when he personally supervised creation of the pirate exhibit. In his day, the Hollywood pirate was always singing yo-ho-ho and pinching or ogling females, or wenches, as the ladies were called.

But we are in a different era with different standards. About the only way you can see pirates act that way is to watch old films on the American Movie Classics channel.

If you switch over to the up-to-date cable movie channels, there is little pinching or ogling. They don't waste time. The females fling off their clothing and spring atop the compliant male for a few filmed minutes of joyous moaning, writhing and grimacing.

So by today's entertainment standards, the behavior of the mechanical pirates is restrained.

But that doesn't mean that the protesting feminists were wrong. I can understand how a woman might feel, taking her little daughter through the show and hearing her ask: "Mommy, why are those men chasing the ladies?" What does the parent say? "Oh, they want to propose marriage or living together for a while to see if they are on the same page?"

On the other hand, if zealots wanted to make a big deal out of the pirates' conduct, they could question why they are shown guzzling what is obviously booze.

Do we want the kids to see the glorification of drunken bums? Could this not offend those who are going through the pains of a 12-step program?

And if the pirates are assumed to chase the women for the food on their platters, doesn't this make a humorous statement about the serious problem of gluttony? Are those with weight, cholesterol and blood pressure problems supposed to be amused?

So if we start demanding that it be too realistic—or not realistic enough—who knows where these paths might lead?

Remember, these pirates are men who spend long periods of time in the company of other men.

So would it be unreasonable to wonder if some of the pirates might not prefer the company of other men? In more ways than singing yo-ho-ho together?

If so, would not gay men be justified in asking the Disney people to acknowledge them by maybe having a few of the pirates hold hands and do a bit of smooching?

Sometimes life in these strange times is just one can of worms after another. ∎

'Good old days,' bad old attitudes

TUESDAY, AUGUST 18, 1992

"I like this Republican pitch about bringing back traditional family values," said Slats Grobnik. "Yeah, those were the good old days."

What good old days are you talking about?

"When my wife zipped her lip."

What kind of family values are you talking about?

"Hey, don't you remember? There was a time when a guy could give his old lady a whack in the head without having it turned into a federal case."

You condone wife abuse?

"Well, not every day. I'm no insensitive mug, you know. Only when it's needed to keep peace and quiet in the family. And in the good old days of family values, a woman didn't run out and get a lawyer and break up the family."

That's true, the divorce rate used to be much lower.

"Sure, because she knew what side her bread was buttered on. She'd have to go out and get a job. But there weren't lots of jobs for women, so she took her lumps like a man or a good woman and kept the family together."

A heart-warming observation.

"Yeah. A guy used to go to work, come home, and supper was on the table. Or if he wanted to stop for a few pops after work, that was his right, right?"

I'm not sure there is anything in the Bill of Rights about the happy hour.

"It should be. Now what ya' got? My kid comes home from work. Does his wife have dinner on the table? Not a chance. It ain't gonna be on the table until he puts it there because sometimes she works longer hours than him, so he has to share in the cooking. And you know what else she does? Sometimes she stops with the girls after work."

Uh, they don't like being called girls.

"Yeah, I know. Or Doll, or Baby, or Honey, or Cutie Pie. And you can't even say a babe is a bimbo even if she is a bimbo."

Of course not. You should not be making moral judgments.

"See? You don't believe in traditional family values. In the good old days, we was always making moral judgments. Like if there was a chick in the neighborhood and she was what we used to call 'easy,' then we used to call her a bimbo or even a slut. Now, there's a word you never hear anymore. Slut. But back when we had traditional family values, we called a spade a spade and a slut a slut."

Some people might say that was cruel.

"Hey, sometimes you needed a little cruelty to keep those traditional family values going. Like if you had a kid who didn't have no respect. So you might have to whack him around a little. That was your business. Now you might get some busybody calling up some social worker outfit, and the next thing you know, you're in court for a child-abuse rap. Or maybe your own kid will sue you. How can you have family values when you can't even use your own property the way you want?"

But there are those who don't consider a wife or a child as property.

"Yeah, that's because of the liberals. It was the liberals who made it so I can't give my wife a jolt when she needs it. Now if I do it, she's out the door. And she can get a job. If she was younger, she could even become a cop or a fireman, instead of staying home and cooking my supper and ironing my shirts like God meant her to do. And, poof, there goes the family, and the values. Jeez, she could even get to be a bartender."

What's wrong with that?

"You got a short memory, pal. What was it, about 25 years ago, a woman couldn't tend bar in Chicago? Not unless her father or husband owned the joint. Then the liberals stuck their noses in, and the law was changed, and you go in a joint now and you can't even swear the way you want to because there is a babe behind the bar. Like that one over there."

There's nothing wrong with that woman being a bartender. She has a child to support.

"Yeah, and I happen to know that the kid ain't legit."

That is none of your concern.

"Well, in the good old days of family values it would have been my concern. Everybody in the neighborhood would have been giving her and her kid the old fish eye. And it would have said on the kid's birth certificate that he wasn't legit."

Another cruel practice that was eliminated.

"Yeah, it got changed because of more heat from the troublemaking liberals. By the way, I happen to know that she's shacking up with that guy at the end of the bar."

Who is?

"That female bartender. The unwed mother, as we used to call them."

Yes, they live together. They have been for a long time. It is nothing unusual, and they seem quite happy. By the way, people don't refer to it as shacking up anymore.

"See? In the days of traditional family values it was called shacking up. And you sure wouldn't invite somebody like them over to the house for pinochle. And that kid would be the biggest disgrace in the schoolyard. Those were the days."

I really doubt that many Americans want a return to those sorts of traditional family values.

"Then what kind of values are the Republicans talking about?"

I'm not sure. Maybe something along the lines of the old Andy Hardy movies.

"The ones with Mickey Rooney?"

Yes, he played Andy Hardy.

"Then I'm all for those traditional values. He was a great guy."

Yes, Andy Hardy was a fine character.

"Nah. I meant Mickey Rooney. He had six wives. He knew how to treat 'em." ▪

Clinton's big lead easily explained in age of indulgence

THURSDAY, MAY 16, 1996

Why would anyone be surprised that President Clinton has a huge lead in all the political popularity polls and would win by a landslide if the election were held today?

The answer is so simple and obvious, and it has nothing to do with political ideology or executive capabilities.

The glib, youthful Clinton is almost the perfect man for these fast-paced times and the future. But the grim, aging Bob Dole is a carry-over from a past that to many Americans is gone, except in the grainy films shown on the American Movie Classics channel.

We know that television is the most powerful of all political tools. Clinton was born into the TV age. He knows when to be softly serious, when to grin and chuckle, when to be bold and play the statesman, when to feel our pain and when to whip off a crisp commander-in-chief salute.

And he can do any of the above in a snappy 10-second sound bite, nibble or hickey—whatever the script requires. He can even play rock on his sax and gyrate his hips with considerable soul.

He would make a masterful daytime talk-show host, possibly the equal of Geraldo or Oprah.

In contrast, Dole was already a grown man and a heroic war casualty before TV began shrinking the national brain. He has never bothered to learn the art of the 10-second bite, much less the nibble or the hickey. I can't think of one industry that would hire him to sell its product on the tube. Well, maybe hernia trusses. If he dances, it has to be a dignified fox trot.

Then there are their voices. Clinton's voice is high-pitched. Dole's is much deeper.

Does that matter? You bet it does. Clinton has a voice for today. Just listen to popular rock music. All of the singers have high-pitched, eunuch-like voices. It's almost impossible to tell the men from women, if there is any difference.

There was a long-gone time when a baritone such as Perry Como or a bass such as Vaughn Monroe topped the hit charts; when a deep-voiced singer would bellow: "Old Man River, that Old Man River, he don't plant taters, he don't pick cotton."

But today, the lyrics would have to be changed to "Old Person River, that Old Person River, he or she does not plant potatoes or pick cotton because the work is demeaning."

And today's deep-voiced singers are found only in the country music field, self-pitying losers groaning about their two-timing women going honky-tonking and leaving them with a sink full of dishes and not one beer in the fridge. Their fans will be too hung over to vote.

If anything should have delighted the Clinton backers, it is a couple of non-traditional political polls that were widely reported.

One asked who people would trust to baby-sit their kids. The other asked which candidate they would ask to choose the toppings for their pizza. Clinton easily outdistanced Dole in both polls.

This tells us that most American parents are indulgent and wouldn't want someone such as Dole telling their kids: "Sit down, shut up, turn off the TV, eat your vegetables. I will tell you a story about the government bureaucrat in wolf's clothing that ate children who didn't finish their dinners." They would prefer someone who would gently say: "I feel your pain, I feel your diapers, have another Twinkie."

It also tells us that most Americans don't know much about pizza if they would trust a guy from Arkansas to pick their toppings.

These silly polls were brought to my attention by an angry Dole supporter who said: "Why doesn't someone do a poll in which they ask people this question: 'Who would you ask to walk down to the OK Corral with you—Clinton, the slick draft dodger, or Bob Dole, the pain-wracked World War II combat soldier?'"

Nice try, but a poll that asked such a question would be inconclusive.

That's because this is 1996, and most of the answers would be something like:

"I'm not asking anybody to go there with me because I have no intention of walking down to the OK Corral. It is not my fight, and I'm not going to get involved. And if anyone tries to involve me, they will hear from my lawyer."

A far better measure of true voter sentiment would be a poll in which people were asked: "If you wanted to borrow money from someone with no intention of ever paying it back, would you bring your hard-luck story to Bill Clinton or Bob Dole."

It would be a landslide. ∎

Designer label flies in face of tradition

WEDNESDAY, JUNE 14, 1989

I'm not fashion conscious, but while sitting around a back yard party, I couldn't help but notice the young man's fashionably rumpled and baggy black trousers.

It wasn't that they were shaped like the trousers that we called zoot suits during my youth—wide in the knees and narrow at the ankle.

In those days, zoot suits were worn by street toughs and sissies who wanted to be mistaken for street toughs. Now they're popular among yuppies. I guess this is known as cultural evolution.

But what caught my eye was something on the front of the trousers.

At first, I thought he had dribbled some food on himself. Then I realized it was some sort of white label, about an inch long and half an inch wide.

So I said: "Excuse me, but you seem to have some sort of label there on the front of your trousers."

"Yes," he said, "it's the designer label."

"But it is on the fly of your pants. On the crotch. Why do you have the name of the designer on your crotch?"

With the clear logic I admire in yuppie creatures, he said: "Because that's where the designer put it."

Of course, how stupid of me.

However, my curiosity had not been satisfied. I said: "What is the name of the designer."

He said: "Why don't you take a look."

I prefer not to study anyone's fly at close range. Republican National Chairman Lee Atwater might spread rumors. But the young man's wife was standing nearby, and she did the honors.

"It says: 'Girbaud,'" she told me. That figured—a Frenchman. You won't find anybody named O'Malley or Szamanski sticking their names on somebody's fly.

I'm familiar with the practice of clothing makers putting their names on garments, although it is usually on the hind end. I refuse to buy such products. My position is that if Calvin Klein or Mr. Levi or the others want to use my bottom for advertising purposes they should pay me just as they'd pay for a billboard.

But this was the first time I had seen a designer's name on someone's crotch.

To determine why they do this, I contacted the New York office of this Girbaud outfit.

A spokeswoman named Joni Fiori said the designer-crotch pants have become quite popular among people ranging from their teens to their 50s, but they've hit it biggest among people in their 30s.

Or as she put it: "It's very thirtysomething," which made me glad to be very fiftysomething.

Joni did concede that the crotch is an unusual location for a designer label.

In fact, she said, "I'm like fixated. I find myself staring at people's crotches."

An interesting fixation. I'm sure some people think it strange. On the other hand, this fixation might also help her make the acquaintance of many lonely young men.

"Hi, miss, I notice that you're staring at my crotch. Would you care to come home for dinner and meet my mom?"

As a loyal employee, Ms. Fiori wears the company's product, and she says: "People do look at you kind of askew, and I have to explain to them that I work for the company that puts the label on the fly."

This confused her mother. "I remember the first time I wore them, my mother said they made a mistake and I should take them back."

But the question remains: What is the logic of putting the name of the product on the crotch?

The answer was provided by Girbaud publicist Richard King.

"It's just a little difference, and that subtlety can make all the difference in the world. Like a tie, as the fashion changes, so does its length."

True, but I have yet to see anyone dangling a tie from his fly.

King said Francois (Girbaud's first name; why aren't any designers named Wally?) put the label in front to be different. But he conceded that it could be suggestive.

"Francois said he has a particular preference for something unique, but there may be something subliminal about putting a label right over the crotch. Maybe it's like an open invitation."

An open invitation? A rather bold fashion statement, I'd say. But what does the guy do who doesn't have a Girbaud crotch label? I suppose he could just drop his trousers, although that would be less than tres chic.

However, this fashion trend has given me an idea. I might take a few pairs of trousers to a tailor and have little labels sewn on the fly.

Then when someone stares, they will read:

"This is my fly. Don't you feel silly looking?" ∎

Dillinger would be 2-bit criminal now

FRIDAY, MARCH 12, 1993

It's hard to believe that John Dillinger was once the best-known criminal in America.

And that his fame lives on. Movies have been made and books written about his crime career. His biography is in almost any encyclopedia.

To this day, crime buffs stand in front of the Biograph Theatre on Lincoln Avenue and say: "Wow, that's where the FBI gunned him down."

How big a story was it, when he was killed? Under the giant headline of the

July 23, 1934, Chicago Tribune—"KILL DILLINGER HERE"—were three Page 1 stories.

And the index listed these stories inside:

- Dillinger's audacious crimes and his spectacular escapes captured the imagination of the public like no other criminal in American history. Page 2.
- High points in the life of John Dillinger from his birth in Indianapolis in 1902 to his death in Chicago last night. Page 2.
- Attorney General Cummings 'gratified' by shooting; Chicago agents praised. Page 2.
- Highlights in the career of America's most dreaded criminal. Page 2.
- Crowds gather at morgue to catch glimpse of Dillinger's body. Page 3.
- Examination at morgue reveals Dillinger had seared his fingers with acid. Page 3.
- Two eyewitnesses tell story of slaying. Page 3.

And not only in Chicago but all over the country. It was the end of the most sensational crime career of its time.

So why am I telling you this? To illustrate what a terrifying, wacky society we have become.

By today's standards of criminal behavior, Dillinger was a nickel-and-dime guy. If he were killed today, he probably wouldn't rate more than five paragraphs on an inside page, if that.

We're talking about a thief, not a killer. Sure, a higher-class thief than most because he robbed banks rather than 7-Elevens. But a thief, nevertheless. His bank-robbing career brought in about $300,000, which he had to share with his gang. Even if you consider inflation, he didn't make as much as recent savings and loan swindlers.

Today, we don't even consider bank robbery news. Last year there were 9,381 banks, S&Ls and credit unions robbed of $61 million. The death toll: 16 robbers, six bank guards, one bank employee, one customer. How many did you read or hear about?

And Dillinger was once ranked by the FBI as America's Public Enemy No. 1.

Now compare what Dillinger did to what you have been reading about or seeing in your newspaper the past week or two:

- An anti-abortion demonstrator, wearing a gray business suit, waits outside a Florida clinic with other protesters, then takes out a gun and puts two bullets into the back of a physician who performs abortions. Earlier, the killer said he prayed that the doctor would "give his life to Jesus." He apparently decided to speed up the doctor's spiritual transition.

- In Waco, Texas, a religious nut and his loony followers use their huge arsenal of military hardware to kill four federal agents. At last report, it was a standoff. Inside the compound, the head loony says he is waiting for God to tell him what to do; outside the compound, there are military tanks. The tanks are needed because—who knows?—the loony might say God told him to bring out the bazookas.
- In New York, they are rounding up suspected terrorists for blowing a huge hole in the world's second-tallest building. The explosion, the smoke, the chaos, were so dramatic that within a few days we forget that at least five people were killed. That's five more than Dillinger did in.

Those are the main crime stories of recent days. There isn't enough space in the papers or time on the news shows to deal with the run-of-the-mill street gang killings, the dope-deal murders, the punk gunman who robs a grocer then shoots him between the eyes to see if the pistol really works, the morons who toss their girlfriend's kids out of windows.

A few weeks ago, the big story was the mass murder of seven people in a fast-food restaurant in Palatine. And there were the random highway killers in Florida. But those crimes are already dim history. It's been shoved aside by bombs in New York, the gun-toting messiah in Texas and the bible-quoting doctor killer in Florida.

Just for a moment, let's forget Dillinger and switch to Jack the Ripper, who is probably as famous. He's been the subject of at least 100 books, thousands of magazine articles, several movies and millions of words in newspapers.

What did he do? He was a fiend, no doubt about it. He roamed London's seedy section about 100 years ago and carved up a number of prostitutes. He was never caught, but he has become a lasting symbol of evil and danger.

Compare him to our modern mass killers. Unlike the weirdo in Wisconsin, Jack the Ripper never cooked and ate his victims. Unlike John Gacy, he didn't bury them in his suburban basement. And he didn't slaughter entire families because a dope deal didn't go down.

We live in the greatest country in the history of the world. And everything else considered, maybe the craziest.

A final thought on John Dillinger. Whatever mischief he may have done, and it really wasn't that much, he never once said that Allah, Jesus, the Lord or even the devil told him to do it.

God bless the lad for his self-sufficiency. ∎

Just the fax paper, ma'am, not the facts

The young woman behind the checkout counter in the electronics store said: "May I have the last four digits of your telephone number?" She was looking at the computer and her fingers were poised over the keyboard, ready to type in my data.

Her question caught me off guard. All I was doing was buying two rolls of fax paper, not exactly a big-time purchase.

And I was holding a $20 bill in my hand. Not a credit card or a check. Cash on the barrel head.

So I responded with a question of my own:

"Huh?"

Again she said: "May I have the last four digits of your telephone number?"

I had to stop and think about that. She was young and attractive. I am not young and . . . well, I am what I am. So I had to assume that she was not after my phone digits for reasons of impropriety.

After giving it a bit of thought, I said: "No."

"No?" She looked a bit bewildered.

"That's right, no."

There was a long moment of silence. And again she said: "No?"

I said: "Look, I have selected these two rolls of fax paper. I want to buy them from you. Is that OK?"

She nodded, but still looked doubtful.

So I said: "I will give you money. You take my money. I will take the two rolls of fax paper. Then we will have a deal. Is that OK?"

I said all of this in as pleasant a tone as I could muster. Having worked behind bars, counters and other such places, I know it is not the best way to spend a day, so I am never unpleasant to those who are in what we laughably call the service industry.

She nodded again. But I could tell that she didn't care much for my pitch.

"This is what I call a business deal," I said. "I want this fax paper. It makes my life easier because I don't have to deal with the drug heads, boozers and ruling bureaucrats who lounge at the U.S. Postal Service.

"And I will give you money. Cash money. No checks, credit cards or other forms of IOU. Hard cash. Reduces paperwork for both of us. I give you money, I take the two rolls of fax. We will then have a deal. Can you live with that?"

She nodded. By her eyes, I could tell she now thought she was dealing with the sort of demented person who makes the evening TV news, and probably feared that in a moment she would be taken hostage.

I tried to ease her fears.

"Look, when I was a kid, my family was in the tavern business and I tended bar. The neighborhood men would come in and have a shot or a beer, and maybe both. We never asked for their phone numbers. In those days, half of them didn't have phones, anyway. We just poured the drinks, took their money and life went on. It was a simple business deal.

"Later I worked at an outdoor sausage stand on Western Avenue. I would make an Italian sausage or beef sandwich, with or without peppers, and it was a straight cash deal. We never asked names or phone numbers. It would have offended the customers, and they might have cracked our kneecaps."

Her nodding became more vigorous. And she glanced at the phone. I think she wanted to make a mad dash to call the cops.

"Really," I said, "I'm not trying to be difficult. It's just that I don't believe that in order to buy a couple of rolls of fax paper, I should share personal details of my life. I bet if I give you part of my phone number, you will want my name. And my address."

"We're supposed to ask," she said, pointing at a poster on a nearby wall.

It was from the president of the corporation, explaining why his company wanted my name and address.

He said he wished to give me a good deal. He could send me catalogs and other puffery about when I could pick up a bargain. And he vowed never to sell my name and address to anyone else.

I had no reason to distrust the president of this national chain of electronic stores. But I was not persuaded. I didn't have his phone number, and I would bet it was unlisted.

And I would also bet that if I tried to phone him in his office, I would wind up talking to a public relations person. (I know that is true, because I later tried.)

So here he was, asking me to provide all of this personal information so he could bend the back of my hard-working postman with a lot of dumb mail about electronic junk I don't need.

After reading the message from the president, I turned back to the young lady behind the counter and said:

"I want the fax paper. Do you want my money?"

She nodded and took the $20 and gave me my change.

"Nice doing business with you," I said, as I headed for the door.

"Yes," she said. But I'm not sure she meant it. ▪

Some numbers will just kill you

THURSDAY, NOVEMBER 22, 1984

My sister sounded depressed. Earlier that day, she happened to drive past our mother's old house. "It's gone," she said. "It looks like it burned down."

That was no reason to feel bad, I told her. If anything, the fire was a civic improvement.

The last time I was there, about two years ago, the house was still standing. But it had become an outpost for the Insane Idiots or some other such gang.

When I stopped my car and got out for a sentimental look, the various louts who were draped across the porch or hanging out the windows scattered like roaches. They apparently mistook me and a large friend for narcs.

I thought about the house and the neighborhood after listening to Mayor Harold Washington's number-jugglers try to justify cutting the size of the police department.

They say that in recent years, the city's population has been shrinking, while the police force has remained just as big as it used to be.

If you believe as they do—that in numbers there is truth and wisdom—it stands to reason that the police force should now get smaller.

But in the words of Inspector Wang, a fictional detective: "Only one thing wrong with your theory: It's stupid."

Consider the neighborhood I just mentioned, only a stone's throw from Humboldt Park. Or, as measured today, only a bomb's throw.

In all the years we lived there, I can remember only one street murder.

Oh, there was violence. Energetic tavern brawls. Post-softball game fights. Even neighborhood gang confrontations.

But nobody was killed. The worst damage was usually a split lip, a cracked tooth or a broken nose.

And we had our share of criminals. The neighborhood produced some of the city's leading career burglars and car thieves, although they usually went somewhere else to steal. Not out of community loyalty. There just weren't many diamond brooches to be found near California and North.

But in general, it was a safe neighborhood. Kids could wander around. Women could go to a store at night. A young guy and his girlfriend could take a stroll to the Crystal Theater on a warm summer evening. Teenagers could walk a few blocks over to the next neighborhood to get a hotdog from Nick the Greek's pushcart.

And on hot nights, something happened that now seems hard to believe: People slept in the park.

Nobody had air conditioning. So hundreds of families would leave their sweltering flats, carry blankets and pillows into the park, spread out on the grass and sleep until dawn.

Today, if you see somebody lying on the grass in Humboldt Park at 3 a.m., call the cops, the paramedics and the undertaker. He's surely got a blade in his ribs or a bullet in his bladder.

The whole area is now a war zone. The streets and alleys and parks and gangways and doorways belong to the Insane Idiots, the Deranged Disciples and the Latino Lunatics.

Nobody says "put up your dukes" anymore and settles for a bloody nose as the mark of victory. Step across the wrong street or give somebody the wrong salute and it's the fast draw and a bullet in the head.

On Friday or Saturday nights, the hospital emergency rooms look like a scene out of "M*A*S*H." Except nobody is laughing.

When I was a kid, one cop could have taken care of the whole neighborhood. Now, one cop wouldn't be *safe* in the neighborhood.

It's not just Humboldt Park—it's big hunks of the entire city. Much of the South Side, the West Side, the long strip of meanness through the entire North Side.

Sure, the population has grown smaller. But it's also grown nastier. There are more guns in the hands of more crazies, young and old. The sociologists can try to explain why. What matters is that it has happened.

And if this city needs anything, it needs more, not fewer, cops on the street.

So pay no attention to the arguments of number-jugglers in City Hall. They can juggle all the numbers they want, but I'll give them a few numbers to remember:

He was 6-8. Three gang punks stopped him on the street in broad daylight. One punk fired a .22. He lost 10 liters of blood.

He was dead at 17.

I don't know how a smaller police force is going to get rid of those kinds of numbers. ∎

Old story is news to Baby Boomers

THURSDAY, DECEMBER 3, 1992

The sobbing came from the next booth. Glancing over, I saw an attractive couple, tears streaming down their cheeks and dripping on their veggie lunch plates. And I spotted the source of their grief.

On the table was the latest copy of Newsweek, with a cover story revealing the shocking news that countless Baby Boomers have reached or are now approaching middle age. This issue of the magazine has traumatized many of those born in the 15 years after World War II.

"It's so cruel and unfair," the woman gasped.

"Yes," said the man. "I don't know if I can cope."

Then they saw me staring and the woman shrieked: "Look, it is an old person, an ancient."

The man indignantly said: "Hey, you have frightened my companion. The least you can do is cover your face."

Draping a napkin over my head, I apologized for intruding and asked if I could be of any assistance in their time of sorrow.

"No," he said, "there is nothing you can do or anyone else. As incredible as it may sound, I am going to turn 40 in a couple of days. And she will do the same next month."

That admission brought on another fit of sobbing. When it subsided, she sighed and said: "And just when we're getting through that, we pick up this magazine and discover that some day we'll have to become 50. It says so right on the cover. How much bad news is a person expected to endure?"

But we all go through it. I once turned 40.

They stared suspiciously. "I don't believe that," she finally said.

It's true. Did you think that the rest of us were always middle age or elderly?

"As a matter of fact, yes," she said. "Weren't you born that way? I mean, as far back as I can remember, people like you have looked old. Are you trying to say you were once young?"

Sure. Did you think yours was the first generation to experience aging?

He nodded. "We thought this was some sort of new disease that was infecting only Baby Boomers. I was going to write my congressman and demand to know why the government isn't spending more money to find a cure. But you say it actually happened to you once? Turning 40?"

Absolutely. Happened about a year after I turned 39, as I recall. Back in 19-something or other. Way back before the CD, the PC and even the VCR. But it was after the LP, FM and TV.

Leaning forward, he said: "Tell me, what was it like? How did it feel? How did you cope?"

Don't remember.

"Ah-hah, it was so painful an experience that you have blocked it out of your memory."

"No, I simply forgot it like most other birthdays."

"That's impossible," he said. "How could you possibly forget something like that."

Easy. You see, there was a time when turning 30, 40 or 50 was no big deal. Sixteen was a big deal because you could get a job. And 21 was a very significant milestone because it meant you could order a drink without worrying about being carded. But 30, 40 or 50 just quietly happened to people. Magazines didn't put it on the cover like it was a national crisis. And every columnist who turned 40 didn't write about his or her new age of enlightenment. You just got up and went to work, or went outside the cave to fight a dinosaur.

The woman said: "Are you trying to tell us that this sort of thing has been going on for a long time?"

Oh, sure, for centuries, since before recorded history.

Becoming angry, she said: "Then why hasn't anything been done about it? How could you just sit there and let it happen?"

But there isn't anything that can be done. You're born, you have birthdays, you turn 30, 40, 50 and so on, if you're lucky. And then, phfft.

"Phfft?" he said. "What do you mean, 'phfft'?"

I mean, phfft: The bell tolls, we have our exits and our entrances, the long sleep, adios amigos. You know, phfft, and it's all over.

He looked shocked. "You mean actually dying? Like in the movies and on TV shows, but for real?"

That's it. Happens all the time, and in the best of families too.

She waved the magazine at him and said: "Was there anything about that in here?"

He shrugged and said: "I didn't get that far."

"Well, isn't that a fine kettle of tofu," she said. "How can a person make vacation plans?"

They were silent for a moment, then he grinned and said: "You're just trying to scare us, aren't you? A real kidder."

I'm afraid not. But don't worry. You have a lot of time left. With modern medicine and diet, you're a good bet to make it to 80.

His eyes narrowed in deep thought, then he took out his portable wallet-sized computer, called up a spread sheet, punched in some numbers, studied the results and said: "He's right. Eighty is 40 plus 40, so we've used 40 but we have another 40 left. Not bad."

She looked relieved and said: "Then we can plan that vacation."

"Yes," he said, hitting more keys, "and it looks like we'll have time to pay off the credit cards."

Having eased their concerns, I paid my check and left.

While walking away, I heard him chuckle and say: "You know, I still think he's just a kidder."

She said: "Who?" ∎

CHAPTER 10
Ain't Too Proud to Beg

As I mentioned in the introduction, Dad ignored his editors' requests to write a column about the Tribune's charity drive for his first couple of years at the paper, a reflection of the ambivalence he felt during his transition. But when he gave in, he produced columns far outshining the usual "good cause" pieces most of his colleagues created. While there are a few instances of repeated quips and references, he managed to find a variety of ways to make the pitches entertaining.

The first time he acquiesced, it was at the end of a "Letters" column, and it isn't hard to tell who really wrote the tongue-in-cheek letter. —D.R.

Some letters ripe for the spiking

THURSDAY, DECEMBER 11, 1986

Letters, calls, complaints and great thoughts from readers:

Chip Kaliher, Arlington Heights: Which of the following do you personally find most disagreeable: aldermen, bumpkins, chess players, MBAs, mullahs, wimps, yuppies or Green Bay Packers?

Comment: What I find most disagreeable are grown men with names like Chip.

Lynn Sagrillo, Forestville, Wis.: I read your recent column on Green Bay's "football thugs."

There is one point you missed. At least in Green Bay, the thugs are confined to the football field.

In Chicago, the thugs run loose on the streets.

Comment: True, but in Chicago I have yet to hear of a street thug spiking someone's wallet.

Tom Kochanski, Cicero: You have a lot of gall belittling Green Bay. . . . What would you know about Green Bay?

I lived in Green Bay for many years. I go back every year to visit friends. There is absolutely no reason to label Green Bay as a backwoods town because of one football player's actions.

Compare Chicago corruption to Green Bay. Compare Chicago bribery to Green Bay. Compare Chicago crime to Green Bay.

Comment: Yes, we're better at all that, too.

Lon Bishop, Milwaukee: Although the stupid remarks by the mayor of my city provoked your remarks, I found your allegedly humorous observations about Green Bay and Milwaukee to be offensive.

To hear you, Green Bay is a hick town where everybody hunts deer and wears long red underwear, and all we do in Milwaukee is drink beer and burp.

For your information, Wisconsin is not a hick state. You will find restaurants that serve continental cuisine in many cities and stores that provide the height of fashion.

I don't believe you have spent much time in Wisconsin. If you had, you wouldn't have made all those ill-advised remarks.

Comment: I have been in Wisconsin hundreds of times. The last time I was there, I went in a restaurant and ordered meat loaf. The waiter said, "We don't serve French cooking."

M.J. Davis, Cleveland: What is wrong with the news media? Aren't you happy unless you are trying to drive a president from office?

What is it that President Reagan has done wrong? He has tried to make friends with Iran. Is there something wrong with that?

Just because he didn't blab his plans to the press, everybody is jumping on him. Why should he tell the press anything? You'll just lie and distort it anyway.

If I had my way, everybody in the media would be locked up in jail or put against the wall and shot. We'd be better off without the whole bunch of you. You just destroy our freedoms.

Comment: Look, Ron and Nancy, if you're going to write to me, don't use phony names.

Helen Watson, Chicago: Why is there such a big fuss about where to build a new "world-class" central library in Chicago? Most of the people in this city don't read anyway.

Just take a look at the neighborhood libraries and see how many people are actually using them.

They're not. People are watching television. Those who read books buy them. And most of the books on the best-seller list are trash anyway.

If you gave people a choice between a new library or cable TV, they'd vote for the tube.

It's a myth that we need a "world-class" central library. We're just wasting money on a fancy building to store books that nobody's going to read.

Take a poll of your readers. Ask them how they feel about books.

Comment: I did as you suggested and asked Slats Grobnik whether Chicagoans care about books. He said: "Of course we do. If you don't know a book, how you gonna put a bet on a football game?"

J. Warren, Chicago: I am a person of considerable means, and at Christmas time I always feel slight pangs of guilt because I have so much while the poor have so little.

I've tried to find ways to alleviate these feelings of guilt but haven't found a satisfactory solution. One of my friends said that I should go among the poor and give them money. That doesn't appeal to me because while I have compassion for the needy, I don't care to associate with them. I have a dread that being poor might be contagious.

Yet, I feel that at Christmas time I should do something to help them, if for no other reason than that if the poor become too dissatisfied, they might revolt and take what I have. Then I'd be poor, and I have little experience at it and probably wouldn't survive one cold night. So how does someone such as myself make himself feel better with a minimum of discomfort or embarrassment.

Comment: The perfect solution for people such as yourself is to send a check to Chicago Tribune Charities Christmas Fund, P.O. Box 5120, Chicago 60680. Besides helping the needy now, next April you will have the warmth and satisfaction of writing it off your income tax. ∎

A straightforward approach to giving

TUESDAY, DECEMBER 8, 1987

Those who believe in the great media conspiracy won't believe this, but in the 24 years I've been writing a column, no editor has ever told me what I should or shouldn't write about.

With one distasteful exception, and this is it.

As some of you may have noticed, this paper runs a Christmas fund for the needy.

So the editor suggests to all the columnists that we do one piece putting the arm on the readers for contributions.

Now, I don't mind giving my own money. Actually, I do mind, but I do it anyway because I don't want somebody looking at my tax return and thinking I'm a cheapo.

But for several valid reasons, I object to using an entire column for a purpose that could be interpreted as an act of kindness and charity, which makes my friends laugh at me.

First of all, almost all such columns are boring. By the time a reader gets to the third paragraph and realizes that he's being suckered into reading about the needy, the hopeless, the downtrodden, the hungry and the destitute, he says: "Oh, man, I don't need this kind of downer."

And he promptly turns the page, seeking a story about murder, lust or political mischief—something to brighten his spirits.

I'm convinced that the only people who enjoy reading stories about the downtrodden and needy are social workers. And that's because the stories reassure them that they'll keep their jobs.

It also bothers me that our society spends 11 months of every year hustling a profit and saying of the needy: "Yeah, if they'd get off their butts and go to work, they wouldn't be mooching off me. They should do what I did—get a job in my father's company."

But along comes December, the lights twinkle, Bing Crosby starts mooing about a White Christmas, and suddenly these same people are saying: "Oh-oh, Christmas time. I better find a good deed to do."

A few years ago, a woman called me a week before Christmas. She was distraught because she wanted to invite an orphan to her home for Christmas dinner. But all the social agencies said their orphans had already been booked.

"What can I do?" she asked.

I told her to wait until July, when the demand for orphans had subsided.

She said: "But it isn't the same in July."

That's why I almost never write sappy, sentimental Christmas columns. Nor do I read them or watch any of the alleged classic Christmas stories.

For example, there's the ever-popular O. Henry short story about the poor but devoted young couple—the husband with the fine pocket watch his father left him, and the wife with the long gorgeous hair.

She wants to buy him a splendid watch fob, so she sells her beautiful tresses to a wigmaker. Meanwhile, the husband sells his fine watch to buy her an expensive, ivory comb.

So she winds up with a comb but little hair, and he gets a fancy fob for a watch that's gone.

The dips. If they were going to sell her hair and his watch, they should have used the money for a week at a Club Med like any smart Yuppies would have done.

Then there's Dickens and the bum rap he put on Scrooge, who was no worse than T. Boone Pickens, Lee Iacocca or the other leading money-stackers of our era. There was nothing wrong with Scrooge that a good sleep therapist couldn't have cured. As for Tiny Tim, I still think the kid was faking that limp so he wouldn't have to take out the garbage.

I can think of only one sentimental Christmas column that I've ever written, and that was many years ago.

It was about an old neighborhood friend of mine who finished work in his factory job on Christmas Eve, had a couple of drinks at the company party, then drove home through Humboldt Park.

As he went past the frozen lagoon, he saw kids on the ice. Then he saw one kid fall through.

A crowd gathered, but nobody knew what to do. My friend leaped out of the car, tore off his jacket and dashed onto the ice. He fell through, too, but he rescued the kid.

When he got home and stopped shivering, he phoned me. It made a good story. Especially the part about discovering that while he was in the water, somebody in the crowd stole his pay envelope and Christmas bonus from his jacket.

Anyway, I'm sorry to have put you through this, especially if you've read this far, which I doubt.

But if you feel guilty for being prosperous, you can ease your middle-class conscience by using the form printed below to send a few bucks into the fund.

But please, don't tell anyone I asked you to do it. I have a reputation to uphold. ∎

Giving probably won't hurt anyone

FRIDAY, NOVEMBER 25, 1988

Do-gooders sometimes ask me to write columns hustling money for the poor, the downtrodden and the needy. I always tell them to bug off.

Not that I lack compassion. I have a tad of it, although the average prison guard probably has more.

But experience has taught me that most people don't want to read about the poor and the downtrodden. Such columns make them feel depressed.

If I depress them often enough, they'll quit reading my column and I'll be out of work. Then I'll become poor and downtrodden. I can handle that, but my wife couldn't, and she'd quickly dump me for some guy with oily hair, a gold chain and tickets to a Club Med.

However, over the years I have made a few exceptions to my rule. And I'll tell you about one of my most successful fund drives.

It happened about 20 years ago, when I worked for the Chicago Daily News.

There was an unfortunate young woman who lived in the Taylor Homes housing project. She had three kids and a husband who dumped her.

One evening, she was on the sidewalk and saw a man shot to death by a street gang.

The gunmen were brought to trial. The woman was the key witness. She was put on the stand and asked to identify the murderers. But she refused to testify.

The judge demanded that she describe what she saw. She said she couldn't. The judge asked why.

She said that if she testified, the gang would surely kill her. And she wasn't going to make orphans of her three children.

The judge warned that he would hold her in contempt and jail her. She said jail was better than a grave, so the judge ordered her locked up.

I went to the jail and interviewed her. It was heart-rending. All she wanted was to live in peace. Her dream was to move from the Taylor Homes to a decent apartment, away from the violence. Buy some decent furniture and warm clothes for her kids and raise them properly. That wasn't asking a lot.

So I wrote about the case, rapping the judge and asking readers to kick in a buck or two to help her achieve her dream.

The judge, who disliked publicity, decided he couldn't keep her in jail forever and released her.

Within three or four days, readers sent in about $3,000. With inflation, that's probably $8,000 in today's dollars.

I phoned and asked how she wanted the money delivered. She took the CTA to my office, wearing an old housedress and a cheap coat. She wrapped the money securely in a sack, thanked me and left.

The money kept coming. In a week, there was another $2,000. I again called her.

She arrived wearing a slinky red dress, spike heels and a coat with a fur collar. She was with a tall young man who wore what was then known as a Super Fly outfit. He didn't smile or say much.

They took the money and left. I figured, what the heck, after what she'd been through, she was entitled to a little fling.

That was the last I saw of her.

But a few weeks later, I was in a bar that was a hangout for off-duty cops. Two of them struck up a conversation and said:

"That was a nice thing you did for that woman from the projects."

I thanked them.

But they added: "There's one little problem. She hasn't moved out yet. You know why?"

Maybe she was having trouble finding an apartment.

They said: "No, we worked on that case. And she's still there because she's War Lord for the gang that killed the guy. She's the gang's Big Mamma. That's why she wouldn't testify. See, he was a member of the gang, too, but he was giving her a bad time. She had him hit. We couldn't prove it, but we know it. So I think you've been had, pal."

I later checked with other cops on the case and the prosecutor's office. They said the same thing. As one of them put it: "You are the patsy of the year."

It crossed my mind to ask the lady for a refund. But I figured she and her Super Fly friend might be offended.

Anyway, that experience is one reason I avoid do-gooderism.

However, there's an exception. Every year at this time, the editor gives my arm a twist and asks me to put in a plug for a worthy cause.

It's for the Chicago Tribune Christmas Fund, which helps needy children, the hungry, the homeless and the mentally retarded.

Since today is the day when America begins its annual Christmas spending orgy, I thought that some of you might want to put aside a few bucks to help those who are truly needy.

The coupon is right below. Fill it out, and send a check.

I guarantee that none of it will go to any Big Mamma War Lord. At least I hope it won't.

Ah, what the heck, take a chance. ∎

Me first, second, third, fourth . . .
MONDAY, DECEMBER 18, 1989

Once a year, the executives of this newspaper ask me for a favor. They want me to put the arm on you for a few bucks for charity.

The first time this happened, I said: "I don't think you starchy underwear types understand. I am a fan of the late Feodor Chaliapin."

One of the managers said: "Who is he?"

"Are you a holder of MBA degree?" I asked.

"Yes, with pride," he answered.

"Then your abysmal cultural ignorance is to be understood. To enlighten you, Feodor Chaliapin is considered to be one of the greatest, if not the greatest, basso profundos who ever rattled the rafters."

Clearing his throat, he said, "Hmmm, and what is a basso profundo."

Pathetic. So I explained that a basso profundo sings in a very deep voice. Because I have a very deep voice, I'm partial to them. Unfortunately, most singers who are popular with the masses today have such high, squeaky voices, I suspect that certain manly parts of their anatomy have been snipped off.

Also, in most operas the basso profundo sings the role of a villain, a rogue, a mean guy. Since those are my basic instincts, I'm usually the only person in the audience laughing when he commits his dirty deeds.

"All this is interesting," the executive said, "but what does this have to do with our seeking your help in raising funds for the Christmas fund?"

"I thought I made that clear. I am an admirer of Chaliapin."

"I'm sorry, I still don't understand."

"Then I'll enlighten you. Many years ago, when the great Chaliapin was at the height of his world-renowned powers, his manager booked him for a performance in Paris.

"In those days, this was no small journey. He and his entourage—flunkies, in the corporate jargon—had to travel by slow train all the way from Moscow.

"When he finally arrived, he asked his manager how much he was to be paid to sing for all those perfume-soaked, snail-eating Frenchies.

"His manager told him that it was a charity benefit performance. Chaliapin said something like: 'I come all dees way on train to sing for noddink?' The manager pleaded that it was for a worthy cause.

"Chaliapin said: 'I am worthy cause. I no sing for noddink and you are fired, dumb-head.'

"And with that, Chaliapin got back on the train and went home. There were a lot of unsold frog legs at that opera house, I guarantee you."

The executive said: "He must have been a stone-hearted man."

"Yes, today he would probably have an MBA and be the deepest voice on Wall Street. But now you understand why I can't solicit readers for charity. I would betray my devotion to Chaliapin and his many admirable qualities. Of course, if you want to give me 10 percent off the top of anything I raise, I might see my way clear to. . . ."

"No, no," he said. "You see, one of the fine things about our efforts is that we have virtually no overhead. Virtually everything that comes in goes to the needy."

"Well, I thought it was worth a try. But, like Chaliapin, I must be on my way. I cannot subject my readers to a weepy, blubbery appeal to their generous natures. If they had generous natures, they wouldn't be reading me in the first place."

The executive looked stricken, which is the way I like to see them. He whimpered: "Isn't there anything you can write that will help?"

I hate seeing a grown man whimper. No, that's a lie. I enjoy it. So I said I'd try to think of something.

And I have. Here is my pitch.

If you are a kind-hearted, gentle, generous person, who is concerned about the plight of our society's unfortunates who have less and are in genuine need, then you've probably given already and don't need me to goose you.

Who does that leave? The rich and selfish, the comfortably greedy, the me-first indifferent. My kind of guys.

So as one louse to another, let me put it to you this way. Think of it as insurance, protection money.

Imagine what would happen if all the poor really got frustrated and angry. They would rise up, storm your palatial dwelling, strip you of your ill-gotten BMW, your high-tech stereo, your multi-disk CD player and carry off your mink-draped chick. Even worse, they might take the mink and leave the chick, who would then dump poor, penniless you.

To avoid this living nightmare, just tear out the coupon printed below, write a check and send it in quick. Then you can turn on your burglar alarm and get a good night's sleep.

Oh, and it's tax deductible, which always feels good.

There, I've done my part for a worthy cause. And I feel so good about it, I think I'll listen to an old Chaliapin record. Oh, those Frenchies who bought tickets that evening must have been steaming. ▪

Season's greetings from Scrooge's pal

TUESDAY, DECEMBER 18, 1990

It's time for my annual begging, mooching, sniveling, blubbering column of gooey Christmas cheer.

If you're smart, you'll stop reading and move on to something more entertaining, such as stock tables, because I'm going to put the arm on you for money for a worthy cause.

This isn't my idea. I don't believe that columns should be used for worthy causes. It's the columnist's role to spread hatred, distrust and make people hyperventilate.

But this newspaper wishes to be a responsible corporate member of the community. Despite its rather somber, sober manner, it wants to be thought of as loving, caring, kind and gentle.

So every year the executives ask the columnists if we will write something to twang your heartstrings and goad you into writing a check for the Chicago Tribune Holiday Fund, which gives money to the needy.

They ask us to do it because they can't do it themselves, since they all have grim faces and wear charcoal gray overcoats, charcoal gray fedoras, wingtip shoes, and look like certified public accountants. They even wear their fedoras and wingtip shoes to bed. So who would give money to them?

That's why they stick us with the mooch job: Columnists have kindly, honest faces. And we don't wear our wingtip shoes to bed. Only our socks.

So they want us to write wimpy, bleeding-heart columns about how we should all do something to help our less fortunate fellow man during this, the season of joy. And that's supposed to bring a tear to your eye and a check to the fund.

But I can't do it. I'm sorry, but I've never seen a reason to get sappy and sentimental because merchants string gaudy lights along Michigan Avenue, or because some of my former neighbors put plastic wise men and mangers on their lawns.

Especially since the neighbors were intolerant. One year, I decided to outdo them. I gathered a group of my tavern friends together, including one very short fellow, and they all dressed up in exotic, ancient Eastern garb and stood on my lawn. We draped some shaggy rugs on a few stray dogs to make them look like barnyard animals.

When cars went by, my friends waved at them. I thought it was an impressive display, especially when the real short fellow sat up in the manger and held a beer can aloft. But the grouches down the block called the cops and they insisted that we cease and desist. And there is supposed to be religious freedom in this land? Hah.

And cable TV has made the season even worse, because now it is impossible to get through one evening of channel clicking without stumbling across Scrooge and Bob Cratchit and Tiny Tim and that crowd.

Actually, it's a good story, but most people don't understand it.

There was nothing wrong with Scrooge's flinty attitude. Until he turned into a wimp, he was a smart, hard-nosed businessman, and if we had more like him today the Japanese wouldn't be buying all our golf courses.

When Scrooge had all those bad dreams, he should have spent a few bucks on a sleep therapist. Then he could have fired Cratchit and had a clear conscience; told his smart-aleck nephew that he had written him out of his will; and forced the truth out of Tiny Tim. The truth, in case you have not read the Dickens memoirs, was that there was nothing wrong with Tiny Tim's legs. He just faked being gimpy so he wouldn't have to take out the garbage, the lazy kid.

If it was up to me, I would ask readers to contribute to a special fund for the saxophone player.

In case you haven't heard him, the saxophone player hangs out on Michigan Ave., across from the place I work. And all day he plays "Jingle Bells" over and over again, exactly the same way every time. Because the tall buildings create an echo chamber, it's as if he's blaring right in my ear. Since the beginning of December, I've heard him play "Jingle Bells" exactly the same way—in a polka up-tempo—2,185 times.

What I'd really like to do is ask people to contribute to a fund so I would have enough money to hire thugs to snatch him from the street, stuff him in the trunk of a car and drive him out to the suburbs where the executives of this newspaper live. And force him, at gunpoint, to play "Jingle Bells" in front of their houses all night long.

Then we'll see how loving, kind and gentle they feel, the stiffs.

Anyway, the coupon is right under the column. If you feel like it, send a check. There's a chance your name will be printed in the paper so you can show your friends how kind and generous you are, although they'll just laugh.

But just so you don't think I'm a complete grouch, I leave you with this final Christmas thought:

It's tax-deductible. ∎

This begins with a true story about our drunken uncle—Frank Duckman, my maternal grandfather's twin brother. —D.R.

Ok, uncle, Mike's jingling the bell

FRIDAY, DECEMBER 6, 1991

I had an uncle who sometimes drank too much. Actually, that's an understatement. For years, he was a helluva lush. And a nasty one. There was the time he and his girlfriend had a spat and he threw her out of his flat. This can happen in a relationship. But in uncle's case, he threw her by way of a second-floor window. Fortunately, she landed in a soft snowbank. She left him for good, though, saying the magic was gone.

For years, uncle was a city bridge tender. And he always worked the late shift. He preferred being at his job during those lonely hours because the taverns were closed anyway.

However, his bridge-tending career ended one night when he raised a bridge and passed out before he lowered it. It was an hour or two before a supervisor arrived and found him snoring. He was fired, despite his argument that all the other bridges were in place and people had alternate routes.

Somehow he ended up at a Salvation Army shelter, where he dried out. He not only got his eyes uncrossed but found religion. And he stuck around the Salvation Army center, doing odd jobs and pouring coffee into other wayward boozers.

But the best part of his new life was manning a pot and clanging a bell. He would go out during the Christmas season and spend hours in the cold, clanging the bell and saying: "Thank you, brother" or "Bless you, sister" to those who dropped coins in his pot.

He would come over every Thanksgiving and talk about how pumped up he was for the coming bell-clanging season. And he would look across the table and say something like: "That's your third glass of wine, huh? Just keep it up. One of these days you'll be ringing a bell too." He was a fun guy at dinner.

He'd stop by at Christmas too. And he'd say something like: "How many eggnogs is that? Yeah, when I go, I'll leave you my bell. You'll be ringing it." Because of him, I became the only sneak eggnog drinker in the family.

He was ringing his bell almost to the end. And the last time we talked, he said his only regret was that he didn't leave a bridge up years earlier. He also repeated his prediction that if I didn't mend my ways I would some day clang a bell. Then he was gone, the family's only full-time do-gooder.

So in respect for his memory, I am going to now clang a bell. Sort of.

As you have probably noticed, this paper indulges in an annual orgy of do-gooderism. It raises money for all sorts of worthy causes through its Tribune Holiday Fund.

(I think it does this because the Tribune used to be known as the voice of Midwestern Conservative Republican Isolationism and Inhumanity to the Downtrodden, and it has a guilty conscience.)

However, the executives here have a problem. They can't ask you for the money themselves. They know what many of you would say:

"Why are you asking me for money when your parent company is stupid enough to pay $3 million to pitchers who only win one game all year?"

I know you would ask that because I ask that same question myself. In fact, I have suggested that they demand that all of those millionaire Cub pitchers go stand on corners with a coin pot and clang bells.

When I made this proposal, someone in a gray fedora and wingtip shoes—I don't know his name since every executive here looks the same to me—said: "We can't make them ring bells. Their arms are too sore."

Imagine that. Three million a year and they are too frail to clang a bell. And there was my uncle, with icicles on his nose, doing it for three squares a day and a flop.

Uncle leaves one bridge up in the air and he loses a job. These pitchers walk the bases loaded and give up a home run and then send another $100,000 paycheck to their brokers to invest in blue chips.

Anyway, the gray fedoras have asked me to twist your arm, and I've done it. There's a coupon at the bottom of the page. You can fill it out and send in a few bucks. If you've done anything nasty lately, it will make you feel better. That's cheaper than going to a shrink.

OK, uncle, wherever you are. I clanged the damn bell. ∎

Charity is fine, but let's talk about . . .

TUESDAY, NOVEMBER 24, 1992

It's remarkable that in one week there should be two scientific advancements that will fantastically enhance the sex lives of millions of Americans.

First, there was the announcement of the new pill that will increase the potency of men of all ages, even the elderly, by 200 to 300 percent.

As the developers of that pill said: "In tests of more than 1,200 men of all ages, the results were astonishing. One 85-year-old man turned into an absolute jack rabbit."

Then came the announcement of the development of the Orgasm Patch, designed to be worn by women. Tests show that when wearing the patch, even the most sexually inhibited women experience gratification unheard of anywhere but in the Forum Section of Penthouse Magazine.

The patch will soon be on the market under the brand name. . . .

Got you, didn't I? If I could take a readership survey, it would show that 99.9 percent of all those who began reading this column, made it this far.

No, there is no new sex pill or sex patch. I told a sleazy lie just to get your attention.

But before cursing me and slamming the paper to the floor, hear my excuse: I lied for a worthy cause.

As some of you have observed, every year at this time the Tribune engages in an orgy of do-gooderism.

Throughout the paper are pleas for readers to "Give From the Heart," by sending contributions to the Chicago Tribune Holiday Fund. The money goes to help children, the hungry, homeless, other needy.

Every columnist is asked to join in, and most do because they have warm hearts and are decent people with throbbing social consciences. They know how to write columns about the unfortunate that will bring a tear to a reader's eye and a choked sob from the throat.

On the other hand, I have a heart of stone and have no more conscience than Jack the Ripper. I can't write heartwarming stories. Heartburn is my product.

But I take part because I try to have a cordial relationship with the executives who run this outfit.

We have an arrangement. They permit me to dress like a bum, turn my office into a slum and be rude to readers who phone when I'm taking my afternoon snooze. Also, they never make suggestions as to what I should write about. That's probably because they don't read what I write anyway. They like reading spreadsheets.

All they ask in return is that once a year I put the mooch on you for their Holiday Fund.

The fund is important to them for two reasons. First, it is a fine charity with not one penny spent on administrative costs. Second, it eases their guilt for being well-paid executives, most of them Republicans to boot. Not that they feel very guilty about their condition. If they did, they'd enter therapy and seek a cure.

So that's why I resorted to cheap trickery to get you into this column. But admit it—would you have read more than one sentence if I began by saying: "Today's essay is about a worthwhile charity and why you should contribute to it." You'd have yawned and moved on.

Now, let me make my pitch. There are additional benefits you receive for giving to this fund.

First, the Tribune prints names of all contributors in the paper (except those who wish to remain anonymous).

Think about that. Most people never get to see their names in the paper unless they are politicians, disk jockeys, murdering fiends, members of the British royal family, weirdo rock musicians, newspaper columnists and other disreputable characters.

The only time the average decent law-abiding citizen gets in the paper is when his death notice is printed, and it's too late for him to see it.

So why wait for that sad day? Here's your chance to see your name in print. You can all have a lasting memorial to your generosity, suitable for framing.

The other part of my pitch is this: The Tribune Co., which owns this paper, also owns the Chicago Cubs. It is trying to persuade a young pitcher named Greg to remain a Cub—working every fifth day—for about $32 million.

I own a paltry few shares of Trib stock. So I give you my word that if he accepts their deal, I will go to the next stockholders meeting and represent all level-headed people by saying to the board: "Are you people nuts?" It won't do any good, but I'll feel better and maybe you will too.

You'll also feel better if you use the coupon below.

There, it's done for another year. And, who knows, maybe next year there actually will be a miracle pill and patch, and won't we have fun? ▪

Honest—it's just like in the movies

TUESDAY, DECEMBER 14, 1993

This is a true story.

Several years ago, I was walking down Michigan Avenue on a cold evening. A poor wretch sat against a building rattling a tin cup.

In a tired voice, he said: "Help a needy person, sir, and you'll have good luck."

But I was in a hurry. I was on my way to meet a beautiful movie actress (you would instantly recognize her name) for a candlelight dinner. She had arranged the evening because she hoped to persuade me to write a screenplay for her.

So I didn't pause to drop some coins in the poor wretch's cup.

In a few minutes, I was in a cozy French restaurant sitting next to the movie actress. She was even more stunning in person than on the screen.

That may be why my hand shook when we clinked our champagne glasses together and she wet her lips and fluttered her eyelashes at me. This caused the glass to slip out of my hand and the champagne to splash across the front of her dress.

I quickly grabbed for a napkin to dab her dress. She mistook my intention, slapped my hand and said: "Don't be so aggressive, you naughty fellow."

Embarrassed, I pulled my hand away. In doing so, I knocked her water glass over. I tried to grab it, but instead I knocked the candle over, causing hot wax to splash down her considerable cleavage. With a shriek of pain, she jumped up. I grabbed an ice cube and dropped it down the front of her gown, thinking it would soothe the wax burns.

"You boor, you moron," she shouted.

I tried to make amends by attempting to retrieve the ice cube. Again she mistook my intentions and slapped my face.

Then she turned and dashed from the place to her waiting limo. I slumped into a chair, and the maitre d' approached and said: "Will Madame not be with us tonight?"

"I guess not," I said, "so I'll dine sad and alone."

"Come with me," he said, leading the way to a tiny table between the kitchen's swinging door and a dirty dish bin.

I looked around and saw the other diners pointing at me, snickering and giggling.

Before I finished dinner, I had a terrible toothache. And I could feel the flu coming on.

Walking home, I felt a pain in my foot. I could tell I was developing a corn.

Then I passed the same poor wretch. Again, he said: "help a needy person, sir, and you'll have good luck."

I stopped, turned around, came back and stuffed several dollars into his cup.

"Bless you, kind sir," he said.

The toothache began fading away.

So I added a five-spot.

My foot stopped hurting.

I followed the five-spot with a 10-spot. Suddenly my feverish brow felt cool.

As I walked on, I heard his voice: "Good luck will follow you, and a Merry Christmas."

The next morning, I was awakened by the ringing of the phone. It was the beautiful actress. In a soft voice, she said: "I want to apologize for my shameful loss of temper last night. I have not slept a wink, I feel so bad. I hope you don't hate me too much."

I told her: "Hey, forget it. Like I always say, life is too short to hold grudges. Let's do it again some time. But without the ice cube, he-he."

"You are such a mature, understanding man," she said, which showed that besides being a knockout, she was a good judge of character.

So we did a repeat on the dinner, and the evening went off without a hitch, if you know what I mean.

And later, when my schedule permitted, we spent a week or so on her yacht cruising those sultry little islands in the Bahamas. But I won't bore you with details. You've seen one sultry little island with a beautiful movie star, you've seen them all.

Anyway, I learned something from that experience. If you ignore the needy, as I did, you can have really bum luck.

But if you help the needy, as I did when I had a second chance, your luck can change.

So if you're smart, you'll clip out the coupon below this column and send a contribution to a wonderful cause—the Chicago Tribune Holiday Fund, which helps thousands of needy people.

Thank you very much.

P.S. The editor just returned this column to me and said he didn't believe a word of it and that I should write the truth. OK, I made up a little bit of it, such as the business with the beautiful movie star. But the part about the panhandler and the toothache was true.

Look, would I have dragged you this far if I just rattled a tin cup? ∎

Studs was Studs Terkel, the Pulitzer Prize–winning author, broadcaster and good friend of Dad's. —D.R.

Do yourself a favor, pull out the wallet

FRIDAY, NOVEMBER 25, 1994

Once again it's time for the distasteful chore of mooching off readers without sounding like a weepy, hand-wringing, blubbering do-gooder.

I must because all the other columnists do. If I refuse, the executives will whisper that I'm not a team player.

They'd be right, of course. I've never been a team player. That's why my favorite sports are fishing (me against the mighty bullhead), pinball (me against tilt) and arm-wrestling (me against the wife).

So this isn't easy. When I began this work many years ago, a wise old editor told me: "This is Chicago, so never write warm and cuddly columns because they will make the readers puke. Remember, you don't see many cute bunny rabbits in Chicago, but the rats survive."

Words to live by, and I have. But the mooching must be done, so let's get on with it.

I won't preach or tell you what your contributions to the Tribune Holiday Fund will be used for. Take my word, it's a worthy cause.

Instead, I will give you practical, hard-headed reasons why you should send in a few dollars. Here we go.

If you are rich, you should give because history tells us that if the needy become frustrated, they might rise up and storm your palatial home to loot, pillage, ravish, burn and carry away your womenfolk and graphite-shafted golf clubs. To save a trifling sum, are you willing to risk losing all the rewards of success you worked, cheated and lied for? Send a check before an angry mob drags you to a wall. Think of it as revolution insurance.

If you are not rich but not poor—sort of in the middle—you should give because you can list it as an income tax deduction. Do you want the fat cats to hog all the loopholes?

If you are a conservative, you surely believe that private charity, not tax-squandering government programs, should provide for the needy. OK, this is an excellent private charity, with hardly any overhead. So put your money where Jesse Helms' fat mouth is.

If you are a liberal, you know deep in your heart that you are really a nice, caring, compassionate, sensitive person who loves the downtrodden and shares their pain, although you would feel lost without them. You definitely should give because if you don't, you are a fraud and I will tell Studs on you, so there.

If you have a guilty conscience for having mistreated your fellow man or woman, you should give because it will ease your guilt without leaving you with a terrible hangover and not knowing where you parked your car.

If you don't have a guilty conscience about anything, then you are either a saint or a sociopath. If you are a saint, you are dead or broke. In either case, you are off the hook. But if you are a sociopath, you should give generously because there's always a chance that some day you will stand before a judge, accused of some foul deed, and your lawyer can wave around the canceled check to show that you are one swell guy.

If you are one of the many who bought those amazing toenail clippers that I recommended, you owe me because I brought comfort and ease to your life.

If you didn't buy the toenail clippers, then you have a spare $2.95, so send it in and maybe a needy person can tend to the needs of his toes.

If you are a politician, judge, socialite, industrialist, financier, disc jockey or a celebrity of any sort, this is a warning: You'd better kick in right now, and I'll tell you why. I scrutinize the names of all the people who give, and if you aren't there I will use the vast power of this column to destroy your careers and ruin your lives and leave you miserable and destitute. Among those who didn't give in the past were Richard Nixon, Herbert Hoover, Ivan Boesky, Michael Dukakis, Al Capone, General Custer, Dan Rostenkowski and that Bobbitt fellow. Look what I did to them. I warn you: I am pitiless and vindictive, so save yourself a lifetime of grief. Remember, I enjoy being cruel. So give generously and ruin my day.

If you've come this far, you are an easy sell, and all you have to do is clip out the coupon, send in the trump and you will be assured of going to heaven. And if you don't make it, well, I lied. ▪

Fund donation works better than a street handout

THURSDAY, DECEMBER 7, 1995

Because of superstition, I seldom stiff a panhandler unless I suspect he is Walter Jacobson on a quest for ratings.

Nor does it matter to me what the panhandler plans to do with my small gift.

I was with a stuffy colleague one day when an old guy shuffled toward us and made a raspy request for a contribution.

His eyes looked like two festering wounds. His hands trembled, and his stubbly chin was nicked from failed attempts to shave.

Before I could get the usual dollar out of my pocket, my companion shook his head and said: "I'm not going to give you money to spend on liquor. But I'll tell you what I'll do. I'll go in that diner and pay for a sandwich and coffee for you. How about it?"

The guy looked sad and said: "But coffee makes me nervous."

So I quickly gave him two bucks, and as we walked on, my companion said: "You're not doing him any favors. He's just going to buy a bottle of cheap wine."

Which was ridiculous. Of course I had done him a favor. The man was clearly in touch with his body and its needs. What he needed most was a touch of old skull popper to settle those millions of humming nerve endings.

Besides, he might not buy a bottle of cheap wine. He could wait and save enough for a bottle of cheap vodka. Had I thought of it, I might have given him an extra dollar and urged him to buy a few olives to drop in the vodka bottle. Then he would have a martini, which is more socially acceptable.

In any case, what he didn't need was a mini-lecture on what he needed. The do-gooders and reformers have done enough harm to guys like him.

If you look around Chicago, you'll see that we no longer have a genuine, identifiable, established Skid Row.

We used to have a fine Skid Row on West Madison Street. Block after block of flophouses, cheap liquor stores, greasy spoon diners and a Salvation Army office.

Everything, in fact, that a full-time or even a part-time lush needed.

Then the do-gooders, with prompting by sly real estate developers, decided it was a blight and had to go.

So they urban-renewed it out of existence, depriving all the boozers of inexpensive housing, reliable liquor and food prices and plentiful companionship.

And they deprived the machine precinct captains of a core of reliable voters who asked nothing more than a bottle of muscatel for doing their civic duty.

People like my pompous companion fail to appreciate the many qualities of your basic no-nonsense panhandler.

This man was honest. He didn't come up with any far-fetched story about needing train fare to visit an ailing relative back on the family farm.

No, he needed a drink, and he knew that we knew he needed a drink. So by not trying to con us, he demonstrated an admirable faith in his fellow man. We'd need fewer lawyers if everyone was as forthright.

And by having the personal initiative to hit the streets and panhandle, he was not a burden on government and the taxpayer.

Which brings me to one of my gripes about our tax system. We are supposed to be able to deduct charitable contributions for tax purposes. This encourages us to do something for the needy. Yet, I can't deduct the $2 I gave to that guy. Or any of the many similar contributions I've made over the years.

Is that fair? Can anyone deny that this poor stiff is any less needy than those who get a wide range of government handouts and don't even say thanks?

I once suggested to my accountant that we deduct my street contributions. He said no because I would risk the terror of being audited and not having proof that I gave some lush a couple of bucks.

So I've been thinking about printing up some simple receipts that say something like this:

"This is to certify that I (blank for name) received a street contribution of (blank for amount) from this kind gentleman for the worthy purpose of helping me avoid a bad case of the shakes and snakes and ending up as a burden on society. Sincerely yours, (blank for signature or X)."

But in the meantime, if you want to help someone and get a tax writeoff, too, you might consider clipping out the coupon below this column and sending a contribution to the Holiday Fund.

It helps thousands of needy people. Who knows, maybe some even have the shakes. ■

It's time to help others before the 2nd helpings

THURSDAY, NOVEMBER 28, 1996

Oh, joy. Now it begins again. The holidays! Frenzied shopping, recorded voices pounding our ears with elevator music about a white Christmas, chestnuts roasting and that deer with a hangover-induced red nose.

Forced smiles from those who pretend to be cheerful while getting more and more depressed. And Scrooge, a practical businessman still maligned and misunderstood on TV every night. He should have sued Charles Dickens.

Then there is the turkey. Millions of Americans hate turkey. We are the ones who have been intimidated by cholesterol-obsessed doctors into avoiding sandwiches made with salami, corned beef, liverwurst and other manly foods. So all year, we obediently chew turkey sandwiches at lunch. We're not even permitted to douse them with ketchup or mustard because condiments are salty, which the docs warn is a blood pressure no-no.

Now the holidays begin, and what do we get—more turkey. Why couldn't the Pilgrims have eaten pork shanks with dumplings and red cabbage? Or prime rib and a baked potato with sour cream? If only the early settlers had been carefree Italians instead of uptight WASPs. We would all be eating lasagna, sausage with green peppers and garlic bread.

It wasn't always like this. There was a time in another life when I worked at a place that provided me the means to a cheerful holiday season.

That's because every year at this time it would launch a reader participation called "My Most Unforgettable Christmas."

Readers would write in with their most unforgettable tales. Most of the stories were touching, poignant, almost certain to bring a sentimental tear to the eye.

But the person who handled all of these stories would keep a folder of those stories that were a bit eccentric.

And every few days, she would drop a folder with these stories on my desk, and I would share them with my readers.

That's how I got the story of John H., who recalled as a little boy being taken to a neighborhood department store to get up on Santa's knee to tell him what he wanted.

And how, on Christmas Eve, his mom told him to trot down to the neighborhood tavern and tell his dad to come home for dinner.

And how, when he walked into the neighborhood tavern, he saw his dad duking it out with the very same Santa Claus on whose knee the boy had sat.

It is still one of my favorite "unforgettable Christmas" stories.

Then there was Sidney, whose father was a machine precinct captain. And just before Christmas, the father and little Sidney would drive around the precinct and little Sidney would go to the front doors of loyal Democratic voters and give them a turkey.

And years later, Sidney recalled ringing the doorbell of one little bungalow. A young man opened the door, and little Sidney introduced himself and handed the young man the turkey.

And, as Sidney told it, the young man turned around and yelled: "Hey, pa, there's some little Jew here who wants to give us a turkey."

But this paper doesn't solicit poignant stories. So that leaves me with the most unpleasant chore of the year: putting the mooch on readers to kick in to this paper's do-gooder charity.

I figure this is as good a time as any since many of you are sitting there, filled with food, drink and contentment. Vulnerable.

Now, think of those who have so much less while you have so much more.

And think of what might happen if you don't write a modest check and send it in with the coupon printed below.

I'll tell you what might happen: Those who have less might get fed up and rise up in a revolution—storming into your neighborhood, your home, looting, pillaging and carrying off your womenfolk.

Do you want that to happen? Maybe your womenfolk do, but you don't. So think of your contribution as survival insurance.

And this is a good time to do it since you probably haven't gone out and blown your wad on a new computer that will just make your life more complicated.

One other thing: By giving, you improve your chances of going to heaven. Don't you want that? Believe me, it is true. When you arrive, just tell them Mike sent you. Really, not one person has told me they were turned away. Clout. Don't leave this world without it. ∎

CHAPTER 11
War—Been There, Done That, Seen It, Hate It

Dad saw action in Korea with the Air Force. However, he wasn't exactly military material. If you'd like to read about his experiences, observations and attitude about life in the service, pick up "Royko in Love: Mike's Letters to Carol" (University of Chicago Press), a series of letters he wrote to his future wife, my mother, from the base he was transferred to after the war ended. It's vintage Royko, at age 21. —D.R.

War's toll doesn't end with last bomb

FRIDAY, SEPTEMBER 25, 1992

There was this squib of a news story that came over the wires the other day. It wasn't much longer than a baseball box score or an interview with a rock star about his next tour. It said:

"Boston (AP)—The death rate among Iraqi children rose dramatically in the months after the gulf war, largely because of an outbreak of diarrhea caused by disabled water and sewage systems, researchers reported today.

"In the first seven months of 1991, about 46,900 more children died than would have been expected, according to a study in the New England Journal of Medicine.

"It said the death rate for children under 5 was triple that before the war.

"The study was conducted by Dr. Alberto Ascherio of the Harvard School of Public Health and other researchers from the United States, England, New Guinea and Jordan. It was paid for by the United Nations Children's Fund.

"The researchers said they worked independently of the Iraqi government."

That's it. About 15 lines of type.

But then, it's old news. The war has been over for a year and a half. The parades have ended, the yellow ribbons have been taken down and the last proud, chest-thumping speech has been made.

Still, if you like numbers, 46,900 is an interesting figure. And you can play with it in different ways.

For example, there are baseball and football stadiums that have a seating capacity of about 46,900.

So we might try picturing one of these stadiums with every seat occupied by a child 5 years or younger.

Try it. Close your eyes and imagine Comiskey Park in Chicago or Shea Stadium in New York with a little kid in every seat.

That's a lot of noisy kids.

Now, imagine that somebody pulls a switch and sends a jolt of electricity into the seats and every one of those 46,900 noisy kids dies.

That would be a lot dead kids. So you'd better open your eyes, since it isn't a pleasant thing to imagine.

Or we can look at it another way. The biggest hotel in the world is in Las Vegas. It has 4,000 rooms.

So if you put 11 kids in each room, you'd have stuffed the place with 44,000 kids. Put the extra 2,900 in the grand ballroom.

Let's imagine that someone pushes down on a plunger, setting off a huge explosion that blows the hotel away, really flattens it.

Now that would rate more than a squib of a story. It would be front-page headlines all over the world: "Hotel explodes killing 46,900 children."

Which just shows that bad water leading to diarrhea and other intestinal disorders doesn't have the dramatic impact of an explosion, although the results are the same.

Or we can play with the number another way.

The average daily attendance at Disney World is 72,233.

Of course, all 72,233 people aren't there at the same time. Some come in the morning and are gone by mid-afternoon. Some come in the afternoon and leave when the big parade is over.

So let's take a guess and say that at about 2 o'clock on an average afternoon, there are about 46,900 people there, many of them children.

And a terrible thing happens. A giant meteor comes roaring out of space and lands smack dab on Disney World, leaving nothing but a giant crater. (Scientists say something like that could happen, but it's a zillion-to-1 shot, so don't change your vacation plans.)

Now that would be a super-big story. It would stun the world and would go down in history as one of the greatest disasters.

Which shows that if you want to make history, get hit by a meteor instead of stomach cramps.

Which also shows that there is more to modern wars than that which the Pentagon allows us to see on CNN.

What we see on TV is kind of fun, all those videos from high above of targets far below suddenly blossoming like tiny flowers when a bomb lands. The graphics are not yet as good as Super Mario 4, but maybe by the next war, they'll catch up.

And we see the parades, the strutting politicians and the cheering sports bars that have become cheering war bars.

But what we don't see is described in the full report by the doctors who made this study:

"The destruction of the supply of electric power at the beginning of the war, with the subsequent disruption of the electricity-dependent water and sewage systems, was probably responsible for the reported epidemics of gastrointestinal and other infections.

"These epidemics were worsened by the reduced accessibility of health services and decreased ability to treat severely ill children."

In other words, we don't see those invisible but deadly killers in the water or the children screaming because their stomachs hurt and their fevers are raging. And we don't see them weaken, fade, then die.

But who would want to see a downer like that, anyway?

In a classic understatement, the doctors concluded: "War is never good for health. But the full effect of war and economic sanctions on morbidity and mortality is difficult to assess, and the number of civilian casualties caused indirectly is likely to be underestimated.

". . . During the gulf war, it was suggested that by using high-precision weapons with strategic targets, the Allied forces were producing only limited damage to the civilian population.

"The results of our study contradict this claim and confirm that the casualties of war extend far beyond those caused directly by warfare."

Forty-six thousand nine hundred kids. Give or take a few tots.

So what color ribbon do we wear for that triumph? ▪

Gulf II has bomb written all over it

WEDNESDAY, JULY 29, 1992

Some sequels work, but others don't. For example, "Godfather II" was a hit. But "Godfather III" was a clinker. The original "Alien" movie was a smash. The last one was a yawner.

So the White House should give that some thought before it goes into production for Desert Storm II.

There's no question that the original Desert Storm was one of the smash TV hits of all time.

It made instant superstars out of Stormin' Norman Schwarzkopf, Colin Powell, as well as Blitz Wolfer and the entire cast at CNN. And almost overnight, it transformed George Bush from a near flop into the biggest box-office draw of 1991.

The plot wasn't all that original: the ruthless and powerful Saddam riding roughshod over his weak and helpless little neighbor, only to be driven back when the forces of the heroic George Bush galloped in.

We've seen it before in "Shane," "The Magnificent Seven" and countless other shoot-'em-ups. Sometimes it's the ruthless and powerful cattle baron against the humble sheepmen or homesteaders. Or the ruthless and powerful railroad builder against the farmers or the small-town folk. Or the ruthless and powerful mining company against the small grubstakers.

However, the Desert Storm script had an unusual twist. The ruthless and powerful bad guy almost always gets it at the end. When John Wayne, as Rooster Cogburn, chased down Lucky Ned Pepper and his gang (including the Original Mexican Bob), he didn't say: "OK, Ned, you've learned your lesson, by golly, now go and sin no more." No, he left Ned and his gang dead in the dust.

But when Desert Storm ended, there was Saddam (far more evil and powerful than Lucky Ned Pepper or even the Original Mexican Bob) in excellent health, wearing his tailored uniforms and merrily knocking off helpless Kurds.

Not that most people noticed, with all the parades, welcome-home ceremonies and national chest-puffing, back-patting and yellow ribbon-waving in the joy of our having restored the frightened emir of Kuwait to his throne, thus reuniting him with all of his teenage wives.

But the survival of Saddam, not as powerful but still ruthless, should have been the tipoff that we might see a sequel someday. Any scriptwriter will tell you that's the only reason to let the villain slip away before the credits roll.

And what better time than now, with Bush once again slipping at the box office. Which is why Washington is now buzzing with talk that a sequel might be in the works.

As I said, though, sequels can be risky. Bush has his qualities, true, but he's no Batman, although Dan Quayle would have made a fine Robin if they hadn't written him out of the script.

For one thing, the special effects might not be as effective the second time around. All those smart bombs, brilliant missiles and other exploding intellects provided some of the finest visuals Americans had seen since the creation of Super Mario and his brother Luigi.

And the generals and other Pentagon cast members turned in fine performances. As a critic said: "They give good briefing."

But as we later learned, some of the bombs weren't all that smart; some missiles were absolutely dimwitted. We would be told: "Now what we see there, that little dot, is an Iraqi tank." Then, poof, the tank would be gone and we would cheer and wave our yellow ribbons.

Later, it turns out that it wasn't a tank after all, but may have been a moth-eaten tent in which an old biddy was cooking a pot of camel hump stew.

Or if it was a tank, it might have been one of our own, which is really counterproductive.

So if there is a sequel, the audience might be harder to impress. When some general turns on the video and says: "Now, that little spot we see here is an Iraqi missile site, aimed right at Disney World. Ah, and now you see it and now you don't," this time some reporter might pipe up and ask: "General, how do we know that tank was not really a moth-eaten old tent, in which a toothless hag was stirring a pot of lizard stew, huh?"

Or someone else might even say: "OK, General, assuming that thing you blew up was a bridge and not a row of olive trees; and assuming the bridge was in Iraq and not in New York or San Francisco, since we all know mistakes can happen; and assuming that you have blown up every bridge in Iraq, some of them five times, how come Saddam is being shown on CNN, wearing a brand-new uniform while throwing a Kurd out of his office window?"

So it might be best to forget about a sequel. Just go with reruns. But leave out the ending. ∎

Leave flag debate to the war heroes

THURSDAY, JUNE 21, 1990

During the braying that passes for debate in Congress, one political patriot leaped to his feet and declared that those who oppose a flag-burning amendment are "deliberately gagging 10 million veterans throughout this nation."

That's one of the standard arguments for tinkering with the Constitution: a few publicity-seeking ninnies who burn a Taiwan-made flag in public are somehow insulting anyone who served in the military.

Or that all veterans agree on the need for an amendment.

Or, for that matter, that every person who served in the military had the common goal of fighting for the Grand Old Flag.

Oh, come on. Let's stop dealing in silly myths about veterans.

First of all, the vast majority of all living veterans never saw the enemy, whether the enemy was German, Japanese, Italian, Korean, Chinese, Vietnamese, Cuban, Grenadian or Panamanian.

That's because the majority of veterans were not front-line grunts, combat pilots or battleship gunners. They were behind the lines transporting, repairing, communicating, supplying, training, planning, shuffling papers, banging on typewriters, running a PX, guarding a gate or just goofing off. Someone had to do it, and those who did had no regrets.

Those who were in combat might have been thinking about how fine it was to be ducking bullets, slogging through mud or snow and bleeding for Old Glory, baseball, apple pie, motherhood, truth, justice and the American way.

And if you believe that, you've seem too many John Wayne movies.

Every combat veteran I've known said that what they thought about most was staying alive. When all hell was breaking loose, there was little thought given to political ideologies. If they felt loyalty, it was to the guys on their left and right.

It strikes me as being presumptuous for anyone, vote-hustling politicians included, to say what someone died for. In every war, many men die because of the arrogance and stupidity of politicians and generals. If that's a noble cause, why don't more generals and politicians get up there and bleed?

Yes, there are heroes, men who were uncommonly brave and self-sacrificing. But who is to say why they were heroic? Did the young man charge up the hill at the enemy pillbox because he had visions of Old Glory flapping in the breeze at a baseball game while 40,000 beer-drinking fans sang or yawned? Or was he simply furious, terrified or acting on impulse? If you talk to heroes, some of them aren't sure why they reacted as they did. Some say they just did it, period. But you won't hear many saying: "Well, I began thinking about the Stars and Stripes and what it represents, so I picked up my. . . ."

I know a man who was pinned down at the bottom of a hill with his wounded commanding officer. The only way to safety was to go up the hill. He told his CO to wrap his arms around his neck and hang on. Then, with the wounded officer on his back, he ran up the hill while Japanese bullets whizzed past him.

They said he was a hero for saving his CO's life and gave him a medal. As he later told me: "I figured that with him on my back, he'd catch the bullets instead of me. He got hit once in the ass, so I was right."

I also know a former politician who won the Medal of Honor. The things he did were beyond a screenwriter's imagination. He wouldn't talk about it, but I once discussed his heroics with one of his closest friends.

The friend chuckled and said: "Yeah, but they left one thing out of his citation. He was drunk."

So maybe the politicians should let the heroes speak for themselves. If they did, we would find that there is no consensus.

Sen. Robert Dole, the Kansas Republican, qualifies as a war hero. He was shot to pieces in World War II and still shows the scars and the pain. Dole is in favor of the flag amendment.

Sen. Robert Kerrey, the Nebraska Democrat, also qualifies as a war hero. He won the Medal of Honor in Vietnam and came back with only one leg. He's against the flag amendment.

So what does that tell us? That Dole is a patriot and Kerrey isn't? Show me your stump if you believe that. ∎

War is heaven—if you believe

THURSDAY, MAY 31, 1984

The punishment seems harsh for that young marine corporal from Chicago who wouldn't go to Lebanon because of his Muslim religious beliefs. He's been sentenced to four months of hard labor and a bad-conduct discharge.

On the other hand, a line has to be drawn somewhere. And whether or not Col. Alfred Griffin realized it, he was trying to goof up the ancient rules and traditions of warfare.

He said that because he practices the Muslim religion, he could not kill another Muslim. And that's why he didn't show up when his outfit shipped out.

Well, what kind of attitude is that? If soldiers refused to kill somebody simply because they practice the same religion, it would be damned hard to get a war going.

Why, you don't see Iraq and Iran quibbling over questions of faith. They're all Moslems, and very devout. But with Allah's name on their lips, and their holy men urging them on, they've been eagerly slaughtering each other by the tens of thousands.

Nor have Christians ever been squeamish about waging wars on other Christians. If they had been, most of the liveliest wars in Europe would never have occurred.

Germany is loaded with Christians of all denominations. But every so often, it feels the need to shoot its way into France, Poland and other Christian nations. France, in its Napoleonic heyday, didn't hesitate to stomp all over other European Christians.

If anything, faith sometimes helped get their blood pressure pumped up, although it's doubtful that Christ intended His message to be used that way. Some wars were fought precisely over the issues of who prayed loudest, who ought to be leading the prayers, who kicked in the most loot to holy men and who should be admitted to heaven. The issues never stayed resolved for much longer than it took to count and stack the bodies of the faithful, but all the killing seemed like a good idea at the time.

If everybody thought the way that marine corporal does, World Wars I and II, which set records for Christians killing Christians, could never have occurred. Pilots and bombardiers and cannon-shooters would have been saying to themselves: "I wonder if any of my fellow Lutherans are down there?" Or: "I'll be darned—that guy I just shot crossed himself just the way I do just before he expired." Which is negative thinking of the worst kind.

Actually, there are benefits to waging war on people of the same faith.

For one thing, if you're taken prisoner and you die, you have a good chance of receiving a Christian burial, which is always nicer than being tossed out with the leftovers. And on religious holidays, the prison guards might be warmed by the spirit of the day and give you one less kick.

Also, both sides usually try to avoid destroying churches that have significant histories or architectural value. In Italy, for example, a lot of bystanders were killed, but a surprisingly large number of fine churches were undamaged. That's good because it means that there will be attractive settings available for the funerals of civilians who happen to be blown up.

Also, when both sides have the same religion, it's reassuring to know that the other guy might not have a heavenly edge. Maybe the enemy's holy man is telling him the Lord is on his side, but since your holy man is assuring you of the same thing, the worst you figure to get is a draw.

Then again, there are advantages to fighting wars with people who have different beliefs. Some religions promise heavenly reward to those who zap nonbelievers. Most at least imply that it's a little less sinful to knock off somebody from an off-brand faith. And it does make for a more interesting variety of religious souvenirs and trinkets to be plucked from enemy corpses.

I have to suspect that the marine corporal has little knowledge of his own nation's history, which includes our own bloody Civil War, fought between people not only of the same faith, but of the same nation and, in some cases, of the same families. That's the beauty of a civil war: Everybody has to put aside all those petty personal considerations for the overall social benefits of blowing somebody away.

All things considered, our present situation is probably the best arrangement, at least from the point of view of those who might think like the corporal, since the next big war would probably pit us—a religious nation—against the Soviets and godless Communism.

It could be the world's biggest and final opportunity to finally find out once and for all if God really takes sides in these differences.

Boy, if He doesn't, won't all those earlier holy warriors feel silly? ∎

War's end no time to pass up a buck

TUESDAY, MARCH 5, 1991

In winning the Iraq War, we did more than slap down Saddam the naked aggressor. It appears that we also put on one of the biggest and most successful trade shows in business history.

And the TV war that we saw—all those roaring jets, fast-moving tanks, muscular helicopters, intellectual missiles and night-vision goggles—was viewed by rulers and generals in other countries as a terrific TV commercial for our high-tech weapons industry.

As Monday's Wall Street Journal reported, American defense contractors are already "salivating" at the prospect of selling a wide range of death-and-destruction gadgetry to countries in the Middle East as well as other parts of the world that were dazzled by the live demonstration they saw on CNN.

Of course, this country could take the moral high ground and say, no, we will not help any of you short-tempered nations build bigger and nastier armies and air forces so you can start acting goofy again.

But the Journal, which always has its finger on the racing pulse of the world's fat cats, indicates that it's unlikely we will let galloping morality make us do anything giddy and foolish.

Because if we don't do the selling, somebody else will.

As one weapons merchant put it: "The Europeans will look at us and say, 'By gosh, you guys are moral.' But we're going to see what our Middle Eastern comrades-in-arms need. We're open for business."

Of course, foreign weapons merchants are at a disadvantage right now. Iraq used lots of European stuff and it was a marketing disaster. Soviet tanks, for example. They have a huge surplus inventory. But after the way their tanks clunked around in the desert, the Soviets might have to mark them down below dealer cost and offer a factory rebate.

There are those who might scoff at our cars, our stereos and our almost-vanishing TV industry. And did you know that just about every American golf club is manufactured by people who can't even say "fore?"

But when it comes to turning bridges into ink blots or turning a tank into an old Weber grill, we're No. 1. If Consumer Reports ever did comparative testing on causing terrified guys with mustaches to pop out of the sand, the products of the U.S.A. would be rated "best buy."

No, thanks to the war, we're perfectly positioned in the marketplace. Now that Saddam the Great Eye Plucker gave his neighbors a big fright, the Saudis and all the other oil-glut countries are going to be on a shopping spree. And the more weapons one country buys, the more its neighbors will want in case somebody else decides to become a Great Eye Plucker.

A lot of countries already have Scud missiles. That means there will be a big market for our Patriot missiles to shoot down the clumsy Scud missiles. And that, in turn, means that they'll want something that is less clumsy than the Scud missiles at avoiding the clever Patriot missiles. That's the wonderful thing about the weapons business: For every offense, you can develop a new defense. And for every new defense, there will be a need for an even better offense. It makes you wonder if the first ancient warriors weren't football coaches.

Of course, there will be those who will argue that the Iraq War should have taught the more industrialized and allegedly civilized nations of the world a lesson about selling weapons to erratic personalities. And some congressmen and other do-gooders will try to impose limits or even outright bans on the sale of such merchandise.

But they are overlooking the friendship factor. How can we tell countries that are friends of ours that we won't sell them the means to protect themselves? Is that any way to treat a friend?

As a result of our Iraq triumph, we happen to have a lot of friends right now. Countries whose UN delegates used to put their thumbs to their noses and wiggle their fingers at us and say "nyah, nyah" are now all choked up at what a swell guy President Bush is.

And how can we tell our weapons industry that it can't grab a share of the eager foreign market? Just when we're bursting with pride at the high IQ of our missiles and other amazing gadgets, are we to ask our American businessmen to stand with yearning eyes and empty pockets while the French sell missiles that couldn't go around the block without getting lost?

We should also remember, as President Bush has pointed out, that we could not have won this war as decisively as we did if it hadn't been for the weapons developed by American companies.

But have any of these companies asked to be honored with a confetti parade? Of course not. Confetti is nice, but a cashier's check is nicer.

So to those who might object to American companies cashing in on the next international arms race, I say this: Yes, war is hell. But business is business. ∎

Now, here is how to really honor vets

TUESDAY, NOVEMBER 9, 1993

I just phoned six friends and asked them what they will be doing on Thursday.

They all said the same thing: "working."

Me too.

There is something else we share. We are all military veterans.

And there is a third thing we have in common. We are not employees of the federal government, state government, county government, municipal government, the Postal Service, the courts, banks or S&Ls, and we don't teach school.

If we did, we would be among the many millions of people who will spend Thursday goofing off.

Which is why it is about time Congress revised the ridiculous terms of Veterans Day as a national holiday.

The purpose of Veterans Day is to honor all veterans.

So how does this country honor them?

By letting the veterans, the majority of whom work in the private sector, spend the day at their jobs so they can pay taxes that permit millions of non-veterans to get paid for doing nothing.

As my friend Harry put it:

"First I went through basic training. Then infantry school. Then I got on a crowded, stinking troop ship that took 23 days to get from San Francisco to Japan. We went through a storm that had 90 percent of the guys on the ship throwing up for a week.

"Then I rode a beatup transport plane from Japan to Korea, and it almost went down in the drink. I think the pilot was drunk.

"When I got to Korea, I was lucky. The war ended seven months after I got there, and I didn't kill anybody and nobody killed me.

"But it was still a miserable experience. Then when my tour was over, I got on another troop ship and it took 21 stinking days to cross the Pacific. When I got home on leave, one of the older guys at the neighborhood bar—he was a WWII vet—told me I was a —head because we didn't win, we only got a tie.

"So now on Veterans Day I get up in the morning and go down to the office and work.

"You know what my nephew does? He sleeps in. That's because he works for the state. And do you know what he did during the Vietnam War? He ducked the draft by getting a job teaching at an inner-city school.

"Now, is that a raw deal or what?"

Of course it's a raw deal. So I propose that Congress revise Veterans Day to provide the following:

1. All veterans—and only veterans—should have the day off from work. It doesn't matter if they were combat heroes or stateside clerk-typists. Anybody who went through basic training and was awakened before dawn by a red-neck drill sergeant who bellowed: "Drop your whatsis and grab your socks and fall out on the road," is entitled.

2. Those veterans who wish to march in parades, make speeches or listen to speeches can do so. But for those who don't, all local gambling laws should be suspended for the day to permit vets to gather in taverns, pull a couple of tables together and spend the day playing poker, blackjack, craps, drinking and telling lewd lies about lewd experiences with lewd women. All bar prices should be rolled back to enlisted men's club prices. Officers can pay the going rate, the stiffs.

3. All anti-smoking laws will be suspended for the day. The same holds for all misdemeanor laws pertaining to disorderly conduct, non-felonious brawling, leering, gawking and any other gross and disgusting public behavior that does not harm another individual.

4. It will be a treasonable offense for any spouse or live-in girlfriend (or boyfriend, if it applies) to utter the dreaded words: "What time will you be home tonight?"

5. Anyone caught posing as a veteran will be required to eat a triple portion of chipped beef on toast, with Spam on the side, and spend the day watching a chaplain present a color-slide presentation of the horrors of VD.

6. Regardless of how high his office, no politician who had the opportunity to serve in the military, but didn't, will be allowed to make a patriotic speech, appear on TV or poke his nose out of his office for the entire day. Any politician who defies this ban will be required to spend 12 hours wearing head phones and listening to tapes of President Clinton explaining his deferments.

Now, deal the cards and pass the tequila. ∎

CHAPTER 12
The Funniest Guy in the Room

Gong in your head rings in the new

This is the morning when millions of people ask a series of age-old questions. They seek answers, truth, wisdom, guidance, which I will now try to provide.

Question—Why, oh why, did I do it?

Answer—Because you are stupid.

Q—But what choice did I have?

A—Choice? At 1 a.m., she said: "Let's go home." But you wouldn't listen, dummy.

Q—But I was having such a good time. I deserve to have a good time, don't I?

A—You only thought you were having a good time. If someone from another planet saw you, he would think that it is normal for humans to walk at a 45-degree angle.

Q—I wasn't that bad, was I?

A—You weren't? Do you remember pushing that attractive female into a corner and trying to nibble her earlobe?

Q—Vaguely.

A—That was a lamp.

Q—No wonder the earlobe tasted funny. Is that why my tongue is this strange color?

A—No, your tongue is a strange color because you kept drinking from glasses that had cigarette butts in them.

Q—I thought they were odd-looking olives. So is that why I have this bad taste in my mouth?

A—The bad taste was from something you ate.

Q—But I ate some of the pizza, and it was good.

A—Yes, but when you eat pizza, you're supposed to remove it from the cardboard.

Q—Why am I so overwhelmed by feelings of guilt and shame? I was just trying to have some laughs.

A—There is nothing laughable about hiding behind the shower curtain and yelling "boo" at females who used the washroom.

Q—I can't believe I did that.

A—The females couldn't, either.

Q—But I only did it a couple of times.

A—That's because your host asked you to stop.

Q—And I'm sure I did, didn't I?

A—Yes, but only after turning the shower on him.

Q—I hope he didn't get too mad.

A—Not as mad as he did later, when you insisted on playing with their cat.

Q—But I like cats. What's so terrible about playing with the cat?

A—In the litter box?

Q—I don't remember that.

A—And I suppose you don't remember going outside to walk around and get some fresh air.

Q—There's nothing wrong with that.

A—No, but do you remember finishing your walk and coming back inside and taking off your clothes and getting in the Jacuzzi?

Q—That's impossible. My host doesn't have a Jacuzzi.

A—No, but his next-door neighbor does.

Q—I'd rather not hear any more.

A—Wait. Do you remember being dragged out of the Jacuzzi and trying to nibble that attractive woman's earlobe?

Q—Another lamp?

A—The neighbor's Labrador retriever. And when you finally returned to the correct party, do you remember dancing?

Q—What's wrong with a little dancing?

A—On the buffet?

Q—Enough. What I'd like to know is why construction crews are permitted to work on holidays and make so much noise?

A—There are no construction crews nearby.

Q—I can hear them. The pounding is deafening.

A—That is your heart.

Q—What can I do to make myself feel better? There is a painful tightness in my jaws and chin.

A—You can cure that by removing the rubber band that is holding the party hat atop your head.

Q—Thank you. But why do I feel so hot and clammy? Is that some kind of symptom?

A—Yes. It is a symptom of having gone to sleep while still wearing your winter overcoat.

Q—My back aches something awful. I suppose that means I need a firmer mattress.

A—Or a softer bathtub, which is where you slept.

Q—Please, how can I make myself feel better? Isn't there something I can do to relieve my feelings of misery? Isn't there some cure for this?

A—Sure. You can try stripping to your shorts and going out in your back yard and jogging in place for about 15 minutes.

Q—My Lord, that could kill me.

A—I didn't say it was a perfect cure. ∎

In 1993, John Bobbitt's penis was chopped off by his wife, Lorena. How could Dad resist? And it's likely he wrote all of these himself. —D.R.

Bobbitt limericks hit below the belt

THURSDAY, NOVEMBER 11, 1993

During lunch with several co-workers, one of them brought up a disgusting subject.

"I've written a limerick about that Bobbitt couple," he said. "Want to hear it?"

Despite my protests that it wasn't a fit topic for a lunch conversation, the others urged him to go on. So he recited his crude little poem:

Big John was a lad of great lust
Had a wife who was filled with distrust
One night while he slept
With a knife, in she crept
As a lover Big John's now a bust.

To my disappointment, everyone hooted and laughed. But news people are notoriously insensitive.

Even worse, they took out notebooks and began composing their own limericks and reading aloud. It was appalling. But I'm going to suppress my revulsion and pass some of them along to show how callous people can be about the misfortunes of others.

There once was a Bobbitt named John
Who thought he was quite the Don Juan
His wife disagreed
So the next time he wee'd
John couldn't locate his wand.

Isn't that loathsome?

Lorena wished John could be nicer
But he wasn't much of a de-icer
If she finds a new spouse
Let us hope he's no louse
Or we might have our first serial slicer.

Odious isn't a strong enough word to describe such inhumanity.

Big John Bobbitt might have been hipper
Had he kept his hot hands from his zipper
But to his wifey's dismay
Big John leaped to the fray
The results would have pleased Jack the Ripper.

Absolutely vile. But they refused to desist.

A surgeon was filled with great tension
Trying to sew on a thing we can't mention
He stitched and he sewed
Used all the skills that he knowed
But the wee thing won't stand at attention.

John Bobbitt was never a loner
In fact, he was known as a roamer
His wife seized his prize
And cut him to size
Now he is his own organ donor.

There was once a crime most venal
One might say 'twas inches from renal
It wasn't for sport
That she made him so short
Her intentions were nothing but penal.

I ask you: What ever happened to compassion?

The Bobbitt case sure is a dilly
Though it sounds a little bit silly
He said she's the hacker
Who lopped off his whacker
She said she was only trying to Free Willy.

Such low humor. In the future I will lunch alone.

There once was a man from Manassas
Who was fond of sleeping with lasses
His wife had enough

So she chopped off his stuff
Now let's see him try to make passes.

People at the next table chuckled. There are boors everywhere.

There once was a lady named Bobbitt
Who got so fed up that she lopped it
She said, "I'm sorry honey,
But your conduct's not funny,"
And she very efficiently stopped it.

I don't know if I can go on. But I'll try.

There once was a place in Virginia
Where a gal snipped it off like a zinnia
She whipped back the sheets
Ignored his sad bleats
And attacked like a professional ninja.

Fortunately, the waiter was bringing the check.

John Bobbitt's detractors will scoff
For it seems the judgment's been soft
He's been retrofitted
And now he's acquitted
That's the last time he ever gets off.

Now with dread I await the mail. I know there are many sadists out there who will try their hands at the limerick form at poor Bobbitt's expense.

I should point out that most of the above trash was written by men. What ever happened to male bonding?

By the way, anybody got a good rhyme for "bonding"? ▪

Faint occurrence gets activists' goat

TUESDAY, MAY 7, 1991

Although I'm not an animal-rights activist, I am somewhat troubled by the latest example of man's inhumanity to four-legged beasties. This time it is the Fainting Goat.

You probably haven't heard of fainting goats. I hadn't either, until I read an Associated Press report on them.

These goats don't actually faint. But they have an inherited muscular defect that is activated when they are under stress. Their muscles tighten and they roll over on their backs with their legs sticking straight up in the air.

Others don't roll over, but their legs stiffen and when they run, they bounce along like rabbits.

The muscle contractions don't last long. And they suffer no permanent harm. But they look undignified, as would anyone who might roll over with his legs sticking straight in the air.

Animal-protection groups are angry because the fainting goats are being bred and sold to people who, for one reason or another, want to own a fainting goat.

In fact, there is a group called the International Fainting Goat Association. And there are various state fainting goat associations. These are rather exclusive, since you have to own a fainting goat to become a member.

Some of the fainting goat owners hold an annual contest to see which fainting goat faints the fastest and stays down the longest.

But the fainting goat owners say that what they do isn't cruel. They just enjoy saying "boo" to a goat and seeing it roll over with its legs pointing at the sky.

The animal-protection groups disagree. While they concede that it isn't illegal to make a goat faint, they say it's obvious that the goat doesn't enjoy the experience, so they try to discourage people from saying "boo" to goats or supporting organizations that hold goat fainting contests.

This is one of those difficult legal and moral situations for which there are no easy answers.

On the one hand, we have the right of an American to sneak up behind a goat and shout "boo" or "baaah" or "hey, there, goat." Although it has not been tested in the courts, I'm sure this right is protected by the 1st Amendment. I doubt that the Founding Fathers gave much thought to the sensibilities of fainting goats.

On the other hand, there are many local laws that prohibit cruel treatment of animals. So the question is whether it is cruel to yell "boo" at a goat and cause it to roll over with its legs in the air or hop like a rabbit.

I don't have the answer. And the only goat owner I know is Sam Sianis, the Greek who owns the Billy Goat Tavern. Because he has owned many a goat, even displaying some of them in his saloon, I asked him if he thought fainting goats suffer.

He said: "Nah, goats ees dumb. I got some customers who roll over jus' like dat and they no suffer, either."

So who really knows what goes on in the mind of a fainting goat? The only experience of this kind that I've had involved a cocker spaniel.

This cocker spaniel belonged to my sister and her husband. By chance, I discovered that I could make it perform a strange act.

If I stared at it, the cocker spaniel would collapse and roll over on its back with its legs in the air. Then it would . . . I'm trying to think of a word that will not offend the editors and readers of this newspaper. How shall I put it? Well, in plain English, the dog would wee.

Was I being cruel? I don't think so. I never caused the cocker spaniel to do this more than once a visit. If I had done it five or 10 times, I suppose that might have been cruel, but I didn't because my sister would have demanded that I mop her kitchen linoleum.

And I don't think the dog considered it cruel, since it always leaped back to its moist feet, wagged its moist tail and tried to fling its moist body into my arms.

For a while, I considered taking the dog over to the neighborhood movie theater that, in those days, had live, amateur stage shows on Saturday nights. I had seen acts in which dogs jumped through hoops and did back flips and things like that. But no dog did anything like my sister's cocker spaniel. It could have been a show biz first.

But my sister was fond of the dog and said she didn't want it held up to public ridicule. She always had the softest heart in the family. ∎

A critical look at contact lenses

MONDAY, OCTOBER 28, 1985

He was bent over a sink in the office men's room, poking a finger into his eye and muttering.

I asked him what his problem was.

"The air. Must be a lot of pollution or something. It goofs up my contact lenses."

No, I scoffed, his problem wasn't the air. His problem was the vanity of those who insist on wearing contact lenses because they think it makes them look better and conceals a minor physical flaw.

They can't be like the rest of us normal, well-balanced, weak-eyed people who are not embarrassed about perching regular glasses on our noses.

They are so concerned about their appearance, so lacking in self-confidence, so vain and filled with conceit, that they go to the trouble of sticking a tiny piece of plastic to their eyeballs.

While poking at his eye, he indignantly offered a long, lame explanation about how much better he can see with contacts.

I've heard it before. But there is only one reason to wear them, and it is vanity.

I used to hear the same stuff from the right fielder on my softball team every time we had to stop the game while he crawled around on all fours, looking in the grass for a lens that had somehow leaped from his eyeball.

And I used to hear it from a handball partner, as he crawled on all floors, peering into the cracks between the floorboards.

There is also the golf partner, who in the midst of a game will suddenly clap his hand over an eye or begin poking at the orb with a finger.

That's the most offensive part of it—when they stick fingers in their own eyes.

Never once in my entire life have I touched either of my own eyeballs. Nor have I permitted anyone to touch them.

And I never will. To touch the eye is against the laws of nature. No creature on earth wants its eyeball touched.

You can make a test to confirm that statement. Take the nicest, gentlest cat you can find. Or the most docile, tail-wagging, droolingly happy dog.

You can pet them. You can rub their ears. You can ruffle the fur under their necks. You might even be able to get away with pulling their tails.

But just dare to try to touch their eyes. Those friendly little beasts might nip off your finger, as they should.

Or try it with a friend. You can pat a friend's back, put a hand on a friend's shoulder, take a friend by the arm, even pat a friend on the cheek.

But make the test. Go up to any friend, even your best pal, and try to touch his or her eyeball. They will leap away.

And it isn't mere surprise that causes that reaction. Give them warning. Ask your friend, "Would you mind if I touch your eyeball with my finger?"

You do that once or twice and your friends will begin shunning you.

There is also the inconvenience. People who wear those things can't just yank off their glasses and toss them on the dresser or under the bed when they go to sleep.

They have to mess around with their eyes to remove them, put them in miniature cookers, simmer them or whatever they do overnight, then go through the whole thing again in the morning.

And we've all heard the stories about people who awake thirsty during the night and, in reaching for a glass of water on the night stand, accidentally drink their contact lens.

There is something else they can't do. When provoked in, say, a barroom debate, they can't make the menacing gesture of removing their glasses, putting them on the bar and serving notice that the talking is over. Now there is action.

A person would look pretty foolish saying, "I don't have to put up with your guff," and then begin poking himself in the eye.

Finally, I have long suspected that there is a potential health menace in contact lenses. Eye doctors will deny it. But logic tells me it exists.

The danger is this: What is to prevent those things from sliding off your eye and up behind your forehead and even farther up, into your cranium? What do you do then, when this tiny object is up there in your head, rattling around between your skull and your brain?

Think about that. And be careful about rolling your eyes. ∎

Cat's best friend? Look right here

TUESDAY, OCTOBER 9, 1990

Although I'm not superstitious, I've long believed that if I do something good and kind, it will come back to haunt me. And once again, I've been proved correct.

The other day, as we strolled in the neighborhood, my wife spotted a kitten sitting near our alley.

"Isn't it cute?" she said, moving toward it.

I said: "Careful. If it bites and you come down with rabies and go mad, I'll have to chain you to the water pipes in the basement."

She made a clicking sound and the kitten came over and rubbed itself against her leg.

"See?" she said, "it's friendly."

"If it weighed 200 pounds," I said, "it would have you for lunch."

She's learned to ignore my observations about cats, so she picked it up and said: "I wonder if it's hungry."

"Then let it catch a bird," I said. "I have no respect for cats that aren't self-reliant."

She carried it to our yard and brought it food and milk, which it gobbled down.

An examination showed that it wore a collar, but no name tag. "What should we do?" my wife asked. "It's getting cold and rainy. We can't just leave the poor thing out here."

See? One minute I'm walking along minding my own business. The next, I'm responsible for the well-being of a strange cat.

We conferred. We couldn't bring her in the house because my wife already has two cats. Only strange old ladies have three cats. And I refuse to be married to a strange old lady, so two is my limit.

Besides, she could have some strange disease. (The cat, not my wife.) And the other two cats could catch it, and they aren't covered by my company medical plan.

So we put her in the garage, left food and water and slapped "Kitten Found" signs on trees, light poles and the neighborhood convenience store.

The next morning, we went in the garage to check her well-being. We heard a meow, but couldn't see her. I looked under and behind every piece of garage junk.

I heard her again. The sound came from under the car. I crawled around, getting an oil stain on a good pair of slacks, but couldn't see her.

It appeared that she had somehow crawled up into the body of the car. That meant that if I started the engine, she might be mashed. My car warranty doesn't cover that.

I considered jacking up the car and trying to find her, but if the jack slipped, my wife would be a widow. And after a suitable period of mourning, she'd take the insurance money and run off with a fortune-seeking yuppie.

"We could call a garage and have them come out with one of those professional jacks," my wife said.

See? I'm minding my own business, and all of a sudden I've ruined a pair of $40 slacks and I'm bringing in an emergency road crew to find a cat in my transmission.

If I didn't get her out of my car, I couldn't use the car. I'd have to take the bus and subway to and from work, which means I'd probably be mugged before the day ended.

That's what kindness gets you.

I decided to lure it out with a few shrimp. A mouse would have been cheaper, but the store didn't sell them.

It worked. So my wife took her to the animal hospital to see if she carried plague.

As it turned out, we were right not to bring her in the house. The vet said she had a few ticks or mites or some such problem. Nothing serious or uncommon, but the other cats might have caught them. Then I'd have three itchy cats, and who needs that?

But otherwise, the vet said, she is healthy. He provided some stuff to spray on her and said the little nasties would all be gone in a week or two.

"Now what do we do?" I asked. "The vet cost $65. The ruined slacks are $40. That's more than a C-note, not counting the shrimp. When I was young, an evening with a harlot cost less."

My wife phoned three animal shelters, the humane kind that say they won't give cats to mad scientists or zap them after a couple of weeks. But it appears that it takes longer to get a cat into a shelter than a kid into Harvard.

So now I have this kitten living in my garage. That means I have to park my car on the street, where it will surely be snatched by chop-shop pirates. Before this is over, I could be out a fortune.

That's what I meant about being punished for acts of kindness.

Therefore I'm putting her up for adoption. The vet and my wife tell me she's a fine looking little thing. They also said she seems alert and smart. I'll take their word for it, although I wonder why a smart cat would crawl into the innards of my car.

So if you want this creature—it's about 9 months old, incidentally—you can call me at 312-222-3111. I'll toss in the stuff the vet gave me to spray on her and foot the bill for any other shots she might need.

But don't ponder it too long. There are limits to my kindness and decency. I have a canvas sack, some rocks and there is a park with a deep lagoon nearby. All I have to do is put her in the sack and . . .

Oh, stop weeping, all you hysterical children, I'm just making a little joke.

Or could it be that the bad man in the newspaper isn't joking? We shall see, hmmm? ∎

Killer? Murder? Many find they can live with it

WEDNESDAY, MARCH 13, 1996

A man in Canada recently made a bit of news when he took legal steps to change his family's name.

His name has been Arthur Lawrence Death. He wants it changed to Arthur Lawrence Deeth, which is the way it has always been pronounced, except by those who snicker and make wisecracks.

The request for a name change is understandable. But what is surprising is the large number of people born with unusual and potentially embarrassing names who choose to live with them.

By searching a national phone book program, I came across a wide range of names that could bring smirks from store clerks, bank tellers and traffic cops.

For example, there is a Martin Pecker, a businessman in Boca Raton, Fla.

He is one of several dozen Peckers scattered across the country.

Of his name, Pecker says: "Honestly, I love it. As a kid I got a lot of teasing for being a Pecker. But I grew up big—I'm 6-3 and 220—and my sons are big, so people are careful about what they say. And with women, I used to get flattering remarks.

"Here in Boca, I have a physician friend named Zipper. We were in a society page together once. Zipper and Pecker."

Then there is James Pee of Birmingham, Ala., one of a few dozen Pees, who seem to live mostly in Southern states.

Laughing, Pee said: "I've had trouble with my name since I was a kid. Spent 10 years in the Air Force, so I got a hard time there too. I've had nicknames like Pee-Pee, Urine, Little Pee.

"Around Kosciusko, Miss., there are so may Pees that there is a Pee Cemetery.

"I never really thought seriously about changing it. And I asked my son, who's in college, how he felt. He said that if I could get by being a Pee, he'd just as soon stay a Pee too."

Paul Crapper of Lehigh Acres, Fla., one of numerous Crappers, said: "I'm perfectly happy being a Crapper. People make remarks, but I just pass it off or say something like: 'I'm like Alka Seltzer, I bring relief.'"

Walter Crapp of Brownsville, Pa., feels the same way: "I never considered changing it. My grandfather came from Russia and had a long name. So I just decided to keep Crapp and drop the rest."

Of her married name, Suzan Geek says: "I believe we are the only Geeks in North Carolina," which might be a matter of debate.

"People sometimes laugh because they can't believe someone could be a Geek. And when I order a pizza by phone, they almost always laugh. But I'm in real estate, and I assure you that nobody ever forgets my name."

Among the more distinctive names are Murder or Murders.

Danny Murders, 51, of Russellville, Ark., has done considerable research on how the names came about.

"When my ancestors came to the New World in the 1700s, it was Murdaugh, with a Scottish brogue. They were farmers and moved West. Later, in Tennessee, the census takers spelled it phonetically so it became Murder or Murders. Around Hot Springs, there are about 26 families named Murders. There are four brothers known as the Murders Boys. As far as I know, none of the Murders have changed their name."

A Killer named Christine, in Cheshire, Conn., says: "Oh, yes, it is a daily conversation piece. People will say things like, 'You don't look like a killer.' And I've often been asked to show an ID because people don't believe my name can be Killer. The name is of German origin. As for my being teased, not very often. Maybe they were afraid."

Jack Ripper, 60, who runs a sign company in Detroit, says: "Sure, I get called Jack the Ripper about twice a day. Because of the Ripper name, people used to ask my mother, 'Is Jack the Ripper your husband?' And she'd always say, 'No, but my son is.' I like it. That's why I put it on my business. People don't forget a name like Jack Ripper."

Peter Hitler, 54, of Mequon, Wis., says: "Well, it is interesting to say the least. Our family goes back to the 1700s in Circleville, in southern Ohio. There were a lot of Hitlers there. A Hitler Street, a Hitler cemetery.

"There used to be a lot more of us, but they changed their names around World War II. I was just a kid, but my older brother took a lot of flak. My parents took our name out of the phone book.

"There aren't too many Hitlers left. I've run across three or four. I guess the name is outlawed in Germany.

"I'm in real estate and not a day goes by without someone saying, 'Oh, my gosh,' or 'Why didn't you change your name.' Any time I present my credit card, someone makes a remark. But it is something you live with. I don't think about it anymore."

Which is what a New Yorker named Ben Mussolini said: "Hey, forget it. I've been through this before. I don't feel like talking about it."

And the woman who answered the phone listed for Jim Wierdo said: "The Wierdos don't have this number anymore. But so many people keep calling. I don't know why." ∎

If all's fair in love, what about later?

TUESDAY, OCTOBER 11, 1988

B y writing this story, I am not condoning what Gerald did. His conduct was nasty, cruel and vindictive. But it was also funny, and with most of today's news being about the frantic babbling of politicians, anything with a chuckle is welcome.

Gerald lives in a suburb of St. Paul. He's divorced and it is an understatement to say that he doesn't think much of his ex-wife.

That isn't uncommon, of course. Many divorced people loathe their former spouses. That's one of the reasons I almost never write about divorce disputes.

It's my experience that if you ask a divorced person whose fault the breakup was, about 99 percent of the time the man will say "hers," and the woman will say "his." Depending on whom you talk to, in every shattered marriage there was one saint and one fiend.

Or, as an old divorce lawyer once told me: "They all lie. The secret of success is to get your client to tell better lies."

But to get back to Gerald and the nasty thing he did, as reported in the St. Paul Dispatch.

Gerald wasn't violent, as some ex-husbands are. There are countless cases of men beating up boyfriends of their ex-wives. And, although it is more rare, ex-wives have been known to pluck a few tufts of hair from an ex-husband's new flame.

There are tire slashings, obscene late-night phone calls and, occasionally, a guy will get sloshed and drive his car onto his old front porch.

Gerald, to his credit, showed a bit more wit and imagination.

After Gerald was divorced by Sharon, she packed up and moved to another state, while he remained at their old address.

One day a letter came for Sharon. The decent thing would have been for Gerald to send the letter on. But Gerald had bitterness in his heart, as many divorced people do.

So he opened and read the letter.

It turned out to be a questionnaire from someone in Sharon's old high school class of 1958.

This person was putting together a newsletter that was to be sent to the other members of the class, bringing them all up to date on what their old classmates were doing 30 years later.

Those readers with a malicious nature have already guessed what Gerald did.

Yes, Gerald filled in the answers to the questionnaire.

Then he signed Sharon's name and returned it to the person putting together the newsletter.

And a few months later, more than 100 members of the class received the newsletter and read about each other. When they got to Sharon's responses, their jaws dropped.

There could be little doubt that Sharon sounded as if she had had the most interesting 30 years since graduation day.

In answer to "occupation," the answer was: "Retired on 3rd husband's divorce settlement."

There was a question that asked: "Achievement most proud of?"

The answer: "My three divorces and how each time I married into more money to the point where I am now living on the $400,000 settlement and interest from my third divorce."

Another question asked for an "outrageous, unusual or interesting experience."

The response: "Going out to Virginia . . . on my job and having an affair with two different guys while my third husband was back in Minnesota working two jobs."

But Gerald hadn't even hit his stride. For the question about hobbies, he wrote:

"Nightclubbing, partying and looking for new and wealthier husbands."

And for "Secret ambition or fantasy," he wrote:

"Seeing if I can't get married as many times as Liz Taylor and gain my riches through divorces, not work."

When Sharon finally saw the newsletter, she said "eek," or something to that effect. Then she called her lawyer.

And now Gerald has been slapped with a $50,000 lawsuit by Sharon. She says that's what it will cost to soothe her embarrassment and mental anguish. I suppose that if there is a moral to this story, it is that it's a good idea to let sleeping ex-wives lie.

And Gerald had better hope that when this $50,000 case comes to court, he draws a judge who either has a wicked sense of humor or a nasty ex-wife. ▪

A Lhasa apso in every pot!!

THURSDAY, JUNE 21, 1984

It began even before I came to work this morning. A pal and I were sweating up a handball court when I heard a female voice speak my name.

I looked up and there stood a young woman in tennis togs, holding a racket. I smiled pleasantly, since she had nicely tanned legs.

She didn't smile pleasantly. She said: "Mr. Royko, at this moment there are dozens of little dogs up in your office—the kinds of dogs you call *useless*!—and they are all pooping on your desk."

On second thought, her legs weren't that good. Kind of bony in the knees. So I said, "Isn't it kind of early in the morning for you to be smoking grass?"

She glared at me, then wandered off. My handball partner, looking puzzled, said, "What was that all about?"

"I don't think she liked this morning's column."

"What was it about?"

"Tiny dogs. And how useless they are."

"Oh, Lord, you didn't say that, did you?"

"Yeah."

"But you know how people react. Don't you remember the cat owners? What do you write things like that for?"

"You know what the guy said when he was asked why he took off his clothes and rolled in the cactus?"

"What?"

"He said that it seemed like a good idea at the time."

When I got to the office, the phone was bouncing. My assistant looking harried, said, "It's bad."

"You're disgusting," a caller said. "I can't believe you would recommend eating dogs."

I didn't recommend it. I just mentioned that in some Asiatic societies, they eat shish-ka-bow-wow and other canine dishes. But I don't recommend it.

"It is still a horrible, nauseating thought. You should be fired."

Madam, have you ever eaten lamb stew or lamb chops?

"Yes, but . . ."

That is revolting. A sweet, docile, loving, harmless woolly creature like a lamb? They have such sweet eyes. And you devoured its flesh? I will not speak to so heartless a person as you. Goodbye.

Then there was the furious Harriet Sandy, president of the Lhasa Apso Club of Chicago. These are people who own the breed of dogs I wrote about. She demanded an apology and said she is going to bring the full power and influence of the club down on my head. All 30 members.

"You know nothing about the Lhasa apso," she said. Of course. I already admitted in my column that I know nothing except that they're tiny and useless, like all tiny, useless dogs.

Sandy delivered a lecture on the history of the Lhasa apso, which I will share with you.

They were originally bred in Tibet as good luck charms. She didn't say whether they were attached to key chains, like a lucky rabbit's foot.

"They were also fine watchdogs," she said. "They guarded the inside of the palaces."

Who guarded the outside?

"Bull mastiffs."

For Pete's sake, with bull mastiffs outside, a mouse could guard the inside.

"I had one that was only 11 pounds and he was a fierce watchdog. He once took a dislike to a 6-foot plumber who came to do some work and held him at bay in a corner. The man was terrified."

A simple explanation: phobia. I have a friend who is 250 pounds, and he is terrified of tiny, harmless bugs. A ladybug could hold him at bay. But that wouldn't make the ladybug a fierce watchbug.

The calls went on. There was a lady who wept as she said, "How could you encourage cruelty to little dogs?"

Nonsense. I don't encourage cruelty to any creature, except an alderman.

"You said they could be used to wash windows. That it was all they were good for."

I was wrong. You can also spray them with Endust and chase them under the bed. Works well, I hear. By the way, have you ever eaten roast duckling?

"Yes, but what . . ."

How horrible. Cute little ducky-wuckies. They just paddle around a pond, put their little behinds in the air and go quack quack. Little Donalds. And you tear their bodies with your teeth. How can you sleep with that on your conscience and stomach? I gag at the thought. Goodbye.

And a man, voice shaking with rage, who said, "Tell me—what is your real motive for writing something like that?"

I told him that I would level with him about my *real* motive. I could lie and say that I did it because I thought it was an amusing story, a tiny slice of city life, the little dog falling through a crack in the rocks. Or that I poked fun at little dogs because I think their owners take things too seriously, such as perceived affronts to their pets. After all, the pets don't read and aren't offended.

But I won't lie. That's not why I did it.

"Then why did you do it?" he asked.

I did it because it is my goal to rid this great nation of tiny dogs. History shows that the first sign of a great nation's decline is the proliferation of tiny dogs. The Roman Empire fell when the emperor started carrying four or five little dogs under his toga. He said they tickled and he liked it. Greece declined when Alexander the Great took as a hobby the juggling of little dogs.

Only nations with big dogs survive. It is my goal to lead a crusade that will end with every American family owning an Irish wolfhound, a mastiff or a St. Bernard.

"You are a sick man," he said.

Maybe. But you'll never catch me referring to a dog as baby.

MONDAY, JUNE 25, 1984

Letters, calls, complaints and great thoughts from readers:

Pat Shannon, Westchester: You are an opinionated, narrow-minded old man.

Before my husband and I purchased our West Highland white terrier, we were seriously considering purchasing a Doberman pinscher.

We consulted with our vet and he advised against it. He knew a woman who owned one for eight years. It had a beautiful disposition. Then one day, without any warning, it viciously attacked her.

So don't ridicule people who only want a simple, loving pet. Not a killer.

Comment: And I knew someone who owned a 14-ounce, pink Yeppa Lulu. For years it was sweet, docile and did nothing but sleep and eat stuffed mushrooms and *pate foi gras*. Then one day, without warning, it bit off their parakeet's beak. One never knows, does one? It's just a jungle out there.

Marianne Brousard, Elmhurst: I'll bet that way down deep inside, you just love useless little dogs. Your story was a mask for the real marshmallow you. Admit it, you love them, right?

Comment: Yes, I do love them. But never as the entree—only as hors d'oeuvres. ∎

It's hard warming up to 4 seasons

MONDAY, DECEMBER 11, 1989

The young woman was born and reared in southern California. Until a few weeks ago, she had never been in any other part of the country.

Then she relocated to Chicago. Not by choice. It was an upward career move. She works for a national chain of bookstores in one of those huge suburban shopping malls.

I happened to be in the bookstore on business recently, and the first question she asked me was: "How can you stand it?"

No, that's not the way she said it. There was more emphasis. It was more like: "How can you *staaaaaaand* it?"

I asked what it was that I was *staaaaaanding*.

"This weather," she said.

Once again, though, it came out as: "This *weeeeeeather*."

I told her it wasn't a very cold day. The thermometer on my car registered about 37, and there wasn't much wind.

"You don't think that's *coooooold*?" she asked.

Wait until the Hawk arrives, I warned, the howling arctic wind that rips through town in January and February. Go downtown and walk across one of the bridges, into the beak of Hawk, and feel your own beak turn into an oddly shaped ice cube. Then you'll know what cold is.

Even better, stand at a bus stop, peering into the distance and wondering if the bus will arrive before your eyeballs freeze and your ears plop into the snow.

"And you enjoy that?" she asked. Once again, it was more like "*enjoyyyyyy*."

I was about to go into my usual routine about how living through Chicago's fierce winters develops strength of character, a rugged constitution and an appreciation of the arrival of spring, the beauty of autumn and the warmth of summer. In other words, the variety that comes with the changing of the four seasons that those in the monotonous warmer climes don't experience.

And how there is something about living in the frigid North that makes us industrious, hardy and prepared to overcome adversity.

That's what I always tell people from California, Arizona, Florida and other sunshine states.

Instead I decided, just for once, to tell the truth. No, I don't enjoy it. I don't *enjoyyyyyyy* it at all. I hate it. Yes, *haaaaaate*.

She asked. "Then why do you live here?" A reasonable question. Why *do* so many of us live in Chicago? Or Milwaukee, Cleveland, Minneapolis, Buffalo and other long john towns?

If you give it thought, there is something stupid about it. We are the only creatures on earth that have reasoning powers. So why don't we ask ourselves: "Is it sensible to live in a place where you freeze your butt five months of the year?"

Even most birds and many ocean-going fish, which have IQs lower than Dan Quayle, head south when the temperature drops.

So why are millions of us here?

Because we don't control our own destinies.

In my case, the blame can be placed on my grandfather. After getting off the boat in New York, he boarded a train heading west. But he and his friend, Casimir Czentskowski Jr., became rowdy and when the conductor reprimanded them, they hit him on the head with their last bottle of vodka and were thrown off in Chicago.

Had that not happened, he might have gone on to California. And today, I might be named Lance or Rance and be gliding on a surfboard.

Of course, had he gone on, he would not have met my grandmother and I wouldn't be here or anywhere today, so I can't be too hard on the old coot.

We're here because this is where the jobs were, in the factories, the mills, the mines and the stockyards. The only people who settled in the upper Midwest by choice were the Swedes, Fins and other blue eyes because their idea of fun is to sit in a steam room then jump naked into a snow bank. Strange folk.

Besides, until 40 or 50 years ago, when air conditioning became common, the Sun Belt wasn't that appealing. Snakes under the bed, gila monsters on the porch, deadly spiders in your shoes, hurricanes, earthquakes, hurricanes. Given a choice, it is far nobler to drop dead shoveling snow from your sidewalk than being digested by a gator.

After I explained this to the woman in the bookstore, she asked: "But if you hate it, why do you *stayyyyyy*?"

Because it's too late. I'd look silly on a surfboard, and I'm not quite ready to dodder around Wrinkle Village, being mistaken for George Burns. So I stay and freeze.

Then I asked her: "But if you are already so miserable, why are you here?"

And she said: "Because of my *jooooobbbbb*."

Poor girl. And the worst of it is that your frost-bitten grandchildren will blame *you*. ∎

Downloading some lowdown statistics

THURSDAY, JANUARY 12, 1995

Home computer sales are booming, but do most people really need them?
There are those who scoff that it's money wasted on a fad, the national craze to buy the latest high-tech gizmo, whether we need it or not.

They question how many people really need elaborate accounting programs or spreadsheets to balance their checkbooks and track their expenses. To be happy, must we have printouts of precisely how much we spend each year on coffee or toilet paper?

And when did we become so hungry for data that we're all supposed to be surfing the Internet? If there is so deep a craving for significant information, why do millions watch "Roseanne" or "Beavis and Butt-head"?

No, the skeptics say, most of those who go on-line just wander aimlessly, nameless blips passing in the night.

But a computer-loving reader believes he can provide a rebuttal to those who doubt the usefulness of having a lot of RAM and ROM flickering on your own monitor.

He gave me a folder stuffed with computer-generated data, and he asked this question:

"Could you provide an exact count of every putz and schmuck in this country?"

I had to admit that I couldn't. And I doubted that anyone could.

He proudly said: "Well, thanks to my computer and an amazing software program that I bought over the counter, I can do it, and I did. It's all there in the data. Take a look."

An examination of his data proved him correct, sort of.

What he had was a listing of every person named Putz or Schmuck who is listed in a telephone directory.

"With this program," he said, "I can type in any name and it will give me everyone with that name in the United States who has a phone listing.

"After I got this program, I happened to hear someone at work say: 'Boy, there sure are a lot of schmucks and putzes running around.' So I decided to look it up and see how many there are."

It turns out there are 652 Putzes and 464 Schmucks scattered across the United States.

"You probably thought there were more Schmucks than Putzes," he said. "Most people do, but now we know that it isn't true."

Actually, I had never given it any thought. But I suppose it's worth knowing if the question ever comes up on a quiz show.

Of course, there are flaws in this data. They are only published phone listings. It's possible that a lot of Schmucks are unlisted. That would be understandable, because the word is often used in a derogatory way.

The dictionary says a schmuck is a person who is "clumsy or stupid; an oaf." (Incidentally, there are four people named Oaf with phone listings.)

But a co-worker who is knowledgeable about Yiddish words said schmuck has broader meaning. She explained:

"Strictly speaking, it is a male organ, but in popular usage, it has gone beyond that.

"A schmuck is someone's ex-husband or boyfriend who putzed around too much. A creep, a jerk. It can also be used to describe a stranger, as in: 'Hey, schmuck, ever heard of a turn signal?' Or a known person, as in: 'My husband, the schmuck, forgot to come home last night.'

"More recent derivations include schmuck head, schmuck face, schmuck breath and your royal schmuckness.

"But a putz is more of a harmless dolt, that goofy, awkward geek who's the same guy he was in the 3rd grade when everyone spit on him. Weenie, wimpy, wimpish, nerdy, doofy, goofy. It usually replaces someone's name, as in: 'Move it along, putz!'"

So I suppose that a person would be better off being a Putz than a Schmuck, although the proud Schmucks would probably disagree and self-effacing Putzes might not even care.

In any case, it's possible that more Schmucks are unlisted or have bigger families. If so, the Schmucks might very well outnumber the Putzes, despite what this computer program tells us.

The user of the program conceded that point, but he stubbornly said: "It would still be a valuable tool, providing a starting point if someone wanted to do the research and call the Schmucks and Putzes to ask them about their family size."

Possibly, but I doubt if people would appreciate their phones ringing and a stranger asking: "Would you mind telling me how many Schmucks there are in your family?"

To do something like that, you would have to be a real putz. ▪

These heretics pay through nose

FRIDAY, FEBRUARY 17, 1989

Our government and many others have denounced the Ayatollah Khomeini for the death sentence he placed upon the author of a novel that has offended the Islamic world. And for offering a bounty of up to $3 million for anyone who bumps off the writer.

Individuals throughout the world are expressing horror that a "hit" should be ordered for someone merely for writing a work of fiction.

As Studs Terkel, the famous Chicago author and radio interviewer, told me: "I was going to have Salman Rushdie on my show to talk about his book. And now he's got to hide in England 'cuz they're going to kill him. Has the world gone nuts?"

But I can't share this indignation. Death, after all, is the punishment for heresy in the Moslem religion.

And I can sympathize with the true believers of that religion whose sensibilities have been offended.

That's because I belong to a religion that also carries a severe punishment for those who would dare scoff at our beliefs.

As I've written before, I am a member of the Church of Asylumism and believe it is the one and only true faith.

For those who are not familiar with the Church of Asylumism, I will provide a brief history. Then I'll explain how we punish heretics.

Our church was founded by Dr. I.M. Kookie, one of the world's leading experts on lots of things. In our church, he is called the Prophet Kookie.

As Prophet Kookie has revealed in the Book of Kook, man is not native to this planet. He did not evolve from monkeys, as some people believe, or descend from Adam and Eve, as others insist.

Millions of years ago, a highly advanced race of peaceful, happy beings on a distant planet had a perfect society. But they developed a social problem. A few hundred of them became deranged. Their madness took different forms. Some stole or became violent. Others tried to become lawyers. Some wanted to form political parties. And a few claimed that God spoke to them and told them how everybody should live.

So they were rounded up, put on a spaceship, and a search was made for an uninhabited planet that would serve as an asylum. They found this planet.

As the Book of Kook reveals: "The spaceship crew that dumped them here named this planet Earth, because in their language, the word Earth means 'booby hatch.'"

Thus, we are all descended from this group of transplanted lunatics, which explains man's eccentric behavior throughout recorded history.

Many people don't share our beliefs. And that's fine. We don't impose our faith on others. In fact, we try to limit the membership of the Church of Asylumism. As Prophet Kookie wrote in the Book of Kook:

"It would be unwise to convert masses to our faith. There are not enough shrinks to go around."

However, we do expect to be accorded the same respect that we extend to those of other faiths.

If others wish to fight holy wars, blow each other up, whip, flog, discriminate, ostracize, highjack, riot and murder—all in the name of religion—we do not criticize or deny them their means of showing devotion to their faith.

To the contrary. As the Book of Kook tells us:

"It just shows that we're right. This is one big booby hatch."

However, we expect the same respect to be shown to our faith. And we have ways of punishing those who fail to show proper respect.

Unfortunately, this has occurred in recent days.

After I revealed the existence of the Church of Asylumism, I received numerous calls and letters from those who were, to say the least, rude.

One woman called and shrieked: "You and this guy Kookie sound like a couple of nuts."

A man phoned and said: "That is the most ridiculous religion I have ever heard of, and this Prophet Kookie ought to be in a nut house himself."

And a letter came from a person who said: "You and this Kookie person will fry in hell for spreading this kind of garbage."

Well, it is one thing to insult my faith. I hold only the title of High Inmate in the Church of the Asylumism. We do not have titles such as deacon, bishop, rabbi or ayatollah.

Our rankings are Inmate, High Inmate, Ward Attendant, Shrink, High Shrink and, of course, The Prophet. (Should we ever have our own religious TV show, his title will be changed to The Profit.)

There is no penalty for insulting the rest of us. But we do not tolerate any slurs against the Prophet Kookie. As the Book of Kook says on this subject:

"The Prophet Kookie is not to be insulted, abused, ridiculed or have his hubcaps stolen.

"The punishment for these offenses is severe. Anyone who violates this rule will be sentenced to having his or her nose tweaked."

So, with the greatest solemnity, I must announce that those who have insulted and ridiculed the Prophet Kookie now face retribution.

You have been sentenced to having your noses tweaked. And, as High Inmate, I am offering a $1 reward to those who tweak the nose of those who have committed the offense.

This bounty has been approved by the Prophet Kookie. In fact, he is so offended, he has said:

"If the offender has a cold and a runny nose, the bounty is $1.50."

You have been warned. ∎

Norwegians and Swedes, you have not been forgotten

WEDNESDAY, APRIL 3, 1996

As any sensitive person knows, especially those of the modern liberal persuasion, ethnic jokes are considered socially offensive.

So I was appalled by an e-mail letter from a man who actually asked me to tell an ethnic joke in my column.

He said: "Having read you over the years in three Chicago newspapers, I have noted that you manage to upset just about every ethnic and racial group at one time or another.

"However, I can't remember your ever saying anything infuriating about Swedes or any other Scandinavians. In fact, I don't remember ever hearing a Swedish joke in my entire life.

"Because I am of Swedish ancestry, I feel left out and a little hurt at being ignored. So does my wife, who has some Norwegian in her background.

"We lead quiet lives, except when the holiday season requires that we drink hot glogg, and we would appreciate having you write something that would get our normally tepid Scandinavian blood boiling with rage.

"With your knowledge of ethnic matters and your gift for giving offense, even when it is not intended, I am sure that you have a Scandinavian joke tucked away. If so, please share it so we, too, can feel part of the insulted mainstream of American life."

Well, that is what I call a lot of gall. And selfishness too.

Just to satisfy his warped need to feel insulted, he expects me to expose myself to the anger of one of the largest and oldest ethnic groups in the Chicago area.

That's all I need these days—thousands of blue-eyed blond people named Sven and Ole and Inge gathering outside my office, wearing Viking helmets, flinging smoked herrings and boiled potatoes at my window and chanting: "Fire dee boom."

On the other hand, there is something in what the man says about his feeling left out of the "insulted mainstream of American life."

His complaint is that he has nothing to complain about. In that sense, he is a victim because he is being made to feel dull.

If I ignore his plea for help, I will be shirking my journalistic duty to try to help society's victims.

So as much as I abhor ethnic humor and ethnic jokes in any shape or form, just this once I will stifle my nausea and fulfill this man's request.

At this point, I will understand if sensitive readers choose to flee to another part of this paper where they can find something more uplifting.

In fact, I encourage it, since I want to offend as few people as possible, which has always been my policy.

Having said that, I will now grit my teeth and get on with this distasteful business.

One day this Swedish guy walks into a dingy little storefront travel agency, holds up a page out of a newspaper and says: "You say in this ad that you have a voonderful luxury cruise for only $69.95. I vant to go on this voonderful luxury cruise."

The guy behind the counter says: "Sure. Do you have the $69.95 in cash?"

"I sure do," says the Swede, plunking the money on the counter.

At that point, two big thugs leap out of a closet, whack the Swede on the head, drag his unconscious body out the back door, stuff him in a barrel and drop the barrel into a river that flows past.

A few moments later, a Norwegian guy walks into the same dingy storefront travel agency, holds up the newspaper and says: "I vant to go on this $69.95 voonderful luxury cruise."

The guy behind the counter says: "Sure, you got the fare in cash?"

"You betcha," says the Norwegian, slapping the money on the counter.

Again, the two big thugs leap out, pound him on the head, drag his limp form out the back door, shove him in a barrel and drop it in the river.

After a while, the Swede and the Norwegian regain consciousness, and they find that their barrels are bobbing along together.

The Norwegian says: "Good afternoon. Tell me, do you happen to know if they serve dinner on this cruise?"

The Swede shakes his head and says: "No, I don't think so. They didn't last year."

There, the foul deed is done and I really feel dirty. So I must go and bathe before someone asks me to tell the really disgusting one about the Italian general and the German field marshal. ∎

Sex's still right down their alley

WEDNESDAY, JANUARY 23, 1985

The response to my Sex or Bowling survey of men has been so huge that it will be days before we can scientifically tabulate the results and read the thousands of shocking letters.

But based on early returns from all over America, it appears that the majority of men prefer sex with their wives (or other companions) to bowling, fishing, golfing, watching TV or even sitting at a bar with their pals.

As Louie in Chicago put it: "When it comes to sex with my wife or bowling, I prefer sex with my wife because I don't have to change my shoes."

And most of them emphasized that they reject cuddling as the sole sexual

activity, which puts them in conflict with the majority of the women who responded to an Ann Landers survey.

It was the Landers survey that inspired mine. As you recall, 72 percent of her
readers said they just wanted to cuddle and pet and preferred not to go all the way.
Some said they disliked sex so much that they were relieved when their husbands
expired or became infirm.

As Joe from Cicero wrote: "If all my wife wants is cuddling and petting, she
don't need me. She can go to the pet shop."

Ron in LaPorte, Ind.: "I was loved and fondled and cuddled a lot when I was a
baby. And burped, too. Now I want to get on with it!"

I suspect that many of the men who responded to my survey are married to
the unhappy women who responded to Landers. As a fellow who signed himself
"Frustrated in Omaha" put it:

"Forty years ago, on our wedding night, my wife suddenly said: 'Is this supposed to be fun?' Sex was never the same to me again. I opt for fishing."

And Hank in Davenport says he has no doubt that the Landers survey was
accurate. He wrote: "She said that showed that 65,000 of her readers don't like sex.
I'm sure that is true. I think I've met every one of them. They are everywhere."

Some men wrote that they have joyous sex lives with their wives, including
some who have been married for 25 to 50 years, such as the retired minister in
Alaska who said: "At 65, my bedroom is still my favorite playground and my wife
the only playmate I need."

And George in Evanston said: "Why choose between sex and bowling or everything else? A good man can do everything. It's a matter of priorities. I know,
because I am a good man."

But others were less enthusiastic.

Fred in Orland Park wrote: "Any activity is better than sex with my wife. Going
to the dentist runs a close race."

Depressed in Detroit: "When people say to me: 'How's your wife?' I always
answer: 'Better than nothin.'"

Deprived in Kansas: "Because of my wife's attitude, my sex life can be compared to sitting down to an eight course dinner minutes after losing my upper and
lower dentures."

Weary in New York: "I get more pleasure and satisfaction out of scratching my
athlete's foot than anything from my wife."

Eddie in Gary: "When my wife is home, her hair is never washed or brushed,
no makeup, and she wears a bathrobe even a bag lady wouldn't pick up and a
pair of slippers that look like dogs with the mange. But when she goes out, she's
in 5-inch spikes, black fishnet stockings, a dress cut down the back and a slit up
the leg to the thigh, every hair in place and a push-up bra that would make Dolly
Parton jealous. When she comes home and I say: 'Come here, honey,' she says
'One minute.' And in one minute, out comes the bag lady again."

Exhausted in L.A.: "In my marriage, foreplay consists of 15 minutes of me begging."

Among those who said they prefer bowling (or some other activity) to sex with their wives was Bill, from a western suburb, who showed a certain amount of malicious glee in writing:

"The greatest feeling in the world is going to a bowling alley and bowling and drinking beer with your friends and knowing that your wife hates you because she knows that you are in seventh heaven without her."

He might not be so gleeful when he learns that I have received another letter from a man in a western suburb, who signed himself: "Friendly Neighbor."

He wrote: "I have a neighbor who prefers bowling to sex with his wife. So when he goes bowling, I have sex with his wife."

I'll have more later. Man's quest for knowledge never ends.

JANUARY 24, 1995

"You must be jesting to even ask. Five hours on 150 acres of perfectly manicured beauty, breathing fresh air, experiencing the excitement of pars and birdies with my best friends, compared to five minutes of subpar lovemaking with 150 pounds of not-so-manicured woman who constantly complains about my income and lack of understanding? It is no contest. I will take the birdies over the old bat any day. Sign me, Two handicap in Naperville."

And from R.R.R. in Villa Park: "For me, golf is more fulfilling. It provides four hours of uninterrupted pleasure in contrast to—what? You get to set your own pace without nagging for speed or performance. A golfer is guaranteed 18 opportunities for success in one round. While playing, your partners give you encouragement and praise—even when you aren't doing well. I don't remember that ever happening in my bedroom."

M.H., who wrote on stationery of the Forest City (Ark.) Country Club, said: "I salute your sensitivity and insight. At least when my buddies on the links are amused by my inadequacies, inabilities and ineptness, they are laughing with me—not at me."

Pat of St. Louis: "In responding to your survey, I mentioned to my wife that I had to put down whether I preferred sex with her or sinking a 40-foot birdie putt. She told me the odds of either happening in the near future were about the same."

Jeff of Chicago: "Hitting a great golf shot is like having an orgasm. Sadly, during the average man's lifetime, he will probably orgasm a lot more often than he will hit good golf shots."

A dissenting view on golf or sex is found in a tiny poem from an elderly fellow who signs himself "Old 88 in Cleveland."

"When I was young and in my prime,

"I'd rather swing my golf club any time

"But now that I am old and gray,

"I'd rather have sex twice a day.

"P.S. If you print this and get deluged with fan mail, please refer my phone number to females age 70 and over."

After golfers, fishermen showed the most willingness to flee the bedroom. Their views are reflected up by John H. of Chicago, who said: "Let's face it, sex just can't compete with the feeling one gets in landing a 7-pound bass. Perhaps my feelings are screwed up because my wife looks like a 7-pound bass."

And Richard of Ashtabula, Ohio, said: "Include me as someone who thinks that a woman is only a woman, but a 6-pound bass is a trophy. Besides, a man can hire a taxidermist to mount the bass for him, whereas in the case of a woman he is pretty much stuck with that chore himself."

Most bowlers reject their sport as a substitute for carnal delights.

Shaky Jake of Cleveland said: "Any time my wife gives me the nod, I'll drop my bowling bag and stay home. I can always go bowling when we finish."

A similar view was expressed by Jim of Hoffman Estates: "I would like to say that given a choice I would rather be having sex with my girlfriend and go bowling with my wife."

One bowler, Roy of Oak Lawn, said that my survey has caused him confusion: "I find it difficult to state my preference for sex or bowling since I have taken to making love to my bowling ball."

Leaving sports, another trend is being predicted by a sociologist, who wrote from the Washington, D.C., area.

He said the trend will be a result of Ann Landers' survey of women in which 72 percent of them said that they prefer cuddling with their husbands to going all the way. That survey, of course, inspired my survey.

The sociologist said that if cuddling does indeed become the most popular of sexual activities, it could lead to a dramatic change in American street language.

In the future, he predicted, we will hear people saying things like:

"Cuddle off." "Cuddle you." "Go cuddle yourself." "You are a complete cuddle up." "Go take a flying cuddle." "You are a real mothercuddler." And "Hey, baby, let's go to my place and cuddle our eyes out."

JANUARY 29, 1985

Says Big B of Cleveland: "Talk about cuddling! I should be the one cuddled so I could get turned on by my wife, who has developed a figure like the Pillsbury Dough Boy. The only part of her that is in shape is her right wrist, from turning the TV knobs all day."

Jim of Memphis: "I really can't complain about my wife because being married to her has really improved my health. I used to smoke two packs a day. Then I took a vow that I would only have a cigarette after we have sex. I've cut down to less than a pack a year. And as fast as she gets into her hair rollers and flannel nightgown and hits that pillow [she starts] snoring like a bear; I'm going to be in shape to run in marathons before long."

Charlie from Virginia: "I suggest that a total, loving commitment between a man and a woman includes sex—but as a manifestation of a marital union, not the totality. But I have to honestly say that intimacy with my wife is so incredibly dull, perfunctory and mechanical that I would much rather do one of the following: Watch the grass grow, watch them unload the trucks at the supermarket or go down to the highway and count out-of-state license plates."

Don of Westchester: "Enough, I say. I refuse to beg!"

Eddie of Seattle: "When I married her, she was 20 and a beauty. We had one child almost immediately. After that, it was aches, pains, cards with the girls, hours on the phone with her mother and spending my money as fast as she could grab it. But I'm patient. This year, our one child finishes college and I have stashed a bundle and will be on my way out of state. She can have the house—but I'll have the satisfaction of knowing she can't pay the mortgage, the lazy . . ."

But not all men feel that way. Just as many wrote about the happiness of their lives, including many who are in their 60s and 70s and say they still have satisfying sex lives.

Tony of New York says: "I don't know what it is. Maybe just luck. But I'm 72; it's still as great as it ever was. Maybe a little slower, but so what? I don't have anything else to do."

And there are the happy men who offer advice to the unhappy men.

Sherman of Glen Ellyn says: "After 35 years of marriage, I have come to the conclusion that there are no frigid wives, but only inconsiderate, ignorant and boorish husbands who neither know or care about the sexual needs, responses and desires of their wives. Get with it gentlemen!"

And Tom of Youngstown, Ohio, in a burst of candor, says: "I have a gorgeous, sexy wife. She is a great wife; works full time; is a great mom, cook, homemaker; and really tries to please me. Yet, all I do is pick at her, rarely take her out or spend enough time with her. I am lucky. But I must also be sick. How many of you guys see yourself in this letter?"

Bob of Evanston says: "I'm afraid that the message many unhappy women try to get across is that those women want to make love, not make sex. I can't blame them for feeling unhappy."

That last letter might be of interest to Nick of Chicago who wrote: "I prefer my wife in stockings with the seam up the back, a pink garter belt, high heel, furry slippers. That's the way I want her dressed when I get home, and she's got the house cleaned, has made dinner, walked the dog and wants to listen to me about my fishing trip with the boys, ha, ha."

Or Macho Jack of San Jose, who said: "I think the trouble with the unhappy broads in this country is that the wimps don't know how to treat them. Believe me, women like a guy who tells them what to do and when to do it—and if you have to rough them up a little, they might complain but down deep they love it. I'm divorced now, because she nicked me with a kitchen knife then called the cops and left me. But that was in a fight over money, not sex. I'm still trying to get her back."

Good luck. And maybe next time she'll stab you over something less crass than money.

MONDAY, FEBRUARY 11, 1985

Letters, calls, complaints and great thoughts from readers:

Karen N. McCarthy, Memphis: Regarding your sex and bowling column, in the interest of fairness, I hope you will allow a word from the ladies:

There once was a fellow named Fred
Who would bowl 'til he almost dropped dead;
No romance for him
He worked on his spin
And his wife found a spare for her bed!

A fisherman, name of McTish
Had a wife who was really a dish;
While his lines went kerplunk
She reeled in a real hunk
And got rid of McTish, the cold fish.

Old George loved to guzzle his beers
In the pub alongside of his peers;
He learned one day, amazed,
Coming out of his daze
That his wife had been gone now for years!

Our Thor loved to golf and cry Fore!
He considered that sex was a chore;
While he played the links
She was up to hijinks
And eventually dumped Thor, the old bore.

Comment: I think that puts the whole thing in its proper perspective. ∎

326 | CHAPTER TWELVE

To tell the truth, he's a real loser

TUESDAY, SEPTEMBER 4, 1984

When the winning lottery numbers were announced on TV, there was moaning and swearing up and down the bar. But Herbert took it calmly. He shrugged and said, "Unlike these fools, I was absolutely certain I wasn't going to win."

But how could you be sure? Anybody with a ticket has a chance.

"No, that isn't true. I don't know how it's done, but somehow things are rigged so that certain people can't win. People like me."

What do you mean, people like you?

"We have certain characteristics."

Such as?

"Well, let's start with Hawaii. I don't like Hawaii. I would never consider going there."

So?

"So this. About half the people who win a big lottery say the same thing: They're going to use some of their winnings for a vacation in Hawaii. Never Paris or a villa near Rome. Never Martha's Vineyard or Palm Springs. It's always Hawaii. Why do people who suddenly get rich want to fly thousands of miles to eat a pig cooked in a hole in the ground?"

An interesting question.

"Yes, and another reason I don't qualify is that I don't have a sister in California."

What does that have to do with it?

"The ones who don't go to Hawaii usually say they are going to use their winnings to visit their sister in California. How's that for life in the fast track?"

I suppose it could be livelier.

"Yes, and I'm not going to buy any new furniture or a new TV set or add a rec room to my house, which winners always say they're going to do. I would announce that I was going to burn down the dump and every dull object in it."

Your wife wouldn't like that.

"That's probably true. So I also would announce that I was going to retain the best divorce lawyer in America to rid me of her."

That's rather callous of you, considering all those years she's given you.

"Actually, it's generous of me. It's not like I was going to hire someone to bump her off, which I could well afford to do if I won the lottery. Now that would be callous. And I wouldn't do it unless she was unreasonable."

But what would your friends think?

"As friends, I hope they would understand. I would write them letters, explaining everything and telling them how I was going to save our friendship."

How would you do that?

"By having nothing further to do with any of them."

That's not very friendly.

"Of course it is. Human nature being what it is, if I won they would all become terribly envious. This would cause friction in our friendship. So to save them from this painful situation, I would tell them that I didn't want to see them again. And if they showed up, I'd have my bodyguards throw them out."

But wouldn't you share some of your new wealth with them?

"That would be a terrible thing to do to my friends. It would make them dependent upon me, which would be wrong because they would never know if they would have succeeded in life on their own. Naturally, they'll fail on their own. But at least through failure they will come to know themselves. That precious self-knowledge would be my true gift of friendship to them."

But how can somebody live without friends and loved ones?

"Oh, that's no problem. I would simply go to the French Riviera and put up a sign on my yacht saying: 'I have $90 million. Do you love me?' Believe me, the world is filled with loving people. They would probably love me so much they would be willing to do light housekeeping and my laundry, too."

But you can't just spend your life as a playboy.

"Why not? Why can't there be just one lottery winner who looks into the TV cameras and says: 'I am going to quit my job, dump my wife, shed my friends and use my wealth to do all the unspeakable things most of you dream about but are ashamed to admit.'"

Because that would discredit the lottery. It isn't intended to shatter marriages and turn decent men into sinful idlers.

"You might be right. So if I ever win, I'll revise my plan. I'll stay with my wife."

That's the way.

"Yes. And I'll get six mistresses." ∎

Ugly secret told! Reading scandal!

THURSDAY, FEBRUARY 1, 1990

When I returned from vacation, a co-worker asked me what I thought about a major national news story that had occurred while I was away.

I told him I hadn't read it. Looking surprised, he said: "It was in all the papers. Front page."

Then he mentioned a big international development. I told him I had missed that one too.

"Don't you read papers while you're on vacation?"

As a matter a fact, I don't. When I'm working, I read four or five papers a day, plus the various national and international news wires. By the time I go home, I have news squirting out of my ears.

So when I take time off, I try to ignore the great issues of the day. I figure that if something really big happens—the start of World War III or the arrival of Martians—I'll hear people screaming in the streets and will become informed.

Because most news people are news junkies, my co-worker seemed amazed.

"You actually don't read *any* newspapers?"

So I confessed to a dark, dirty, little secret. Yes, when I'm on vacation, I do read one newspaper. And I read that paper only when I'm away from Chicago.

This requires a brief explanation. It begins with the fact that normally I don't do the food shopping. So I don't get into supermarkets.

But while I'm on vacation, I share shopping chores. And as I'm standing in the checkout line, my eyes are drawn to a supermarket publication called Weekly World News.

Because I work for a serious, responsible newspaper, I shouldn't admit this. But I love the Weekly World News.

You may be a regular reader of this publication—especially if you lack several front teeth, have three junked cars in your front yard and your favorite sport is TV wrestling.

If The New York Times can be considered the Mozart of journalism, then the Weekly World News might be described as a journalistic Geraldo.

So I always grab a copy and slip it among the groceries and mumble to the checkout lady: "Uh, it amuses my wife."

Then I devour every amazing story.

The last issue I read, which I brought back with me, contained nothing about the upheavals in Europe, Bush's budget, the reunification of Germany or other weighty matters.

But it had a screaming headline (all of its headlines scream or, at the very least, shriek) that said: "Bulldog Rips Mercedes To Shreds!"

It seems an Australian's car stalled on a country road. Suddenly a big bulldog came out of a hedge and began chomping his car. "I feared for my life," the man said. The dog's owner said: "I don't know what got into Barney, he's normally a good boy. I guess he just liked the way the car smelled."

A few pages over was the headline: "Rock Music Cures Deaf Girl!"

There was no scientific explanation for this miracle. Maybe the kid had a waxy buildup and the bass guitar burst through.

In most stories, the headlines tell it all. For example:

"Fatal Reunion! Divorced Couple Die When Their Cars Collide On The Way To Patch Things Up!"

"Old Lady Locked 55 Hours In Coffin-Sized Closet!"

"World's Biggest Cat—51 Pounds And Growing!"

"Chain-Smoker Kicks 30-Year Habit . . . Then Chokes To Death On Wad Of Nicotine Gum!"

"Naked Thief Turns Into Human Icicle . . . After He Gets Stuck In Restaurant's Vent And Freezes!"

"Angry Man Guns Down His Bean-Eating Buddy. He Just Kept Passing Gas, Says Gunman!"

But in that issue, my choice for top headline was: "Love-Starved Hippo Tries To Mate With Scuba Diver."

(For those who demand the sordid details, it happened in a river in South Africa where some blokes went swimming. The diver, who suffered a few cracked ribs and considerable indignity, said: "He thought I was his mate." An animal expert said the young man was lucky. "Hippos are fierce lovers who don't stop until completely satisfied, and they are used to getting their way.")

Keep that in mind if you plan to swim among hippos.

A close second to the hippo headline was the one about an incident in Swaziland, which also is self-explanatory:

"Cannibal Steals Accident Victims' Corpses And Eats Them!"

And this country became hysterical when California motorists were shooting at each other?

Finally there was the story about a West German man who was slicing some salami for a snack before his favorite TV show came on. The knife slipped, and he cut his hand.

Apparently he was a TV addict. The headline tells it all:

"Man Bleeds To Death While Watching TV! He Wanted To Finish His Program Before Going To Get Help!"

But the vacation is over, so I'm back to significance. Will Jesse run? Will Gorbachev survive? What about Bush's budget? And how will we solve the problems of the inner city?

I think maybe I'll start doing the food shopping. ∎

To Dad, Donald Trump was nothing more than a clownish foil for a few funny columns. Here are two of them. Little did he know what was to come. —D.R.

$20 million hardly worth it for Ivana

WEDNESDAY, FEBRUARY 14, 1990

My jaw dropped when Slats Grobnik gave his views on the breakup of the Trump marriage.

"That guy Don Trump is a louse, the way he's treating his old lady," said Slats. "Even worse, he's a cheapskate."

You, of all people, are sympathizing with Trump's wife, Ivana?

"Sure, ain't you? The way he was playing around. He was bringing his young dolls on ski trips when his wife was there, and taking 'em to parties. I mean, if a guy is going to play around, he ought to have the decency to do it on the sneak."

I suppose that's true. In other times, he would be called a cad, a cur and a scoundrel. But I don't understand why you call him a cheapskate. From what I've read, she will receive $20 million, a palatial house and surely a judge will award her substantial child support payments. I don't consider $20 million to be a trifling sum.

"That's what I thought when I first heard about it. I said, wow, $20 million ain't just walking-around money. And I got to admit that if my wife walked up to me and said, 'Hey, bozo, scram out of my life,' and handed me a certified check for $20 mill, I'd shake her hand, tell her we would always be friends, grab the dough and hop the next plane for the French Riviera."

Then why are you calling Trump a cheapskate?

"Because I looked at the big picture. See, that's the trouble with most people. They think small. They say the babe is getting all that money, she ought to be doing backflips instead of saying she's going to sue him for more."

And what is the big picture?

"For starters, this Trump is supposed to be worth at least $1.7 billion, maybe more. You know how much money that is?"

Lots.

"It's more than that. I figured it out. I'd have to work for 6,666 years to earn $1.7 billion."

With mandatory retirement, you'd never make it.

"Right. So I took my calculator and I figured out what percentage of his bundle this Trump is giving his wife. With the big house and everything, it barely comes to 1.5 percent. He probably makes that much in interest in 2 or 3 months, the cheapo. So what do you think a judge would say if a guy walked into Divorce Court and said: 'Your honor, I'm worth $200,000. So I figure that I'll give my wife here $3,000 and we'll call it quits.'"

I think the judge might tap him on the head with his gavel.

"Sure. But here's Trump running around with different dolls and now he's trying to stiff his old lady with a measly 1.5 percent."

Ah, but you overlook the fact that she entered into a prenuptial agreement—a contract that established the sum she would receive.

"I know that. But if he was any kind of a guy, he wouldn't hold her to it. Just because he's a rat don't mean that he can't be a fair rat. What about all those golden parachutes big companies give executives when they get the boot?"

Well, what about them?

"Some of those guys get millions. But did any of the executives ever go through 9 months of labor like Trump's wife did three times? Did any of them get stretch marks from anything except eating big lunches on their expense accounts?"

You have a point.

"Sure. There she was waddling around in a maternity dress, with water on her ankles and all that stuff, while he was downtown getting some steam and a massage at his private gym. And don't forget, she just didn't sit around the house looking at People Magazine. She was at his big casino in Atlantic City. From what I read, she was running the joint, watching the bottom line, making sure the dealers weren't pocketing chips and giving a big smile to the high rollers. She kind of reminds me of my Aunt Stella."

Who?

"My Aunt Stella. When my little Uncle Chester was a neighborhood bookie, and a guy didn't pay, Aunt Stella used to go see the guy and threaten to stick both her thumbs in his eye balls. She had big thumbs so they always paid. You can bet that Uncle Chester wouldn't have tried to dump Aunt Stella with only 1.5 percent. Not if Chester didn't want to wear two eye patches the rest of his life. But to get back to the Trumps, you can tell she was devoted to the guy and was trying to please him. She even had her mug hoisted to look young."

Her what?

"Her mug hoisted. You know, one of those Joan Rivers jobs."

You mean cosmetic surgery?

"Yeah. And that can't feel good. The doc has to stick needles in your head and grab your skin and yank on it like a pair of tight stockings. I almost pass out when the dentist cleans my teeth. But Trump's wife goes through that so that when they go to a party she don't look like a dog and embarrass him. Just having a doc stick needles in her head ought to be worth 1.5 percent."

Well, these profound questions will all be resolved in court, as well as in the National Enquirer. And I commend you for your enlightened views.

"Thank you. And I got one piece of advice for Trump's girlfriends."

What is that?

"If he marries one of them, and the preacher says, 'Do you take this man to be your lawful wedded husband,' she ought to say, 'Yeah, and I want at least 20 percent.'" ∎

Trump stumped on Marla, er, Carla

FRIDAY, JULY 5, 1991

NEW YORK—While strolling along 5th Avenue, I was surprised to see The Donald walking along, a beautiful woman on his arm.

I stepped up and said: "Hello, The Donald, I am from the press. Any startling new revelations to make about your personal life today?"

The Donald withdrew a printed statement from his jacket pocket and said: "I assume you are familiar with my recent utterances about the terrors of modern dating because of the threat of AIDS?"

"I read that. You really do ask your female friends to undergo medical testing?"

"One can't be too careful."

"I'm curious. Just how do you go about diplomatically making such a request. Do you send them a note or what?"

"Oh, no. The first time we go out, I make it a double-date. Then when I go to the young lady's home, I tell her: 'I'd like you to meet Charles here, he is my personal physician. And this is Lucille, his medical technician.' Then I hand her some flowers. I always bring flowers. And I say: 'I hope you don't mind if Charles takes a little of your blood and Lucille analyzes it? It will take only a few minutes, then we can go to dinner. I've made reservations at a wonderful place.'"

"That's very tactful. But I assume that is no longer necessary, since you are now engaged to Marla."

The Donald blinked and said: "No, I'm engaged to Carla."

The young lady on his arm frowned and said: "What are you talking about? I am Marla and you are engaged to me."

Then she waved her left hand, showing a diamond the size of a turnip.

The Donald looked dazed. "You are Marla, not Carla?"

"Of course I am Marla, not Carla, you silly but lovable tycoon."

The Donald scratched his head, recombed his hair, gave it a squirt of goo and said: "I don't understand this at all."

I interrupted to say: "Yes, she is right. It has been in all the papers. You dumped Ivana for Marla, but then you were reported to have dumped the beautiful Marla because you were smitten with the gorgeous Carla. But then you announced that you had become engaged to Marla, and indicated that you had never been anything but 'friends' with Carla."

The Donald shook his head and said: "There seems to have been a mistake made here. I would have sworn that I dumped Marla and had become engaged to Carla."

The young lady laughed and said: "No, you foolish but adorable real estate mogul, you originally said you dumped me, the beautiful Marla, for Carla, but then you dumped Carla and proposed to me, Marla."

The Donald peered at the young lady and said: "You're saying that you are Marla and not Carla?"

She sighed and said: "Of course I am Marla and not Carla, you debt-ridden but still rich darling, you."

The Donald reached into his jacket pocket and took out a stack of photographs of women. As he riffled through them, he kept glancing at the young lady. Then he stopped and stared at a photograph and said: "I'll be darned, you're right. You are Marla, not Carla."

"See?" she said, giggling delightedly. "I told you. And we're engaged and will live happily ever after, unless the banks peel you like a grape, in which case I will have to reconsider my options."

The Donald shook his head and said: "I think I know what happened."

I said: "Do you mind if I take notes?"

"Not at all," he said, "since it is my duty as The Donald to share with the American public every detail of my private life, my every emotion, my every thought, as banal and tawdry as they might be."

"Yes, you owe it to history. So what happened?"

"I think it is because I've always been bad on names. By the way, what's yours?"

"Mike."

"Nice to meet you, Ike. Anyway, I get names mixed up. Iraq, Iran, I still don't know which is which, not that they matter in my glamorous life. So when I announced that I had become engaged to Marla . . . ."

"Ah-hah, you meant to say Carla."

"I think so. I mean, it doesn't make sense for me to become engaged to Marla if I dumped her for Carla, does it?"

"To an impartial observer, no."

He turned to the young lady and said: "Then I'm very sorry, Marla, but there seems to have been a mistake. I'm supposed to be engaged to Carla. I hope you understand."

"Of course," she laughed gaily, "but I have a simple solution. You can just call me Carla instead of Marla."

The Donald thought for a moment, then said: "Yes, I suppose that would solve the problem. Then I'd be engaged to Carla. By golly, I'll do it."

He smiled and said: "Spike, I'd like you to meet my new fiancée, Carla. I dumped Marla for her, you know."

As they strolled toward his limo, I heard him say: "By the way, you have passed your blood test, haven't you?"

"Twice, you credit-risky but still fun-loving playboy, you."

"Good," The Donald said. "Now let's go get your teeth checked." ▪

I was in Dad's office for a few of the AT&T calls, and it was a blast to watch him torment these poor callers, few if any ever knowing they were getting to play the straight man (or woman) to one of America's greatest humorists. Nothing displays Dad's improvisational wit—fast as a John Wayne quick-draw—better than these gems. The calls went on for years; AT&T never changed the phone number. The columns Dad got from them were huge hits with readers, and I have appended calls from later columns. —D.R.

The number you have dialed . . .

WEDNESDAY, NOVEMBER 28, 1984

I have a confession to make. It's directed at hundreds of people whose names I don't know.

These are people who have tried to dial AT&T, the phone company, and wound up talking to somebody who sounded a little strange.

Let me explain how this happens:

Somebody wants to find out where the nearest phone store is or how to plug the phone in or complain that it doesn't work or something like that.

So he looks up the number in the directory, calls information or looks on the bottom of the phone.

The number is a toll-free 800 number. Simple enough. Just dial 1, then 800, then the number.

For reasons I don't understand, many people don't bother to dial 800 first. They just dial the seven-digit number.

When they do that, they don't get AT&T. They get one of my three office phone lines.

This can be a nuisance. There are days when five minutes don't pass without the phone ringing and somebody saying something like:

"Hello, I live at 67th and Kedzie. Where's the nearest phone center?"

Or: "I got this phone and I'm trying to plug it in but it doesn't seem to work."

This has been going on all year. From morning 'til night, day after day, hundreds, thousands of calls about telephones.

The calls disrupt my work. Even worse, they sometimes jar me out of a sound sleep. They drive me and my one assistant crazy, since there's nobody else here to answer the phone.

Being a normal human being, my nervous system sometimes becomes frayed. After a dozen calls in one morning, I begin mumbling to myself: "Why can't they dial that damn 800 first? Do you have to be a genius to dial 800 when the phone book specifically says 800?"

So I sometimes react impulsively. And that has led to the following, actual conversations:

Hello.

"Hey, I live at Milwaukee and Kedzie, and I want to know where the nearest phone center is."

Oh, it's around there somewhere.

"Well, what's the address?"

Guess!

"Wha—?"

C'mon, guess. Pick a number from 1 to 10.

"Hey, are you crazy?"

Don't say I'm crazy. If you say I'm crazy again, *I'll kill you*!

Click.

Hello.

"Yeah, I picked up a new phone but something's wrong. I plug it in and it doesn't work."

I see. Have you tried plugging it in your ear?

"My what?"

Your ear. It says right here on Page 10 in my employee's manual: Suggest customer stick plug in ear. Oh, wait a minute, you can also try sticking it in your nose.

"Is this the phone company?"

To tell the truth, I don't know. I haven't worked here very long.

Click.

Hello.

"Uh, I got this phone, and there's something the matter with it."

Oh, how terrible. Are you suffering much? I know how you must feel. My heart goes out to you. Oh, if there was only something I could do, I'd do it, believe me, anything, anything. But I feel so powerless.

"Hey, I'm just calling about my phone."

Have you tried praying? That can help. I once had a toaster that didn't work, and I prayed and prayed and . . .

Click.

Hello.

"I want to know where the phone center is in my neighborhood. I live at . . ."

Forget it. You shouldn't have a phone.

"Whad'ya mean?"

Your voice is unpleasant. Raspy. Too loud. A person who sounds like you should not have a phone. I forbid you to ever have a phone. This is your final warning, do you understand?

Click.

Hello.

"I want to know where the nearest phone center is."

I will tell you that if you will tell me something.

"What?"

What is the meaning of life?

"The what?"

The meaning of life. What is truth? What is beauty?

"Hey I just want to know where the phone center is."

Phone center? I'm trying to talk to you about life, beauty, truth, and all you want to talk about is phone centers? What kind of insensitive person are you? You disgust me.

"You can't talk to me that way. Let me speak to your supervisor."

"Madam: I am the supervisor."

Click.

So if you have to call that number, remember, dial 1-800.

If you don't, the voice you hear might say: "Ah, your new phone doesn't work? Well, phones can be shy little things. Have you tried giving it a kiss?"

Click.

JULY 23, 1985

"My phone isn't working right," someone would say.

"Then bang it against the wall," I would tell him. "If that doesn't work, you might chant a mantra. That always makes me feel better."

Monday morning a woman said, "I want to get my phone repaired."

"What's wrong with it?"

"There's a buzzing noise."

"Whom were you talking to when it made a buzzing noise?"

"What's that got to do with it?"

"Just answer my questions, please, if you expect us to help you."

"It happens when I talk to everybody. My friends, my daughter."

"Ah-hah, that explains it. Your daughter and your friends are making a buzzing sound at you."

"What are you talking about?"

"Sure. They're trying to make you think you are batty so they can have you committed and divide up your wealth. Happens all the time."

"Say, who is this?"

"Buzzz, buzzz, buzzzz, buzzzz."

She hung up.

Then there was the man who spoke with a foreign accent. Actually, I use the same response for everyone with foreign accents.

"I'm sorry, sir, but AT&T will not provide service for your phone needs."

"Why not?"

"Because you have a foreign accent. For all we know, you are a spy for a foreign power, and AT&T does not want to assist those who would undermine and subvert this great nation. You probably use our phones to transmit our top secrets."

"Hey, wait a minute . . ."

"You're probably a dirty commie, and it is not this company's policy to assist dirty commies in doing their dirty work. We demand that you turn in your phone and surrender to the FBI immediately. Goodbye, and may the Lord have mercy on your treasonous soul."

Most of the calls are from people who want to know where their nearest phone center store is. So I ask them what their address is and give them one of my standard replies.

"There's one right around the corner from Jake's Bar."

"Where?"

"Jake's Bar. You know where that is, don't you?"

"No, I don't. What is the address?"

"You don't know Jake? Little bald guy with a thin mustache? Nice guy, give you the shirt off his back. But he drinks too much these days. His wife left him, you know. Ran off with one of the customers. But Jake's the kind of guy who'll buy a drink and cash a paycheck if he knows you."

"What are you talking about? I want to know where to take my phone for repairs."

"Oh, you don't even care about Jake, do you? Wife's gone, took the kids, cleaned out the bank account, but that doesn't bother you. No compassion for your fellow man. Jake can just drink himself to death, but you don't care. Well, if you're going to be heartless and selfish, I don't want any more to do with you. Goodbye and good riddance from AT&T."

Or sometimes, when they tell me where they live, I'll say:

"Wow, you live *there*? I grew up in that neighborhood. I lived there for *years*."

"You did?"

"Yeah. Boy, how do you stand it? What a cruddy neighborhood. The real pits. I hated it. And the people. I never saw such weird people. No teeth, or two noses or an eye in the middle of their foreheads. They're like mutants. It must have something to do with the water. Do you look like that—real weird, I mean?"

"What are you talking about?"

"Look, I'm sorry about your phone, but I'm going to have to hang up. Just talking to you gives me the creepy-crawlies. Ugh and goodbye."

SEPTEMBER 9, 1985

"Where's the phone center around Ford City?"

I said, "What is your ethnic background?"

"What'd ya want to know that for?"

"Please, sir, just answer the question. What is your ethnic background?"

"Irish. So what?"

"Well, I'm afraid we won't be able to help you."

"Why not?"

"We are discontinuing all service to people of Irish ancestry."

"What? Why?"

"Look, you just don't pay your bills. We don't know if you spend it all on beer or what, but you can't be trusted."

He burst into a string of appropriate swear words.

"And you are also crude," I added. "Goodbye."

Seconds later he called back and demanded an explanation.

"I told you, we are no longer servicing the Irish. We will be cutting off your service shortly. Goodbye."

I assume that he has since told all of his friends and relatives of the anti-Irish bigotry he encountered and that they are as outraged at AT&T as he is. Or else he has learned to dial 1-800.

Then there was the woman who called from the Jefferson Park neighborhood. I asked her name, then said, "Isn't that a Polish name?"

"Yes it is," she said.

"Ah, then I'm very sorry. We can't help you if you are Polish."

"What are you talking about?"

"We don't like the Polish."

"That's the most terrible thing I've ever heard. Why are you saying that?"

"Corporate policy, I guess."

"You have a corporate policy that you don't like the Polish?"

"That's right. I'll tell you what, why don't you have your name changed to something that sounds American? Try Smith or Jones."

"How dare you."

"We dare, madam, because we are big and powerful. And you ain't. Goodbye."

Later there was the man of Italian ancestry who was struck speechless when I told him that we were refusing service to Italians because our technicians didn't like working on phones that were garlicky.

A woman of Norwegian parentage vowed to call federal authorities after I told her that she and all Norwegians were being cut off. "You Norwegians are just so dull," I said, "that we don't believe you have anything worthwhile to talk about on a phone anyway."

And I've managed to alienate, on AT&T's behalf, many blacks. A conversation with one black man went something like this:

"Tell me, are you of the black persuasion?"

"Yeah, what about it?"

"We are discontinuing service to all blacks."

"Say what?"

"Yes. You people use all that jivey language and, frankly, you laugh too much.

And that causes a confusion in the electronic equipment. Our equipment is designed to handle traditional American speech, not all that jive talk."

"I don't believe this."

"Well, that's the way it is. If I might offer a suggestion, you try to become a white suburbanite. G'by."

I don't know how much AT&T spends on public relations. I'm sure it's a considerable sum. But in the face of my campaign, it's going to be a big waste.

So wise up, AT&T, and get a new number. Why, I haven't even gotten around to the Hispanics, the Chinese, the Lithuanians, the . . .

SEPTEMBER 7, 1994

"You say your phone doesn't work properly? Well, that is your tough luck, bozo. This company has been bought by Yawoola, an oil-rich Arab nation, and we are going to teach you lazy Americans not to abuse precious phone privileges. As of tomorrow, you are forbidden to use a phone. If you violate this order, your ear will be cut off. This is your last warning. Goodbye."

Sometimes I ask for the caller's name. If it is ethnically or racially identifiable, I might say: "I am sorry, but we no longer provide service for people of your ethnic or racial background because you are notorious for being drunks, deadbeats, cutthroats, philanderers, degenerates and you have no need for a telephone because you have nothing intelligent to say since your genes and DNA are inferior. May the Lord have mercy upon your worthless soul, farewell forever."

And once in a while, I might say: "You got problems with your phone? Hey, we all got troubles. My old lady just cleaned out the checking account and ran off with my favorite bartender and best buddy. And I got a prostate problem. And my boss hates me. And you are calling me about some stupid buzzing in your phone? Hey, I am a human bomb ready to explode. Don't mess with me, you hear?"

They usually hang up, and I'm sure it gives them something to think about until they finally dial the correct number for AT&T.

So if you must call AT&T, be sure to follow the instructions. ∎

CHAPTER 13
Me, Myself and I

These are Dad's first two columns for the Trib, after which he moved on and didn't refer to his "move" or Murdoch (in this context) again. —D.R.

New address sits fine, thank you

WEDNESDAY, JANUARY 11, 1984

I was born in the wrong generation. If I'd had any choice in the matter, I would have arrived years later, so that I would have been growing up during the 1960s.

Say what you will about the youths of that era—dope heads, flower chompers, mantra chanters—they had an attitude toward work that appealed to me. They tried their best to avoid it.

My old pal Slats Grobnik, also born before his time, summed up our attitude this way:

"Everybody says that work is so good for ya. Well, if work is supposed to be so great, how come they got to pay ya to do it?"

That's always made sense to me. I've known a few people who were born rich and never had to work, and they always struck me as being a little dumb, but very happy.

Oh, those born rich will try to con you into believing that with all their money they're still capable of being miserable. Occasionally, one of them will fake a nervous breakdown and blubber to People Magazine about how his or her wealth has brought nothing but sadness, tension and blotchy skin.

But don't believe a word of it. They only say that because they're afraid that if the rest of us knew what a good time they're having, we'd storm their estates, drink their wines, ravish the maid and eat their polo ponies.

Consider that Onassis girl, the one with the bowling ball thighs. Every so often, we read about how her inherited millions have not made her happy. But every time I see a picture of her, what is she doing? She's on the deck of her yacht, wolfing down figs, baklava, snifters of Metaxa, all brought to her, ordering around a crew of handsome beach boy types.

If she's miserable, then the night scrub lady in this office would gladly trade in her mop and pail for that type of torment.

On the other hand, just go stand outside Union Station or a Loop 'L' stop or a factory site in the morning and study the faces. Grim, grim, grim. You can almost hear the stomach acid eating away at the lining.

Why? Because they're going to work, that's why.

So why do we do it if it is so depressing? The obvious answer is that we have to eat, pay the rent, clothe the kids, feed the cat, cover the bar tab and put something aside for a good hairpiece in our old age.

But beyond that, we have been taught that it is good to work. Every generation, except that of the flower children, believed it. The Depression generation feared the soup lines. Today's generations fear Sony and Honda.

And we were taught that anybody who didn't work was a bum. [Many Republicans still believe that. Except those who are unemployed.]

It's this dread of being considered a bum that has motivated me to work, without missing a payday, since my 15th birthday.

My first job was setting pins in the old Congress Bowling Alleys on Milwaukee Avenue. I was amazed to find that many of my fellow pinsetters were bums. That's when I discovered that life can be so tough, even bums have to hustle a living.

Later I tried other occupations: working in a screw machine shop, on a loading dock, in a lamp factory, a department store and behind the bar of a tavern.

These jobs taught me a lesson that I still live by, in work or physical fitness: Don't run if you can walk; don't walk if you can just stand there; don't stand there if you can sit down.

That philosophy led me to my present line of work. It's not that I particularly enjoy chasing news stories, although it can be fun watching a frightened alderman crouch behind his wallet. And it's not that I enjoy writing opinions, since it is much easier to lean on a bar and mumble them instead. The true appeal of this job is that I can do it while I'm sitting. The only thing that would be better would be to find a job I could do while lying down. But hardly anybody, except Hefner, has that kind of luck.

So that's what I've been doing for the past 20 years or so—sitting and avoiding being a bum. To be truthful, I'd rather be doing nothing, leading the life of a boulevardier or a playboy, but that costs a lot.

Until today, I've been doing my sitting at another place about a block from here.

And I was content until this fellow came into town with a large sack of money and decided to buy that place.

As sometimes can happen between boss and employee, we didn't see eye to eye on a few things, so I decided to do my sitting over here.

That doesn't strike me as being any big deal. I would think that any self-respecting, international tycoon would be delighted to get rid of somebody who sits as much as I do.

And if he wants somebody for a sitting job, heck, I know people who are much better at it than I am. My friend Slats once tried for a world record in sitting. And he would have made it, too, if he hadn't become so fatigued that he had to lie down.

Anyway, that's how I landed on this page.

But now this international tycoon's aide says they are going into court to prevent me from doing my daily sitting here.

What a problem. I don't want to do my sitting there. But he doesn't want me to do it here. Can you imagine a guy coming all the way from Australia just to tell me where to sit?

So what option will that leave me? Sitting on a park bench, I suppose. And I wouldn't mind it, but it doesn't pay much, unless you work for Ed Kelly.

Life is strange. All those lousy jobs loading trucks, working in factories, slinging hash, digging holes and running a punch press—nobody ever said they'd sue to make me stop.

Ah, Rupert, where the hell were you when I needed you? ∎

In Alien's tongue, 'I quit' is 'vacation'
THURSDAY, JANUARY 12, 1984

A Chicago politician called today and chortled: "Congrats, you're one of us now, you sly devil, you."

One of you? What are you talking about? I've never been indicted, convicted or even nominated.

He chuckled knowingly and said: "C'mon, you turned out to be a real double-dipper."

A double-dipper? Me?

"Sure. And you remember how many times you've rapped us for double-dipping, don't you?"

You mean for somehow managing to be on two payrolls at the same time?

"Right, you slicker, you. But now you've done it yourself. When are you going to run for alderman? Believe me, you've got all the instincts."

Despite my protests, he was still chuckling when he hung up.

A moment later my Uncle Chester called and said: "I want to apologize. I just told your aunt that you're not as dumb as I always thought you were."

I appreciate that. But what changed your mind?

"Because I see that you managed to get two papers to print your stuff at the same time. How'd you swing that? I was always amazed that even one would do it."

Me, too, but this isn't my idea. I'm against it.

"Then I'm wrong. You really are dumb."

Let me explain.

"Don't bother. You probably don't understand it yourself. G'by."

He might be right, but I'd like to try to explain this bizarre situation anyway.

As people who read both Chicago newspapers might have noticed, my columns have appeared in both of them the last couple of days.

The columns in this paper are new. The ones in the other paper are reprints of columns that were written and published in past years.

The reason there are new columns in this paper is that I now work here.

The reason old columns are appearing in the other paper is that I don't work there anymore. But The Alien who now owns it doesn't seem to understand that. So he keeps printing my old columns and saying that I'm on vacation.

I don't know why The Alien is doing that. Maybe it's a custom in his native land, which is about 6,000 miles from Chicago.

If so, it is a very strange custom.

I mean, in this country, most employers know when somebody does or doesn't work for them.

Around here, if somebody walks into the boss' office and says something like, "You're kind of a disreputable character and I don't want to work for you, so I quit and here is my resignation," the boss would surely understand.

And the boss would say something like: "Good riddance. Turn in your key to the underlings' washroom."

But apparently it doesn't work that way in The Alien's native land. There, I suspect, when a person quits and walks out, the boss smiles brightly and says: "Ah, he has gone on vacation."

If so, they must have some really confused payroll departments.

Or maybe there's another explanation. It could be that The Alien, in trying to learn about our customs, has been studying City Hall.

If that's the case, then I can understand why The Alien is acting so strangely.

In our city hall, it's always been difficult to tell if people are working, on vacation, retired or even dead or alive. And it's made little difference. The work level has been about the same.

There have been documented cases of aldermen's young nephews being hired as city inspectors and immediately vanishing, not to be seen again until they showed up for their retirement party.

It is said that a City Hall supervisor once showed up at the wake of a foreman from streets and sanitation. As he stood over the coffin, somebody said: "Did you know him well?" The supervisor said: "He worked for me for 30 years, so I came here to see what he looked like."

But if that's what The Alien believes, somebody should straighten him out. That's the way it's done in City Hall, but not in the private sector. The custom is for the rest of us to work in order to support our ancient political tradition.

I suppose this is the kind of confusing problem that we're going to have to get used to in this modern world, with rich foreigners running in and out of each other's countries to buy up each other's businesses.

And it could be worse. As an anthropologist friend said:

"It's a good thing for you the other paper wasn't bought by somebody from the wealthy but distant and remote nation of Manumbaland."

Why?

"It is the custom there that when somebody resigns from his job, he is beheaded."

I guess I was lucky.

But there's still time. ∎

Frankly, I debated whether to include this one. It was his first column since Tuesday, December 13. The following Sunday, as Jon Hilkevitch reported in the Trib, "Chicago Tribune columnist Mike Royko was charged with driving under the influence and resisting arrest after he and another motorist were involved in a minor traffic accident Saturday afternoon."

That May, he pleaded guilty to drunk driving and was sentenced to two years of supervision; ordered to refrain from drinking during the supervision period; had the automatic six-month suspension of his driver's license extended by four and a half months to mid-December; was hit with a $1,000 fine and two years of probation on the resisting arrest charge; and was ordered to complete 80 hours of community service. He read to the blind.

It was a low point in Dad's life. But he didn't try to hide, minimize or rationalize what happened. Dad never accepted the label alcoholic, preferring to refer to himself by the term used in the world he grew up in—a drunk. He struggled his entire adult life with booze, sometimes successfully kicking the habit, but more often than not, suffering from it.

I often wonder if Dad's drinking would have become a problem had he chosen a different profession. It would be hard to exaggerate how different the newspaper business is now compared to his era. The bar was an extension of the newsroom, and it was the rare columnist or reporter that went right home after work. It was also the era before 24-hour cable news. Newspapers were central to people's lives, columnists were celebrities and Dad was the reigning rock star of that world. Add to that the fact that Dad grew up in a tavern, tending bar at age 12 and living above the place his father owned and ran. The bar was, literally, his second home.

This column, Dad's first after the DUI arrest, was his confessional. The reason it's here is because I think it's a great one, uniquely so, written under the most trying personal circumstances since the death of my mother. Leaning on Slats to help him out, Dad could make you chuckle while he was laughing through the tears. —D.R.

Enquiring minds don't need to know

TUESDAY, JANUARY 3, 1995

When we met for our traditional New Year's drink of Ovaltine, Slats Grobnik said: "Tell me about those pills. You buy them across the counter or does a doc have to write a prescription?"

Pills? What pills?

"Those Stupid Pills I figure you been taking lately. Boy, they really did the job, didn't they?"

I am not familiar with Stupid Pills and have not used them.

"You did it all on your own? Boy, then you're a natural like that baseball movie with Robert Redford. Maybe they'll make a movie like that about you, except at the end the only fireworks will be in your head."

Do you mind if we talk about something else?

"Hey, no problem."

Thank you. I gather that you, too, have been on vacation. Did you have a pleasant time?

"Sure. And I didn't get arrested even once."

That wasn't what I meant. Did you go anywhere?

"Yeah, I took a little trip. You wanna hear about it?"

Sure.

"Well, I got where I was going without having to put up any bail money."

Forget it.

"Just making conversation. But I guess you don't wanna talk about it, huh?"

About what?

"How you got to be public enemy No. 1."

That's a slight exaggeration. But, no, my attorney advised me against saying anything until we go to court.

"Oh, that ought to be fun with the cameras being shoved in your face and the TV reporters asking you how you feel, and if you regret being a jerk, and if you're ever going to do it again, and if you are thinking about hanging yourself, and how now you ain't got no credibility no more, and are you going to get in another line of work, and did your boss say you ought to go to the Betty Ford clinic, and how are you going to get around without wheels, and is your wife going to get a divorce, and how are you ever going to write something bad about someone else when now you are such a bum, and if you decide to hang yourself will you do it where they can get a good shot for the 4 o'clock news, and . . ."

Excuse me, I said I would rather not discuss it.

"But you ain't; I am. When you come out of the courthouse, you gonna take a swing?"

At who?

"The reporters or the camera guys. Even if the punch don't land, it would make a great bite for the 4 o'clock news, and they'd probably use it again at 10. You might even make the networks again."

Of course not. Why would I do something like that?

"Well, as long as you're taking those Stupid Pills, you might as well get all the benefits."

I told you, I am not taking any such pills. And let us change the subject, please. How are things at work?

"Just fine. And when I pull into the company parking lot, everybody don't run to call their insurance agents, and nobody asks me if I can walk a straight line and touch my nose. Speaking of that, with your nose, you should have been able to pass the test by touching it with your foot."

And how is the family?

"Everybody's fine. Why not? When they go out, they don't have to wear bags over their faces because of me. How about yours? Have they tried to have you committed yet?"

No, but it's nice of you to ask.

"What about Oprah or Geraldo?"

I don't watch their shows, but what about them?

"Have you thought about going on? I'm sure they'd be glad to have you even if you didn't wear a sequined gown and high heels."

Why in the world would I do that?

"Geez, to talk about your rise and fall—how you went from being a highly respected bum to a pathetic, sad, down-and-out bum. They'd probably bring on some other once-mighty bums—maybe ol' Spiro Agnew, Darryl Strawberry the ballplayer and that guy Keating from the S&L scandal—so you could compare notes on how you turned into social outcasts. Then the audience could ask questions about how it feels to be such lousy lowlifes.

"It could be a heck of a show, and you could get a tape to leave to your grandchildren so they'll know what a live wire you were."

Thanks for the suggestion, but I believe that I'll decline the honor and instead go through the normal legal process.

"That's all? Just go to court?"

That's customary, isn't it?

"I guess so. But it don't seem like enough. Hey, how's about if I go rent a white Bronco with a car phone, then we can go for a ride on the expressways, and I'll drive, and you can announce that you're going to end it all, and . . ."

How about if we just have another Ovaltine.

"You're no fun."

Yes, and it's about time. ∎

Flying is great, but the log tells a different story

TUESDAY, OCTOBER 17, 1995

This is going to be a diary. A very short diary. It is being written with trembling fingers on a laptop computer.

Sunday, 9:40 a.m.: For the last 20 minutes, I have been strapped into a seat in a large metal tube. This tube is about five miles above the state of Colorado. It is moving in an easterly direction at about the speed of a bullet.

In other words, I'm in a commercial jet airliner, and I don't belong here.

That's because I don't fly. I have a phobia. Several, in fact. I'm a control freak, and I fear heights, confined spaces and terrorists, both domestic and foreign.

The last time I got on one of these things was about 20 years ago. But that doesn't count because some friends poured an afternoon's worth of vodka into me and I thought I was on a fast bus.

But this time I did it without even one drink. Which shows that sobriety is overrated.

So what am I doing way up here, thousands of feet from the surface of the planet I love and already desperately miss?

It's the fault of the sadistic blond woman sitting next to me, calmly reading a magazine. She loves flying, and she bullied, cajoled and shamed me into getting on this thing with her.

By the time I changed my mind and decided to leave and catch a night train out of Denver, it was too late. We were already along the ground and hurtling into the sky.

My life didn't flash before my eyes because I had my hands over them.

When I opened them, I nudged my wife and said: "Look at that poor guy. He either fainted or died of fright."

"No," she said, "he started taking a nap as soon as he got on."

"Then he must be that lunatic Chuck Yeager."

Sunday, 10:05 a.m.: It still hasn't crashed. But, then, there is always a calm before the storm.

The stewardess came by and asked if I wanted something to drink. I said yes, some scotch, and leave the bottle. My wife said: "He'll have coffee."

When the stewardess brought the coffee, I told her I would like to speak to the pilot. She asked why. I said I wanted to see his driver's license. She chuckled. I don't know why she thought that was funny. The pilot is an absolute stranger. How do I know what his qualifications are?

Sunday, 10:30 a.m.: Neither of the wings has fallen off yet. I asked my wife to look out of the window and keep her eyes peeled.

"For what?" she asked.

"Birds. All it takes is one dumb goose or even a sparrow flying into an engine and we've all had it. I don't want to end it that way, screaming the Lord's Prayer as we plunge toward a Nebraska cornfield. I want to go out with dignity in my own bed, surrounded by my loved ones and watching their faces when I tell them they've been cut out of my will."

Sunday, 10:45 a.m.: My wife said, "You don't have to keep your safety belt on for the whole flight."

"Like hell I don't. If the door accidentally pops open, I don't want to be sucked out. I still can't understand why we aren't issued parachutes."

Sunday, 11 a.m.: The door to the cabin has opened and a man comes out and talks to the stewardess.

"There's the pilot," my wife said.

"My god," I said. "Who's flying the plane?"

"The co-pilot."

"What, some rookie kid? That's outrageous. If we make it alive, I'm going to write to the FAA."

Sunday, 11:20 a.m.: The plane dips to one side. Then it starts to lose altitude. In my steadiest hysterical voice, I tell my wife: "I knew it. We're going down. We're doomed. Forgive me for not being a better husband. Or don't forgive me. What's the difference now. I'm about to become a charred lump."

"Shhh, relax, we're just landing," she said.

"Oh, boy, that's when it always happens."

"We're fine. Look, you can see O'Hare."

"What are those cars doing on the runway? This is insane."

"That's the toll road, silly."

"I hope the pilot knows it."

Sunday, 11:40 a.m.: There is a tiny thump.

"We've had it," I moaned.

"We've landed," she said.

I open one eye. Then the other. She's right.

The napping guy on the other side of the aisle yawns, stretches and rubs his face. So I yawn, stretch and rub my face. It's a guy thing.

Sunday, noon: We're in a cab. The driver asked: "How was your flight?"

"Smooth as silk," I said. "Slept most of the way."

The blond snickered and said: "Should I call a travel agent tomorrow?"

"Why not? It's a small world." ∎

A middle-age man white from start

WEDNESDAY, AUGUST 15, 1990

There was a time when being a middle-age white man wasn't a bad thing to be. He was considered a pillar of society, a worldly source of wisdom and experience, even a leader.

But over the years, the middle-age white man has fallen into disrepute.

It began in the 1960s when young adults, their consciousness heightened by love, flowers and a few joints, declared middle-age white men guilty of greed, cruelty and liking dull music. (They conveniently forgot that middle-age white men had invented such wonders as the light bulb, the telephone and Popeil's Pocket Fisherman.)

And now middle-age white men stand in shame for dominating most corporations; for being the congressmen who caused the S&L mess; and for belonging to the golf clubs that exclude minorities and won't let women share the choice morning tee times.

This can be very depressing if you are a middle-age white man. Or to use more contemporary language, if you are part of the middle-age white man community, which I happen to be.

I don't apologize for my condition. In the words of a great philosopher, I'yam what I'yam.

Nor do I take any great satisfaction in it since it was none of my doing. If nature had decided otherwise, I might be a middle-age turtle or yak.

But as fate or chance decreed, I am a middle-age white man. However, unlike other middle-age white men, I have always been one.

Yes, strange but true, I was born that way. It created quite a stir at the hospital when the doctor said: "You are the parents of a very small middle-age white man. Congratulations, I think."

My mother was disappointed, but my father said: "Look at the bright side. Now we don't have to save for college."

Most of the supermarket papers of that era had headlines saying: "Woman Gives Birth To Tiny Middle-Age White Man."

Naturally, being born a middle-age white man, my childhood experiences were different than most.

When the nurses brought a bottle to my crib, I said: "What is that stuff?"

"Formula," they said.

"If you don't mind, I would rather have a martini, with two olives."

"On the rocks?"

"Straight up, please."

"And for dinner?"

"A strip steak with baked potato and sour cream."

I recall the pediatrician leaning over and saying: "I don't recommend that diet."

I said: "Why not? That is middle-age white man's food."

"Cholesterol," he said. "You're better off with fish or skinless chicken. And watch the butter."

Damn. The middle-age white man's burden.

He also said: "You should quit smoking."

I said: "I haven't started yet."

"Well, after you start, you should quit."

"I'll try," I said, "but it won't be easy."

When I left the hospital for home, another problem arose.

"Please," I said, "I would rather not be wrapped in this silly little blue blanket."

"What would you prefer?"

"Single-breasted gray suit, button-down shirt collars, striped tie and wingtip shoes. I want middle-age white man's clothes."

"Wouldn't you prefer something more festive for this occasion?"

"Hmmm, then make it lime-green polyester golf slacks, a red golf shirt, yellow socks and white Footjoy shoes."

Suitably attired, I was taken home only to face other conflicts. When I was being put to bed, one of my aunts began singing a lullaby.

"Would you please stop that?" I said.

"Don't you like lullabies?" she asked.

"No. I would rather listen to a Glenn Miller record, or Bing Crosby."

And when they bought me my first birthday toys, I could not conceal my dissatisfaction.

"Look at the pretty red wagon," they said.

"I don't want a pretty red wagon."

"What do you want?"

"I would like a vehicle appropriate for a middle-age white man. Possibly a big black Oldsmobile. And for my second birthday, I will want a big black Caddy, fully loaded. Moving up—that's one of the few pleasures of the middle-age white man."

On my first trip to the playground, they asked if I wanted to play in the sand box.

"Not unless you get me a sand wedge," I said.

When I started nursery school, I took one look and said: "Ixnay. There are girls and minority groups here."

"What's wrong with girls and minority groups?"

"Nothing. But what if I choose to exercise the constitutional right of the middle-age white man to tell a dirty, sexist, racist joke?"

"But you shouldn't tell such jokes."

"Then what's the fun of being a middle-age white man? I can't run fast, I can't jump high and I don't even know Bo Diddley. No, they can't take that away from me. . . ."

So that's the way it went. Now, through no fault of my own, I am one of the millions of my kind, viewed with suspicion and contempt.

In my next life, maybe I will come back as a yak. ∎

I've fully paid my victim tax

THURSDAY, JUNE 28, 1984

The detective put two photo albums on my desk and said: "If he's in there, you might recognize him."

The albums were huge. They were filled with front and side pictures of thugs, stick-up men, muggers, pimps, purse snatchers and all-around thieves.

Halfway through, I said: "You must have every bum in Chicago in here."

The cop shook his head. "No. Those are just the ones from your area."

It was an awesome thought: all those mean, moronic mugs plying their trade in my neighborhood alone. And if you add together all the mugs in the other neighborhoods, they're the size of an army. In fact, there are probably many nations whose armies aren't as big as Chicago's street mug population. Or as mean. Or as well armed.

In a way it made me feel better about having been robbed. If there were that many of them out there, being robbed seemed almost natural. Not being robbed was unnatural.

As a friend of mine put it: "It's sort of like a tax we pay for living in the city. A victim tax."

If so, I'm a solid taxpayer. Looking back, my victim tax adds up like this:

Robbery: This is my second one. The first time was about 15 years ago, when I was covering a story on the South Side and a group of large punks took my money and watch. They didn't have guns, though. They relied on muscle.

I also had a near-miss a few years ago. They came out of a dark gangway, but because they were wearing those goofy high-heeled shoes, I outran them.

Burglaries: Three. The last time was when they battered down the door of my old house. Eventually they were caught and turned out to be kids from prosperous suburban families. When he learned that his son was a burglar, the father of one of them pitched over with a massive heart attack. The judge sentenced them to see a shrink.

Car theft: Three. Once, they went joy riding, then dumped the car in front of an alderman's house. I don't know if that was a coincidence or they had a sense of humor. The next time they stripped it and left it in a forest preserve. The last time, it vanished forever, probably in a chop shop.

Actually, I'm getting a little tired of it. My neck is stiff from looking over my shoulder. While city life has its charms, I don't like having to guess whether the guy walking toward me on the dark side street has a shiv up his sleeve. He probably doesn't like the feeling either.

It's not the money. The two punks in my building's outer lobby got about $95. My stolen cars were insured. So was the stuff taken in my house burglaries.

But I don't like looking down the barrel of a gun. Especially when the guy holding it is nervously hopping from one foot to another, twitching, breathing hard, and I'm wondering if the stupid bastard is going to blow me away.

It's also the indignity of it all. I'm a grown man. I've fought in a war, married, raised my kids, buried my dead, paid my bills, worked hard at my job and never mooched a dollar from anyone.

And there I was, wondering if it was all going to end on an impulse by an illiterate punk with the IQ of a turnip. It lasted less than a minute, but it isn't a pleasant feeling to know that your life is in some punk's grubby hands.

But what do you do? An hour after I was robbed, I was depressed because I realized I wasn't my father's son.

It happened to the old man many years ago. He was a milkman. One morning, before dawn, a guy with a knife started to climb into his truck. The old man kicked him in the face. The guy got up and ran. The old man slammed his truck into gear, drove on the sidewalk, floored the gas pedal, and—bump, bump—the world had one less stick-up man.

I could have done the same. My car was at the curb, only a few feet away. I could see them running down my street. In a few seconds, I could have caught them. I'm sure the insurance would have covered any damage to my bumper.

But it didn't even cross my mind. In my father's day, people fought back with ferocity. In my day, we pay the victim tax and wonder what sociological forces brought the poor lad to a life of crime.

All things considered, running them over is a much better idea.

Of course, his mother would probably sue me. And collect. So I guess I got off cheap. ∎

Condo man back down to earth

WEDNESDAY, OCTOBER 9, 1985

I suppose the tomato was a factor. I like tomatoes. But the kind sold in most stores taste like the plastic they're wrapped in. So I figured that if I wanted a good tomato, I'd have to grow my own. To do that, I'd need a back yard.

And that's why I am no longer Condo Man. About a week ago the moving truck came, and I have reverted to my natural state of Bungalow Man.

As I explained four years ago when I moved from a house on a side street into a lakefront condo, I was launching an anthropological study of those relatively new urban creatures, Condo Man, High-Rise Man, Lakefront Man, Health Club Man, Singles Bar Man and all the others.

To do this, I knew I couldn't watch from afar. I had to immerse myself in their native cultures, as social anthropologist Margaret Mead used to do. I had to become one of them.

Now the study is over, and I have to admit that it was a complete flop.

Oh, I tried. One of the first things I did was buy a genuine Bargongini 34-speed racing bike with a talitanium frame that weighed only 4½ ounces.

Slipping on my designer bike suit, I walked my bike into Lincoln Park, swung aboard and began pedaling along the lake. The bike creaked once or twice, then collapsed under me.

I carried the twisted wreckage into the bike shop and demanded a refund. The proprietor said: "We are not responsible. You are too heavy. It says right in the warranty: 'To be ridden only by the fashionably lean.'"

So I joined the New Vo Reesh Health Club and, in my velour running suit and my Nike shoes, set about creating a lean Lakefront Man body.

"This," the hulking instructor said as he patted the derrick-like machine, "is the state of the art in exercise equipment. It will develop your quadrafeds, reduce your blats, strengthen your flipadids and do wonders for your claphs."

I strapped myself in and began lifting and pumping and kicking every which way. I found myself gasping and everything suddenly turned black.

When I came to, the instructor was standing over me with smelling salts, saying: "A close call. You caught your gold neck chain in the weight rack. Maybe you ought to try jogging."

So it was back to Lincoln Park, where I tried to learn the ways of Jogging Man. And many of the experienced runners were generous in sharing their wisdom, such as the lean runner who said, "I don't want to intrude, but it really isn't good form to jog with a Pall Mall dangling from your lips."

Within a week I had increased my distance from 10 yards to almost half a block. And I checked my pulse and found that, at the height of my workout, my rate went from its normal 100 beats a minute to almost 400.

When I mentioned that to my doctor, he turned pale and said: "Why don't you just try walking? It's just as good for you, and it reduces the odds of your collapsing while running and the momentum carrying you into the lake."

So I took to taking brisk walks along Sheridan Road, Lake Shore Drive and Lake View Avenue.

But after only two days I displaced my hip socket and sprung a kneecap while leaping to avoid the sidewalk droppings of a pair of 200-pound Mastiffs. Their owner, a facelift under blue hair, said, "I'll thank you not to frighten my dogs."

During my recuperation, I decided to check out the scene at the singles bars. But I quickly left when a man appeared from behind a fern and said, "Looking for your runaway daughter?"

But it wasn't all bad. From my living room window I had a splendid view of the sun coming up over the lake. And over the Dopemobile, a camper that arrived in the park each morning to sell strange herbs and spices while a nearby policeman slipped tickets under windshield wipers.

And I fulfilled one goal: I found the elusive perfect pesto sauce for pasta.

When I told a neighbor of mine about my triumph, she waved her copy of Chicago magazine at me and said: "You're so out of date. Nobody cares about pesto sauce anymore. We're into Ethiopian cuisine. No silverware. You scoop up the yak stew with pieces of round bread."

So that was it for me. If I'm going to eat stews without silverware, I might as well do it somewhere in the direction of Milwaukee Avenue.

And if somebody runs past my front door, I'll expect to see a cop chasing him. ∎

He could fill book with pithy phrases

FRIDAY, NOVEMBER 27, 1992

A flattering invitation recently arrived. It was from Joseph Neely, an author in Michigan, who wrote:

"I am compiling a book which features the favorite saying of successful persons such as you. This book is intended to inspire people and to give them some insight into the philosophies which help certain people to accomplish significant tasks.

"Essentially, I am looking for a saying which has given you comfort, kept you focused on your goals or inspired you during your life. The saying can be one which you composed or it can be from some other source.

"As of this date, I have received contributions for this book from a diverse group of persons, including former NATO commander and White House Chief of Staff Alexander M. Haig Jr.; minister and author Norman Vincent Peale; Dr. Deborah McGriff, the first African-American woman to serve as superintendent of a major urban school system; and Notre Dame's head football coach Lou Holtz, to name just a few."

That's an impressive group, and I'd like to be in it. But I've never had one favorite saying that inspired, comforted or focused me throughout my life. And I don't have any that would be likely to inspire someone else to lead a better life.

At different times, a variety of sayings have helped me in one way or another.

Like most young men of my generation, I believed in the saying our mothers passed on to us: "Always wear clean underwear, so if you get in an accident and go in the hospital, you won't be embarrassed." That's still a good idea, although I would add, "and no pastel colors."

As a lad, I abided by a saying in my neighborhood that went: "Don't go on the other side of Chicago Avenue, because the Italian kids there will always jump a

Polack." The one time I became careless, a group of young men surrounded me and demanded my name. I said: "Rocko Rico Royko," which I thought was a clever ruse.

But they jumped me anyway.

That experience led me to believe in the saying that is familiar to many Cub fans: "You win some and you lose some, but mostly you lose some."

Then there was my grandfather's favorite saying: "Never trust a Russian." He said that long before the Cold War began. So I asked my grandmother what he meant by it, and she provided another saying: "Never trust your drunken grandfather."

Later, when I was in the military, I placed great faith in the popular saying: "Don't never volunteer for nothing." But it didn't make much difference, because if you didn't volunteer, they made you do it anyway.

Early in my newspaper career, a wise old reporter passed along a saying that helped me become thrifty. He said: "Always stash away some [deleted] money, so if you got a boss you hate, you can say, '[Deleted] you' and quit." I'm still saving.

And another mentor had a saying I tried to follow: "Be nice to the copy boy, even if he's a mope, because he might grow up to be your boss some day." And sure enough, several mopes did.

Some co-workers once tired of hearing me complain about not having anything to write about. So they put an inspirational plaque on my wall that showed a little sailboat with limp sails and a man pulling some oars. It bore the words: "When there's no wind, row."

But I've since taken it down and replaced it with a sign that says: "When there is no wind, book a cabin on a cruise ship, sit by the pool, order a cool drink and look at the babes."

Several of my friends have had sayings that I like, although I'm not sure what they mean.

For example, Studs Terkel always ends his radio show by saying: "Take it easy, but take it." I once asked him if that was something he learned when he went to law school, but he denied it.

The late Marty O'Connor, a Chicago reporter, used to say: "Only suckers beef." He said it was an old South Side Irish expression. While it sounded manly, it wouldn't make sense today, when the most successful special-interest groups are those that beef the loudest and most often. Now the saying should be: "Only suckers don't form an organization, compile a list of unreasonable demands and hold a crabby press conference."

I used to be impressed by the line John Wayne uttered in so many of his Western movies: "A man's got to do what a man's got to do." But when feminists heightened my social sensitivities, I realized it was a sexist saying. After all, the feminists pointed out, we could just as well say, "A woman's got to do what a woman's got to do." For that matter, a puppy's got to do what a puppy's got to do. That's life, which is a favorite saying of Frank Sinatra. Or maybe Mike Ditka.

So I guess I won't qualify for Mr. Neely's book of inspirational sayings. Unless he would consider using one of my friend Slats Grobnik's lines.

Slats has always tossed off this salutation when saying goodbye to friends: "Stay out of the trees, watch out for the wild goose and take care of your hernia."

When I ask what it means, he shrugs and says: "Just do it; you won't go wrong."

He's right, but I'm not sure it's something to live by. Unless you have a hernia.

Anyway, I appreciate Mr. Neely's kind invitation. Although I haven't been able to contribute to his book, he did give me something to write about.

As I always say: "Another day, another dollar." ∎

Why be a writer? Think of your feet

FRIDAY, MARCH 16, 1990

The letter began with a question: "Do you recall an event from your childhood that first inspired you to write?"

The question was posed by a worthy organization called Child's Play Touring Theatre. It's a professional theater company promoting writing literacy among children.

To raise funds, they're asking writers: "Will you please take a few minutes to help the cause of literacy by sharing your own memory with us?" They plan to hold an auction and sell the writers' responses.

I'd like to help their cause. But I have a conflict.

On my wall there is a quotation from Samuel Johnson that I try to live by. It says: "No man but a blockhead ever wrote except for money."

So if I write something free for this worthy cause, I will be a blockhead.

On the other hand, I'd like to help them out. The solution is to answer their question in my column. That way, they will have their answer, and I'll be paid by the Tribune.

To answer their question: Yes, I recall several events in my childhood and young manhood that inspired me to become a writer.

When I was a child, my father was a milkman. Those were the days when most people had fresh milk, cream, butter, cheese and other dairy products delivered to their doors each morning.

Most of his customers lived in three-flats, so he would grab a couple of metal trays, load them with bottles and run up the back steps. During the summer, when school was out, I went along as his helper. Because I was only 7, he had me handle light first-floor deliveries.

Watching my father dashing up those steps at 5 a.m., sweat pouring down his face, I learned two things: 1. Being a milkman was hard work. 2. I didn't want to be a milkman.

A few years later, when I was about 12, I became my grandfather's helper. He was an independent house painter.

So I spent another summer vacation going with my grandfather on jobs, helping him with the dropcloths, ladders, scaffolds, putting on masking tape and doing some painting myself.

This was before the days of rollers and paint that could be washed off brushes with water. Painters prized their brushes like the fine tools they were. They had to be thoroughly cleaned with chemicals.

Working with my grandfather, I learned several things. Painting walls wasn't bad, although it could get tedious. Doing woodwork and floors was murder on the knees. Ceilings got paint in your face and a crick in your neck.

I also discovered that house painters drank a lot. My grandfather and his cronies said that was because fumes from the paint were hazardous but shots and beers were an effective antidote. However, one day my grandfather had too much antidote and fell off a scaffold and broke his leg. So I decided that I didn't want to be a house painter. Besides, I was a sly scamp and knew that you didn't have to paint ceilings to drink antidotes.

After that, I had other jobs setting bowling pins, working on a landscaping crew, in a greasy machine shop, a lamp factory and pushing carts around a department store. I learned one thing from these jobs. They made my flat feet hurt.

So I decided that if I was going to find my life's work, it would have to be something that wouldn't make me run up and down steps, get paint in my face or give me aching feet.

Then, while still a young man, I read a magazine article about Ernest Hemingway, the great novelist. It described his typical workday.

He would arise, have a bit of breakfast and write until about noon. Then he and a pal or two would get in his cabin cruiser and spend the rest of the afternoon sipping tall cool ones and fishing.

Except on days when he didn't feel like fishing. He would write until noon and go sit at an outdoor cafe with his pals and sip tall cool ones.

This impressed me as a sensible way to earn a living, and that was when I began thinking about becoming a writer.

But I almost changed my mind. I later saw another article about Hemingway, and there was a picture of him in the act of writing. His typewriter was on the mantle and he typed while standing. According to the article, he always stood while he wrote.

While that wasn't as grueling as running up three flights with six quarts of milk and two pounds of butter, I knew that standing over a typewriter all morning wouldn't do my fallen arches any good.

So I gave up thoughts of becoming a writer and set a new career goal. I would become a disc jockey. I knew that they sat while jockeying their discs. And one of my teachers told me I had a natural gift for that sort of work. Actually, she didn't say I should become a disc jockey. But she mentioned that I often babbled like an idiot, so it amounted to the same thing.

Fortunately, I read still another article about Hemingway. And that one said that he wrote while standing only because he had hemorrhoids and they hurt more when he sat.

That clinched it, and I set out to become a writer. And while I haven't achieved Hemingway's success, the job has never given me aching feet.

On the other hand, I can modestly say that I've been compared with Hemingway. Well, sort of. Readers sometimes tell me that I'm a real pain in the what-chamacallit. ∎

Franklin, Edison, now the toenail guy

THURSDAY, OCTOBER 20, 1994

We live in a time of so many amazing high-tech inventions. And I have just happened upon one of the most useful products ever seen.

The way I found it is an interesting story in itself.

I am one of those people who hates to cut his toenails. It is a stressful, acrobatic chore, involving bending, stretching, twisting, grunting and hoisting a stubborn leg onto a sink.

Nature made toenails very thick to allow man to kick smaller creatures, as was his destiny. This makes them difficult to clip.

And if your clipper is sharp enough to do the job, the slivers of toenail can shoot through the air like shrapnel missiles. We can only guess how many people have been scarred for life by their own toenail shards or those of a loved one.

Because of these hazards, I sometimes go long periods of time without clipping my nails.

And recently I was walking barefoot through my home when I heard a terrible yowling.

I looked down and was shocked to find that I had impaled the cat on my uncommonly long nail.

Deciding it would be bad medical practice to remove the wounded cat from my toenail, I hopped on one foot to the car and raced to an animal clinic. It wasn't an easy drive with a leg sticking out the window, so as not to dislodge the cat.

"You handled it just right," the veterinarian said as he removed the angry creature, stitched its wound and declared it healthy.

Then he chuckled and said: "The same thing happened to me once, except it was a tiny in-law instead of a cat. But since I discovered Easy Hold by Trim, the world's finest toenail clipper, it is no longer a problem. I highly recommend it."

And that's how I bought my own Easy Hold toenail clipper, a wonderful device that makes clipping one's toenails almost a pleasure.

It is sharp and powerful and has clever thumb and finger grips that prevent slipping. Through extra leverage, it requires so little strength that even an arthritic should be able to hack through the most monstrous nails.

And it somehow gobbles up the clippings. That eliminates the danger of your being wounded by one of those tiny, sharp missiles.

In opening the wrapping it came in, I happened to glance at the printing and saw these words: "Developed in cooperation with the University of Mississippi Medical Center."

I've always been proud that the University of Chicago leads the world in Nobel Prizes, many of them for scientific discoveries.

Yet I don't remember ever dashing out and buying something discovered by any of the Nobel Prize winners. I don't even know if their discoveries have made me happier or healthier.

But here we have the far less prestigious University of Mississippi helping create a product that will make life easier for the many millions of us who have toes.

A call to the university put us in touch with the man who invented the amazing Easy Hold—the widely unknown Eric "Ric" Rommerdale, 52, a retired Navy dental lab technician who now runs lab technology at the university's School of Dentistry.

"Well, well, well," he said, "you found me. I usually stay out of the limelight."

(His modesty explains why we have not seen him on "60 Minutes.")

"You really want to talk about this?" he asked.

Of course. There are an estimated 2.5 billion toes in this country. And around the world, I can't even comprehend such a number.

"Well, it isn't that glamorous. In about 1988, I was getting gas at one of those stop-and-go places that have soda pop and stuff, and I saw this old fella trying to cut his nails. But the thing kept slipping out of his hand. He said: 'I wish someone'd come up with something that'd help me hold onto these things.'

"So I went home and played around with the idea in my workshop. And I finally came up with this thing. I had friends try it, and everybody seemed to like it."

After a while, he called Revlon, the biggest seller of all sorts of nail clippers.

"Some Mr. Vice President told me, 'We're not interested in anything you're doing.'"

Probably some Ivy League guy with an MBA.

So he called the much smaller W.E. Bassett Co., and the president came to see him, looked at his invention and asked him to redo his entire line of implements—scissors, tweezers and, of course, nail clippers.

The rest, in the toenail world, is history. The clippers have sold by the millions. And because he has a dozen or more patents, Mr. Rommerdale shares in the profits of each and every item.

"Now, the part that catches the clippings? Be sure to say that wasn't my idea.

They already had it. Boy, that was a great idea, so Mama don't have to pick 'em up off the floor."

Mr. Rommerdale declined to say how much he has raked in since his contribution to gracious living went on sale two years ago. "I'm just a poor retired sailor." But he conceded that he makes 2 percent of the sale royalties.

And he deserves it all for his vision and creativity. The rest of us look at our toes, and what do we see? Just our toes.

He looked and saw his fortune.

"I've done a lot of things," Mr. Rommerdale says, "but I guess this is what I'll be remembered for."

By me, that's for sure. And my cat too. ∎

Hard to face up to pie prank now
THURSDAY, APRIL 11, 1985

I thought the pie-in-the-face fad was long and gratefully dead. You probably remember—about 12 years ago pies were flying everywhere. People went into the prankster business, calling themselves Pie in the Eye Inc. or Pie in the Face Ltd., and charging $50 or $100 to hit somebody with a cream pie.

Some disgruntled victims filed lawsuits. One woman collected $5,000 because being hit by a pie made her so nervous she had to start seeing a psychiatrist. So the craze faded away. But not completely.

In Connecticut, a judge is trying to make sense out of a recent pie-throwing incident.

It seems that a woman was angry because a junior high school principal had been strict with her daughter.

She hired a guy to hit the principal with a pie during a graduation ceremony. The principal, not amused, had the guy pinched.

The woman, fearing exposure, allegedly offered the pie thrower a bribe to conceal her identity. And she allegedly offered a relative a bribe to take the blame.

This has led her to being charged with breach of the peace, tampering with a witness and bribery.

I could have told the woman not to mess around with pie throwing. I tried it once and it involved me in one of the most embarrassing episodes in an already shameful career.

When the pie fad began, I was writing for the Chicago Daily News, and on a slow news day I asked the readers which well-known Chicagoans they thought should be hit in the face with a pie.

They responded by the thousands, suggesting dozens of celebrities, including politicians, athletes, actors, actresses, broadcasters and disc jockeys.

But the most votes were for a TV weatherman, known at the time for his boisterous behavior on camera.

So I hired a guy who had just gone into the pie-tossing business to carry out the readers' wishes.

After finishing his evening broadcast, the TV weatherman came out of his studio on State Street, strolling along with his fellow anchormen.

Up stepped the pie man, who gave him a cheerful hello, and shoved the whipped-cream mess into his face.

A photographer, who had been lurking nearby, recorded the scene for history, and the next day it was in the paper.

This led to two immediate developments:

First, my phone screamed and my mailbox overflowed with the reactions of civilized people who said I was an idiot, a boor and an adolescent.

I couldn't argue with them. Having somebody hit in the face with a pie sure wasn't an example of subtle British wit.

But it became worse. A couple of days after the pie was thrown, this newspaper came out with a story on Page 1, gleefully raising questions about the character of the pie thrower I had hired.

To the pie thrower's embarrassment, and my amazement, the story disclosed that he was an ex-convict and a confidence man who did creative things with credit cards.

So there I was, in the public's perception, plotting and collaborating with a shady character to carry out an assault on a nice, jovial weatherman.

People called to accuse me of being everything from a puppy thief to a schoolyard flasher.

And it got even worse.

The disclosures about his past caused the pie thrower to lose his regular job. And he blamed me for his troubles, which was somewhat unfair, because I hadn't told him to moonlight as a pie thrower.

He was so upset that he threatened to sue me. But after thinking about it, he realized that he wouldn't have much of a case.

So he threatened to bump me off, although I assured him that, given a choice, I'd rather be sued.

After awhile, he calmed down, so did the publicity, and the whole silly thing faded away.

But for a long time, many people, including my friends, would ask me, "How could you do something that stupid?"

And I've never been able to come up with an explanation except the one given by a guy who took off all of his clothes and jumped into a cactus patch.

When asked why he did it, he said, "Well, it seemed like a good idea at the time." ∎

It's not technicolor, but it's dream coat

WEDNESDAY, JANUARY 18, 1995

A fter all these years, I have discovered a hidden benefit in doing this job.
It came in a letter from a nice lady who lives in Arizona.

She had read an old column about my wife's disgust with my winter overcoat, which is 17 years old and has threads hanging from the sleeves and collar, mud and soot stains, missing buttons and holes from cigarette burns.

Other than that, though, the coat is structurally sound and fends off the wind as well as it did the day I bought it.

And it doesn't smell bad, except in the summer, when I don't wear it anyway.

Like most of my clothes, the overcoat is old and raggedy because I like old, raggedy clothes. Also, I don't believe in wasting money on something new when something old does the job just as well.

In the case of clothing, the purpose is to prevent me from walking around naked. Old clothes do that just as well as something designed by a skinny Italian with one name.

And when I wear my old overcoat, panhandlers never approach me. If anything, they say: "Hey, I got here first; go hustle the next street."

When she read about my overcoat, the nice lady in Arizona sent this letter:

"I have been a widow since 1990. All this time I have been trying to find a good home for my husband's beautiful and seldom worn overcoat.

"Would you please accept it in memory of my husband, who was a very kind, gentle and peaceful human being.

"Please do not divulge my name, as I live alone and it could jeopardize my safety."

The letter arrived in a box. With it, neatly packed in a plastic garment bag, was a splendid, blue-black overcoat that appeared to be made of the finest soft wool.

As the lady said, it had been seldom worn and looked new. It was finer than any coat I have ever owned.

I slipped it on and it fit perfectly. Her husband and I must have been the exact same height and weight.

Just then, two female co-workers dropped in. They immediately ooed and aaahed, as womenfolk do when looking at spiffy garments, and said: "What a gorgeous coat . . . where did you buy it . . . how dressy . . . looks like cashmere."

I showed them the letter. They sat silent for a while, then one said: "You aren't going to wear it."

Of course I'm going to wear it. Perfect fit. The deceased must have been a fine figure of a man. Why wouldn't I wear it?

Looking queasy, she said: "Well, he's, you know, it belonged to someone who, you know. . . ."

"He's dead," the other one said. "Don't you think there is something kind of morbid about wearing clothes that belonged to someone who died?"

I thought about that for a moment or two. Then I pointed out that in this country's wealthiest communities are great mansions and estates that have been handed down from generation to generation.

Wouldn't it sound odd if an heir said: "I cannot live in this 24-room mansion with stables, dining hall, billiard room, tennis courts and 10 full johns because it belonged to my father and his father before him and my great-grandfather, who built it with money he stole fair and square."

Or if an heiress said: "I will not accept this pearl necklace, the diamond earrings, the sapphire brooch, the platinum bracelet or any of the other baubles because my mum wore them and I would feel a bit morbid."

No, the rich are practical in such matters. That's why they stay rich and get richer. Waste not, want not. And that, incidentally, is why the Arabs are in such a sad pickle today.

"What do the Arabs have to do with it?" they asked.

The answer is obvious. Back in the old days, they used to bury guys like King Tut with their valuables. They'd put the poor mummy and his jewels and money and credit cards in a tomb inside a pyramid. How dumb could they be? They could have held an estate sale and cleaned up. And look at all they lost in compound interest over a few thousand years.

"But that coat belonged to someone you didn't even know. It might be different if it belonged to someone in your family."

True, but is it my fault that he didn't have any relatives with the same sleeve length?

They looked unconvinced, but one of them said: "I hope that you write her a nice thank-you note."

Of course I will. There's something I wanted to ask her about anyway.

"What?"

I wonder if he had any ties. ∎

Just a fin-de-siecle kind of individual

TUESDAY, MARCH 16, 1993

It came as a pleasant surprise to learn that I am on the cutting edge of men's fashion.

I discovered this after reading an article in The New York Times about a new magazine devoted to the kind of clothing worn by today's male.

The story contained this capsule view of men's fashion trends by one Woody Hochswender, who is editor of the new magazine, which is called Esquire Gentleman.

Mr. Hochswender said: "If you take an anthropological view of fashion today, it's all happening in men's fashion.

"Take a walk on any street in New York and look at the hair, the pants tucked in the work boots, the jewelry, the tattoos. You have two currents—the hippy and the dandy. You have your deconstructed Salvation Army grunge and your neo-Edwardian Beau Brummell, brocade vest, foulard tie and pocket square.

"It's all very interesting, very fin de siecle."

Yes, I found it interesting, but for different reasons.

There are two kinds of stories that appear in newspapers that I can never understand.

One is any rock music review. Most rock critics write in terms that are understandable to only other rock critics, rock musicians and people who have cooked their brains with strange substances.

The other is any story written about fashions. I mean where else do you find phrases like "deconstructed Salvation Army grunge," or that today's fashions are very "fin de siecle"?

It shows how journalism has changed. There was a time when an editor would have said to a reporter: "Fin de siecle? Are you talking about Vinny Di Cicco, that West Side precinct captain?" Or an anthropological view of fashion? I don't even take an anthropological view of anthropology, since the only old bones that interest me are my own.

Which shows why I have never considered myself in the mainstream of fashion: I don't even know what "fin de siecle" means. And I doubt if the clerk at Kmart, which is wear I buy my wash-and-wear trousers, would know either.

My fashion statement has always been as follows:

1. Wear clean shorts and underwear because, as our parents taught us, if you get in an accident, you don't want to be embarrassed in front of the emergency room nurse.
2. Wear socks that match, although if one has a hole in the toe and the other doesn't, most people won't notice if you remember to wear shoes.
3. Own one dark suit for going to funerals. If you take good care of it, you can even wear it at your own.
4. Always wear the same tie to Italian restaurants, and a different tie to Chinese restaurants, so you won't get gravy stains that clash.

These rules have served me well. I have never been tossed out of a restaurant or any other public place, although I am often seated near the fire exit.

But Mr. Hochswender's statement aroused my curiosity. Especially about things being very "fin de siecle."

He was kind enough to take a phone call and explain what he was talking about:

"Fin de siecle means end of the century," he said. "It is said the last decade looks back.

"So today's fashions are a nod to the 1960s and the 1890s."

That is why we have some guys dressing like dandies—"the neo-Edwardian, Beau Brummell brocade vest . . . it's ruffled blouses, long, cutaway coats, high buttoned weskit. It's the watch chain, the walking stick, the hat, the half-boot shoe. That is now the urban style—everywhere you look the half-boot shoe. Look on the street."

(Actually, I do look on the street. And maybe Chicago is different from New York because the only neo-Edwardian types are hotel doormen.)

At the other extreme, he said, "is your deconstructed Salvation Army grunge look. There is a neo-hippie or '60s revival going on in both men's fashion and women's fashion.

"Secondhand store clothes, patchwork clothes, wearing the same clothes day after day. The American Grunge movement is related to this deconstruction. It's anti-fashion. It's a very strong style statement. They're torn, ripped, tattered; they're recycled."

That's it. That is me. I have never heard my wardrobe described any better than that, except that I don't buy my clothes at the Salvation Army because they wouldn't accept my wardrobe as a donation in the first place.

But American Grunge? Yes. Not merely torn, ripped, tattered, but stained, frayed, blotched and—my own, personal signature touch—peppered with tiny cigarette burn holes. (That is why I never wore a polyester leisure suit; I was afraid of meltdown.)

So I'm a fashion plate without having known it. Maybe that's why when I meet a panhandler on the street, we both get confused about who is supposed to give a buck to whom. Sometimes I come out ahead. ∎

This athletic feat sprains credulity

THURSDAY, MAY 6, 1993

The cry of horror came from the TV room. I rushed from the kitchen, where I had been fetching a beer, and found her wide-eyed and gape-jawed.

"Look," she said, pointing at the TV.

Writhing in pain, almost in a fetal position, was Michael the Magnificent.

"What happened?" I asked.

"He slipped and twisted his ankle and fell," she said in a choked whisper. "Oh, this is terrible. It could be the end."

The phone rang. It was a friend, a Korean War vet, a hard-case of a barroom brawler in his younger days. He sounded near tears.

"What if it's busted?" he said. "Look, they're carrying him off! He can't put any weight on it. Oh, [obscenity], how could this happen?"

I urged him to have a drink and try to think positively. Then I hung up and tried to console her.

But she seemed to be sinking into a dark pit of despair.

Hoping to distract her, I said: "I am having severe chest pains."

"Take a Maalox," she muttered.

But in a few minutes, the great one was back. And as all Bulls fans saw, on a gimpy ankle he still performed his usual heroics.

Now filled with joy, she said: "Have you ever seen anything like that?"

The phone rang and my friend said the same thing: "Nothing like it, ever, right, huh?"

Well, yes, I have witnessed an athletic achievement that was similar to, and even surpassed, the feat of Jordan and his ankle.

As a matter of fact, today, May 6, is the 17th anniversary of that heroic event.

I'll tell you the story. But because the main figure is a man of uncommon modesty, never boastful, always self-effacing, I must omit his name.

It was on a softball diamond on the Northwest Side of the city. The first inning and the pitcher-manager was at bat.

He hit a line drive to left and slid into 2nd base. But his cleat snagged on the bag and he struggled to his feet, hopping on one leg.

The team gathered around. "I think it is sprained," he said.

"But if you come out," a teammate said, "we forfeit because we don't have anybody on the bench and won't have enough guys for a legal team."

"I'll play," he said. "What's a little sprain?"

So he remained in the game. The next batter singled and our hero somehow hobbled past third and scored.

Twice more, he came to the plate. And each time he lashed a hit. By the third hit, he was hopping to first base like a one-legged man.

When the game ended, he was helped to a car. The team gathered at their post-game bar, where he propped his leg up on a chair. His teammates marveled at how quickly the ankle was increasing in size.

"That must really hurt," they said.

"Agony," he said, with a laugh. "But as Vince Lombardi always said, you got to play with the little hurts."

In the morning, the leg was almost twice its normal size. So he went to see his bone Doc.

The Doc, an Armenian, rushed him in for X-rays, then said: "How you did this?"

"Hook slide. Should have gone in head first like Santo always did."

"What you talk about?"

"I ripped a double and slid into second base. Felt something pop."

"You do this playing baseball?"

"Softball. Sixteen-inch. This is Chicago, you know."

"Why you didn't come here right away?"

"What, and forfeit the game?"

"Game? You are a big jerk sometimes, you know that?"

The X-rays arrived. The Doc shook his head. "You know what you did? You broke your fibula."

"I don't know what that is," the heroic fellow said.

"It is a bone. And you know what else you did? You broke your tibia. That's a bone, too."

"I thought it was just a bad sprain."

"Yes, and you also have a bad sprain."

"Well, next time I'll slide head first."

"Next time will be a long time," said the Doc. "I can't believe a grown man can be so stupid."

"Hey, Lombardi said you got to play with the little hurts."

They stuck him in a hospital bed, wrapped the leg to stem the swelling and hoisted it in the air.

A nurse asked how it happened. "I slid into second. But I played the whole game. Got two more hits and scored both times. As Lombardi always said . . ."

She shook her head and said: "And I thought my husband was a goof."

His family and friends came to visit, saying things like: "You played the whole game with two broken bones and a sprain?"

"Well, as Lombardi used to say . . ."

"You are a real —head."

A few days later, he arrived at his job on crutches. He went in to see his boss and said: "You can be first to sign my cast."

His boss took a felt tip pen and in big letters wrote: "To the biggest [obscenity] idiot who ever worked for me."

About three months later, the Doc removed the cast and said: "Don't do anything but walk for the next two weeks."

"Sure," the hero said. Then he went home, put on his uniform, rejoined his team and pitched a double-header, getting a total of six hits.

A week later, the Doc examined him again and said: "OK, you're fine." The hero laughed and said: "I knew it. That's why I played a double-header the day you took off the cast."

The Doc nodded and said: "And I knew you would do something like that, so that's why I left the cast on an extra two weeks. You are a very stupid person, you know?"

So this week we have a guy playing with a mere sprain and he is hailed as a hero by an entire city. Back then, there was a guy playing with a sprain and two busted bones and he is hailed as a —head, an idiot and a goof.

I wonder—could Vince Lombardi have lied? ▪

CHAPTER 14
Poopery, er, Potpourri

Bald facts leave no doubt that hair just isn't worth it

TUESDAY, APRIL 9, 1996

During a recent interview, the noted actor Ben Kingsley was asked about his baldness.

Like the late Yul Brynner's and the late Telly Savalas', Kingsley's scalp is totally without hair. No fringe, sideburns or fuzz.

Kingsley said he does not discuss personal matters. That was surprising for two reasons:

First, people in show business seldom consider anything too personal to talk about. They don't hesitate to blab about who they are sleeping with or have slept with and if it was fun.

And when they get too old to sleep with anything but a denture holder, they write books with detailed accounts of everyone with whom they've had even a brief snuggle.

Kingsley should be praised for having the dignity to refuse to discuss a personal matter. Of course, he's English, and English actors are more reserved than their American counterparts, except those who perform after drinking a quart of gin.

But of all the things he could consider "personal," why baldness? Unless he wears a hat or a toupee, his hairless dome is there for everyone to see. Including the reporter with whom he chatted over lunch.

Baldness is normal to hundreds of millions of men across the planet. Some are totally bald, as is Kingsley. Others are bare on top with a fringe on the side and back, which makes them the barber's 10-minute delight. And some shamelessly let the side fringe get long and comb those few sad side strands across the bare top.

But baldness is no more a personal matter than your height, eye color or the size of your shoe. One way or another, it is a matter of genetics.

Unless, of course, there are peculiar circumstances involved in Kingsley's baldness.

Let's say, for example, that until recently, Kingsley had a lush head of hair. But then, during one of those lover-spats shows for which show-biz people are famous, every strand was plucked out by an enraged girlfriend.

Under those circumstances, it would be understandable that he would say his lack of hair was a personal matter. You couldn't very well expect the man to say, "Well, I have no hair because my gorgeous live-in lover and I disagreed over the Oscars, and she plucked my entire thatch."

But that's highly improbable. At least I hope it is, for Kingsley's sake.

It's more likely that at some point his hair started falling out, either receding at the forehead, which is the most graceful way to lose it, or on top, creating that empty round spot, which is less desirable unless you are about 6-5 and nobody can see it.

The arrival of baldness can be traumatic, especially for men who are young. Young used to mean someone in their 20s. Later, it became the 30s. Now, because of the Baby Boomers, it covers those up to and in their 50s. Before long, we'll hear ex-Boomer males in their 60s greeting each other with, "Hi, kid," and "What's up, lad?"

But as a great philosopher once put it, "Hey, doo-doo happens, man, dig? So be cool."

And that's the way it is with baldness. Just as some people become nearsighted or farsighted or have prominent noses, overbites, big ears or poor hand-eye coordination, others lose their hair.

Some young man staring with terror at a dozen hairs in his sink might disagree, but there are benefits to baldness.

For one thing, a young man who knows baldness is a family trait might be more inclined to seek an early, stable family life. He looks at his father, who has a head like a cue ball, and tells himself: "Uh oh, I'd better find a willing female and marry her now before I look like old dad."

So young men who are inclined toward future baldness tend to marry young. Of course, when his hair falls out, he notes that his wife now weighs 180 pounds and has big blue veins in her legs. So she, too, was looking ahead. But that's the breaks.

Of course, men who are confident enough to wait until they are bald before seeking a mate will know that they have found someone who is not a ninny concerned only with appearances but is an intelligent, serious type who gives deep thought to a man's net worth.

And as I've written before, there is nothing more time- and cost-efficient than baldness.

It takes me about two or three seconds to prepare my hair in the morning. I haven't owned a comb for 15 years and spend nothing on sprays, shampoo or a blow dryer.

In contrast, a friend who is a TV anchor creature spends a minimum of 30 minutes a day at home and in the health club on his hair. Think about that. It comes to about 182 hours a year. That's more than 7.5 full days. And if he keeps his hair and job, over the next 20 years he will have spent 150 days—or more than 21 weeks—using his blow dryer, comb and brush to tend the useless thatch.

If you think of the millions of man-hours that are wasted each year by the millions of men who are overhaired, it is an awesome economic waste by this country.

Because we are in a highly competitive global economy, maybe we should have a law requiring all men to have their heads shaved each day.

Women too. I don't want to be accused of discrimination. ∎

Khomeini's wrath is a writer's dream
MONDAY, FEBRUARY 20, 1989

Many famous writers have rallied to the defense of Salman Rushdie, the author who has been sentenced to be bumped off because he wrote a book that offended Moslems. They have decried the death threat of Ayatollah Khomeini, the strange old bird who rules Iran.

Besides decrying the threat, they have expressed deep distress, horror, anger, indignation, shock and outrage at efforts to censor Rushdie's novel.

I'm not sure if all of them are really that worked up. Any self-respecting writer is expected to at least pretend that he's in a tizzy when something like this happens.

In fact, I suspect that, down deep, many of them envy Rushdie. I sure do.

Until a week or so ago, at least 99.9 percent of the world's population had never heard of Salman Rushdie or his current book. Or any of his previous books.

He was known to some admiring book critics and literature professors. And he was read by those who fancy themselves members of the literati, which means they read the New Yorker and claim to understand Ingmar Bergman movies.

As far as popular success goes, any old movie star could write her memoirs, list all the leading men with whom she had tumbled about a stairwell and get on more best-seller lists than Rushdie.

But suddenly riots were erupting in countries where his book wasn't even being sold, and rioters were dying.

Then the ayatollah, who's pretty murderous for a holy man, ordered a hit on Rushdie. Some other Iranians put a $3 million bounty on his head, and the little-known author was an instant international figure.

In Chicago, where Rushdie wasn't exactly a household word, his books were sold out in a day or two. A friend of mine, who was not familiar with Rushdie's work, rushed to buy one.

"I wanted to know what the big fuss was all about," he said.

And?

"Now that I've read the book, I'm even more confused because I'm not sure what the book is about. It's just weird."

Terrified book chains, which make literary judgments based on what their computers tell them, have stashed the books in the back rooms, fearing that Moslems will blow their stores up if they see a window display.

And in some countries, publication of the book has been postponed or canceled for the same reason.

But that's only making the book a bigger seller in places where it is available.

What it amounts to is that Rushdie has been given the greatest blessing any author can have.

He's being censored.

Despite the outrage writers display at the mention of the word censorship, it is every author's dream to be a victim.

That's because a sincere censorship effort can take a book that is just sitting there gathering dust and turn it into a big seller.

A few years ago, I discovered that one of my books had caused a flap in a small New England town. Some parents didn't want their high school children reading it as a class project because they thought I didn't respect authority.

I called the parents and told them that I fully supported their efforts to have the book censored and I would gladly sign a petition to ban me.

They were surprised. "You want your own book banned?" they asked.

Of course, I told them. And I asked them if they'd mind publicly condemning it for being obscene, erotic, filthy, perverted, filled with dirty words and deeds and a danger to public morals. It wasn't any of those things, but I figured we should go for broke.

Unfortunately, the censorship movement didn't spread beyond that one town, or even the one school. It would have helped if they had held a book-burning. I offered to send them a dozen copies so they could get a nice fire going in the town square, but they declined. So my hopes were dashed. It takes more than a few irate small-town parents to get a lucrative censorship movement going.

But Rushdie has hit the jackpot. While other authors would be thrilled to have their books thrown out of a couple of bookstores, be damned by one or two preachers and picketed by a few fat ladies, Rushdie gets riots, diplomats exchanging indignant notes and a multimillion-dollar bounty is put on his head. If you spread all those goodies around, there would be enough to create a dozen best sellers.

True, Rushdie has to endure the tension that goes along with a death threat. So for a while, he will have to lie low in England. Although the ayatollah has already rejected Rushdie's apology, maybe someday the contract on him will be lifted.

Then it's unlikely he will be killed by any Moslems, unless he rides a cab in New York or Chicago, which is a risk many nonauthors take every day. ∎

The real message? God only knows

THURSDAY, MARCH 4, 1993

Looking up from his newspaper, Slats Grobnik shook his head and said: "You ever wonder if God has a drinking problem?"

A what?

"You know, if he goes on benders once in a while, really gets tanked up."

No, I have never wondered about that or given it a passing thought, and I don't think it is an appropriate topic of conversation. I don't even know why you would ask such a question.

"OK, I'll tell you why. I'm reading the paper about this guy in Texas who shot it out with the federal agents."

Yes, the leader of the Branch Davidian, a rather violent religious sect. What about him?

"Well, he was going to surrender. But then he said he talked to God and God told him not to, so he's going to stonewall it for a while."

What does that have to do with your question about God's drinking habits?

"Lemme go on. Now I look at another story in the paper, and I read about people who are worried about the national debt. So some of them are sending their own money to Washington to help cut it."

Yes, one can make a donation of that kind. So?

"So this. There's this woman in North Carolina, and she's putting the arm on her friends to send in some dough, and you know why she's doing it?"

A misguided sense of patriotism, I assume.

"No, she's in some religious group and she says, here, I'll read it to you, she says: 'The Lord talked to me about it and I asked what should I do, and that's what he told you to do.' Now, I ask you, can you picture that?"

Picture what?

"God looking down and telling some woman in North Carolina: 'I know you and your friends work hard for your money, but here's what I want you to do. Everybody chip in a few bucks and send it to Washington to reduce the deficit so Congress don't have to cut out some of the swindle projects they put in for their lobbyist pals.' Does that sound like something somebody sober would say?"

You should put your questions to an expert on such matters: a theologian or maybe a bartender.

"And if he was sober, would God say to that guy in Texas: 'Look, young man, don't surrender to those federal agents. You got enough good ammo to hold them off for another week, so do it.'"

Obviously, that would not be rational advice. But you can't attribute two separate incidents to heavenly imbibing.

"I'm not. But it's part of a pattern. I look at the news, and I see people all over the world doing crazy things because they say God wants them to. You got Israel and the Arabs, and both sides say God is on their side. Then you look at the countries around India, and they're going at each other because they say God wants 'em to do it. Same thing in Bosnia. And you're saying you don't see a pattern?"

What kind of pattern?

"A guy gets loaded, and the next day he says: 'Oh, boy, did I say that? I told them to have a war? I told 'em to shoot it out with the feds? I told them to send their money to Washington. I think I better go on the wagon.' Except with God, time not being too important when you got eternity to play with, the binge could last 50 years before the hangover sets in."

I suppose if you believe all the individuals, the religions and the nations that attribute their action to God, one might think that booze could be the problem. Or even a malicious sense of humor. But I really doubt it.

"Well, it's just something to think about. See, there was a time when I thought that maybe God was a bookie."

A what?

"A bookie. You know, someone who takes bets."

What gave you that idea?

"You mean you never noticed? All you had to do was watch TV and every time somebody would win a championship, the star of the game would go on TV and say something: 'I guess the good Lord wanted me to score that touchdown.' Or some fighter would knock another guy's head halfway to the balcony and then he'd say: 'I just trusted in God.' So I started thinking, why would God want one big bunch of clunks to beat another bunch of clunks? Or one palooka to deck another palooka? And the only think I could figure was that God was making book and wanted to cover the spread or something."

That sounds unlikely.

"I know, because every bookie I know stays sober because he's got to be careful with his odds. So if God is a boozer, he can't be a bookie or he'd lose a bundle."

Look, I don't think either of your theories are credible. Nor would most theologians.

"Why not?"

Because the more reputable ones believe that God lets us determine our own destinies.

"You mean God is sort of an innocent bystander?"

I suppose that is one way to put it, yes.

"Then I'm right about God being a boozer after all."

What makes you think that?

"Because sitting up there watching what goes on down here would be enough to drive anyone to drink." ▪

Call for sympathy is enough to bring tear to your eye

TUESDAY, NOVEMBER 26, 1996

D avid Schlessinger is seeking public sympathy. Yours, mine, everybody's. He went to a restaurant and was unhappy with his steak dinner. So he called the police, got a lawyer and sued, and it kicked around the courts and finally became a federal case.

Here is how the U.S. Court of Appeals just summed up Schlessinger's unhappiness:

"David Schlessinger and two friends visited Anthony's Steakhouse in (Lake) Geneva, Wis., for dinner on January 8, 1994. Schlessinger ordered his steak medium-well done. Before the main course arrived, Schlessinger deemed that he was 'receiving substandard service at the restaurant, so I demanded better service.'

"Judging the meat he received 'burned,' Schlessinger complained long and loud. George Condos, the owner, told him that the food had been properly prepared and asked him to stop disturbing the other patrons.

"Schlessinger was unwilling to eat the food, to leave, or to pay until his demand for a new entree had been met. Schlessinger's affidavit continues: 'I feared trouble by the escalating situation and called the police from my cellular phone to get the situation corrected.' George Salimes and another officer answered the call. Condos suggested to the officers that Schlessinger might be under the influence of drugs. Salimes told Schlessinger that, unless he paid the tab and left, he would be arrested for disorderly conduct and theft of services. The trio then paid and left."

The court went on: "Most people dissatisfied with a restaurant's service or cuisine would tell their friends not to go, resolve not to return, and perhaps write a letter to the editor of the local newspaper or the Better Business Bureau, then let the matter drop.

"But having played the wise guy in calling the police, Schlessinger encored that performance by filing this suit against Condos, Salimes and everyone else in or out of sight—including the town of Lake Geneva, the Town Board and its members, the town's police department and the town's chief of police."

Then the appeals court comes to this stern conclusion:

"This goofy lawsuit deservedly met an abrupt end in the district court. Frivolous at the outset, and likely maliciously retaliatory as well, the case has deteriorated on appeal.

"Schlessinger's suit is absurd and likely malicious. It trivializes the constitutional rights he asks us to vindicate. If your meal is not tasty, you do not throw a tantrum, upset the other diners, and then sue the mayor of the town where the restaurant is located . . ."

"Suits and appeals such as this not only bring the courts into disrepute but also divert scarce judicial time from other litigants who have serious claims or defenses . . .

"We therefore direct Schlessinger and his attorney to show cause, within 14 days, why they should not be penalized . . . for pursuing a frivolous appeal."

You might think that after being called "goofy" and a "wise guy" by a panel of federal judges, a person would be embarrassed and quietly slink away.

But not David. He called here because he feels like a victim. (Who doesn't, these days?) And he wants everyone to know about his suffering and indignation.

"How dare a judge call me goofy and a wise guy because I called the police . . . I'm president of a company."

(Which is true. Schlessinger, who lives on the Near North Side, runs a Chicago insurance agency that his dad started 31 years ago, the year David was born.)

He went on: "They (the restaurant and the police) humiliated me. I was on high blood pressure medication when this happened. I went on vacation with two friends to calm down and relax, and my blood pressure got worse. It was a horror story."

That isn't the way George Condos, the restaurant owner, remembers it:

"He walks in like he's Donald Trump and we're a bunch of mice. and then he insults everyone in the place. We've never had a customer like that before."

"He was running up and down the main dining room with the cellular phone and complains to the waitress about the table, the salads and the meal, everything. She offered to give him something else. He said our food was garbage.

"He acted like an immature punk, threatening my father and saying he was going to take our restaurant. . . . He smarted off to other customers. He went up to a local business owner and told him that he probably didn't know what a cellular phone was. Obviously, he was daddy's little boy . . ."

Now, after being called a goof, a wise guy and malicious and frivolous by a federal appellate panel, he is going to have to go to court and show why he isn't any of these things.

If the court isn't satisfied that he isn't a goof and a malicious and frivolous wise guy, it can tell him to pay all the legal fees run up by everyone he sued.

That could wind up being quite expensive, since everyone involved had to hire lawyers to defend themselves against the charge that they violated his constitutional right to have his steak done just so and be treated with the respect due a wealthy young guy from the Near North Side.

Now he wants our sympathy. I'm sure he'll get it. Yes, when a guy orders a steak medium-well and it turns out to be well done, what else can he do but throw a tantrum and sue everyone.

I can imagine the readers sobbing as tears run down their cheeks.

Oh, stop giggling, all of you.

THURSDAY, MARCH 20, 1997

Letters, calls, complaints and great thoughts from readers:

Pat Lawrence, Chicago: I saw a brief story in the Tribune about a David Schlessinger being arrested as a pedophile for using liquor, marijuana and gifts to sexually seduce teenage boys.

It said that he ran an insurance company on the North Side.

Is this David Schlessinger, by chance, the same David Schlessinger you wrote about after he thought his steak was too well done, and he sued half the community of Lake Geneva, Wis.?

The story didn't say so, but the name is the same and so is his occupation.

Comment: Yes, I'm sorry to say that David Schlessinger, the accused predator of young boys, is David Schlessinger, finicky diner. If he is convicted of these very serious charges, I doubt that he will be sending any of his meals back. In prison, he might be considered a main dish himself. ∎

Day after St. Pat's, it's time to ponder luck of the Irish

TUESDAY, MARCH 18, 1997

I liked St. Patrick's Day much better before scholars and pundits took to pondering its significance and analyzing the role of the Irish in American life. When the whole idea of the celebration was to give City Hall a day off so politicians could strut on State Street and their admirers could get drunk.

Now panels of experts gather on TV to talk about why the Irish have had such remarkable political success in big multi-ethnic cities such as Chicago and New York.

This question has been kicked around for years and the answers aren't at all complicated until academic types try to complicate them.

First, there is language. When the great waves of immigrants came here in the late 19th and early 20th Centuries, the Irish had the advantage of being able to speak English. Not only speak it, but with a charming and musical brogue.

This meant they could get jobs that required their talking to people and understanding what was being said to them.

That was no small leg up in the unskilled job market. My favorite example of what it could lead to was a young man who got off the boat in New York and immediately boarded a train to Chicago. He was met at the station by relatives who took him—not home—but directly to the Maxwell Street police station, where he was given a uniform, a badge and a gun, and put on the Police Department payroll.

Then he was taken to a nearby intersection, where he went to work directing traffic only hours after arriving here.

Eventually, he rose to captain and district commander, with all the clout that went with those ranks.

There was another young man who landed a job as a conductor on the streetcars, a prized job for many Irish immigrants.

He later laughed about how he palmed nickels and dimes until he had stashed away enough to pay a politician to get him on the Police Department.

In time, he became a renowned robbery detective, a sergeant, a lieutenant and a captain, and when he retired he was the superintendent of police.

That was not an uncommon story in the Police and Fire Departments, the many jobs in City Hall, county government and anywhere else political clout could get someone on a payroll or in one of the building trades unions.

Of course, to have political clout, they had to win elections and hold the political offices. And that is where loathing and distrust became great assets for the Irish.

Of all the immigrant groups that came to Chicago, they were the only one that didn't bring with them the baggage of Old Country wars and hatreds.

Just about all the other groups had, at one time or another, marched across their neighbors' borders, shot at, oppressed, looted and pillaged each other.

So when they looked at names on ballots, they could recognize the ethnicity of candidates and were likely to say: "Why should I vote for that bum. His people rode in and burned down my village and stole my grandfather's best ox."

But Ireland was so busy being oppressed by the English, it didn't have the time or inclination to get involved in Europe's many crazy conflicts.

So with all the ethnic and racial distrust and loathing in Chicago, the Irish politicians became the compromise of choice. Sure, the English hated them, and the Irish reciprocated, but so what? The English in Chicago found politics too grubby and moved to the suburbs as soon as they stole enough to afford it.

To this day, an Irish name is an asset on the ballot. Candidates for judge have been known to change their names to something Irish sounding in order to get elected. I know one judge who was elected despite being found less than qualified by the various bar rating groups and having virtually no organizational support. But he has a fine Irish name, although he is black. I'm not sure, though, if he marched in this year's parade.

Part of that mystique flows from the kindly way the Irish have been treated by Hollywood.

Take John Wayne. He liked having Irish names in the heroic roles he played, as did other Hollywood stars.

When John Wayne played the lead character in a movie called "McClintock," it probably never crossed his mind to call the movie and hero "Ginzberg," "Svenson," "Papadopoulis" or "Brzezinski."

During prohibition days, the Irish bootleg gangs in Chicago were just as murderous and corrupt as any others. They tried hard and would have become the city's dominant gangsters had not Al Capone's lads been more efficient shooters.

But who do we see in the gray fedoras in all the gangster movies, from the old-time "Scarface" to the modern "Godfather" and "Wise Guys" films? It's one snarling Italian mobster after another. Unless, for a change of pace, the producers decide to give us Hispanic or black drug dealers.

The best thing about St. Patrick's Day is that it gives us an extra New Year's Eve in the early spring. In fact, it is better than New Year's Eve because the restaurants can't jack up the prices for a plate of corned beef and cabbage and beer dyed green.

The worst part is the rather boastful and patronizing statement: "There are only two kinds of people—those who are Irish and those who wish they were Irish."

To which Slats Grobnik always responds. "Not me. I never wanted to grow up to be an alderman, even if I didn't get caught." ▪

Earth Day message is lost on the slobs

TUESDAY, APRIL 17, 1990

Somebody from an environmental group recently called to ask if I would record a radio public service message as part of their Earth Day awareness campaign.

When I declined, she asked why. I explained that it would be a waste of time because Modern Man is a slob and nothing I could say would change that.

"Don't you care about the environment?" she said.

Of course I do. Or at least I once did. And I had a practical idea for improving the environment. But when I proposed it, I was ignored. So now I say that Modern Man can wallow in his own muck.

A persistent creature, she wanted to know what my practical solution was. So I shared it with her.

The idea came to me some years ago, on a pleasant Sunday morning, when my softball team was playing in Lincoln Park.

One of my players slid into second base and beat the tag for a double. But when he stood, his face was twisted in pain, he was clutching his backside, and saying "owee."

We surrounded him, so as not to shock female spectators, lowered his trousers and examined the stricken area. There we found the source of the pain: a jagged chicken bone.

We plucked it out. And to prevent infection, we poured Jim Beam on the wound, which we kept on hand for such emergencies.

But I began wondering how a chicken bone had found its way to that base path. Since chickens are not native to our softball diamonds, it's doubtful that one had just died there.

There could be only one answer. Someone had eaten a piece of chicken and tossed or dropped it, without regard to the environment or my player's hind quarters.

So I took a thorough look around the softball field. There were chicken bones all over the place. And hamburger wrappers, plastic cups, shards of glass, a diaper or two and all sorts of glop.

The next day, I called the park district and asked how much trash they picked up from the ground each week and how much it cost. The figures were astonishing. I calculated that if all the trash from one summer was piled in a heap, after the first big snowfall, we would have a ski run that would rival those in Aspen.

I asked a veteran park official if anyone had ever been arrested for tossing a chicken bone, a rib or a wad of Kleenex in the grass.

"To the best of my memory," he sadly said, "I don't think anyone has ever been pinched for littering."

That's when I hit upon my idea. Obviously, the police don't have the manpower to arrest every litterer. Even if they did, the courts and jails couldn't handle the crush.

So the answer was a tougher law. Not some slap-on-the-wrist fine. Or a stern lecture and probation from a judge.

I proposed that an adult litterer be hanged from the sturdy branch of a park tree and left to dangle there until he became unsightly. We could have even imported vultures to circle overhead for dramatic effect.

That way, the police wouldn't have to arrest every litterer. The sight of one stiff in each park twisting in the wind would be enough to make most people think: "If I drop this hot dog wrapper here, rather than be a good citizen and walk 20 paces to that waste basket, the vultures might pick my bones. I will be a good citizen."

The public response was immediate and, to my disappointment, negative. Readers accused me of being sadistic and cruel.

Well, of course I was. That was the idea. We know that Mafia hit men, sex fiends and berserk spouses who prefer knives or guns to marriage counselors, don't worry about Death Row. But most litterers are, in other ways, sane and rational. So in their case, the threat of being strung up would definitely be a deterrent.

And isn't it even more cruel and sadistic to befoul the environment, abuse Planet Earth and leave our grandchildren hip deep in old chicken bones and Kleenex? What kind of legacy is that?

The do-gooders and faint of heart would not be persuaded by my plan to hang 'em high. And that's when I dropped out of the environmental movement.

But I still believe my approach would be effective. And not just for chicken bone tossers.

Consider the big corporate polluters. When they are caught, the corporation is taken to court. The corporation is fined. So the corporation's stockholders receive a smaller dividend. And business goes on.

But what if, say, the laws were changed for oil companies that goof up and dump gunk in the sea? Let's say that the punishment was to take the board of directors out to the middle of the oil spill, toss them overboard and say: "Now you will experience what those birds and seals have experienced. Sink or swim, gents."

Or those companies that slyly dump waste into a waterway. Why not ladle up a pitcher of it for the corporate officers and say: "You dumped it—so drink it." Those whose great smokestacks befoul the air could be taken to the top, turned head down and dropped in the chimney so they could take a few deep whiffs of their product.

After I explained this to the environmentalist, she stammered that this was not the sort of thing they had in mind for a radio public service message.

I wasn't surprised. Maybe the meek will inherit the Earth, but they'll all be plucking chicken bones out of their butts. ∎

Legal marijuana—a pot of gold

FRIDAY, MARCH 8, 1985

I've been playing around with a fascinating number—14,000 tons. That's the amount of marijuana—foreign and domestic—that's said to be consumed each year in this country.

Actually, the federal narcs think it might be even higher. A recent raid in northern Mexico turned up 10,000 tons. The narcs were stunned because they thought that Mexico produced only one-fourth that amount.

But for this column's purpose, let's stay with the 14,000-ton figure.

If you break that down, it comes to 448,000,000 ounces.

I'm told that an ounce of marijuana will produce 20 to 40 joints, depending on whether you are frugal and make skinny ones or are self-indulgent and make them stogie-sized.

There's also a waste factor—seeds, twigs, bugs, spillage and so on.

So let's be conservative and figure 20 joints an ounce.

That's just under 10 billion joints a year.

If you divide that by the population of this country, it comes to about 40 joints for every man, woman and child.

Now, we can assume that millions of little toddlers and pre-schoolers don't smoke it. We can even assume that most kids in elementary school don't, since most of them don't have the purchase price.

And we can assume that millions of old codgers in nursing homes or two-room flats don't use it.

So who's doing all this grass-smoking? Recent studies say that teenagers are smoking less and less pot. So the biggest users are the age groups that range from young adults to middle-agers.

And they're a huge part of the population. If they aren't the majority, they're not far from it.

That tells us something obvious: There's a great demand in this country for marijuana.

As any Harvard economist—or dry-goods salesman—will tell you, when there's a great demand for something that isn't hard to supply, somebody is going to supply it.

Obviously, it's happening. Whether you live in a big city, a suburb or a small town, you can easily buy marijuana. If you aren't sure where to get it, just ask the nearest teenager.

So I have a simple question: If so many Americans want and use marijuana, if they are already getting it so easily, if they insist on spending billions of dollars a year on it, why are we screaming at Mexico, why are hordes of narcotics agents floundering around in futile attempts to find it, why are the police and courts still wasting time and money trying to put dealers in jail for selling it?

It ought to be obvious by now that the politicians in Washington can talk all they want about stamping it out, but they can't do it. It's become one of this country's biggest cash crops. It's a big part of Mexico's economy.

So maybe it's time to give up trying to stamp it out and consider legalizing it, thereby controlling it.

If it were legal, we wouldn't have gun-crazy dealers spraying Florida and other big import states with machine-gun bullets. They wouldn't be bribing politicians in this and other countries. In other words, it would be taken out of the hands of the criminal dope dealers, who are quickly becoming some of the world's wealthiest creeps.

It would allow the narcs to stop wasting their time trying to stop it, which they can't do, and would let them concentrate on chasing far more harmful drugs, such as heroin and cocaine.

And, best of all, it could be taxed. A $10 or $20 an ounce federal tax would bring in more than $5 billion or $10 billion a year. And every local government could slap on a little tax of its own.

Who would sell it? Private enterprise, I suppose. The day it became legal, we'd see nationwide pot franchises springing up.

And we could stop feuding with Mexico, since our own needy farmers could grow enough to meet all local demands.

Why, they'd probably wind up dealing in marijuana futures on the Board of Trade.

The sale could be regulated just as we now regulate the sale of booze. TV and radio advertising of pot would be banned, just as we've banned the advertising for hard liquor and cigarettes. Minimum age limits would be set.

Sure, it would be impossible to enforce the laws 100 percent. But the fact that teenagers find ways to buy beer doesn't prevent the rest of us from drinking it.

And, yes, I'm aware that marijuana isn't good for us, although scientists still aren't sure what the effects really are.

However, the scientists do know a lot more about the effects of even the finest scotches, the most elegant gins, the most regal cognacs. Even if you pay $5 a shot and tip the bartender a deuce, they will still quiver your liver and strain your brain.

So it might be time for us to stop pretending that we can do something to stop marijuana from being sold and consumed. In a country where the citizens—and even illegal aliens—have unlimited freedom of movement and where there is almost no control of its own borders, we can't do it.

Then why not try to at least regulate it and let our own farmers and businessmen make a buck.

Are we ready for a McJoint? ∎

Florida kid's case worth cheering for

THURSDAY, APRIL 23, 1992

Some lawyers and social workers are worried because a kid in Florida is trying, in effect, to divorce his parents. They say that if he wins his lawsuit, it will set a terrifying precedent that will threaten the structure of American family life.

Fine. A lot of family lives in our society could use some threatening.

In many communities, the family courts can't keep up with the incredible volume of child abuse, neglect, indifference, abandonment and general stupidity.

Over in divorce court, they are swamped with vicious child-custody battles that seem to never end, as furious parents use their kids as weapons of revenge against each other.

So why should the kids be regarded as mute bystanders or pawns or property when they are the victims of all this adult idiocy?

In the Florida case, the parents are divorced. The father is an abusive drunk, the mother has been rapped several times for neglect. The child, now 11, has been in foster homes for more than two years.

Now he wants stability. He has asked to remain with his present foster family, and they want to adopt him.

So the boy's lawyer has asked the court to legally end the parent-child relationship.

The state social workers don't like the idea. They say that one of their priorities, besides protecting children, is reuniting families.

Ah, yes, reuniting families. That's always a priority. And I've written about many families that have been reunited. Unfortunately, the cases I've written about usually involve a child being dead or maimed after having been reunited with abusive or neglectful morons. There are so many such cases that I could probably write about nothing else for a year. But then I'd be too depressed to keep writing, and you'd be too depressed to keep reading.

The lawyers are concerned because they say the Florida case could lead to other kids suing to dump their parents because they were denied the latest Nike shoes or Ninja Turtle game.

If the lawyers really believe that, it doesn't say much for their own profession. Are there attorneys who would handle some brat's Ninja Turtle-deprivation case? Not likely, especially if the kid didn't have a fat retainer fee in his piggy bank. And are the lawyers saying there are judges who would take a frivolous suit seriously, and not toss it out as nonsense?

No, if the Florida boy wins his case—and I hope he does—what we'll probably see are other suits filed by kids who will be saying that they have had it with parents who are dopeheads, drunks, sadists; parents who don't know how to take care of children and are unwilling or incapable of learning. And that they've had it with social service agencies that don't provide social services.

One of the biggest scandals in this country is the failure of the legal system to protect neglected and abused kids from people who, through the simple process of a romp in the sack, have become parents.

There are supposed to be legal safeguards, but all too often they don't work. We would like to have enough skilled social workers to track the abuse and neglect cases and to rescue the kids quickly. But we don't want to pay the taxes to hire the social workers. We'd like to be sure that each case is closely examined by a judge so that he can make the proper decision. But we don't want to pay the taxes needed to hire enough judges. We'd like to have enough family counselors to work with mopes who show promise of learning how to take care of their kids. But we don't want to pay the taxes to hire them. We'd like to have a system that doesn't have cracks through which so many kids fall. But we don't want to pay the cost of filling the cracks.

I'm sure there are all sorts of deep and complex legal principles involved here. Lawyers can find deep and complex legal principles in a parking meter ticket.

But it seems to me that what we're talking about is the principle of self-defense, which is pretty simple. If you are in danger, and the agents of the law aren't there to protect you, you have a right to defend yourself. Can anyone quarrel with that?

Well, the Florida boy is in danger of being reunited with either a father who has a history of being an abusive drunk, or a mother who has a history of abuse and neglect. The state, through its agencies and the courts, has had more than two years to resolve the boy's problems. It hasn't.

So now the boy is saying that if the state isn't willing or able to protect him, he's going to use the legal system to defend himself.

Why not? Every day, thousands of people turn to the courts with far less serious problems than this kid has.

And you can bet that if every kid in America had $10,000 in his piggy bank, you wouldn't hear many lawyers express grave concerns about legal precedents.

They'd be standing in line at the schoolyard. ∎

Unthinkable deed just part of show

THURSDAY, FEBRUARY 2, 1995

I'll never understand the thinking—or lack of same—that goes into television news.

For example, a few nights ago an anchorman-commentator at the Fox Network station in Chicago (Channel 32) expressed his opinions about the Baby Richard case.

He was furious with the Illinois Supreme Court for ordering the child returned to his biological father.

And he was especially angry at Justice James D. Heiple, who wrote the court's opinion.

He told the viewers: "Justice Heiple, it seems to me, is not only evil, he is dangerous."

A moment later, he emotionally told the viewers what they could do to let the judge know they disagreed with the court's ruling.

"Call him and beg him. We beg you, your honor Judge Heiple, please stop destroying the lives of children."

And the Fox anchorman did something that is unthinkable in the news business. Or at least it was in more thoughtful times.

He broadcast the judge's home telephone number. It was displayed on the screen and the anchorman read it aloud.

The results were predictable. Almost immediately, the phone began ringing in the judge's Downstate home.

The judge, we're told, was stunned. So was his wife, who is seriously ill. When you are seriously ill in the privacy of your home, you don't expect to spend the night hearing weird strangers saying terrible things.

John Madigan, spokesman for the court, says:

"I don't want to sound scary, but they have received some calls that you or I would say were obscene. And calls where the person doesn't say anything, and just hangs up.

"It's one thing to debate an issue openly: abortion, the death penalty, nuclear power. But when you start giving out someone's home telephone number like that, well, there are kooks out there, as we all know."

Madigan spent 51 years in the news business, as a reporter, commentator and newspaper and TV executive, but he says: "I can't recall anyone ever doing something like that."

The reasons this isn't done should be obvious to anyone in or out of the news business. All you have to do is look at the headlines about doctors being shot outside of abortion clinics; judges who have been shot in their courtrooms; other public people being assassinated.

So if you tell a large TV audience that someone is "evil" and "dangerous" and is "destroying the lives of children," that could easily be taken as an invitation for some wacko to do something about it.

And once you give out that person's home phone number, it wouldn't take the CIA to track down a home address.

It's also malicious. Emotionally urging people to phone was obvious harassment, an attempt by the anchorman to punish Judge Heiple. I didn't know that it was the job of a news operation to prevent people from sleeping in their own homes.

The maliciousness goes beyond the judge. By broadcasting someone's home number, a station doesn't just punish that individual. There is also the family.

As I said, the judge's wife has a serious illness. (The nature of her illness is nobody else's business, although the Fox station might consider poking a camera in her bedroom window.) Threats and obscene phone calls from Fox's viewers aren't the best medicine.

But apparently the right of the judge and his wife to have privacy in their own home didn't blink a light in the brain of the anchorman, the Fox station's news director or the producer of the show.

However, the station appears to have a deep sense of its own right to privacy.

When Madigan, the court spokesman, asked the station for a transcript of the broadcast, he was brushed off. The station wouldn't return most of his persistent phone calls.

And when he finally got a few news department people, he says, "I was told that it is Fox's policy that they do not give out transcripts.

"He (the anchorman) told me it was the station's policy and that there was nothing he could do about it.

"I've never heard of a policy like that. When I was news director at Channel 2, if someone was mentioned in a commentary, we immediately supplied them with a transcript."

That seems only fair. Even fundamental. If you use the power of TV to bray that a public person is "evil," "dangerous" and a destroyer of children, the least you can do is put it in writing.

But more and more, TV news sets its own rules, which have little or nothing to do with fairness, decency or even common sense. You keep a sick woman awake all night with nutty and scary phone calls—hey, her husband is a public figure, right?

And the show must go on.

There is an ironic twist to this.

Back in the days when he was the news director at Channel 2, Madigan gave a young hustler his big break by hiring him as a TV reporter.

That hustler is now the anchorman at the Fox station.

I guess that's what they mean when they say: "What goes around, comes around." ▪

Take it from one who knows: Ann meant no harm

FRIDAY, DECEMBER 1, 1995

An old pal from the Northwest Side called and sounded like he might pop a blood vessel.

"Are you going to do something about that . . . that . . . woman?" he sputtered.

What woman?

"That Ann Landers woman. Are you going to let her have a blast?"

Of course not. Ann Landers, also known as Eppie Lederer, has been a close friend for more than 30 years. I don't go around blasting close friends. Especially when they are as cute as a bug.

"But you know what she did? What she said?"

Of course I know.

"She called the pope a Polack. A POLACK!"

So what? The pope is a Polack.

"What? What? You said the pope is a Polack? You said it?"

Of course I said it. And if you ask the pope if he is a Polack, I'm sure he would agree.

"I can't believe this. You're part Polish and you can use a slur like that?"

What slur?

"What do you think? The word Polack."

I don't consider it a slur, and I'm surprised that so many Polacks and others think it is. They have been calling this paper and howling for a sweet lady's scalp.

So once and for all, let us get it straight. If you are truly Polish, you are a Polack.

Who says so? The Polish language says so. In Poland, the word for someone who is Polish is Polack.

Thus, when Eppie, as we call her, described the pope as a Polack, she was 100 percent correct.

If you went in a bar in Warsaw, hoisted a vodka and said: "Here's to the pope, a really great Polack," you would get cheerful nods, especially if you bought the round. Except from the unreconstructed godless commies, the rats.

That's why I've never understood someone being offended by a perfectly valid word.

It's not like calling an Italian a wop or a ginzo, a German a kraut or a heinie, a Frenchman a frog, a Hispanic a beaner or other words that were created as slurs by old WASPs and rival ethnic groups.

This was explained to me at an early age by Big Chester, who used to tend bar at my father's tavern and was the toughest guy I've ever known.

Big Chester was born in Poland, and he would thump his chest, fix Irish Harry with a steely gaze and say: "Oldest university in Europe is in Krakow. We have university when Irish wore fur underwear. We conquer most of Russia when Irish wore fur underwear. I am Polack and proud of it. You want to fight?"

Irish Harry, who hoped to live long enough to become an alderman, would just smile weakly and buy the house a round.

But let us return to my friend Eppie.

Most of the angry people who called hadn't read the article in the New Yorker that caused this flap.

They had heard it on radio and TV, as reported by bubble-headed broadcast boobs who hadn't read it either.

So let's get to it.

In the article, which was about what a great babe Eppie is—and she truly is— she was giving insightful thumbnail impressions of the many famous people she has met. And she has met more of them than anyone but Kup.

About Pope John Paul II, the Polish pope, she said: "Looks like an angel. He has the face of an angel. His eyes are sky blue, and his cheeks are pink and adorable looking, and he has a sweet sense of humor."

Now, I ask you, did any of the TV yahoos and radio babblers tell you about Eppie saying that the pope looks like an angel and has a sweet sense of humor?

Of course not. The broadcast rodents knew that would not serve their malicious purpose.

They zeroed in on the rest of her quote: "Of course, he's a Polack." Laughter. "They're very antiwomen."

What she obviously meant was that Poles of the pope's generation don't always treat women as equals. And she's right. There are countless Catholic women—Polish and otherwise, nuns and housewives—who will tell you they aren't nuts about this Polish pope's attitudes toward women.

And that is a valid issue that can be debated. But it is not a blanket insult of all Polacks.

So I would ask my fellow Polacks to calm down. This lady ain't got a bigoted bone in her trim bod. And when life gets tough, you couldn't ask for a better friend.

That's from one proud Polack to another. ∎

Here's a great way to tick off friends
WEDNESDAY, DECEMBER 17, 1986

Most of us have habits that can irritate our friends and loved ones. With me, it's my wristwatch.

Ever since I discovered this make of watch several years ago, I've infuriated friends, co-workers and even casual acquaintances with conversations such as this:

"Nice watch you have there."

"Oh, thanks."

"One of those oyster-shell jobs, hmmm? Must be expensive."

"Gift from my wife."

"Beautiful. But tell me, what can it do?"

"Do? It tells the time."

At that point, I feign amazement and say: "That's all? For all that money, it only tells time?"

They usually fall into my trap by saying something like: "What do you expect a watch to do?"

I pull back my cuff, display my watch and show them.

While jabbing at the tiny buttons on its front and side, I say: "Besides keeping time in civilian or military mode, I expect it to be a fully functioning calculator. I also expect it to be an alarm clock. And to be a stopwatch. And to give me the day and date. And to beep on the hour."

In the past, I've had the model that not only did all those things but could play my choice of three popular tunes.

As well as light up in the dark.

But this year, I'm capable of being even more infuriating because I have the newest model, with the most amazing feature yet.

After I have run through the above tricks, I now say:

"By the way, let me have your unlisted phone number. I want to store it in my watch's data bank."

That really pops their eyes.

But it's true. Through the genius of Japanese technology, I can store 50 names and phone numbers in my watch.

I merely touch a button and the names and numbers scroll across the watch face.

And I usually conclude my performance by saying: "All that for $32.95 plus tax. Let's see, your watch cost about $500, right? Well, if I buy the latest, improved model of my watch every two years, at the end of 30 years. . . ."

I pause to do some fast figuring in my watch's calculator mode, and say:

" . . . At the end of 30 years, I'll have spent less for all of my amazing space-age, science fiction technology than you spent to, ha, ha, to find out what time it is."

It never fails to get a rise out of them. In fact, I have a friend who owns a $5,000 Rolex and no longer speaks to me.

That's because people like him feel foolish. They spend hundreds or even thousands of dollars, and for what? To get information that is hanging on the walls of most homes and offices—the time of day.

But for only $32.95, I can tap a button and call up the unlisted number of my bookie. Or set the alarm to be sure that I don't oversleep at my desk and miss the cocktail hour.

I've never had as much satisfaction from a material possession.

That is, until I recently had a drink with an old friend I hadn't seen for a few years.

He was wearing one of those delicate, wafer-thin watches, made in France, I believe, so I couldn't resist going into my put-down routine.

"Must have cost a pretty penny," I said.

"A bundle," he said.

In a moment, I was putting my watch through its paces. But he just roared with laughter and said:

"I can't believe this. You? Wearing a nerd watch?"

"A what?"

"That's the kind of watches the nerds wear."

"Uh, you don't understand. This watch is also a calculator, a stopwatch, a phone directory, an alarm. . . ."

He laughed again. "I know all that. That's why the nerds love them."

"Nerds? What do nerds have to do with it?"

"The computer nuts. The calculator freaks. The number crunchers. I've got a kid working in my office who has one exactly like it. Classic nerd. Keeps a slide rule, three pens, a tiny flashlight and a peanut butter sandwich in his shirt pocket."

"Uh, it's got a, uh, a two-year battery, you know?"

He slapped the bar and laughed uncontrollably. Then he said: "Who would have thought it? You, a nerd? Tell me, whatever possessed you to buy a watch like that?"

"Gift from my wife." ∎

When TV news does weather, it takes idiotic to new level

FRIDAY, DECEMBER 20, 1996

"Look around this joint," Slats Grobnik said. "What do you see?"

People. Yes, that's what they are.

"And what are they wearing?"

Clothing. Do I win a prize?

"Some got on sweaters, right? Coats, hats, regular winter stuff?"

Yes, you are a keen observer. So what is your point?

"Uh-huh. And most of them look normal, right?"

Compared to what?

"I mean you don't see none of them drooling or sitting on the floor and talking like babies?"

The day is still young.

"What I'm saying is that they don't look like a bunch of idiots, do they?"

Not to the naked eye.

"Would you say that Chicago and the suburbs are a big community of idiots?"

Other than on opening day of the baseball season, no.

"So Chicagoans are not known to be any more stupid than people in other cities, right?"

I'd say so.

"Then how come the local TV stations talk to us like we're all a bunch of helpless morons?"

In what way?

"OK, what kind of weather do we have today?"

It is very cold. A biting wind.

"But it's supposed to be warm out, right? Beach weather, golf weather?"

Of course not. It is late December and this is Chicago. It is always cold and wintry in late December in Chicago.

"So do you see anybody walking around outside in T-shirts and shorts?"

Don't be ridiculous.

"See? That's what I mean. You know it is cold. I know it is cold. Everybody knows it is cold."

Right. It is cold. It is supposed to be cold.

"OK, but I turn on the TV news and there is this guy with a microphone in his hand and he's standing out at some shopping center and he's saying that even though it is cold, people are still going out to do their shopping. Like this is some big surprise or they are swimming in the lake."

Yes, people do shop. And they go to work. They stand at bus stops or on commuter platforms. They take out the garbage. They go on the porch to bring in the paper. They even jog or take wiggly health walks. They stroll from here to there, or there to here. Been doing it for years, as long as I can remember.

"Right. But this TV guy acts like it is really an amazing deal. I mean, not one of those people he shows us on camera is trapped in a corner, being chewed on by hungry wolves. Not one of them was walking around naked. They were all dressed real warm and walking along just like people do all the time."

Yes, we Chicagoans are hardy, sturdy people.

"And then you know what he says? I couldn't believe it. He says he's going to give us some advice on what we should do in this weather."

Call in sick and stay home in bed?

"No, that would have been original."

Let me guess. Order out for some pizza and beer and have some friends over to play poker until the icicles melt.

"Great idea, but no."

How about this: Cash in the kids' college fund, get an equity loan on the house, leave a goodbye note for the wife, buy a hairpiece, put on a gold chain, and grab the next plane for Bermuda, and sit next to the pool and buy drinks for a bimbo?

"No, that would have made it a great news show."

So what did he say?

He said we should all dress warm if we go out.

Ah, it is the old dress-warm-when-it-is-cold trick.

"Yeah. I sat there thinking, what did we do before there was TV to help us? And you know what else he said?"

Beware of petting polar bears?

"Better'n that. He said that if we go outside, we should be careful about our skin getting numb or turning unusual colors."

Very good advice. One should always take note if your nose turns deep blue and falls off. Pick it up, pop it into your pocket and go see your physician to get it reattached. And try not to sneeze.

"So after I watch that, I start thinking about the way they are going to rate TV shows so we can keep the kids from accidentally watching the kind of kinky stuff the rest of us like. And I'm wondering why they can't put some kind of warning on news shows."

Because news shows are a special category and it is assumed that news directors have the judgment and maturity and professionalism to avoid putting trash on the air.

"But why can't they put a rating on the different items. Like rating something 'M,' which would mean: The next news item contains material that is moronic. Or an 'I' for idiotic."

You can't do that with news shows. That would be something more appropriate for Beavis and Butt-head.

"There's a difference?" ▪

A word about debate 'poopery'

THURSDAY, APRIL 2, 1987

L̲ike many Chicagoans who watched the debate, I was puzzled by a strange new word used by Mayor Washington.

The word was "poopery." The mayor used it twice, referring to a poopery of tax proposals.

Because I had never heard the word "poopery" before, I looked in my dictionary to see what it meant. In fact, I looked in several dictionaries.

I was surprised to find that it was not listed. So I asked a co-worker, who has a degree in English, if he knew what "poopery" meant.

"Sounds to me like it might be some kind of fancy outhouse," he said. "You might ask somebody who lived on a farm."

I doubted that the mayor would be discussing outhouses during the debate, but in this campaign, you never know.

So I called an acquaintance who had been reared on a farm and asked him if they had referred to their outhouse as a poopery.

"First of all," he said, "we did not have an outhouse. And if we did, we would definitely not have called it a poopery. My guess is that a poopery is what they call a washroom in the gay bars."

Pursuing that suggestion, I called a gay publication. The young man who answered the phone said: "If that's some kind of April Fool joke, it isn't funny," and hung up.

Someone else suggested that it might be another word for a cat's litter box. Someone else said it might have something to do with a child's potty training.

None of that applied to anything I heard in the debate. On the other hand, maybe it did.

Anyway, I finally did what I should have done in the first place: I called an aide to the mayor and asked what a poopery was.

"A what?" he asked.

I repeated it.

"Is that something Vrdolyak or somebody called us?"

I explained that the mayor had used the word during the debate.

"He did? Poopery? How is that spelled?"

Just the way it sounds.

"Naw."

Yes, he did. I heard it twice, and I have it on tape. He said "poopery."

"Let me check and I'll call you back."

In a few minutes the phone rang and he said: "The word the mayor used was— I'll spell it—P-O-T-P-O-U-R-R-I. That's potpourri."

Aha! That explained it. The mayor had made the mistake of using one of those French words. And, as is often the case when Americans toss around French words to show how erudite they are, he screwed it up.

He had said poopery when he meant to say poe (as in toe) and pyu, (as in pee-you), ree (as in whee).

Poe-pyu-ree, not poopery.

At least, that's how a friend who took high school French explained it to me. But he cautioned: "It's very difficult to write something in French phonetically. The second syllable in that word is sort of between a long O and a U."

That's what I meant when I said that using French words in an American conversation can be disastrous. I don't know how to make a sound somewhere between an O and a U, and I wouldn't want to, unless I was snoring or sick to my stomach.

But the mayor, who loves flaunting his vocabulary, tried to slip a French word past us, and it came out as poopery. Serves him right. Mayor Daley would have fired anybody he suspected of even thinking in French. And if somebody had used the word "poopery" in the presence of ladies, Daley might have ordered his arrest.

After looking up potpourri in the dictionary, I assume that the mayor was using it to mean: "a miscellaneous collection."

So why didn't he just say: "A miscellaneous collection?" If he had, we would have understood what he meant. He could have even said: "A mixed bag," and we would have dug him.

Instead, he had to show off. And the result was that thousands of confused Chicagoans have been pondering the meaning of poopery.

However, since the mayor introduced this new word to the world, we might consider making it part of the vocabulary. It has a certain ring to it. It could be used in a conversation such as this:

"What did you think of the mayoral debate?"

"I thought some of it was pooporious, at times pooperific, and a few moments that were pooperendous."

"And your overall reaction?"

"Overall? I'd say it was a lot of poopery." ▪

These 7 were special people

WEDNESDAY, JANUARY 29, 1986

Pick up this or any big newspaper, and there will be a page of death notices and obituaries. People die every day. Some die young; more die old. Some suddenly, some after long illness. Rich, poor, unknown and famous.

We pay little or no attention to most of them. In smaller cities, people might look a little closer at the obits because there's more likelihood that they'll know someone.

But in the big cities, most people don't even give them a glance. Or if they do, they just skim the names.

And nobody says that this or that death is a great tragedy, a terrible loss. We don't say that about the death of strangers. People die. That's part of life.

Yet, millions of people around the world were plunged into deep sadness Tuesday because of the death of seven individuals who were strangers to almost all of us.

On the streets, you could find ordinary people staring into store windows at TV sets that showed the explosion of the spacecraft and weeping at the sight.

People phoned me, most of them shaken, subdued, depressed, just wanting to talk to someone about the tragedy.

I asked one elderly woman, who had surely seen much death in her lifetime, why she was so moved at the deaths of people whose names she wasn't sure of.

She said: "It's because they were doing it for us. They were representing us up there, weren't they? They were special."

And I suppose that's part of it. Yes, they were representing us. The human race is going to explore space because it's in our nature to go where we've never been. And maybe we have to if we're going to survive. But we can't all do it. We have to delegate. And they are our explorers. They push back the boundaries for the rest of us.

In a sense, it's the same reason we mourn strangers in the uniforms of cops and firemen who die while doing their jobs. It's because they're representing us. We delegate, and they do our dirty and dangerous work.

And there was truth in what the elderly woman said about the seven being special.

They're special because they were among that small minority who don't do what they do for the paycheck.

They were the fortunate ones who have the brains, the drive, the vision, the physical gifts, to accomplish things that the rest of us can only marvel at. In Tom Wolfe's phrase: "the right stuff."

So it's doubly shocking when we see such special people die literally before our eyes, when we see a great, inspiring adventure turned into a video horror.

And it's a jarring reminder of our mortality. How sure are any of us that there will be a tomorrow when even the very special, the very gifted, can be gone in an instant; when all the dazzling technology, the brilliant minds of the space agency, the meticulous planning, the countless safeguards can't guarantee that a disaster won't occur.

It was a tragedy, yes. But I can't help but think that even in death, maybe they were still among the lucky ones.

I've known so many people, and you probably have, too, who have quietly slipped away after lives of frustration, drudgery, failure, disappointment and sickness. People who never had a chance to climb the mountains of their souls. Or who had no mountains.

The seven people on the spaceship, including the schoolteacher, had all chosen to climb. They wanted to walk the edge, with all the risks it involved.

I'm not sure that the risk wasn't worth it. Maybe it wouldn't be for you and me and most of us who prefer to play it safe. But the next time a spaceship is launched, there will be people aboard who believe that what they're doing is more than worth the chance. There will always be such people, and each of them will tell you that they consider themselves lucky, no matter the outcome.

So in feeling grief, remember that the seven were special in what they did with their lives, right up to the end.

As someone once put it: "If I reach for the stars, I might not touch them. But I won't come up with a handful of dirt." ∎